Dr. Phillip Cary is Director of the Philosophy Program at Eastern College in St. Davids, Pennsylvania, where he is also Scholar-in-residence at the Templeton Honors College.

Augustine's Invention of the Inner Self

Augustine's Invention of the Inner Self

The Legacy of a Christian Platonist

Phillip Cary

OXFORD
UNIVERSITY PRESS

2000

BT
741.2
.C37
2000

OXFORD
UNIVERSITY PRESS
Oxford   New York

Athens   Auckland   Bangkok   Bogotá   Buenos Aires   Calcutta
Cape Town   Chennai   Dar es Salaam   Delhi   Florence   Hong Kong   Istanbul
Karachi   Kuala Lumpur   Madrid   Melbourne   Mexico City   Mumbai
Nairobi   Paris   São Paulo   Singapore   Taipei   Tokyo   Toronto   Warsaw

and associated companies in
Berlin   Ibadan

Copyright © 2000 by Phillip Cary

Published by Oxford University Press, Inc.
198 Madison Avenue, New York, New York 10016

Oxford is a registered trademark of Oxford University Press

All rights reserved. No part of this publication may be reproduced,
stored in a retrieval system, or transmitted in any form or by any means,
electronic, mechanical, photocopying, recording, or otherwise,
without the prior permission of Oxford University Press.

Library of Congress Cataloging-in-Publication Data
Cary, Phillip. 1958–
Augustine's invention of the inner self : the legacy of a
Christian platonist / Phillip Cary.
p.   cm.
Includes bibliographical references and index.
ISBN 0-19-513206-8
1. Augustine, Saint. Bishop of Hippo—Contributions in doctrine
of soul. 2. Soul—History of doctrines—Early church, ca. 30–600.
I. Title.
BT741.2.C37   1999   99-21119
189'.2—dc21

1 3 5 7 9 8 6 4 2

Printed in the United States of America
on acid-free paper

JESUIT - KRAUSS - McCORMICK - LIBRARY
1100 EAST 55th STREET
CHICAGO, ILLINOIS 60615

For Nancy
Beloved Other, One Flesh

Preface

*Of Traditions, Inventions,
and Ancient Fathers*

This is the story of the invention of something new, and like all such stories it is not as straightforward as one could wish: one arrives at new things only after exploring a great deal of other territory and poking into many blind alleys. I hope to have made the story easier to follow by providing summaries of each chapter, so that readers can always have a map of where they are in the whole exploration, and those who like to skip around in the more familiar parts of the story can do so. The problem is that even the chapters that fill in background information contain a great deal that will be unfamiliar to the non-specialist, as well as controversial to the specialist, and hence for both reasons could not be omitted. My test of whether all that background material was really needed is my sense of how very bizarre the climactic narrative (in chapters 6 through 10) would be without it. You are welcome to try the test yourself.

Throughout, it has been my concern to make this book accessible to non-specialists (i.e., everyone who has not studied Augustine's debts to Platonism) while also addressing the deep issues raised by the specialist scholarship. The two non-specialist audiences I have had most in mind are those interested in philosophy and general intellectual history on the one hand, and those interested in theology and the history of Christian thought on the other. I have often stopped to explain things to the one audience that I would take for granted as familiar to the other, and vice versa. And in both cases, even the most familiar themes, I have often found, had to be handled in unfamiliar ways in order to make sense of the astounding phenomenon of Augustine.

It will help you follow the twists and turns of this story if I tell you that I think of intellectual history or the history of ideas primarily in terms of intellectual traditions and their problems.[1] A tradition involves the handing on (*traditio*) of something from generation to generation. In an intellectual tradition this includes not only doctrines or teachings but also the problems raised by them.[2] Such problems, in addition to encounters with other traditions, are prime movers of inquiry in a tradition, and thus a prime source of new ideas in human history.

An inquiry is a kind of adventure or exploration, a search to find a solution to a problem. This "finding" is the root sense of the word "invention" in the book's title: originally, the Latin word *inventio* meant finding the right word or thought for an occasion, hence also finding the solution to a problem. Ancient *inventio* eventually became modern "invention"—the making up of something new rather than the finding of something already there—because an invention in the modern sense is typically the finding of a solution to some problem of design, thought, or practice. My story represents the concept of inner self as an invention, in the sense that it is the finding of a solution to a philosophical and theological problem. But of course that leaves open the question of whether inwardness, and in particular the private inner self, is *inventio* in the ancient sense or invention in the modern sense—an old thing found or a new thing produced.

Though I would like to leave the question open as far as I can for you to form your own judgment, it is only fair to let you know at the outset that in my own view the private inner self is in fact something Augustine made up rather than discovered. In this respect you can call him original or creative. I myself shall avoid such terms, however, for they fit the subject badly. Like all ancient thinkers, Augustine would have regarded "originality" as innovation and novelty, which are bad things—opposed to the antiquity of truth. So "invention," with its peculiar ambiguity, is the most neutral term I could find for what Augustine is up to. Besides, the term itself plays a key role in Augustine's concept of the inner self, as shall be seen in the last chapter.

The inner self is the sort of issue on which it is hard not to take sides, so let me try to explain (especially to those on the opposite side) why I think mine is the sort of story that is best told by someone who is not fully in sympathy with his protagonists. I shall portray Augustine (and Plato and Aristotle and Plotinus) as writers offering us solutions to problems that may or may not be our own, depending on whether or not we accept the premises of the problem. If you already believe certain doctrines are true, then finding a good solution to the problems raised by those doctrines gives you reason to believe the solution is true as well. But if you don't think the doctrines are true in the first place, then you can regard the solutions as inventions (in the modern sense of the word). In my experience, not believing the doctrines that produce philosophical problems makes it easier to discern what is actually going on in the solution. Otherwise one's hopes or fears that the solution be true tend to get in the way of understanding it on its own terms, as one either tries to assimilate it to one's prior convictions or else rejects it as a mistake because one can't assimilate it. Since the problems I study here all arise within the Platonist tradition, and I am no Platonist, I do not think the solutions to these problems are true. Yet by the same token they are not mere arbitrary mistakes either. They are inventions, new concepts in the tradition of Western philosophy and religion—profound and beautiful in some ways, wrongheaded and dismaying in others, and immensely influential—and for all these reasons worth careful, patient and sympathetic study.

I tell the story of the invention of something new—a new concept, I will call it, for lack of a better word. A concept is whatever it is that is represented by a term in some discourse—or perhaps it is the term itself. How concepts are related to words is a deep question, on which I shall do my best to avoid taking sides, except to say two things: a concept always belongs to a whole network of concepts that is structured by logical relations such as consequence and inconsistency (which is why a concept can be used to solve conceptual problems as well as be the source of new problems) and a concept in use belongs to a way of thinking and therefore to a form of human life. The concepts I study here became an integral part of Western thought and therefore of the lives of human beings in the West. The conviction that Augustine *invented* the concept of private inner self is thus not inconsistent with the observation that the inner self has long been a formative element in Western experience. But it is part of our experience like Hamlet, say, rather than like Shakespeare. It is an image of ourselves that a great dramatist has set on the stage of our literature, and subsequently it has had much to do with who we are.

My attitude toward this invention and its subsequent history is complicated by the fact that it was invented by a *Christian* Platonist and influenced primarily the Western *Christian* tradition. For though I am not a believer in Platonism, I am a believer in Christ. The complication arises because Platonism and Christianity are not two entirely separate traditions (see chapter 4). Christianity has been using Platonist language since the New Testament and borrowing (or stealing?) Platonist concepts since the Church Fathers, and the latter of course made an art form of reading Platonist concepts into the Bible by means of what they called "spiritual" as opposed to "literal" exegesis. Since the origin of the orthodox traditions of Christianity (which includes not only the Eastern Orthodox traditions, but Roman Catholicism and the Protestant traditions as well) lies with these Fathers, no adherent of orthodoxy can afford to dismiss all things Platonist as if they were unchristian. And certainly such dismissiveness has led to misunderstandings of Augustine (see chapters 3 and 5).

On the other hand, as both an intellectual historian and an adherent of orthodoxy, I am interested in issues of provenance. I argue that the inner self is a Christian idea that originated in the Platonist tradition; but that puts it in the same category as the Fall,[3] the immortality of the soul, and the notion that if we are good our souls will go to heaven when we die.[4] If you can accept these other notions as Christian then you might be able to do the same with the inner self. The difference is mainly that the inner self entered Christianity later than these other doctrines and is therefore not so deeply rooted in the Christian traditions (especially not in the East, which is scarcely indebted to Augustine). It is also particularly fascinating in that it is a Platonist idea that was invented by a Christian. But in any case the historical point is that all these doctrines (and many more) both belong to the Christian tradition and originate in the Platonist tradition. One therefore cannot justly reject them as unchristian simply on the historical ground of distinguishing Platonism from Christianity; to reject them as unchristian means criticizing the Christian tradition from within. But of course Christianity (like Platonism) has always been a self-critical tradition, recognizing and investigating problems in itself, and indeed one widely accepted name for the self-criticism of the Christian tradition is simply "Christian theology."[5] One of my motives for offering this historical study is to provide material for this ongoing self-critical enterprise of the Christian tradition.

It is not a new thing for a Christian to reflect critically on the relation of the Christian and Platonist traditions, but such reflection usually goes by other names, such as "the relation of philosophy and theology" or "the problem of faith and reason." Since with this book we are stepping into this long history of reflection (like stepping into the course of a great flowing stream, it can put one off balance) I had better say something about my own perspective on this theological issue. Readers accustomed to the relation of philosophy and religion in modernity, where "philosophy" typically plays critic and "religion" designates a tradition under criticism, need to adjust to the situation in late antiquity where, despite occasional fierce criticism by pagan Platonists (who were hostile not to "religion" in general but to *Christianity*), Christians found Platonism profoundly attractive. Hence my theological concern in this book is not to counter the critical force of philosophy but to resist the religious attractiveness of Platonism. What I hope for in a Christian theologian's relations with philosophy is something like the medieval notion of philosophy as handmaid of theology—in other words, I think Christian theologians should appropriate concepts from various philosophical traditions whenever they prove useful in saying what Christians need to say, but without any ultimate loyalty to the meaning these concepts had in their original context (e.g., of systematic Platonism).[6] Hence it seems to me quite right that Christian theologians make use of Platonist concepts to describe the eternity and omnipresence of God, for example (and in the current theological environment, that is a rather hefty concession to the value of Platonism).

Where my concerns diverge from those of most medieval theologians is in my awareness that philosophy in the patristic era (i.e., mainly Platonism) did not offer to stand to the Christian religion in the relation of nature to grace, as if philosophy was earthbound human rationality and Christian faith was heavenly and spiritual wisdom. On the contrary, Platonism is *more* "spiritual" than Christianity, in the sense that it is more resolutely focused on the soul and its relation to eternal things (more "other worldly," as they used to say). For example, it is Platonism that gives us the concept of the immortality of the soul, whereas the Christian Gospel proclaims the resurrection of the dead. The one teaches that a part of us does not die, whereas the other teaches that we die but God can give life to the dead.[7] Hence instead of an intrinsic immortality, the Christian Scriptures place hope of eternal life in the proclamation that God has already raised Jesus Christ bodily from the dead. For the distinctive feature of Christian faith is that it finds no God separated from the flesh of Christ.

One of the crucial theological achievements of the Church Fathers in the Nicene doctrine of the Trinity and the Christological doctrines that followed in later centuries was to negotiate the relationship between Platonist spirituality and this distinctive feature of Christian faith—its Christological fleshliness. My placement of Augustine's concept of the inner self in the context of his Platonism is ultimately concerned with its relation to this fundamental issue of Patristic and all Christian thought: what is the meaning and power of Christ's flesh? The critical question I would pose regarding Augustine's Platonist spirituality is this: why should we want to turn to our inner selves if God is to be found in something external, the flesh of Christ? (And what, after all, is more external than flesh?) I am, in the end, a critic of Augustine's inward turn for two reasons: I think it directs our attention toward something that does not exist (the inner self) and away from that in which resides our salvation (the flesh of Christ). But again, that is only my position, and I hope to have portrayed Augustine's inwardness fairly enough for you to make your own judgments.

Let me add, however, for Christians who wish to defend him on this score, that there is much more to Augustine than just his inwardness. I have had to neglect a great deal of Augustine's thought, because this book is not about Augustine but about the concept of private inner self. It tells only so much of Augustine's story as is necessary to trace the origin of that one concept. In several places I have suggested criticisms of the concept, which should not be mistaken for a blanket condemnation of Augustine—any more than this

book should be mistaken for a comprehensive account of his thought. There are indeed
certain problems I think orthodox Christians ought to have with Augustinian concepts of
inwardness. Augustine himself had some of these problems, and he addressed them by developing a new account of the significance of external things, to go with his new concept of
the inner self. But that is the subject for another book. Hence my criticisms of Augustinian
inwardness do not amount to a rejection of Augustine's thought as a whole—for I offer
here no assessment of his thought as a whole. What I do offer, I hope, is a serious warning
for Christians who are attracted to an inward turn.

My desire is that this book will prove useful not only to those who belong to one of the
Christian traditions, but also to those who are simply interested in the history of Western
thinking about the self and what it means to be human. It was necessary that I explain the
complication of my perspective on Christian theology, however, because it accounts for
much that is peculiar about the tone of this book, which you might notice. A great deal of
the peculiarity is perhaps due to Augustine rather than just me. For anyone in the West at
the beginning of the third millennium, whether Christian or not, Augustine must seem
both strange and familiar—startlingly different from yet disquietingly similar to ourselves.
Getting to know him is like going back in a time machine to talk with one's great-great
grandfather from the old country. He speaks a different language, is at home in a far-off
world we can scarcely imagine, and has all sorts of outlandish ideas, yet he undoubtedly
helped bring us into being—and sometimes it is the strangest things about him that are
most important in giving us our present identity. To recognize ourselves in him is to perceive, I hope, something about our own strangeness.

Of course this filial relationship is especially complicated for orthodox Christians in
the West, to all of whom Augustine has the right to speak using Paul's words: "Though
you have many teachers in Christ, you do not have many fathers: for in Christ Jesus I have
begotten you through the Gospel" (1 Cor. 4:15). That is roughly what the Western Christian tradition means by calling him a Church Father: we owe our particular tradition of
Christianity in large part to him, as troublesome and questionable a legacy as that may be.
Augustine does in fact invite us to question his legacy in the name of the truth of the
Catholic faith.[8] But let him speak in his own words, as near as my translation can give them
to you:

> To be sure, in all my writings I desire not only a pious reader but a free corrector. . . .
> But as I want my readers not to be bound down to me, so I want my correctors not to be
> bound down to themselves. Let not the reader love me more than the Catholic faith, and
> let not the correctors love themselves more than the Catholic Truth.[9]

In dealing with this extraordinary, troubling, and beautiful Father, I have been helped
most by the work of Robert J. O'Connell. Many other scholars have filled in missing pieces
of background for me, but it was O'Connell's writings that performed the unique and (by
the nature of the case) unrepeatable service of convincing me I might actually be seeing
what I thought I was seeing. This happened not long after I found that the proof of the immortality of the soul in Augustine's *Soliloquies* required us to believe in the intrinsic divinity of the soul—and was astonished to discover such a thing in a Church Father. Then I
came upon O'Connell's discussion of "the soul's divinity at Cassiciacum"[10] and it was like
being given permission to see with my own eyes. Of course it is not his fault if I have seen

amiss; but if I have seen aright it should help confirm some of the more controversial stands he has taken in the past thirty-five years of his patient and adventurous scholarship.

My other great debts are to friends and teachers at Yale, where this book first took shape, especially Nicholas Wolterstorff and George Lindbeck, my advisors, and Han Frei, who is still much missed. He was the one who reminded us all that one particular human being, Jesus Christ, is central to the whole Christian faith—a reminder all the more valuable because it was so odd it should ever be needed. But that is how Christian theology goes: at its best it is a reminder of what Christians should never have forgotten in the first place. And I cannot say how much I owe to ongoing conversations with the likes of David Yeago, Kendall Soulen, Kathryn Greene-McCreight, Rusty Reno, Sondra and Tom Wheeler, Roddey Reid, Peter Rodgers, and Nancy Hazle. I could wish all my readers such debts.

Contents

Note on Quotations and Citations

All translations from ancient and medieval texts are my own, as are all other translations, unless an English edition is given in the bibliography. Italics in quotations are mine (their purpose being usually to emphasize the part of the quotation on which my exegesis turns). Citations from ancient texts omit the chapter number where redundant: for example *Confessions,* book 7, chapter 10, section 16 is cited *Conf.* 7:16.

Augustine's Invention of the Inner Self

Introduction

There are varieties of inwardness, so it is important to know which one is being investigated in this book. My concern here is with the concept of self as private inner space or inner world—a whole dimension of being that is our very own, and roomy enough that we can in some sense turn into it and enter it, or look within and find things there. This, I take it, is the deepest and most thoroughgoing form of inwardness; other forms shall be of interest in this investigation only insofar as they lead up to it. In this regard all roads lead to Augustine: the thesis I argue here is that he invented the concept of private inner space. The argument for this thesis consists of two narratives: one telling of the tradition of philosophy upon which Augustine drew (part I) and the other of the development of Augustine's own thought (part II). The aim is to watch the concept of private inner self as it is under construction: to discern its Platonist philosophical foundations, its Christian theological connections, its memorable metaphorical texture, and the motives that led to its being constructed in the first place.

The inwardness being tracked down in this book is a concept, a way of thinking about the human self, and therefore an element in human self-understanding. As such it has worked its way deeply into the intellectual heritage of the West and therefore into the experience of Western individuals, many of whom have experienced themselves as inner selves. But the focus of investigation here is the concept, not the experience. Without the concept, people would describe their experiences differently, and there would be no phenomenon of inwardness to track down in the texts. Moreover, as I hope to make clear from the texts, this concept did not arise directly out of experience, as if it was the expression of some deeper, inarticulate feeling. Rather, it is the product of highly articulate philosophical inquiry, arising in a quite definite theological context in order to solve quite specific conceptual problems.

Its use in technical philosophical discourse is the reason why the concept of a private inner space is something more than a metaphor. The inner space of the self is of course not literally "inner" like the space inside a box. It is not literally a space at all and therefore not "inner" in a spatial sense. This is a new, incorporeal sense of "inner," associated specifically with the soul rather than the body, which begins as a metaphor and becomes established as a piece of technical terminology in Neoplatonist metaphysics. Thus it retains much of the imaginative power of metaphor while also gaining a new literal sense, the sense established by its use in a particular philosophical and theological discourse. The inner space is a dimension or level of being belonging specifically to the soul, distinct from the being of God above it (and within it) and from the world of bodies outside it (and below it). It is like a space, however, in that it is a dimension of being that can contain things: things are found and seen there, as well as lost and hidden there.

The inner space has its ancestors and cousins. Part I of this study tells the tale of the ancestors, part II is concerned with the thing itself, and a planned sequel deals with its important cousin, which I shall call "expressionism." This cousin has perhaps the most ancient lineage of all, which can be traced back to very old and widespread talk about how people can hide their thoughts in their heart and bring them forth in speech. Augustine gives new rigor to this talk by identifying the hidden heart with the private inner space and conceiving speech as an expression of what lies within that space. It was an epochal innovation when Augustine classified words as a species of signs, and treated signs as external indications of the inner will of the soul—thus laying the groundwork for medieval understandings of word and sacrament as well as much of modern semiotics and theory of language. But that subject takes us beyond the scope of this book, to Augustine's account of how the inner self is related to external things and especially how signs communicate or express what is within.

Although expressionism is not the variety of inwardness being tracked down here, it does make a contribution to it that should be mentioned now. One of the things that makes the inner space private is that it is hidden from view: other people cannot look within it. That we can hide what is in our hearts or minds is a commonplace that goes back long before Augustine and extends beyond any one tradition: both Homer and the Hebrew Scriptures speak of this sort of thing. The contribution this notion makes to later forms of Western inwardness is unmistakable when, for instance, Paul contrasts being a Jew "in appearance" (i.e., because of circumcision) with being a Jew "in what is hidden" (i.e., in the heart)—and then this is translated in the King James and Revised Standard Versions of the Bible as "outwardly" and "inwardly," respectively (Romans 2:28–29). Paul is not using the vocabulary of inwardness here, but translators in the wake of Augustine find it natural to translate his words into that vocabulary—and the reason they find it natural is because Augustine himself made the connection for them: the inner is that which is hidden in the heart.

Augustine frequently describes the inner as "hidden," meaning that we cannot see each other's minds or souls. But when I speak of the "privacy" of the inner self, I have more in view than just the contrast between what is hidden in the heart and what is outwardly manifest. There is another conceptual contrast whose field of force, as it were, shapes this space, and that is the contrast between what is common to all souls and what belongs properly to one individual rather than another. For a Platonist, this contrast has some distinctive features. Since the best things in reality are One not Many, they are things that souls can only have in common. Thus, for example, wisdom in one soul is not ultimately different from wisdom in another, for there is ultimately only one true Wisdom. This Platonic Idea or Form of Wisdom is common to all, not the private possession of the individual, and it is equally available to all who have eyes to see it. Hence it is not so obvious that the inner self must be private. On the contrary, the natural thing for a Platonist to say (once Platonism acquires a concept of inner space) is that the inner realm is public not private, since the goods in it are common possessions rather than private property.

The new and specifically Augustinian contribution to the notion of the inner space—the thing that distinguishes it from previous forms of Platonist inwardness—is precisely that Augustine's inner space is actually private. However, Augustine is different from most of his successors in the West in that for him this privacy is not natural or good but results from our estrangement from the one eternal Truth and Wisdom that is common to all. The inner self is private only because it is sinful, fallen away from God.

To bring into focus the particular variety of inwardness we are looking for, we can place Augustine's picture of the inner self between representative pictures from two ancestors and a descendant—like putting four snapshots in a row. The oldest snapshot is Plato's picture in the Allegory of the Cave: an eye that has escaped from bondage in the lower darkness is now gazing upward, away from itself, at the sun. There is no inwardness here, but there is a key concept, intelligibility or intellectual vision, which will be at the heart of later Platonist inwardness. The next snapshot gives us the much less familiar picture of Plotinus: the soul is like a sphere revolving around the source of all light at the center of the universe and turning inward to see it. Our particular souls are each points of light on the revolving sphere, capable of looking outward upon the darkness or turning into the inside to behold the realm of light. This inner realm is the Platonist's "intelligible world," which has now become an inner world—although unlike Augustine's inner space it is common to all, not private. Augustine's picture comes third, and it is of an inner palace, with great courtyards open to the sun. To see the light means both entering within and looking upward—combining Plotinus's inward turn with Plato's ascent to vision. The result is that what you find when you turn inward but not upward, is your own private inner space. Last, there is John Locke's picture of a dark room where there is nothing to see but images projected within. No sun shines into this room from above, and even the windows afford no direct view of the external world but only serve as a lens to project images of what is outside onto a blank inner wall. The thread of continuity tying these pictures together (like four beads on a string) is the metaphor of the soul as an eye, based on the Platonist notion of intelligibility as the visibility of something to the eye of the mind. Plato's picture is intellectual vision pure and simple, Plotinus's is intellectual vision construed as inward turn, Augustine's is intellectual vision resulting from a turn first in then up, and Locke's picture is of a self with no direct intellectual vision of anything but its own private inner world, seeing only the images of things outside.

Hence Western inwardness can be traced back to the Platonist inward turn, represented by Plotinus, which is adopted and modified by Augustine to produce the concept of private inner space, which later undergoes modifications of its own in Locke and others. As we go from Plotinus to Augustine to Locke, we find the inner world shrinking—from a divine cosmos containing all that is ultimately real and lovely (in Plotinus) to the palace of an individual soul that can gaze upon all that is true and lovely above (in Augustine) to a closed little room where one only gets to watch movies, as it were, about the real world (in Locke). It is a progression in which the inner self contains progressively less of reality and divinity—from Plotinus's divine inner self, to Augustine's inner self, in which God can be found, to Locke's inner room where there can be literally no idea of God.

The story I tell here will focus on the development that leads from Plato to Augustine, with only a brief glance ahead at Locke. It is a generational narrative: grandfather Plato's concept of intelligibility (chapter 1) gets married to Aristotle's identity theory of intellectual knowledge (chapter 2), whence is born Plotinus's concept of inward turn. The inward turn is then espoused by Augustine (chapter 3) and married to his Christianity in what may be a shotgun wedding (chapter 4). Later this marriage is misconstrued by kindhearted descendants who don't want to think ill of their honored ancestor (chapter 5). In the climactic narrative, Augustine's outgrows earlier flirtations in order to espouse the inward turn (chapter 6), which, after a miscarriage (chapter 7) and a difficult labor (chapter 8), gives birth to an inner self that is private (chapter 9) yet spacious like an inner world (chapter 10).

PART I

PLATONISM: A TRADITION OF DIVINITY WITHIN

The Kinship of Soul and Platonic Form

The invention of inwardness is an episode in the history of the Platonist concept of intelligibility, which defines the relation between the soul and Platonic Ideas or Forms. After glancing at Stoic precursors to Neoplatonist inwardness, this chapter focuses on the history and problems of the concept of intelligibility in Plato's own writing, beginning with the way Plato uses the existence of intelligible Form to define the nature of the soul in the Phaedo, *then proceeding to investigate how the concept of intelligibility took shape in the course of Plato's attempt to solve a problem about the very possibility of Socratic inquiry in the* Meno. *Plato's initial solution, the doctrine of Recollection, raises further problems about the nature of intelligibility, which Plato tackles using a metaphor that becomes fundamental for later Platonism: intellectual vision.*

Seeing the Good in the Soul

For the most part, we in the West still take it for granted that we can talk about an inmost self and conceive of it as an inner world, a sort of private interior realm where we are most at home and most ourselves. Many still find this concept indispensable, as if we human beings would lose sight of some important part of ourselves without it. Yet such talk is hardly universal or necessary for human life. It is not an inevitable part of human self-description, in contrast (say) to such concepts as perception, life, and mortality. Nor is it as widespread in the cultures of the world as the notion that human beings seek happiness, want to know the truth, can be good or evil, can come close to the divine or be far away. Human beings can describe themselves in emotional, ethical, and religious terms without recourse to the conception of a private inner world. Indeed before Augustine everyone seems to have found it natural to do so, having no notion that there was an alternative.

The texts of the Western tradition bear witness to this. Not only the Bible but Plato and Aristotle and the rest of classical philosophy could say what they had to say about human nature without invoking the private inner space that modern Westerners find so familiar and intimate a part of themselves. Of course this does not mean that Augustinian inwardness has no precursors—as if it came out of nothing. There is an ancient language of inwardness that goes back ultimately to Greek philosophers talking about the soul being *in* the body. But such talk by itself does not imply that the soul is a private inner world or that the soul can turn to look within itself. Indeed, quite the contrary: for classical philosophers the soul was perceptive like the eye—it looked away from itself, paying attention to the world around it.

The history of inwardness is the story of how Westerners developed the desire to see within the soul and therefore came to conceive of the soul doing what no eye ever did: turning to look within its own self. Hefty philosophical convictions lie behind this familiar but radically incoherent metaphor of looking inward—more than just the notion that the soul is *in* the body, more even than the notion that the soul is a deeper and better kind of being than the body. Inwardness begins to take shape when the soul becomes the great clue to the nature of ultimate reality and final happiness. In many different forms of ancient philosophy and religion—among Platonists and Peripatetics, Gnostics and Manichaeans, Cicero and the Stoics—inquiry into the nature of the soul was thought to issue in wisdom about divinity and blessedness. The god's command "Know Thyself," interpreted to mean "know thy soul," stood as a motto at the head of ancient treatises on the soul, hinting at a promise of divine knowledge as the fruit of self-knowledge.[1] Thus inwardness involves more than a conception of the self; it is concerned with the divine, the eternal, the ultimate. From its inception, inwardness meant seeking a glimpse of the soul's inner relation to its divine origin.

For ancient philosophers, it was an obvious fact that the soul was "in" the body. But this did not lead them to anything like an inward turn or an inner space, until they began to locate the ultimate goal of human desire within the soul. Hence the language of inwardness first begins to play an important role in the writings of the Roman Stoics, whose ethics laid great stress on the contrast between what is within the soul and what is outside it, in the conviction that the soul's good lies entirely within its own power. So Stoics like Epictetus, Marcus Aurelius, and Seneca thought we should turn our attention within, in the sense of attending to what is our very own, rather than setting our hearts on things outside, which do not really belong to us. Thus Epictetus asks,

> In what is the good, then? . . . If you wanted, you would have found it was in yourselves, and you would not have wandered outside or sought things alien to you as if they were your own. Turn to yourselves![2]

Marcus Aurelius likewise urges us to consider that "the source of the good is within."[3] But this is not an invitation to enter an inner world: the point rather is that our own choices are the ultimate source of good or evil, so that our soul's health or harm is entirely independent of external things or circumstances beyond our control. So for Epictetus progress in wisdom means withdrawing from external things and turning to our own power of choice.[4]

Related to this Stoic turn to the self is the conviction that the soul is divine, made of the same stuff as the gods, and the dwelling place of an immortal spirit. Hence Seneca can say "God is near you, with you, *in* you."[5] He is referring to the guardian spirit that is supposed to be in each one of us, but he also alludes to the Stoic conviction that the soul itself is inherently divine, made of the same living fire as the celestial gods.[6] For the Stoics were materialists, believing that everything that exists, even God and the soul, is made of bodily elements (earth, air, water, or fire).

No doubt this is why the language of inwardness in Stoicism never developed into the concept of self as inner world. For materialism is not conducive to inwardness. It lacks the dissatisfaction with the visible world that leads to the aspiration to find something deeper. Inwardness begins when that deeper dimension, something fundamentally other than the world of ordinary life, is sought within the self. The Stoics contributed to later Western inwardness by speaking so highly of what is within the human soul but did not get as far as inventing the notion of inner self, because they had no concept of something deeper, beyond mortal sight, which could be joined with the concept of soul to make an inner world. For all their talk of turning to oneself, the notion that the soul might turn into itself and find a whole separate world of its own seems never to have crossed their minds.[7]

It was of course Platonism that first conceived of that deeper dimension, that other world that is more real and true than the visible, bodily world—and it is to this other world that we must look for the roots of Western inwardness. Talk about turning to the soul or to oneself does not indicate an inner self until the soul or self becomes a different kind of being than anything in this world. Hence the earliest metaphysic of inwardness, which I call "the inward turn," arises within the Platonist tradition,[8] where it is elaborated in detail by the founder of Neoplatonism, Plotinus, who inherits both Platonist talk about the intelligible world and Stoic talk about turning to the self or soul.[9]

Plato himself did not locate this other world in the soul but rather in what he called "the intelligible place,"[10] a realm of being whose elements are not material and therefore not visible to the eyes of the body, but rather are "intelligible", that is, understood by the intellect alone. This is the place of Platonic Ideas or Forms. Later Platonists called it "the intelligible world." Plotinus was evidently the first to conceive of it as an *inner* world, located within the soul. In any case, Plato himself does not speak this way but locates this other world using metaphors of heavenly height rather than inner depth: one finds the place of Forms not by turning inward but by looking upward and outward, as if gazing from earth to heaven, or looking beyond the whole visible world to that which is outside it[11]—or else as if one were climbing up out of a dark cave into the true light of day.[12] How it is that the world of Platonic Ideas came to be located within the soul (i.e., how the intelligible world became the inner world) is the first part of my story.

Plato does on occasion use a language of inwardness. He will talk of looking into one's own soul, for instance, but unlike Plotinus he does not connect it with perception of the intelligible world and its eternal Forms.[13] Rather, it seems to be a form of ethical self-examination, an effort to discern whether one's soul is well ordered. One may, for example, try to look at the effect that the virtue of temperance has when it is present in oneself[14] or fix one's gaze on the constitution of the republic in one's soul.[15] Evidently, it is possible to see such things because thinking is like talking to oneself,[16] and what one says to oneself is, as it were, written or painted in the soul.[17] The closest Plato comes to an inward turn is when he describes someone "looking in himself" at the opinions and assertions pictured in his soul,[18] and the closest he comes to a concept of inner self is the one time that he describes the soul's talking to itself as an "*inner* dialogue of the soul with itself."[19] But none of this gets very close to the picture of the self as an inner world, which is familiar to us from Augustine and suggested earlier by Plotinus.

The Other World

The deeper dimension in Platonism was always linked to the soul, even if it was not originally inside it. The conceptual link was forged by the argument for the immortality of the soul in the *Phaedo*, which turns on the notion that the soul is somehow "*akin to* what is pure and everlasting, immortal and always the same."[20] Plato portrays Socrates on the day of his death staking everything on this kinship between the soul and immortal Forms, a kinship not only examined but also exemplified by Socrates' practice of philosophical inquiry. In Plato's dramatization, to inquire about the immortality of the soul is as it were to practice one's own immortality—for all philosophical inquiry strengthens the bond between the soul and the deathless Forms to which it is kin.[21]

Thus Plato's Socrates offers, both in theory and in practice, an alternative to the ancient Homeric picture of the soul and its ultimate destiny. In Homer the soul, or *psyche,* is the insubstantial, fluttering thing that escapes the human body in its last breath and is carried off to the shadowy underworld.[22] The *Phaedo* presents an alternative destination for the soul after death, and a practical route to get there. The pure soul does not end up in an insubstantial underworld, but dwells among true realities, divine and deathless Forms. The road to this true home of the soul is philosophical inquiry, in which the soul investigates unchanging truths by pure thought alone, separating itself as much as possible from the body and thus purifying itself and "practicing to die"—for death is not the destruction of the soul but merely its purification, its separation and liberation from the body.[23] Plato's new notion, the "intelligible place," thus implies a new conception of the human soul: not the fluttering last breath in danger of being scattered on the wind but rather a being of higher order than body and breath, somehow kin to the deathless being of the Forms.[24]

A powerful spirituality comes to birth with this text, a project of turning from sensible to intelligible, from the world of transient and mortal bodies to the world of deathless and unchanging Forms. It is a spirituality that divides the human self cleanly in two: there is the body, which inhabits the visible world, and the soul, which belongs ultimately among divine Forms. This famous Platonist dualism of body and soul rests on the logically prior conception of an intelligible realm of being, which gives the soul an orientation, activity, and destiny wholly separate from the body. Without this other world or deeper dimension, "soul" could only mean what it had meant for Homer or for the Hebrew Scriptures: one aspect of the human self among many, overlapping and interacting with the others—heart and mind, bowels and liver, spirit and breath, flesh and body, none of them neatly contrasting to the soul as visible to invisible, mortal to immortal, mental to physical, or outer to inner.[25]

For Platonist spirituality, then, not only our happiness but our self-knowledge depends on the relation between the soul and the eternal Forms. To know our own soul we must know the Forms. That at any rate is how the argument goes in the *Phaedo*, which grounds knowledge of our souls's immortality on premises about the deathlessness and immutability of the Forms.[26] Augustine's inward turn reverses the direction of argument, aiming to arrive at a knowledge of the eternal by first looking at the soul. But whichever way the argument goes (from the eternal to the soul or from the soul to the eternal) the key premise is that there is some kind of link between the two. The nature of that link is a crucial topic of Platonist reflection and a central theme in Augustine's writing up through the time of his *Confessions*.

The relation between soul and Forms is summed up in the Platonist term "intelligible" (*noetos*). To be intelligible means to be understandable, to be a fit object for the intellect or mind (*nous*). Platonic Forms are intelligible, because they are what our intellects can know. (We cannnot, strictly speaking, *know* sensible things, because they are too unstable and deceptive to be objects of certain knowledge; that is why Plato says they are objects of opinion or belief rather than knowledge). Intelligibility thus defines the very nature of the Forms: they are what the eye of the mind sees, in contrast to sensible things, which are what the eye of the body sees. Investigating the relation of the soul to the Forms, with all its implications for human happiness and wisdom, thus boils down to the attempt to understand the nature of intelligibility. The inner world is a concept that develops in the course of that investigation. The invention of inwardness is an episode in the history of the Platonist concept of intelligibility.

Intelligibility has a history because it is a concept that generates problems. One deep problem stems from the soul's presence in the sensible or material world. Plato sometimes seems to divide the universe of things neatly in two: the intelligible and the sensible, Being and Becoming, the world of Forms and the world of bodies. But Platonist ontology cannot really be that simple. There is more to the universe than just bodies and Forms; there is the troublesome existence of the soul itself. Obviously (to a Platonist) the soul is not a body, yet it is not exactly a Form either. The problem is that a Form is immutable, being "always such, the same as itself,"[27] as Plato puts it, while the soul plainly is not. The soul changes, becomes more or less wise, more or less happy, more or less virtuous. If the great boundary line on our map of the universe is drawn betwen the sensible and the intelligible, then the soul appears strangely out of place, far from the immutable realm of intelligible things but not really at home in the sensible world either.

Plato devised the myth of the Fall in part to account for this: how the soul has its true home in the intelligible place but has lost it, falling from heaven into bodies—thither one day to return, as Plato briefly suggests,[28] thus spawning one of the most important and enduring visions of the afterlife in the Western tradition. But until its return to heaven the soul is locked in the body as in a tomb or prison, chained as in a dark cave, in exile from the upper world.[29] The reality of the deeper dimension casts the ordinary world in a dark light—for the authentic light, the true intelligible light, is elsewhere.

It thus becomes an urgent practical question of Platonist spirituality how to find the true light, when it is so unlike what we are used to seeing. For Plato himself the answer is tied up with the practice of dialectic, that is, philosophical inquiry by means of question and answer. If we want to see what the relation of soul and Forms looks like for the founder of Platonism, the best place to look is his portrait of his teacher Socrates. The key theoretical explorations of the relation of soul to Form are found in the places in Plato's dialogues where the character named Socrates reflects on his own practice of dialectical inquiry, its grounds and its hopes. These reflections are the seedbed in which Western inwardness has its roots.

Enlarging the Soul

The history of the Platonist concept of intelligibility begins when Plato, early in his philosophical career, faces a serious problem. He must find an alternative to skeptical interpretations of Socratic inquiry. As the later history of Plato's own Academy shows,[30] such interpretations come naturally. And it is not hard to see why. Plato's early writings present no theory of eternal Forms, only a Socrates who seeks rather than possesses wisdom. The Socrates of Plato's early dialogues is wise only because he knows he has no great knowledge, and he is Athens's great teacher of philosophy because he teaches nothing but a recognition of one's own ignorance.

How he goes about teaching this is familiar to readers of such early Platonic dialogues as *Euthyphro* and *Charmides*. These "aporetic" dialogues, as they are called, all follow the same pattern: Socrates lures someone into philosophical inquiry by asking him to define a key ethical term such as "virtue" or "temperance." Once his conversation partner takes the bait and formulates a definition, the peculiarly Socratic dialectic of question and answer begins, with Socrates asking critical questions about the definition and his interlocutor trying to defend it. In fact, the interlocutor ends up offering a whole series of definitions, one after another, as each is refuted in turn. It is a peculiar kind of refutation. Socrates does not simply criticize or disprove his interlocutor's definitions; that is part of the cunning of his dialectic of question and answer. To answer Socrates' critical questions is to find oneself in the end *agreeing* to the refutation of one's own views, and thus discovering firsthand one's own ignorance. Hence the early dialogues all conclude without finding a right answer (an *orthos logos*), leaving both Socrates and his friend in a state of perplexity or puzzlement (*aporia*, whence the description "aporetic" dialogue).

The point of this Socratic method is that we cannot search for wisdom if we think we already have it. Socratic questioning therefore undermines preconceived notions of the ethical life in order to spur one on to find the truth about virtue—the truth about how to live and what kind of person to be—which one now recognizes one does not know. But the method is undermined by its own success. If the predictable result of Socratic inquiry is simply perplexity and recognition of ignorance, then what hope is there of ever finding a good answer to a question like "what is virtue?"

Plato addresses this problem in a key transitional dialogue, the *Meno*.[31] The first third of this dialogue follows the pattern of the early aporetic dialogues. After Socrates lures young Meno into a discussion about virtue, Meno offers a series of definitions of the word virtue (*aretē*), each of which he comes to see (under Socratic questioning) as inadequate— and he ends up puzzled and perplexed. In fact he gives a classic description of the puzzlement that Socrates induces—and then asks the central question that Plato must deal with in the dialogue. It is like an author being questioned by one of his characters: after putting Socrates' interlocutors through so many interrogations, Plato finds that one of them has gotten lively enough to ask a puzzling question of his own. This liveliness is of course the author's success, not failure. For Meno's question poses one of the most fruitful problems in all of Western philosophy. By challenging the project of Socratic inquiry it helps initiate the project later known as Platonism.

Meno wants to know how it is even possible to inquire, that is, to seek knowledge of what one does not already know. Hence his question concerns the very possibility of philosophy, the search for wisdom that we do not already possess.

> But Socrates, what way is there of seeking this thing you don't know anything about? What sort of thing do you propose to seek, among all the things you don't know? And even if you happened upon it, how would you recognize that this is the thing you didn't know?[32]

Plato's answer is that in a sense we already do have knowledge of the thing we seek, and that what we do in seeking and learning is actually to recollect a piece of knowledge that was present in our soul all along.[33] This doctrine of Recollection is as good a place as any to mark the beginning of Western inwardness. In stating it, Plato often uses a distinctive verb (*en-einai*) which means literally "to be *in*." The verb also has a relevant secondary meaning: "to be possible"—as when we say "she has it in her," meaning, "it is possible for her to do it."[34] The point of the doctrine in any case is that knowledge is possible for us because it is in a certain sense already present *in* our souls. The doctrine of Recollection thus has the effect of enlarging our conception of the soul and its contents. If Plato is right, there is more in our souls than we are apt to realize, and this "more" that is in us opens up the possibility of deep adventures. Inwardness is about these hitherto unsuspected possibilities of the soul.

In particular, this Platonic enlargement of the soul grounds an optimistic epistemology—a specifically Platonist rather than Socratic view of the possibilities of human knowledge. After making a Socratic discovery of his ignorance, Meno needs a Platonic reassurance about the hope of finding knowledge. Hence whereas Socratic dialectic taught him that he did not know what he thought he knew, Platonic Recollection functions to reassure him that he knows more than he thinks he knows. As the dialogue proceeds, "Socrates" tries to bring this reassurance home to Meno by doing something very un-Socratic: he embarks on an inquiry that arrives in the end at the right answer. This is the famous geometry lesson in which Socrates, asking just the right leading questions, gets Meno's slave boy to recognize—or rather "recollect"—the truth of a piece of geometry that no one thought he knew. The first part of the geometry lesson deliberatly mimics the first part of the *Meno*, following the typical pattern of the Socratic dialectic of refutation, which, as Socrates archly points out in an aside to Meno, results in exactly the same sort of puzzlement that Meno himself had lately complained of.[35] But then Socrates does the new, un-Socratic, Platonic thing: he leads the boy, who has just recognized his ignorance of geometry, to see the right answer—and concludes that he had it in him the whole time.

In this geometry lesson Plato is evidently pointing to a phenomenon we have all experienced, that moment of insight when we first glimpse with our mind's eye the right answer, the truth that had been eluding us until now. And he wants to convince us that the reason we recognize its rightness is because we've seen it before. Hence the reason we can seek it is because the knowledge of it is in some way already in us, in our memories and in our souls, so that when we see it we can recognize it the way we recognize something once familiar but lately forgotten, when after long years we see it again. Thus Plato interprets the experience of insight as a kind of recollection.

Problems of Intelligibility

But if the doctrine of Recollection is an interpretation of the phenomenon of insight, it is an interpretation that itself stands in need of explanation. Here more problems—yet more fruitful problems—turn up. To begin with, how did this knowledge come to be in our souls in the first place? What past is it that we are remembering when we recollect in this peculiar Platonic way? And how could we be so forgetful as not to realize this knowledge was present in our soul the whole time Socrates was refuting our preconceptions and leading us into perplexity?

It is important to realize that Plato's answer to these questions develops over the course of his career. The earlier, less developed form of his answer is given in the *Meno*. Like so many of the solutions Plato finds for his unheard-of problems (problems that never arose in human thought before, because they are problems that no one before Plato ever got himself into) this one takes the form of a myth. It is a myth of transmigration and reincarnation of souls, borrowed from Greek religion and poetry. The story is that our soul is immortal, existing both before and after its time in the body—inhabiting in fact a whole series of bodies, each of which it enters at birth and leaves at death. So Plato's suggestion is that if we ever find a good answer to one of Socrates' questions, it will be because we recollect something we learned in a previous life but have since forgotten.

The doctrine of Recollection must be distinguished from this myth of Transmigration, which is supposed to explain it. For Recollection is an enduring Platonist doctrine, while Transmigration is, as an explanation, a failure. It explains how Platonic Recollection is possible but only at the cost of losing the whole point of the doctrine of Recollection, which was to show how it was possible to seek knowledge we didn't already have. If our present search for knowledge is possible only because we learned in a previous life what we need to know, then Plato has only deferred the task of explaining how knowledge is possible, for he has yet to explain how it originated in that previous life.

Augustine makes this point tellingly, in a famous criticism:

> The noble philosopher Plato wanted to persuade us that the souls of men lived here even before they bore these bodies, and hence that what is learned is recollected as something known, rather than known as something new. He relates that a certain boy, questioned about something in geometry, answered as if he were an expert in that discipline—for when questioned skillfully, step-by-step, he saw what was to be seen, and said what he saw. But if this recollection was of things known earlier, then after all not everyone, or hardly anyone, would be able to do this when questioned in this way. For not everyone was a geometer in a previous life, since geomters are rare enough in the human race to be rather hard to find. . . .[36]

Notice that this criticism strikes effectively against the myth of Transmigration rather than the doctrine of Recollection. It does not show that insight isn't Recollection, but rather that Transmigration, even if it happened, wouldn't explain the phenomenon of insight. Plato himself seems to be aware of this problem, for even in the *Meno*, when he restates the doctrine of Recollection it is in a way that evades Augustine's criticism by pointing beyond transmigration. Discussing the meaning of the slave boy's geometry lesson, Socrates draws out the implications of the doctrine of Recollection for the nature of the soul thus:

> So if during the time when he was human and the time he was not, true opinions *were in* him, which were aroused by questioning and became knowledge, then has not his soul been *learned for all time?*[37]

The time when the slave boy was "not human" means the periods when his soul is disembodied.[38] But the point is that whether embodied or disembodied, his soul always already has knowledge or at least true opinion—it always *has been* learned, in the present perfect. The point is clearly meant to be general: this is the state of everyone's soul. So one need not have been a geometer in a previous life in order to recollect knowledge of geometry, as Augustine alleges. The implication rather is that the knowledge we recollect, being present at all times in our souls, was not learned in time at all but somehow prior to all times—in eternity.

That implication is spelled out in Plato's most fully developed account of Recollection, in the *Phaedrus*, where the myth of Transmigration is backed up by the myth of the Fall.[39] While the Fall serves to explain how souls came to be trapped in bodies in the first place, what explains the possibility of human knowledge is the events before the Fall. Before they ever came into bodies, the souls that later were human kept company with the gods in heaven, contemplating eternal Forms that lay outside the very bounds of the universe. So this is how knowledge was first acquired: by *intellectual vision*, seeing the Forms with the eye of the mind long before there was an eye of the body to distract it and make it forget its inaugural vision. The myth is clearly meant to trace the soul's origin back beyond time to eternity, so that the deathless realm to which the pure soul goes when separated from the body in death is the same realm from which it came in the beginning. The other world that is the soul's destiny in the *Phaedo* is its origin in the *Phaedrus*.

Intellectual Vision

Having enlarged the nature of the soul in the *Meno*, Plato was forced to deepen his account of its origin in the *Phaedrus*. Platonist Recollection enlarged the West's conception of the nature of the soul, which then required a deeper explanation of its origin in the Platonist Fall—otherwise, there was no explaining how the soul first got the knowledge it recollects. This explanation of the soul's origin, like the account of its destiny in the *Phaedo*, depended in turn on the existence of something prior to and more stable than the soul, which could be both its point of origin and its destination. Thus Platonic Recollection points to the soul's Fall and Immortality, both of which are inconceivable without Platonic Forms. In this way Plato's doctrine of the soul developed in tandem with his doctrine of the Forms, and especially with the development of their characteristic eternity and separation from the world of bodies. For the Forms are what the soul sees before embodiment, before time, before the fateful Fall from Being to Becoming.

Everything thus depends on the existence of the Forms and the soul's ability to see them. This connection between soul and Form is a central theme of Plato's middle dialogues, the *Phaedo*, the *Republic*, the *Symposium,* and the *Phaedrus*, and thence of the whole Platonist tradition. It was to this notion of kinship between soul and Form, based on the Forms being somehow visible to the soul, that Plato's answer to Meno's question eventually led—though Plato doubtless did not see exactly where he was going at the time he wrote the *Meno*. What he saw, I have been suggesting, is a problem. But as with all seminal thinkers, Plato's problems were fruitful, in that their solutions led to yet more problems—new problems that required more new thoughts to solve them. The doctrine of Recollection arose as the solution to a problem about the grounds and meaning of Socratic inquiry, but it raised the new problem: if the knowledge we seek is already in our souls waiting to be recollected, then what kind of past do our souls have, in which they could have acquired such knowledge? The answer is that the soul's past, its origin, is eternal, grounded in the unchanging Parmenidean world of the Forms.

The notion of unchanging Forms separated from the material world of time and change is not yet present in the *Meno*, but it is on its way. We can sense it coming just over the horizon in the refutation of Meno's first definition of virtue, when Socrates insists that what their inquiry is after is not an example of this or that virtue but rather the one Form (*eidos*) that makes each of the many virtues a virtue. He states this as a kind of criterion of a good definition:

> Even though there are many different virtues, they all have one and the same Form by which they are virtues, and this is the best thing to look at when answering someone who asks you to clarify what virtue is.[40]

Though there is no explicit reference in this passage to the immutability and eternity of the Form of Virtue, or its separation from this changing bodily world, later Platonists will naturally read it as a reference to a Platonic Form—and they will only be half wrong. If we imagine Plato himself rereading the *Meno* at about the time he was writing the *Phaedo*, he would clearly want to interpret the one Form Socrates is seeking here as the Platonic Form of Virtue. That is to say, in completing his account of the grounds and hopes of Socrates' practice of dialectic, Plato is inevitably led to read a search for the Forms into the very marrow of Socratic inquiry—because, as we have seen, the doctrine of Recollection is ultimately dependent on the notion of Platonic Forms if it is to succeed in its task of rescuing Socratic inquiry from skepticism. Plato's answer to Meno's question is thus the beginning not only of Western inwardness but of the Platonist concept of intelligibility—the notion that there is a profound kinship between soul and eternal Form that gives the soul its possibilities and its nature, separating it from the perishable world of bodies in which it is imprisoned. Intelligibility, with all its implications for the nature of the soul, originates as the Platonist alternative to skeptical interpretations of Socrates.

For my purposes—and arguably for any purposes—intelligibility must count as the central concept not only of Plato's middle period but of the whole millennia-long tradition of philosophical inquiry that has come to be called "Platonism." (By this term I mean not merely a set of doctrines but a whole tradition of philosophical inquiry, in which there are serious disagreements between one thinker and another but also a common set of concepts, doctrines, and problems to disagree about. The term "intelligibility," as I use it in this book, refers strictly to a concept within this tradition, not to any more general notion of intelligibility.) But if intelligibility, the kinship between soul and Form, is the backbone of Platonism, then Recollection looks less fundamental than it appeared in the *Meno*. For Recollection must itself be grounded on something logically prior, a present vision rather than a memory of the past. We can recollect the Forms only because in the beginning we *saw* them. And that means we might possibly see them again. The possibility of such vision is at the heart of Plato's mature account of philosophical education in the *Republic*, where it is expounded most fully in the famous Allegory of the Cave.[41] The contemplation of eternal Forms that was at the soul's origin in the *Phaedrus* becomes the climax of its education in the Allegory of the Cave. Yet for both texts knowledge of the Forms is described rather simply, in terms of a metaphor that becomes fundamental for the entire Platonist tradition: the soul or mind "sees" intellible Forms, as the eye of the body sees visible things in the physical light of day. Intelligibility means the possibility of intellectual vision, in which the mind's eye sees eternal things that are invisible to bodily vision.

The recognition that the notion of intellectual vision is fundamental to Platonism is the point of Augustine's criticism of the *Meno*. Indeed, after rejecting the Platonic myth of Transmigration, Augustine proceeds to endorse the Platonic metaphor of vision.

> We should believe instead that the nature of the intellectual mind is fashioned so as to see intelligible things in a certain unique kind of incorporeal light, being linked to them by the natural order the Artificer established.[42]

Augustine is doing more here than rejecting an unchristian myth. He is insisting that intelligibility be understood in terms of eternity rather than time. The phenomenon of insight into intelligible things may have the feel of Recollection and may even point back to a primal Fall of the soul (Augustine's argument does not exclude either of these possibilities), but we must ultimately understand it not in terms of a temporal relationship between our present and our past, but rather as a form of eternal presence, a Light that is always present and shining and available for the intellect to see, if it is looking that way and is not blinded. Augustine is in effect demythologizing Plato, in a way that is quite in conformity with standard Neoplatonist practices of demythologization.[43]

By replacing myth with metaphor in this way, Augustine is aiming to get at what is fundamental, and for him there is nothing in the world more fundamental than the soul's ability to see intelligible truths, for this is none other than the soul's ability to see God, who is "the immutable Truth which contains all that is immutably true."[44] This metaphor in turn becomes fundamental for the next thousand years of Western Christianity, as theologians came to define ultimate human happiness as beatific vision—seeing God with the eye of the soul. But the metaphor is not without its own problems. It does not really explain intelligiblity but only compares it with visibility—that is, it likens intelligibility to precisely what it is not. From the *Phaedo* to the *Confessions*,[45] Platonism insisted that seeing with the eye of the body is a hindrance to seeing with the eye of the mind, and that it is of the utmost importance to know the difference between the two. But that difference is precisely what a metaphor that likens them cannot elucidate.

This is one of the problems Plato left unsolved at his death. It is perhaps the central problem of the Platonist concept of intelligibility. Plato had pointed to the phenomenon of insight, proposing to interpret it through the doctrine of Recollection, an interpretation that in turn needed to be explained by a pair of myths (Transmigration, backed by the Fall) that were finally grounded on the metaphor of intellectual vision. This still leaves us far from a literal explanation of the intelligibility of the Forms that our minds seem to glimpse in the moment of insight. It took Plato's greatest student to find a way of explaining intelligibility without myth or metaphor. This explanation was to become fundamental for Neoplatonist accounts of intelligibility, especially in Plotinus. If the concept of intelligibility is the backbone that gives structure to Platonism, then Aristotle's identity theory of knowledge is the spinal nerve that gives life to Plotinian Neoplatonism and its original form of inwardness. Yet despite his deep fascination with Plotinus's inward turn, Augustine never saw this central nerve hidden in its backbone, as he knew nothing of its Aristotelian source. This ignorance, together with his Christian convictions, gave him new problems to solve, which led eventually to a new form of inwardness quite different from that of Plotinus. This central and hidden feature of Plotinian inwardness is what we must examine in the next chapter.

2

Identity from Aristotle to Plotinus

This chapter attempts to uncover the conceptual structure of Plotinus's inward turn, which underlies Augustinian inwardness. Its central thread is Aristotle's theory that intellectual knowledge consists of a kind of identity between soul and Form. This can be interpreted as a solution to the Platonist problem of the nature of intelligibility, following the lead of Alexander of Aphrodisias, the most important ancient commentator on Aristotle. Thus the Aristotelian identity theory of intellectual knowledge enters Plotinus's conception of the hierarchy of being, a conception whose fine points need to be sketched in some detail in order to provide a frame of reference for Augustine's version of inward turn.

Aristotle: Knowledge as Identity with God

Aristotle is the first to give a wholly literal answer to the question of how the soul is related to the Forms, without recourse to myth or metaphor. The answer is daring and ingenious, yet breathtakingly simple: the soul *is* the Forms it knows. To add the appropriate qualifications: Aristotle says the soul in its fully actualized state of intellectual knowledge is identical to whatever intelligible Form it is presently contemplating. For the intellect, the rational part of the human soul, is potentially identical to all Forms and actually identical to any Form that it is actually thinking about.[1] This identity theory of intellectual knowledge is adopted centuries later by Plotinus, the founder of Neoplatonism, as a central element in his own explanation of the nature of intelligibility and the soul's place in the universe. Thus an Aristotelian theory becomes an integral part of Plotinus's inward turn, which is the earliest version of the inward turn and the progenitor of Augustine's.

It is not hard to see why Plotinus is interested by it. Consider what it implies, for instance, about the soul's kinship with the divine. When Aristotle's identity theory of knowledge is combined with Aristotle's theology, the implication is that the act of contemplating intelligible Forms makes us identical with God. Intellectual knowledge is the exercise of something divine in us, for in using our intellect we human beings become, as much as is possible for us, divine and immortal.[2] The human mind in the act of contemplation is not merely cousin to mythological deities in the visible heavens but is divine in the strictest and highest sense, being no different from the mind of God. At least that is one plausible (albeit clearly Platonizing) way of reading Aristotle, which makes his theology, psychology, and epistemology mutually consistent.

Aristotle's theology is famous for its central tenet that God is utterly separate from (i.e., transcendent to) the natural world and thinks of nothing but himself: God is in fact defined as intellectual activity understanding itself or the understanding of understanding, *noēsis noēseōs*.[3] This seems a very self-centered and uninteresting sort of deity, until one considers that understanding or intellectual contemplation always makes the knower identical with the known, so that the intellect necessarily contemplates itself in *any* object that it understands. Hence all intellectual knowledge is necessarily self-knowledge and self-contemplation.[4] The claim that God knows only himself therefore does not make him ignorant or hopelessly introspective, but rather is compatible with the claim that God's business is precisely to contemplate the world of intelligible Forms separate from matter. In contemplating the intelligible world, God is identical with it, and therefore in knowing the intelligible world God is knowing himself. Hence in knowing himself God is knowing literally everything there is to know—everything that could possibly be an object of intellectual knowledge.

This means that to the extent we human beings contemplate intelligible Forms separate from matter, we know the same things God knows. For to that extent, we are identical with the same things God is identical with, which means that we are (precisely to the extent that we are contemplating) identical with God. To see intelligible Forms is therefore to be God. To put it in terms familiar to the Christian traditions, beatific vision always amounts to deification.

Of course, for Aristotle the human mind is divine only in part and at intervals, because unlike God we begin our lives in ignorance.[5] Moreover, unlike God, we must build our knowledge on a foundation of empirical investigation, because we are dependent on our senses to find Forms outside ourselves, in corporeal objects composed of both matter and Form.[6] Finally, we are unlike God also in that we are unable to contemplate uninterruptedly the Forms we do know, as we grow weary and distracted and need sleep.[7] Hence our mental activity is not self-sufficient like God's, whose contemplating is uninterrupted, always active, and directed solely to himself.[8]

Nevertheless, when in the exercise of our mind or intellect, whose function is to see essences, we come to know what the Form of a corporeal object is, we contemplate that Form or essence in its pure and fully actualized state apart from its "embodiment" in material objects. Hence if the transcendent God, utterly separate from nature, is contemplating separate Forms (separate, that is, from matter) then we human beings, in the exercise of intellectual knowledge, evidently contemplate the same objects as God. On that assumption, then, there is no difference between us and God, at least to the extent that we humans are exercising our intellectual knowledge. So long as we are actively contemplating intelligible Forms, we are, like God, none other than Active Intellect, knowing and identical with pure intelligible Form.[9]

Alexander's Interpretation of Aristotle

It is not hard to see why this particular way of combining Aristotelian psychology, epistemology, metaphysics, and theology would interest ancient Platonists, but the notion that it might actually be a sound interpretation of Aristotle may take some getting used to. At the very least it requires historical comment. Until recently Western scholars used to take it for granted that Aristotelianism and Platonism were two quite different systems of thought. This is a very natural position to take in light of the later history of Platonism and Aristotelianism, and especially the centuries-long influence of medieval Christian Aristotelianism, which produced a powerful interpretation of Aristotle that leaned in a rather empiricist (and therefore anti-Platonist) direction. In the ancient period, however, the prevailing opinion was that Aristotelian philosophy represented a modification rather than a rejection of Platonism. For example, of the philosophic traditions known to Augustine, both Neoplatonism and the Hellenistic Academy held that Aristotle's teaching was distinguishable from Plato's in name only.[10] Porphyry, Plotinus's most influential student, wrote a treatise arguing "That the school of Plato and Aristotle is one,"[11] and the Neoplatonist schools in Athens and Alexandria subsequently incorporated Aristotle's texts into their curriculum, making especially sophisticated use of his logic.[12] As a result of this harmonizing tendency in Neoplatonism, most of the commentaries on Aristotle known to the West prior to the influx of Arabic learning were written by Neoplatonists, including the Christian Boethius and Porphyry himself.

Any scholarship that takes the medieval Christian interpretation of Aristotle as normative will have to dismiss a great deal of the ancient commentary on Aristotle's psychology and epistemology as Platonist distortion. The opposite side of the coin is that a scholar specializing in ancient philosophy is apt to find the interpretation of Aristotle by a Thomas Aquinas exaggeratedly empiricistic, especially in his treatment of the activity of the intellect. Neither side of the coin is entirely wrong, a contemporary Aristotle scholar might well add, because Aristotle himself was both empiricistic and Platonizing—and to different degrees at different periods in his career.[13] His early empiricism seems to have had an influence on the original development of Stoicism,[14] as well as contributing to the criticism and revision of the doctrine of Forms that we find in Plato's later works.[15] The more Platonizing works of his maturity, on the other hand, furnished the later Platonist tradition with some of its most important conceptual resources, as we shall see.

The notion that knowing intelligible Forms amounts to identity with the divine Mind does seem to me to make the best sense of Aristotle's texts over all.[16] One point in its favor is that it first turns up in the work of an ancient Peripatetic philosopher, Alexander of Aphrodisias, who was a member of Aristotle's own school rather than a Platonist. Alexander is in fact the most important and authoritative Aristotle commentator in antiquity, referred to by others in that period as *the* Commentator (*ho exēgētēs*).[17] He works out his interpretation of the relation between soul and Form in his treatise *On the Soul*, which claims to be nothing but an exposition of Aristotle's theory on the subject.[18] Alexander's interpretation of Aristotle's psychology is evidently the earliest and probably the most influential ever undertaken.[19] It is hard to imagine the later Aristotelian traditions, Byzantine and Arabic, medieval and modern, making much sense of Aristotle's treatise *On the Soul* without it. In particular, the condensed, crucial chapter 3:5 (Aristotle's treatment of active Mind or, as Thomists call it, "the agent intellect") might have remained hopelessly obscure without the help that Alexander afforded to later readers and commentators, and through them to us. Among the readers Alexander has helped is Plotinus, who we know studied him carefully and who evidently found his interpretation rather congenial.[20]

Writing early in the third century AD (about when Plotinus was born) Alexander was the leading Peripatetic of his time, head of the Aristotelian school in an era when school loyalties and orthodoxies were important. The various philosophical schools had been polemicizing against each other ever since the Hellenistic era, and as John Dillon points out, the motives of polemic were not only the need to respond to criticisms from other schools, but also each school's need to distance itself from the others in order to maintain its distinctiveness.[21] It seems to me that Alexander's work *On the Soul*, though not polemical in tone, is shaped by the latter sort of motivation: Alexander takes a Platonizing view of Aristotle precisely in order to distance his epistemology from that of the Stoics. (This is not a problem Aquinas faced when he produced his highly empiricist interpretation of Aristotle a millenium later, in an environment that included no Stoics.)

Alexander's treatment of the intellect reckons with an element in Aristotle's psychology and epistemology that reminds one quite strikingly of the Platonist doctrine of the Forms. The feature of that doctrine which Aristotle had criticized most relentlessly— namely, the claim that the Forms are "separate" (*chōristos*) from matter and therefore not present in the particular substances of the sensible world[22]—reappears in modified form in Aristotle's view that the intellect, in knowing the essences of things, contemplates *Forms separate from matter*. Thus Aristotle's epistemology describes the object of knowledge in the very terms that he had rejected in his critique of Plato's ontology. As Aristotle describes it, the object of knowledge—the thing that the mind becomes identical with when it contemplates—looks very much like a Platonic Form. This is the point on which Alexander's exposition of the Aristotelian theory of mind or intellect turns.

Alexander has to solve a series of interconnected problems about the ontological status of the "Forms separate from matter" with which the contemplating mind is identical. First of all, what happens to them when they are not being actively contemplated? The most familiar answer to this day is that given by Aquinas: they are imprinted on the passive or "potential" intellect. This makes the passive intellect look like the same thing as memory—and in fact Aquinas explicitly identifies it with the memory of intelligible forms.[23] If this is an identification that Aristotle intended, then one wonders why he did not say so himself. Moreover, it makes Aristotle's epistemology look very much like that of the Stoics, who also begin with sense-perception and proceed to give an account of how, through experience and memory, one arrives at general concepts that are retained in the mind. Alexander, on the contrary, seems convinced that Aristotle's account of the knowledge of intelligible Form should look more like the contemplation of unchanging essences than like an empirical process of concept formation. The formation of concepts, he says (using the Stoic technical term *ennoia*) is only an incomplete stage in the development of true knowledge of intelligible Form, a stage at which intellectual knowledge is not yet fully independent of sensation.[24]

Now, there is no doubt that Aristotle gives a basically empiricist account of how the human mind extracts intelligible forms from sensible objects through induction (i.e., recognition of universal Forms in sensible objects) and abstraction (i.e., the separation of the universal Form from the matter in the sensible object).[25] Hence in order to make sure that intelligible Form does not degenerate to the status of a mere mental concept as in Stoicism, Alexander must make the surprising claim that when the mind ceases contemplating, the intelligible Form ceases to exist: for the Form embodied in matter is not universal and intelligible, and the Form separated from matter has no place to go once the mind is no longer actively looking at it.[26]

To counterbalance this claim, however, Alexander introduces a second kind of intelligible Form: one that is intrinsically intelligible, that is, one that never needs to be *made* intelligible by any process of abstraction or induction.[27] This is the kind of Form that seems so much like Platonic Forms. This kind of Form is never merely potentially intelligible, like the Forms embodied in matter, but is always and forever intelligible "in act," which implies (since intellectual knowledge is the identity of the knower with the known) that it is always actively being contemplated. Thus it is imperishable and unchanging and independent of the whole sensible world, just like Plato's Forms. Of course in order for it to be always actively contemplated there must be an active contemplator always contemplating it, and this is the role Alexander assigns to Aristotle's "active mind" or "agent intellect"—which means of course that the agent intellect is nothing other than the God described in *Metaphysics* 7, the transcendent deity, separate from nature, eternally contemplating himself.[28] For precisely in contemplating himself, this God contemplates the eternal kind of Forms, with which he is eternally identical. The good news is that the human mind too can contemplate these Forms, thus having a share in God's own self-contemplation.[29] Alexander plainly thinks that this interpretation of Aristotelian contemplation also accounts for the kind of knowledge that Plato described using the metaphor of intellectual vision in the Allegory of the Cave.[30] This means, in effect, that Aristotle's agent intellect is nothing other than Plato's idea of the Good, and that the higher sort of intelligible Forms constitute what the Platonist tradition calls "the intelligible world."

Identity in Plotinus's Hierarchy

Alexander of Aphrodisias was not the only ancient philosopher who saw a connection between Aristotle's theology and Plato's account of the intelligible world. In fact the Platonist tradition leading up to Plotinus (commonly labeled "Middle Platonism" by modern scholars) is well nigh obsessed with the Aristotelian concept of God as Mind or *Nous*.[31] But as Platonists, they must coordinate this concept with Plato's idea of the Good as well as his account of the Demiurge and the World-Soul, each of which is in some sense God. The result is a confused proliferation of divine Minds, some utterly transcendent and unconcerned with the natural world, some creative of the natural world like Plato's Demiurge, and some immanent in the cosmos as a World-Soul.[32]

Plotinus offers a solution to this problem of proliferating divine Minds by constructing a hierarchy that distinguishes three levels of divine being, in descending order: the One, the divine Mind, and the Soul. This ontological hierarchy, completed by a fourth and lowest level, the sensible or material world, provides the basic architecture for Plotinus's view of the universe.[33] Since this is also the architecture that makes sense of Plotinus's talk of the soul turning inward to find the divine, it is something we must examine in detail.

Plotinus introduces a fundamental distinction between the Platonist First Principle and the Aristotelian divine Mind, by way of a fresh reading of Plato's description of the Form of the Good as above being and essence[34] and of Plato's account of the One that is beyond description, limitation, and knowledge.[35] Plotinus takes these to be two accounts of the same First Principle, the very highest and first of all things. This First Principle is not a Mind, but rather is above Mind and beyond all intellectual activity, just as it is above being and essence and Form. Thus the One or the Good is neither knower nor known, and cannot even properly be said to *be* (for true being or essence is *below* it, in the intelligible world, upon which it shines from above like the sun in the Allegory of the Cave).

The divine Mind is at the second level of Plotinus's ontological hierarchy, below the One or the Good. As in Aristotle, Mind is identical with the Forms it knows—so that at this level we find not only Aristotle's God (the divine Mind or agent intellect) but also the intelligible world of Platonic Forms—Platonic Ideas in the Mind of God.[36] At the third level is the Soul, which Plotinus (agreeing with Aristotle against Plato) thinks of as not only incorporeal but non-spatial and immovable—not located at any place in the material world and therefore not subject to motion, which requires change from place to place.[37] Finally, at the fourth and lowest level of the hierarchy of being is the material cosmos, the spatial and temporal world of bodies and motion, birth and death.

This four-tiered hierarchy is the conceptual framework within which Plotinus works at solving key problems of the Platonist tradition, such as the ambiguous place of the soul relative to the sensible/intelligible distinction, and the relation of the soul to the Forms. Aristotle's identity theory of knowledge serves as a key structural element in the conceptual architecture of the hierarchy.[38] For instance, whereas earlier Platonists were content to locate Platonic Forms in the divine Mind, Plotinus based his account of the divine Mind on the Aristotelian premise that it does not just contain Platonic Forms but is identical with them.

Aristotle's identity theory of knowledge is also fundamental to what is perhaps the most distinctive tenet of Plotinus's theory of the soul. For Plotinus teaches that the higher part of the human soul is always contemplating and therefore is eternally identical with what it contemplates. This is the immutable and "undescended" part of the soul, by which we remain in the intelligible world at the true center of our being.[39] Hence when the soul turns its attention upon its true self, it finds the intelligible world, which is identical with the divine Mind.

This is how the intelligible world comes to be conceived as an inner world. In obedience to the divine command "Know Thyself," the Plotinian soul turns to look at its own interior and discovers that it is at root identical with the divine Mind, containing the whole intelligible world. Hence in Plotinian inwardness the soul turns to see not a private inner space but the intelligible world.[40] Moreover, in turning inward the soul necessarily turns away from things outside it—lower and bodily things—thus accomplishing the essential task of Neoplatonist ethics, purifying itself from the stains of bodily attachments.[41] Hence in this earliest version of Western inwardness the inward turn moves from lower to higher, from mortal to divine, from perishable to eternal, and the inner space is not a private realm but the intelligible world, the Mind of God.

Plotinus wants the soul to turn its attention into its own interior because that is where God is. The concept that makes this inward turn conceivable is that of the higher part of the soul, and the distinctively Plotinian feature of this concept is that the higher part of the soul is always contemplating—for this is what eliminates the only distinctions Aristotle could find between God and the soul of the human knower. As we saw, Aristotle took the commonsense view that human contemplation cannot continue uninterruptedly and is moreover dependent on knowledge of things outside oneself. Uninterrupted contemplation, on the contrary, would mean uninterrupted identity with the intelligible Forms in the divine Intellect, so that the human intellect no longer needs to find its object outside itself—and that is the state of a god, not a man. Plotinus is in effect insisting that the highest and central part of the human self is already as divine as can be, and eternally remains so. Thus Plotinus will say of the wise man what Aristotle will say only of God: that he does not look for happiness anywhere but in himself, for he *is* his own well-being.[42]

Unity and Division

The identification of the higher part of the soul with the divine Mind does not simply obliterate the distinction between them. Rather, it is part of a larger pattern of identity-in-difference that pervades the whole hierarchy of being according to Plotinus. The identity theory of knowledge is a structural element subserving an architectonic whose over-arching theme is unity, played off against the theme of disunity, division, and death.

At the highest level of the hierarchy, the One is as it were pure self-identity, with no internal divisions or distinctions, no particular aspect that is different from any other aspect—the doctrine known later in Christian theology as the simplicity of God. This simplicity or absolute unity implies infinity, in the sense of limitlessness or freedom from boundaries. Of course the One is not like an unending sequence of many numbers or an infinitely extended material object, but rather is unlimited in its power and unbounded in its indivisible omnipresence.[43] Still, affirming that the First Principle is infinite is a bold innovation on Plotinus's part, "the first serious bringing together of ideas of infinity and the divine in a serious and mature Greek philosophy."[44] For a Greek philosopher to say something was "infinite" (*apeiros*) meant to deny that it possessed limit or boundary (*peras*)—and hence, in Platonism, to deny that it had form or intelligibility. For Platonic Forms are defined by their limits, just as geometrical figures are defined by their boundaries.[45] Plotinus could affirm the infinity of the One only because he was willing to affirm its formlessness—not of course that it is devoid of Form like mere matter, but rather that it is *above* Form, just as it is above being and knowing.[46] The One is therefore not to be imagined as a complex structure like a geometrical figure, but rather is more like a geometrical point, which has no internal divisions and, unlike geometrical figures, is not constituted or defined by its intrinsic limits or boundaries. To use a favorite geometrical metaphor of Plotinus, the One is the point from which all else radiates, like spheres defined by a single common center.[47] Thus the One, in its absolute simplicity and infinity, gives being to all the multiplicity around it.

Aristotle's identity theory of knowledge comes into play at the next level, that of Mind, where instead of absolute unity there are different things that can be identified with one another. Above all, there is knowledge and therefore identity between knower and known. The Aristotelian concept of identity used by Plotinus should not be confused with the Leibnizian concept of identity usually employed in modern formal logic, which implies that identical things are wholly indistinguishable from one another. On the contrary, for Plotinus a distinction between knower and known remains precisely in their identity.[48] The duality of knower and known is in fact what primarily distinguishes the divine Mind from the utter simplicity of the One, which knows no distinction between knower and known, subject and object.[49]

Moreover, the intelligible world in the divine Mind contains not only duality but downright multiplicity: there are many Forms, all of which can be distinguished from another.[50] Indeed, their distinguishability, the fact that they are defined by intelligible boundaries or limits (the way a geometrical figure is defined by its boundaries) is precisely what makes them knowable and intelligible. Limit sets one Form apart from another, as the outline of a visible object separates it from its background, making it perceptible to the eye. The intelligible world is thus a realm of clearly defined boundaries, like a sharply focused photograph, easy to see for those who have eyes to see—in contrast to the One, which has no boundaries or Form to see, no matter how acute the eye.

Multiplicity begins at the level of Mind, but unfolds into division and actual disunity at the level of Soul. The fundamental constraint or shaping factor in Plotinus's psychology is the soul's ontological location, at the level between the intelligible world of Forms (i.e., the divine Mind) and the sensible world of bodies. The distinctive thing about the sensible world, ontologically speaking, is that it is spatial. Hence only in the sensible world can there be distance in the most literal sense—the kind of separation that puts empty space between one thing and another, or removes a part from its whole. Indeed only bodies can *have* parts in the literal sense, and therefore only in the world of bodies can parts be separated from wholes.[51] Only spatial things can be torn in pieces, broken, fragmented. Consequently, the sensible world is the only ontological level at which there is loss, destruction, and death.[52] Everything else that exists, including the soul, is immortal and divine. Thus everything that is not a body is divine, belonging to one of the three divine hypostases, One, Mind, or Soul.[53]

Soul, however, is capable of a kind of dividedness or disunity which is not possible at the two higher levels, because it is related not only to intelligible things above it but also to the world of bodies below it. The lower part of the soul (but not the higher part) is divided among bodies.[54] The Fall of the soul from heaven into bodies in the *Phaedrus* depicts the lower soul's excessive interest in the separate body that its job is to animate, adorn, and govern.[55] The phenomenon of separated "individual" souls (Plotinus would rather call them "divided" and "particular" souls) is a result of this Fall. If they had not fallen into this excessive interest in things below them, souls would have nothing to divide them.[56] Nor indeed are our souls utterly divided from one another even in their embodied and fallen state. For it would be abhorrent to think of soul as wholly immersed in the the world of bodies. Rather, a part of the soul is still contemplating the intelligible world—the unfallen and indeed unchangeable "higher part of the soul."[57]

One last feature of the theme of unity in Plotinus is important to note. It will not do to speak loosely of the "organic unity" of the intelligible world. The intelligible world is much more unified than any organism. For an organism can survive with some of its members amputated, and moreover is sure to fall apart in the long run. (No "individual" thing in the world of space and time is permanent.) The unity of the intelligible world, rather, is like that of a science and its theorems:

> Mind as a whole is all the Forms, and each particular Form is a particular mind, as the whole body of knowledge or science is all its theorems, but not as if each part of the whole were separated in space, but rather each having its power in the whole.[58]

In Aristotle's theory of science, which is modeled on deductive sciences such as geometry, all theorems or derivative truths are deduced from a first principle. This means that if one theorem is removed, the whole science is removed. (For by the logical rule of *modus tollens*, when the consequent is taken away, the antecedent principle goes with it: i.e., if P implies Q, and Q is negated, then it follows that P also must be negated. Thus to deny one theorem in a science is by implication to deny its antecedents, including the first principle. Hence removing one theorem is tantamount to doing away with the whole science.) So there is a very strong sense in which the whole of the intelligible world is necessarily implicit in every Form.

This tight logical unity is for Plotinus the literal truth behind loose talk of organic unity or of the Forms as Ideas in the Mind of God. We must not think Platonic Forms are located in the divine Mind the same way individual items are located in a container or even the way parts are found in an organic whole; rather, each of the Forms implies and in a sense embraces the whole.[59] Intelligible things are not like sensible things; they can never be simply inert objects of perception separated from other objects. Indeed they are not merely objects within the intelligible world, but subjects as well—minds within the one Mind. For Plotinus combines the Aristotelian identity theory of knowledge with the Parmenidean principle that "to be and to know are the same," with the result that each member of the intelligible world is not only a being that is known but but a being that knows. Hence every intelligible thing is also an intelligence or mind, knowing everything in the intelligible world and therefore being one with it all.[60]

This helps us in turn to understand the relation of particular souls to the one Soul, which is analogous to the relation between the many intelligences or Forms and the one Intelligence or divine Mind. But of course there is the added complication that souls have the job of governing bodies and therefore can get mired in sense-perception, lust, pain, and imagination. Yet even with the complication of embodiment, the fact that there are such things as particular souls does not change the fact that all Soul is at root one and undivided.[61] On the other hand, multiplicity is also a real feature of being at the level of Soul, and there would be many particular souls even if souls were not divided by their relation to separate bodies. For the realm of Soul is many-in-one, like the realm of Mind which it reflects.[62]

The fundamental difference between Mind and Soul is that in the latter there is the possibility of ignorance or merely partial knowledge. In the intelligible world every science is its true self, complete and whole and unified. But souls can suffer defects in knowledge, for their reasoning is temporal and discursive and does not embrace everything at once.[63] Thus in contradiction to all logic and reality, they can grasp part of a science but not the whole. The ordinary human soul therefore mirrors the intelligible world in a broken and fragmentary way, in reflections shot through with darkness and ignorance, incompleteness and non-being.[64] This is important for understanding Augustine, because it means that insight into intelligible things may be incomplete without implying any incompleteness in the intelligible world itself. We can get a partial glimpse of God, but this does not mean that God is divided into parts. It is only our selves, our fallen and ignorant souls, that are fragmentary and divided. You can see why Augustine was so attracted to Paul's saying, "Now I know in part, but then I shall know even as I am known."[65]

Turning into the Inside

Augustinian inwardness has its roots in Plotinian Platonism and its doctrine of the divinity at the core of the soul. Plotinus himself says we must turn inward to find God because the higher part of the soul, continually contemplating, is identical to the divine Mind. Hence turning into the soul's interior is turning to God, and self-knowledge yields knowledge of all that is divine, eternal, and ultimate. In this way Plotinus's inward turn is based on an Aristotelian answer to the question of how exactly the soul is akin to the Forms. According to Aristotle, as read by Alexander and Plotinus, this kinship consists in the soul's capacity to become eternally and blessedly identical with the Forms in the divine Mind. This ultimate identity of the soul explains the experience of insight and recollection,[66] and is the literal truth behind the myths and metaphors of Plato.

Augustine, who never read Aristotle's epistemology and psychology, was in no position to understand the conceptual core of Plotinus's inward turn. All he had to work with was the myths and metaphors. These included not just Plato's notions of intellectual vision, Recollection, and Fall (all of which are found frequently in Plotinus's writings) but also Plotinus's own metaphor of turning inward.

Plotinus's talk of the soul turning "into the inside"[67] belongs to a set of images he uses to give a memorable picture of the relations between the three divine levels of being. He likens the incorporeal universe to a set of concentric spheres.[68] At the center is the One, like an infinitesimal point, simple, without internal structure, parts, or boundaries—but like the center of a circle it is the source of all around it. Radiating from it like a sphere of light is the divine Mind, which contains all the Platonic Forms with their mutual distinctions, complex interrelations, and fundamental unity. Revolving around this central sphere is Soul, which can either look outward to the dim world of bodies or turn "into the inside" and behold the divine Mind and the One. When the soul does turn inward, therefore, it gazes not at a private space, but at the one intelligible world that is common to all; and likewise when the soul is united to the core and center of its own being, it is united to the one core and center of all things.

Plotinus uses this imagery to illustrate the way that the higher part of the soul is literally identical with the Forms of the intelligible world:

> We and what is ours go back to Being; we return to it and are from it at first. We *know* Those Things; we don't just have images or impressions of them. And that being so, we *are* Those Things. For if we participate in true knowledge then we are Those Things, not taking them down into ourselves but being among them. Since others (not just us) also *are* Those Things, all of us are Those Things. Being together with everything, we are Those Things. So we all are one.
>
> Therefore when we look outside of what we are fastened from, we are ignorant of our being one—like *faces which are many on the outside*, but having one head on the inside [*eis to eisō*]. So if anyone could *turn*, either by themselves or by a lucky tug of Athena, *they would see God and themselves and all things.*[69]

It is a brilliant image: we human souls think we are many insofar as we look outward at the bodily world, like faces on the outside of a huge sphere. But if (perhaps with divine help) we could turn our gaze into the interior of the sphere, we would see that on the inside we are all one God. This is not Christianity, but it is a good place to mark the Neoplatonist point of origin of Augustinian inwardness. Although Augustine does not start out using the metaphors of turning and looking inward, his earliest writings are devoted to an exploration of the notion that God is inseparably present in the soul. Very early in his career as a Christian writer he thinks of the Fall as a movement outward away from unity, and he accepts the implication that souls are in some fundamental sense one.[70] What he never accepts (and probably never understood) is the Aristotelian notion that the mind *is* what it knows. Yet that notion is precisely what holds the whole structure of Plotinus's universe together. So it is a foregone conclusion that Augustine's inward turn will take him to a different place in the end from Plotinus's. What he ends up with is not a soul that revolves around the intelligible world but a soul that can enter its own private inner space.[71] Yet the point of his inward turn remains the same as Plotinus's: to find God.

3

Augustine Reads Plotinus

Augustine's inwardness, his concept of what lies within the soul, develops as he reads both Plotinus and the Bible. We can trace this development because we have his writings from the very beginning of his career as a Platonist and Catholic Christian thinker. How Augustine's readings in the Platonist tradition shaped his conversion or return to the Catholic Church in 386 AD is a central controversy of twentieth-century Augustine scholarship, but our interest lies rather in what the author of the Confessions *thinks of these texts fifteen years later. A look at some passages from Plotinus that Augustine could have been reading while writing his* Confessions *gives us a glimpse of the Plotinian inward turn that lies behind Augustinian inwardness. The double movement "in then up" in* Confessions *7 replaces Plotinus's conviction that the inner self is divine. Plotinus's writings also provide Augustine with the basic concepts he uses to relate Christian faith and Platonist understanding or intelligibility.*

Augustine's Early Period

Augustinian inwardness takes shape in the first third of Augustine's career as a Christian writer, the period that begins with his earliest extant writings in the winter of 386 and culminates in the *Confessions* at about the turn of the century. For ease of reference I will call this whole time "Augustine's early period"; bearing in mind that by the end of it he had written works of deep intellectual maturity and great brilliance. Yet for all that there is something preliminary about the entire period. Except for the *Confessions* and its contemporary, the treatise *On Christian Doctrine*, the works that were to make Augustine the most influential teacher of the Western church were all written in the latter two periods of his career, when he was establishing the conceptual basis of Western sacramental thinking (especially in the second period, which can conveniently be labeled "anti-Donatist," after his primary ecclesiastical opponents at that time) and the Western theology of grace (in his last period, labeled "anti-Pelagian" after his main opponents at the end of his life). It is as if in his early period he were forging tools for later inquiries and weapons for later polemics. Prominent among these tools and weapons, in fact, is the concept of the self as an inner space where God is present.

The two great works written at the end of Augustine's early period look in different directions. *On Christian Doctrine* looks forward to the doctrinal tasks of the later periods, laying down key points of Augustinian hermeneutics and theological method that were to guide not only Augustine but most of Western theological inquiry for over a thousand years. It is the door to Augustine's future—while the *Confessions* is the culmination of his past, gathering up and synthesizing most of the key themes of his writing to date, in addition to telling the story of his life up to then. In the *Confessions* Augustine sifts through the previous decade and a half of his philosophical and theological inquiries and he discards false starts, sums up what he found worth keeping, and clothes it in a language rich both in biblical allusions and in astonishing new metaphors. Most important for our purposes, the *Confessions* recapitulates a project of inward turn that Augustine had sketched in several of his earlier works, and then proceeds to elaborate more fully than any of his works, before or after, the conception of the inner self. As a consequence this conception was available for use in his later work—not to mention the work of the thousands of theologians and philosophers in succeeding centuries who read the *Confessions*. However, none of Augustine's later works makes the inner space of the self into so explicit a theme of reflection as *Confessions* does. So we can say that Augustinian inwardness is a development of Augustine's early period culminating in the *Confessions*, like a symphonic theme that receives its fullest exposition at the end of the first movement, though it is echoed and incorporated in themes of the second and third movements.

The early period has polemics against opponents of its own, most prominently the Manichaeans. The distinctive feature here is that Augustine was never a Donatist or a Pelagian, but he had been a Manichaean. Hence in polemicizing against them he was not merely vindicating the Catholic faith against its opponents, but sorting out his own reasons for being Catholic. The themes of the early period are thus in a peculiar sense the inquiries of Augustine's own heart. It is most significant, then, that this is the period when Augustine acquired his Platonist worldview. He was learning Platonist philosophy at the same time that he was learning the content of the Catholic faith. He found the two mutually illuminating, because he thought they were both ultimately about the same Truth.

It is in this early period that Augustine did his first serious reading of the Scriptures and of Plotinus—the one being of course the fundamental writings of the Christian faith, and the other the premier Platonist of late antiquity. However, long before he had assimilated either set of texts, he was already busy writing. As a result we have what is in effect Augustine's juvenilia. They are known as the Cassiciacum dialogues, because they are philosophical dialogues composed at a villa outside Milan called Cassiciacum, to which he retired in the fall and winter of 386/7, in the interval between his conversion at Milan in the summer of 386 and his baptism by Ambrose, the bishop of Milan, on Easter Sunday 387. The Cassiciacum dialogues are the unripe fruits of conversion, Augustine's first work as Catholic thinker who has left heresy and worldly ambition behind him but has only just set foot on the road that leads to his mature theology. They are also a kind of public record of his education, rather late in life, in the two intellectual traditions that were to be of lasting importance to him, Platonism and Christianity. Because he started a serious study of the fundamental texts of these two traditions so late (age thirty-three) and because he began his writing career just a few months later, he has left us a trail of his intellectual development unlike anything in other Church Fathers. This, combined with that unprecedented document the *Confessions*, gives us a fuller picture of the development of Augustine's thought than we have for anyone else in antiquity.

A Central Issue in Augustine Scholarship

Augustine's development begins with very little. In his first extant writings, he displays a quite meager acquaintance with the Scriptures, although he had already appropriated some of the most sophisticated trinitarian theology available in the West by listening to Ambrose.[1] At the same time, his philosophical reading was severely limited.[2] In fact Augustine never was to have much firsthand acquaintance with the classic texts of Western philosophy. At the time of his conversion, he had scant proficiency in Greek and precious little knowledge of the classical philosophical tradition beyond what he could learn from Latin sources like Cicero and Varro.[3] Of Aristotle he had read only a translation of the *Categories*.[4] Of Plato he was never to know much more than the portion of the *Timaeus* translated by Cicero,[5] along with some snippets from doxographies.[6] Prominent among the latter are Cicero's arguments for the immortality of the soul in the first book of the *Tusculan Disputations*, which include reports on the *Phaedo* and the *Meno* and a page or so translated from the *Phaedrus*.[7]

In short, Plotinus is the only great philosopher whose works Augustine ever studied in any depth. And even Plotinus he could not read as extensively and systematically as we can. He did not have a copy of the *Enneads*, the standard collected edition of Plotinus's works published by Plotinus's student Porphyry. All he had to work with were "certain *books of the Platonists*, translated from Greek into Latin,"[8] which probably included some writings of Porphyry (such as the *Sentences*, an introduction to Plotinian philosophy and spirituality) as well as a selection of Plotinus' treatises. Exactly which treatises were included in these "books of the Platonists," however, is a matter of some uncertainty, as well as the focus of one of the central debates of the flourishing Augustine scholarship of the mid-twentieth century.[9] One eminent scholar even contended that Augustine read no Plotinus at all, only Porphyry—though his arguments did not carry the day.[10] The issue is still not entirely settled, but the debate no longer rages, and the opinion is widely shared that Augustine's reading included some Porphyry and a fair amount of Plotinus.[11] This opinion reflects a growing consensus that Augustine's engagement with Neoplatonist thought was long and deep, involving a highly personal, sometimes astonishingly original but in any case never uncritical appropriation of many of Plotinus's most difficult and interesting ideas—something it is hard to imagine him capable of if he had little acquaintance with Plotinus's texts. Since it is largely to this process of appropriation that we owe the notion of the private inner self, it behooves us to give it careful attention. As this has been a topic of intense scholarly controversy for much of the past century, however, we need first to come to grips with the course of modern Augustine scholarship.

Let me begin with a warning. One point that caused some confusion early on in the debate over the content of the "books of the Platonists" was a tendency to focus rather narrowly on the "intellectual conversion" supposedly described in book 7 of the *Confessions*. The phrase is not Augustine's but a scholarly invention. It reflects a deeply ingrained modern tendency to read the biography of Augustine (like other religious figures) as a story whose high point must be a conversion experience. Under such an assumption, the burning issue for interpretation of Augustine's life story is inevitably: which books brought about his conversion? This led scholars to devote a great deal of effort to reconstructing the events that took place in Augustine's mind in the summer of 386—a period for which we do not have contemporary evidence (Augustine's earliest extant writing begins a few months later) but must rely to a large extent on the condensed, oblique, and much later narrative of the *Confessions*. Moreover, this focus on Augustine's conversion experience led to a relative neglect of the question of Augustine's ongoing assimilation of Plotinus in the many years between Cassiciacum and the *Confessions*. And the latter question is of course the really important one for anyone interested in understanding the conceptual structure of Augustine's thought.

It was, Augustine tells us, "a very few books of Plotinus" that set his heart on fire that summer in Milan.[12] And when he retired that autumn to the villa at Cassiciacum, he took Cicero and Virgil along with him, but not Plotinus.[13] So the changes of mind that took place that year seem to have been stimulated by a rather slight amount of Neoplatonist reading. But that is surely not the case with the changes that took place in the next decade and a half, when he was formulating his distinctive program of inward turn. There is no question but that he kept on reading and rereading, learning and changing his mind, assimilating Plotinus as well as the Bible and Christian doctrine throughout this period. And it was this ongoing assimilation of Plotinus, not the "very few books" read that one summer, that made Augustine the most influential Christian Platonist of all time.

Furthermore, that is where the real drama of his mind is to be found. Augustine's growth as a Platonist philosopher and a Christian theologian does not have to be reconstructed from the fragmentary records of one summer's reading but is available to us in the texts we have at hand. In the writings of his early period we can see Augustine solving longstanding problems and stumbling upon new ones, giving up old convictions and achieving stunningly original insights, changing his mind and in the end becoming a rather different person. In my experience, at least, this is a far more thrilling story than the ones that issue from scholarly reconstructions of Augustine's conversion (or conversions) in 386. And that is indeed what we should expect if Augustine himself is right about the nature of the spiritual life. For by Augustine's own account it is not a single conversion experience but rather a lifetime of turning one's mind to seek the truth (punctuated by many blessed moments of insight) that leads to God.

From this perspective it must be said that contemporary Augustine scholarship has come a long way in the right direction. The beginning of modern Augustine scholarship can be dated to about the turn of the twentieth century, when critical historical methods were first applied to the study of Augustine's life and work, and particularly to the *Confessions'* account of the summer of 386.[14] This had a scandalous effect, much like the application of modern critical historical methods to the Bible during the preceding century. It also involved at first many of the same crude mistakes that made early biblical criticism seem both offensive and uninteresting, as the thematic density and interest of the actual texts was ignored in favor of attempts to reconstruct "what really happened."

The most scandalous conclusion, reached by Adolf von Harnack, Wilhelm Thimme, and (most notoriously) Prosper Alfaric, was to the effect that Augustine's conversion in 386 was really more Platonist than Christian and that he only became a good Catholic in the years afterward. This conclusion is wrongheaded, as Pierre Courcelle demonstrated in what is possibly the single most important contribution to Augustine scholarship of the century. Courcelle uncovered a Milan that was steeped in Christian Neoplatonism.[15] For instance, Courcelle found that the sermons of Ambrose, the bishop of Milan, which played so large a role in bringing Augustine back to the Church,[16] incorporated whole paragraphs of the *Enneads* (without attribution, of course).[17] Thus the idea that Augustine's intellectual conversion was too Platonist to be Christian turns out to be historically misinformed. At the time, Augustine would not have formulated his options in terms of an opposition between Platonism and Christianity, nor would most of the elite circle of Neoplatonist Catholics among which he moved. Rather than being converted exclusively to Platonist philosophy or to the Catholic Church, it seems much more likely that he was converted to the latter by means of the former—just as he tells us in the *Confessions*.

Nevertheless, the notion of "Augustine's early Platonism" remains in circulation in the scholarly world and still exerts a kind of mesmerizing effect—as if it were impossible to picture Augustine's intellectual development as anything but a movement from his early Platonism to his mature Christianity. The obvious fact confronting us in the texts, however, is that Augustine's Platonism grew in tandem with his Christian orthodoxy.[18] The story of Augustine's intellectual development does not begin with Platonism and end with Christianity but rather introduces us to a distinctive brand of Christian Platonism in the making. So, for example, the most ambitious philosophical work of his early period, the treatise *On True Religion*, is both more soundly Catholic than the Cassiciacum writings and far more sophisticated in its Neoplatonism. The ultimate reason for this twin development is banal but ineluctable: in his earliest writings he was not as well informed about either Neoplatonism or the Catholic tradition as he was after fifteen more years of reading and learning.[19]

Augustine on "the Books of the Platonists"

It is ironic, then, that some scholars in the beginning of the twentieth century were scandalized by Augustine's Neoplatonism enough to suggest that the *Confessions* was a kind of coverup that made Augustine's conversion out to be less Platonistic than it actually was. For anyone who comes to Augustine's writings fresh from reading the *Enneads* will find far more Neoplatonism in the *Confessions* than in the Cassiciacum dialogues. Augustine is indeed a more orthodox Christian theologian by the time of the *Confessions*, but he is also a deeper and more judicious Platonist. We must bear in mind that it is that deep and judicious Catholic Platonist who presents us with the message of "the books of the Platonists" in book 7 of the *Confessions*.

That presentation confronts us first of all, I would suggest, with a question of genre: is book 7 meant to be a record of particular events—perhaps the story of his "intellectual conversion" or else of some "unsuccessful attempts at Plotinian ecstasy"?[20] If so, it is singularly lacking in any narrative episodes. In this book Augustine proceeds not by telling a story about himself but by interpreting some texts and showing how they helped him solve some conceptual problems; the connections are not those of historical narrative but those of logical consequence. This makes a striking contrast with the next book of the *Confessions*, which is full of narratives and even narratives within narratives. And whereas in book 8 the climactic scene takes place in a garden in Milan, in book 7 the principal stage is Augustine's own mind, and the climactic scene takes place when he steps onto this inner stage and looks around in it. As book 8 is narrative in focus, so its dominant mode of perception is sensible: Augustine tells us how he listened to stories told by his friends, heard distant voices singing, and literally picked up a book in his hand. In book 7 the focus is conceptual, and the perception is of the intelligible and inner things that Augustine saw with his mind's eye: there is not even a narrative of reading, no moment when he takes up "the books of the Platonists" and casts his eyes upon them. Even the description of their content proceeds not by quoting the words he read but by redescribing them in words taken from the Gospel of John.[21]

There is no real narrative in book 7, I suggest, because its focus is not temporal but eternal. It therefore makes more sense to read book 7 as an account of the concepts Augustine learned from his Platonist reading than as a narrative of a definite series of episodes in his life.[22] Assuming we can call the vision of God a "historical" event, then book 7 makes only one historical claim: that he came to see God that summer because of his readings in the books of the Platonists. But Augustine's account of *how* he came to see God (as described particularly in 7:16 and 7:23) is neither a report of a attempted mystical vision nor an interpretation of the Platonist books (that is the business of 7:13-15) but rather a description of the relation between the soul and God as he understands it *at the time of writing the Confessions*. He does not now attempt to describe his experiences in the same terms he would have used at the time they occurred, precisely because his interest is in telling the truth. To serve that interest he must rely on his *present* understanding of what really happens in that timeless moment when a soul here below catches a glimpse of eternal Truth.

If we understand *Confessions* 7 in this way, then we can explain the fact that the text presents discoveries that are *more* Platonist than the line of thought Augustine pursues at Cassiciacum soon after his conversion—exactly the opposite phenomenon from what we would expect to find if Harnack and Alfaric were correct.[23] The account he gives of his inward turn in *Confessions* 7 relies on a far more sophisticated appropriation of Plotinian thought than anything he was capable of at Cassiciacum, and hence cannot be a historically accurate account of his thinking at the time of his conversion, a few months before Cassiciacum. But historical accuracy is not its purpose, because history is not its genre. It is not even autobiography in the usual sense, but rather the representation of a fundamental insight that determines the soul's relation to God. The great event it tells of is the inward turn:

> Thence admonished [by the books of the Platonists] to return to my own self, I entered into my inmost place, guided by Thee. . . . I entered and saw with the eye of my soul . . . the unchangeable Light. . . . [24]

Some Plotinian Readings

It is not a troubled young convert but the formidable bishop of Hippo who tells us he turned inward to see God because the books of the Platonists told him that was where to look. Since the record of his works up to the *Confessions* shows that he has never stopped assimilating the insights of Neoplatonism, we can assume he still has those books on his shelves available for consultation as he writes his spiritual autobiography—and doubtless more than just the "very few" that inspired his conversion in the first place. So let us consider a couple of Plotinian texts that Augustine could have been looking at about the time he writes the *Confessions*, and read them as it were over his shoulder, bearing in mind the problems that he says they solved for him—the problems solved, that is, by the concept of an inward turn.

The problem (as presented in *Confessions* 7:1-2) is essentially: how to find God? This means, metaphorically, where are we to look? or more literally, how should we direct our mind's attention? We know the senses cannot see God or inform us what he is like, but we have a terribly hard time getting sensible imagery out of our minds. If only we could see in a different way, with a different and non-corporeal vision, then we would be on the right road. But how? Where in the world can the mind turn when it is looking for God? Where do we go to find him?

Augustine's favorite passage from Plotinus, to which he alludes twice in the *Confessions*, addresses just this problem:

> What is the way? And what is the means? How can one behold this extraordinary beauty which remains in the inner sanctum and will not come outside to be seen by the profane? Let him who can arise and come into the inside [*eis to eisō*], leaving the sight of his eyes outside and not turning back to corporeal beauties.[25]

Alluding to the myth of Narcissus as well as the notion of lower and higher beauties in Plato's *Symposium*, Plotinus proceeds to warn against trying to embrace mere images and moving shadows of the real Beauty, like Narcissus trying to grasp his real self in a fleeting external image below him—and perishing as a result in dark and formless depths.[26] Rather we must flee to the Fatherland like Odysseus, not content to stay with a Circe or a Calypso:

> Our Fatherland is that whence we came, and *the Father* is there. *What then is our journey, our flight? Not by feet* is it to be accomplished; for feet carry one from here to there all over the earth. Nor should you procure *horse-chariot or ship*; you should leave all such things behind and not look, but *close your eyes and awaken another sort of vision* instead—a sort of vision which everyone possesses but few make use of.[27]

This is not a journey for the feet, because the distance it crosses is not the sort that can be measured in miles. We begin by leaving behind the spatial world of bodies altogether and entering into the non-spatial realm of our own selves. We must leave the senses outside as we enter this inner sanctum and seek for the Beauty at its center; we must awaken a different sort of seeing that belongs to the mind, not the body.

The vision that Plotinus and Augustine long for leaves bodies behind and places no intermediaries between the soul and the divine things it seeks. As Augustine insisted at Cassiciacum, the only things worth knowing are God and the soul.[28] The inward turn arises from the conviction that in order to understand how this vision is possible, we must look first at the the soul itself and understand its superiority to the whole world of bodies. This puts the kinship between soul and intelligible Forms at the center of attention.

In his treatise "On the Immortality of the Soul," Plotinus defends Plato's claim that the soul is "akin to things eternal and divine" (*Republic* 611e) and in the process fills out Plato's claim with some specifically Neoplatonist content.[29] In most souls, he admits, we cannot see any sign of their divinity. But no one would be an unbeliever (*apistos*) in the divinity and immortality of the soul if they could see it when it had "ascended to itself" (l. 14), purified of the desires and passions that arise from its entanglements with the body and other things external to it. To understand a thing's nature, after all, we must look at it in its pure state. So Plotinus invites us to look at ourselves apart from our impurities, and suggests that what we shall see then is

> a mind which does not behold sensible and mortal things, but understands eternal things because of its own eternity, all in the intelligible realm, *being itself an intelligible world*

filled with light, illuminated by the truth of the Good, which shines the light of truth on all intelligibles. (ll. 32–37)

This is the higher part of the soul, eternally contemplating intelligible things, eternally present There in the intelligible realm because it is one with the things of that realm. Hence the higher soul is itself an intelligible world filled with light,[30] as it reflects the whole of the intelligible world in the divine Mind, where every part embraces the whole. Plotinus's concept of the higher part of the soul lies behind later pictures of the soul as an inner world. The soul finds the true world, the realm of intelligible truth, within itself—indeed finds that it is identical with the divine world within. Ultimately, therefore, the inner world *is* the intelligible world, and the inner self is divine in a very strong sense—it is not just immortal like the gods of classical paganism, but is one with the Divine Mind itself.

Plotinus tells us that if we only knew ourselves (as the Delphic oracle commanded) then we could say with the poet, "Greetings, I am an immortal god" (l. 38). Commenting on the description of contemplation in the *Phaedrus* myth, he drives home his point that the divine and imperishable Forms are seen by looking within the soul: "For it is not by running around on the outside that 'the soul beholds temperance and justice' [*Phaedrus* 247d] but itself by itself in understanding its own self" (ll. 43–45). And it is not as if the soul *becomes* divine or recaptures a divinity it had lost. Rather, it is catching a glimpse of its own eternal being, which had for a time been hidden from it by its own ignorance and vice:

> It is as if gold had a soul and, knocking off what had encrusted it, finally saw its own beauty after being in ignorance of it; now admiring and wondering at its own value, it realizes that it needs no beauty imported from outside, since it is itself of the best. (ll. 47–52)[31]

In Then Up

It is hard to imagine a Church Father getting enthusiastic about a philosophy that identifies the human soul with the divine Mind. But the bishop of Hippo is an odd Church Father. I have suggested we read over his shoulder, but a historically more accurate picture would be to imagine ourselves listening to him as he reads aloud, as nearly all readers did in those days. Let us suppose he is working on a draft of *Confessions* 7. In his study or library he has the books of the Bible within easy reach, but in his hand at present is a text of Plotinus that he is pondering as he prepares to write about "the books of the Platonists." We can therefore imagine ourselves listening to the words of Plotinus (translated into Latin) in the voice of Augustine—not the uncertain young man of 386 but the formidable bishop of 400, who has already written words that would echo in monasteries and palaces, homes and hearts for fifteen centuries. The words of Plotinus's text, teaching that we must turn inward to find that we are inwardly God, are not for him mere memories of a questionable conversion experience; they echo today in the room, in his ears, and in his mind. The urgent question for him, as for us, is: what does he make of them now, in the bishop's library at Hippo?

Augustine certainly does not want to teach his readers that in turning inward we find we are no different from God. Yet clearly the thought is not strange to him: he has lived with these texts for over a decade, and he has not flung them away. So there are some things that Augustine is not telling us in *Confessions* 7. There is indeed a great deal about that summer of 386 that he has left in the shadows, but that is hardly surprising: it is not easy to recall the exact chronological order of a series of insights one has had, especially at fifteen years' remove. But the most important thing Augustine fails to tell us is not about his conversion experience so long ago but about the content of the books that are presently in his hands and on the shelves of his library. He does not let his readers know that for these Platonists the reason we must turn inward to find God is that inwardly we *are* God. Over the centuries, millions of people must have read *Confessions* 7 without realizing that the "books of the Platonists" that led Augustine to an inner vision of God insisted on the inner divinity of the soul.

His reason for not giving a full account of these books can only be that he is concerned to teach the truth. Truth is his first love, and teaching it is moreover the bishop's job. He has learned a great deal about the ultimate Truth from the Plotinus, but he is in no position to explain in any detail to his (largely uneducated) audience[32] how the philosopher who taught him where to look to see God misconceived the very nature of this vision.[33] What he does, rather, is silently correct the error of these Platonist books by adding an extra dimension: God is not only *within* the soul but *above* it as well.

With that crucial modification Augustine thinks he can adopt Plotinus's concept of inward turn and use it to understand his own experience of insight into the ultimate Truth, as well as teach it to his readers and his congregation. So we can imagine him putting down the "books of the Platonists" and picking up his own manuscript to write the words quoted earlier, about how those books admonished him to turn inward and how God himself guided him in this, so that in his inmost place he was able to find nothing less than the unchangeable light of intelligible Truth, which is God himself. But as Augustine proceeds to describe what he inwardly found, he speaks not of identity but of difference, stressing not only the difference between the intelligible light and sensible light (the familiar Platonist contrast between the vision of the mind's eye and the vision of the eye of the body), but also the difference between the mind's eye and the divine light it sees:

> I entered and saw, with the eye of my soul, such as it was, above that same eye of my soul, above my mind, the unchangeable light—not the common light obvious to all flesh, nor as it were something greater of the same kind, shining more brightly . . . but other, quite other than all these things; nor was it above my mind as oil is above water or heaven above the earth, but *it was above because it made me*, and I was below because made by it. *Whoever knows Truth, knows it*, and whoever knows it, knows Eternity. . . .[34]

Augustine corrects Plotinus by bringing in the Christian doctrine of Creation, with its sharp distinction between Creator and creature. We are not God because we are made by God; hence the eternal light of Truth, which is God, shines upon the eye of the soul from above, with the superiority of Creator to creature.

This corrective to Plotinus generates Augustine's distinctive version of inward turn, which we shall examine in detail in part II. Augustine's inward turn requires a double movement: first *in* then *up*. In contrast to Plotinus, the inner space of the Augustinian soul is not divine but is beneath God, so that turning into the inside is not all there is to finding God. We must not only turn inward but also look upward, because God is not only within the soul but also above it. In the interval between the turning in and looking up one finds oneself in a new place, never before conceived: an inner space proper to the soul, different from the intelligible world in the Mind of God. The soul becomes, as it were, its own dimension—a whole realm of being waiting to be entered and explored.

This concept of inner space is an innovation, but none of the elements of which it is composed are new and the convictions that lead to it are not un-Platonist. Augustine could have cited the *Timaeus* as well as the Bible as authority for the doctrine that God created the soul, and the notion that the intelligible Light shines on the soul from above is as old as the Allegory of the Cave. So Augustine need not say, and probably does not believe, that he is saying something new and original here. He is simply trying to state what he thinks is the truth: that the soul can turn inward to find God, as Plotinus says, but that it is more complicated than Plotinus makes it out to be, and therefore we need to correct his description using the older Platonist language of height and ascent.[35]

What Augustine omits to tell us about the books of the Platonists therefore serves to downplay his own originality as well as the differences between Platonism and Christianity—both in the interest of highlighting what he thinks is the truth about the inward turn: that it really is a way of finding God, that it is not incompatible with the Catholic faith, and that Augustine did not make it up. Thus for methodological reasons, as it were, Augustine downplays precisely those features of the inward turn that as intellectual historians we want most to know: that on the one hand Augustine's version of the inward turn really is something new, involving an innovative modification of Plotinus's version, and that on the other hand the original inward turn in Plotinus was grounded on belief in the divinity of the soul. Augustine has been so successful in this that for centuries Westerners have supposed that the inner space of the soul was just there waiting to be discovered (by someone with the psychological acuity of an Augustine) and they have hardly suspected that the reason the books of the Platonists admonished him to enter his inmost self is because of their teaching that the inmost self is God.

But the latter at least is something we do not need Augustine to tell us about; it is plain enough in the texts of Plotinus. We could imagine Augustine putting down his manuscript, departing his study, and leaving us with the books there. Now we can read them in our own voice, without wondering what thoughts are running through Augustine's head as he encounters them. Now indeed it does not matter much whether we imagine ourselves in the fourth century or the twenty-first: we still have the texts, and we still have the question: what are we to make of the quite different but plainly related versions of the inward turn in the texts of Plotinus and the texts of Augustine?

Inner Vision and Faith

There is obviously a great deal in the texts of Plotinus that the bishop of Hippo cannot accept. Yet these "books of the Platonists" have, by his own account, performed the fundamental service of showing him where to look to find God. The insight into the incorporeal and intelligible nature of God that he gained through reading Plotinus remains a foundation of his theology as well as his philosophy throughout his career. After all, it is to be expected that one's conception of God will determine lesser theological concepts like faith and love, sin and soul. As intellectual historians, therefore, we would be justified in saying that Platonist conceptuality is decisive for Augustine's understanding of the meaning of Christian faith. But precisely as intellectual historians we must also note that Augustine himself would not put it that way—and for Platonist reasons.

For Augustine, an understanding of God is not something one finds in a text. After all, he believes we must turn inward to find God, and that means we cannot find a conception of God in the books of the Platonists or any other external thing. A conception of God (if it is true) is a memory of a vision of God, by which one retains what one saw in a moment of insight such as Augustine describes in *Confessions* 7.[36] Thus Augustine does not think he has a Platonist conception of God, but rather that he has glimpsed the same God the Platonists have.[37] No text can give such a vision, but it can tell us where to look. That indeed is the best that any created thing can do, and it is (according to Augustine's semiotics) the basic function of signs in general—to admonish and remind us where to look to see the truth.[38]

This general function of signs, and the severe restriction it implies for the usefulness of words, applies as much to the texts of Plotinus and Platonism as to Scripture and the teaching of the Church. It is, however, quite clear that for Augustine the latter has more authority than the former. Whenever a philosopher teaches something contrary to Christian doctrine, then it is Christian doctrine we are to believe. And it is unmistakable that Augustine's practice conforms scrupulously to his theory on this point.[39] However, none of this changes the fact that the conception of God and the soul that we find in Augustine's own texts is derived from the Platonist tradition and determines in a deep way his conception of the nature and purpose of Christian faith.

Here we must beware of reading later views of faith and reason into Augustine. For Augustine faith cannot see as far as reason—although it makes up for what reason cannot see in its fallen and self-alienated condition. Nor is faith the ground, cause or principle of understanding. This may have been what Anselm had in mind centuries later when he spoke of "faith seeking understanding" and "I believe so that I may understand."[40] But Augustine's formulas, although they clearly inspired Anselm's, have a subtly different flavor, the sharp tang of antithesis. It is not faith itself that seeks and finds the understanding of God, but rather "faith seeks, understanding finds."[41] This, I take it, is equivalent to another pungent Augustinian formula, about the point of the religious life: "it is begun by faith, completed by vision."[42] For of course understanding (*intellectus*) is the same thing as intellectual vision, and fullness of intellectual vision (i.e., seeing God clearly with the mind's eye) is the goal and the meaning of faith.

For Augustine, we begin with faith but end up with intellectual vision, which is better and higher. To be sure, faith comes first, but that is only because at first we cannot see. As the corrupt mind's eye is too weak to bear the sight of God, it must first be purified and strengthened by faith, so that it may in the end arrive at understanding.[43] Faith comes before understanding in time but not in meaning or importance, just as we must travel a road before we can get to our destination but it is the destination that gives meaning and value to the journey.[44] Hence insofar as Plotinus defines for Augustine the nature of intellectual understanding, he has also defined the destination of the Christian journey. Neoplatonist understanding determines the ultimate meaning of Christian faith, just as the inward turn determines how we are to use external things like Scripture and sacrament.[45]

Let us consider, then, one last text of Plotinus, which is particularly interesting for the way it relates the inward turn to things outside us, and intellectual vision to faith. In the treatise "On Intellectual Beauty,"[46] Plotinus insists very strongly that turning within means turning away from bodily things. The treatise contains an extended commentary on the myth of contemplation in the *Phaedrus*. In section 10, after expounding the passage about the ascent of souls led by Zeus to the summit of contemplation (*Phaedrus* 246e–248a), Plotinus insists that the soul sees intelligibles by looking within. Souls that are thoroughly permeated by intellectual beauty "are not mere spectators [*theatais*]. For there is not on the one hand someone outside, and then on the other hand something beheld [*theōmenon*] outside, but rather the sharp-eyed see in themselves what they see" (ll. 35–37).

This may be the closest that anyone before Augustine ever came to combining the metaphor of intellectual vision with a conception of the self as an inner space. It is an odd combination, and Plotinus soon backs away from it—or rather transcends it and passes beyond. He is interested not in explaining how it is possible for the soul to turn and look within itself (strange metaphor!) but rather in emphasizing the sense in which contemplation is *unlike* vision, because it unites knower and known. In contrast to mortal vision, intellectual knowledge does not leave us mere spectators of something other than ourselves. Ultimately, contemplation is not like seeing something outside oneself but rather is a way of being reunified with the ground of one's own being, which is the ground of all being. Hence, Plotinus will say elsewhere, in rising from the divine Mind to the One (which is the ultimate goal of contemplative ascent) we leave behind the last shreds of division and separation, even the duality between knower and known; we do not *see* the One, nor even know it, but are *made one* with it.[47] The ultimate contemplation is thus higher than the identity between knower and known, higher even than Aristotle's God thinking the thought of himself—for it is not thinking or knowing at all (which still involves some measure of duality even in the identification of knower and known) but simply being one and itself, as the divine One. The inward turn does not ultimately make sense for Plotinus unless such divinity—the highest divinity of all—is already at the core and center of our being.[48]

Here again we see why Augustine must devise a new and different version of the inward turn. In order to make the soul less than divine, Augustine must adopt the metaphor that Plotinus rejects: inner vision. For that allows him to do precisely what Plotinus does not want to do—establish a gap or ontological distance between soul and God, seer and seen. It is in this way that the odd metaphor of "looking inward" enters the Western tradition.

Plotinus, on the contrary, would not have us regard our inner possessions as if they were something different from ourselves, like an object of vision we could choose to look at or not (ll. 38–40). He would not have us behold intelligible things as a kind of spectacle outside us; rather "we should bring them into ourselves and look at them as one with us, look at them as ourselves, like someone possessed by a god . . . who has the power to see the god within himself" (ll. 40–45). The notion of the divinity of the soul in this passage is thoroughly pagan, yet we must consider what it might signify to a Christian like Augustine who is convinced that Christ is to be found within us. If Christ is both the divine Truth within us and the inner Teacher,[49] then pagan talk about seeing the god within the self may be pointing in the right direction.

Plotinus proceeds in the next section to advise those who are not yet "able to see themselves" (section 11, l. 1) about how they may come to be one with the god within. They must "run into the inside [*eis to eisō*]" and "leave the senses behind," for "if they wish to see something different from themselves, they put themselves outside" (ll. 11–13).[50] Meanwhile, as they are still learning, they must have a kind of faith (*pistin*) in the image or impression (*eikōn* or *tupos*) of the god within them (ll. 13–17). Here is where Plotinus, like Augustine, puts faith before understanding.[51]

But next Plotinus must answer a critical question about our inward identity with the intelligible realm: "How then can one dwell in intellectual beauty without seeing it?" (l. 19) This states a recurrent objection to Plotinus's belief that the higher part of our soul never descended to the fallen state that we presently experience but remains in the intelligible realm, always contemplating and always divine. If this is so, how come we are not aware of it? Plotinus's reply, here as elsewhere, is that the awareness being asked for is sensual, and sense-perception (*aisthēsis*) is necessarily unaware (*anaisthētos*) of such things.[52] External things, things alien to our own being that bump into us and hurt us, are the kind of things that produce the most noticeable sensations. We do not sense that good which is most at home with us and most ourselves—it is like the way we notice when we are sick but not when we are healthy. (ll. 24–33)

> So then, precisely where our knowledge is most intellectual, we are of the opinion that we are ignorant, because we are waiting for the experience of the senses—which say they have not seen it. For of course they have not seen it, nor will they ever see anything of the sort. (ll. 33–36)

It is because of the credence we put in our senses that we find it hard to credit our own intellectual and immortal nature: it is sense-perception that is unbelieving (*apistoun*) about the immortality of the soul (l. 36).[53]

Thus Plotinus provides not only an account of our knowledge of God, but also an error theory: an account of how that knowledge can be hidden from us even though we inwardly possess it. If God shines within, how is it that we do not see God? It is because we are too familiar with bodily vision, too accustomed to looking with the wrong kind of eyes. Hence the spiritual life, by which we come to see the immaterial God, consists in practicing as much as possible a vision that does not look upon things outside the soul. But while we are still practicing (still on that journey which is not for the feet) we must *believe* that we can reach the goal that we do not yet *see*—believe in things that are as yet invisible to the mind's eye.[54] This is what Augustine has in mind when he writes a treatise *On Faith in Things Unseen*.[55] Thus Plotinus instills not only an inward turn and a search for intellectual vision, but also a reliance on faith. Reading Plotinus would strengthen not only Augustine's belief that we must turn away from external things, but also his conviction that we must begin with faith in order to end up with understanding.

Plotinus's philosophy provides Augustine with a great many things: most important, an explanation of the inner connection between God and the soul, but also an account of why we keep failing to recognize this inner connection and how we may eventually come to see it. Plotinus's account of why we fail to see what is in us is perhaps the easiest Neoplatonist teaching for Augustine to accept, the one that requires the fewest modifications when confronted with authoritative Christian teaching. Throughout the *Confessions* Augustine's portraits of the alienation of the soul from God are Plotinian in concept, though usually biblical in language. Reading Plotinus helps us appreciate the air of paradox about these portraits—the attempt of the wicked to flee the Omnipresent, the separation from God that is not a separation in space, the recognition that God "was inside and I was outside."[56] Ignorance of God is contrary to the soul's innermost nature, yet it is the state in which we all find ourselves. Precisely because of the perverse persistence of this unnatural condition we must rely on faith, not sight, believing what we cannot yet understand. Here again Plotinus defines for Augustine the point of the Christian faith. Yet it is obviously about the Christian faith that he has the least to teach him—and it is also here that bishop

Augustine has the most serious responsibilities. For the mature Augustine the course we take in this journey not for the feet is indicated by external landmarks visible only within the Church: the flesh of Christ, the sacraments, the teachings of Holy Scripture. The most important things Augustine has to say in his later periods are about this journey taken in and by the Church, the City of God on its earthly pilgrimage.

4

Problems of Christian Platonism

Augustine's project of finding God by turning inward to the soul assumes there is a special closeness between the soul and God, that of Platonist intelligibility. This poses a problem specific to Christian Platonism: if God is found by virtue of his intelligibility, then what is the point of his taking on human flesh in Christ? The problems of Christian Platonism do not begin with Augustine but have roots in the New Testament's use of Platonist language, such as Pauline talk about the "inner man." But more important for Augustinian inwardness is the notion of finding Christ in the heart, apart from external things such as Christ's flesh. For Augustine, Christ seen in the heart is the eternal Wisdom that the philosophers sought, and Christians can accept the Neoplatonist theory of Forms in the Divine Mind as an explanation of how God is seen by the eye of the soul. This commitment to the intelligibility of God is Augustine's great idiosyncrasy, setting him apart from the rest of the Nicene or orthodox traditions, which unanimously affirm the incomprehensibility of the divine nature, participation in which is mediated to us only by the flesh of Christ.

Life-giving Flesh

The concept of inner self emerges in the course of Platonist inquiries into the nature of intelligibility that are complicated by the fact that they take place mostly within the Christian tradition. The complications are particularly intense in Augustine but hardly unique to him, for Augustine wrote at a time when Christianity and Platonism had been interacting for centuries. The Catholic Church of Augustine's day had already put the results of some of those interactions firmly behind it, such as the Gnostic doctrine of the divinity of the soul. Other forms of Christian Platonism, such as the doctrine that embodiment is due to the Fall of the soul, were not decisively rejected until the middle of Augustine's lifetime.[1] Thus Augustine's career is shaped not only by the Church's rejection of some radical interpretations of the Platonic kinship between souls and eternity, but also by the fact that other interpretations were still open possibilities. As a Christian Platonist, therefore, he had to deal not only with the traditional Platonist problems about the nature of intelligibility but also with the fact that there were certain fundamental commitments of the Catholic faith that had some bearing on how those problems could be solved.

One of these fundamental commitments is well known: the goodness of Creation. Though Catholics retained the Platonist notion that the first sin was a Fall, they could no longer accept the more consistently Platonist notion that it was a Fall *of the soul into bodies*, for that implies that our bodies are a punishment or prison for our souls rather than a part of the original goodness of God's creation. But there is a yet more fundamental commitment of the Catholic faith that has in the end even more profound consequences for any project of Christian Platonism, and that is the commitment to the man Jesus Christ as "the one mediator between God and human beings" (1 Tim. 2:5). The year after Augustine's death, that commitment was formulated by the third ecumenical council, at Ephesus in 431, in the following terms: the flesh of Jesus Christ is "life-giving flesh."[2]

Think of the problems this formulation poses for a Christian Platonist. The language is deliberately paradoxical (not in a modern logician's sense, but in the literary sense of oxymoron) and was felt to be such by those who formulated it. For in late antiquity, one of the things that "everyone knows" (i.e., that everyone takes for granted) is that the soul gives life to the body or flesh, not the other way around.[3] Yet the council of Ephesus taught that the body or flesh of Christ is a source of life, by virtue of the fact that this particular flesh (and no other) is the flesh of God. As if that were not enough, there is a further, deeper paradox for a Christian Platonist to face. Ever since the *Phaedo*, the Platonist message had been that our ascent to divine and eternal things leaves behind things of earth, body, and mortality. But the formulation "life-giving flesh" is clearly meant to indicate something foundational for all Christian devotion, as if all access to divine life was through this one piece of human mortality called Jesus. And indeed this formula became fundamental for subsequent Eucharistic piety.

In short, there is a question about where to direct one's attention. The Council of Ephesus seems to be offering quite a different solution to the problem, "Where can I look to find God?" from that presented by "the books of the Platonists," which admonished Augustine to turn inward and look up to see the immutable and incorporeal Truth. The Platonist notion of intelligibility, even if acceptable to Christians, seems to involve quite a different mode of access to God than the life-giving flesh of Christ. What should a good Christian Platonist make of the relation between the two? To put the question more pointedly: if the way to see the Truth of God is to turn inward and look upward with eyes that are not of the flesh, then what is the point of having "life-giving flesh" in the first place?

This is not a question that can be shirked by any Platonist who takes Christ seriously. Nor can it be answered simply by referring to the doctrine of Incarnation. It is not enough to confess that Christ is God in the flesh; the question is about the *power* of that divine flesh and how it figures in our relationship with God. And it is a question that arises in this pointed form primarily for Platonists, insofar as they think the proper way to find God is by turning away from bodies. The question, in other words, is not whether Christ is God incarnate (that is presupposed) but rather, what is the *point* of God's taking on human flesh? And again, the question arises in its pointed form only for Platonists: what is the point of having "life-giving flesh" if the ascent to divine things requires us to look away from all flesh?

This is a specifically Christian problem about the Platonist concept of intelligibility. It is a deep problem, for it is inseparable from fundamental issues of orthodox Christian piety, which never strays far from one form or other of the presence of Christ's body. And it is an especially challenging problem for Augustine, because of his thorough commitment to Platonist intelligibility as the way to see God. Although Augustine did not participate in the Christological controversies in the Eastern empire that led to the Council of Ephesus, his mature work involves a sustained effort to hold on to his fundamental Platonist convictions about the closeness of the soul to God, while giving the flesh of Christ its due. But these efforts fall outside the scope of this investigation, where we are concerned not with how Augustine tried to do justice to external things, but rather with how he tried to turn away from them and see with eyes turned inward. Hence this chapter deals only with a specific problem, not its (many and various) solutions. The problem is that turning inward leads away from the flesh of Christ.

"Inner Man" Language

Augustine clearly did not think that turning inward was a purely Platonist notion that had nothing to do with Christianity. He was familiar, in fact, with a language of inwardness that had been present in the Christian tradition ever since the New Testament. The key piece of vocabulary in this language is the phrase "the inner man," which appears three times in the Pauline corpus,[4] with no precedent in any earlier literature except one memorable phrase in Plato's *Republic*. Tracing the path of this little piece of vocabulary and its offshoots will lead us deeper into the Christian problem of intelligibility as it posed itself to Augustine in the midst of formulating his distinctive version of Christian inwardness.

Toward the end of the *Republic*, Plato sums up his theory about the three parts of the soul with a striking metaphor. He compares the soul to a "many-headed beast," a lion, and "the man within."[5] Nothing in the context suggests that Plato means anything like an inner self: "the man within" or "inner man" is simply a metaphor for the rational part of the soul, as the other two are metaphors for the appetitive and the irascible parts of the soul. It is a fine metaphor that seems not to have made its way into the technical vocabulary of ancient philosophy, because we have no record of its appearance in any other text until the New Testament. The impression is probably misleading (for it may well have appeared in philosophical texts that are no longer extant), but from the present state of the documents it looks as if "the inner man" leaped straight from the dialogues of Plato into the letters of Paul.

In Paul too the meaning of the phrase is something close to "the rational part of the soul." This is what the Old Testament typically calls "the heart" (which in Hebrew usage clearly means a faculty of understanding and thought as well as feeling).[6] There are of course important differences between ancient Jewish versions of the thinking or rational part of the self and Platonist ones. Perhaps most notable is the fact that the Hebrew Scriptures do not picture the thinking part of the self separately from the body and contain no arguments for its immortality (in this resembling Homer more than Plato). We might add that the rationality of the Hebrew "heart" tends to be connected more with hearing than with seeing, more with understanding what someone says than with observation and examination. Nevertheless, there is plenty of overlap—enough for a Hellenistic Jew (who probably had a Greek education) to talk in the New Testament of "having the eyes of your heart enlightened"[7]—a phrase that would sound very Platonist indeed if the word "mind" were substituted for "heart." The meaning of the phrase does not appear to differ greatly

from ordinary Greek talk of the mind in many Hellenistic texts. The really drastic difference is the particular purpose of its use in this context: for what the enlightened rational
self sees here is not the Platonists' intelligible world or the Stoics' divine Nature, but the
richness of God's purpose in Christ.

The use of the phrase "the inner man" in the Pauline literature is probably best understood in a similar way. The phrase itself must have been readily recognizable as meaning something like the part of the self that has rationality and understanding, and perhaps
the more educated members of Paul's audience would recognize its Platonist provenance
(whether or not Paul himself did is a question I could not answer).[8] In any case the distinctive thing about its use in the New Testament is that the nature and destiny of the
"inner man" is so closely tied to the one man Jesus Christ. The result is a set of passages
that are open to Platonist exegesis but do not require it. These would attract the attention
of Christian Platonists for centuries to come, along with such texts as "for the things that
are seen are temporal, but the things that are unseen are eternal" (2 Cor. 4:18). There seems
no reason to doubt that these passages are borrowing, directly or indirectly, the language of
the Platonist tradition—yet non-Platonist readers could also point out that the eternal
things they have in view are not a Platonist intelligible world but the eschatological reign of
Christ.[9]

In later, more systematically Platonist Christians, the language of the inner man gets
intertwined with more thoroughly Platonist views of human nature. The most important
and formative figure in this development is Origen, the third-century Christian Platonist of
Alexandria. Origen, who studied philosophy under the same teacher as Plotinus,[10] established by precept and example the immensely influential Alexandrian school of allegorical
or spiritual interpretation of Scripture, based on methods that had been developed by
Philo of Alexandria, the Jewish exegete and Middle Platonist of the first century AD In the
preface to one of his most important writings, he expatiates on the Pauline metaphor of the
inner man, distinguishing the desires, needs, and perceptions of the inner man or soul
from those of the outer man or body, and indicating that this is the hermeneutical key to an
edifying reading of the great love song of the Bible, the Song of Songs, which might otherwise be taken in a very carnal sense.[11] Elsewhere Origen speaks of the five "senses" of the
mind or heart—a seeing, hearing, feeling, smelling, and tasting that correspond to the
bodily sense organs but perceive spiritual rather than corporeal objects.[12] From Alexandria this vocabulary of inner or spiritual senses, along with the letter/spirit hermeneutics it
supports, spread to the more sophisticated circles of the Western church. But Augustine
knew nothing of it growing up in Africa, the "Bible belt" of the Roman Empire, whose
great theological hero was the anti-Platonist Tertullian, and where those most committed
to an "advanced" and spiritual Christianity were the Manichaean heretics.[13] He encountered it first in Milan, in the sermons of its bishop, Ambrose, where it was part of the exegetical practice and anthropological theory that helped bring him back into the fold of the
Catholic Church.[14]

For our purposes the chief importance of early Christian talk about the senses of the
inner man, inner vision, inner hearing, and the like is that it must have convinced Augustine that the language of inwardness was part of the very best Catholic tradition. And it
could hardly have escaped his notice that the "inner man" was the subject of concern not
only in Ambrose and Paul, but also in Plotinus and Plato.[15] This convergence must have
struck him as one of the things true philosophy and true religion have in common. At any

rate, Augustine picks up part of this language very early on in his writing career, speaking of an inner eye of the soul already at Cassiciacum[16]—and then frequently, indeed incessantly, for the rest of his career.

Interestingly, however, talk of "the inner man" is not nearly as prominent in Augustine's writings as talk of the inner eye of the soul, and there are reasons to think that it does not play a particularly important role in his thought.[17] For the striking and new thing about Augustinian inwardness is the conception of an inner space that one can enter and look within. This does not consort especially well with talk of an "inner man," because one expects the inner man, like any other man, to be looking away from himself (at Forms in a Platonic heaven, say, or at Christ sitting at God's right hand) rather than into himself. So for instance one of Augustine's most concentrated uses of "inner man" language comes just before, but not during, his most elaborate discussion of inner space in the *Confessions*.[18] Talk of "inner man" and "outer man" in this passage is just another way of referring to body and soul,[19] and Augustine has no further use for it when he moves on to an in-depth discussion of the soul's inner space. In effect he uses "inner man" language at this point as a kind of prelude to inwardness, offering it as biblical justification for describing the difference between objects of the bodily senses and powers of the soul in terms of a contrast between outer and inner. But such language does not prove useful when he gets to work seriously analyzing the nature of the inner self. "Inner man" language likewise turns up frequently in the treatise *On the Trinity*, where once again the contrast between "inner man" and "outer man" serves primarily to indicate the direction of Augustine's inquiry, rather than contributing substantively to his discussion of the nature of the soul.[20]

Christ in the Heart

In what is probably the earliest substantive use of the phrase "inner man" in his writings,[21] Augustine speaks of Christ "dwelling in the inner man" and means to be quoting Paul.[22] In fact he is conflating two adjoining phrases in the letter to the Ephesians:

> [I pray that the Father] might grant you, by the riches of his glory, to be strengthened in power through his Spirit *in the inner man, that Christ may dwell in your hearts* by faith, rooted and grounded in love. . . . [23]

There are motives for this conflation. In this passage Augustine wants the "inner man," which he equates with "the secret place of the rational soul" (*rationalis animae secretis*), to be the temple in which we pray to God, but the New Testament only helps him so far as to say to Christians "Don't you know that you are the temple of God, and the Spirit of God dwells *in you*,"[24] without mentioning the soul as the part of "you" in which God dwells. By replacing the "heart" in which Christ dwells (Eph. 3:17) with the "inner man" (Eph. 3:16), Augustine gets the inner man to look like an inner space or temple where God can be found.

In the end this move is not very promising, for biblical usage does not really support it. But the other passage quoted here (about believers as a temple in which the Spirit of God dwells) is more like what Augustine wants. It belongs to a pattern of Pauline language about Christ or the Spirit dwelling "in you." Such talk is a good deal less common than its converse (such as talk about believers being "in Christ"), and it is more characteristically in the second rather than the first person.[25] But its suggestiveness, for anyone interested in finding God within, must be immense. Especially suggestive for Augustine, it seems, is Ephesians 3:17, where Christ is said to dwell in "your hearts." What exactly this means, and how it is related to New Testament talk about the Spirit dwelling in us and our being "in Christ," are not simple questions and have been the subject of intensive exegesis and meditation for centuries. Somehow it is all connected with Paul's apparent inability to think about the identity of believers apart from the existence of the one man Jesus Christ. In any case, it is important to notice what kind of inwardness is *not* present in this Pauline language: it contains no hint of an inward turn, no suggestion that we should try to find Christ inside ourselves by looking within our hearts. On the contrary, Christ is in our hearts "by faith" and—as Paul says elsewhere—faith comes by hearing the Gospel of Christ preached, that is, by perceiving a word of good news that comes to us from outside ourselves.[26]

Whatever the New Testament originally meant by talking about Christ in our hearts, such talk has quite definite implications for a Platonist such as Augustine, who must think of human beings as made up of body and soul and who will inevitably identify Paul's "heart" with the Platonist "soul." What part of Christ, then, will be found in our hearts? The *body* of Christ cannot be in our hearts, for bodies do not dwell inside souls. Nor does Augustine ever suggest that the *soul* of Christ dwells in our heart: he prefers to speak of souls *united* to other souls in love and friendship[27] rather than of one soul being *in* another. Hence what remains is his divinity, not his humanity. That alone is what we find if we turn inward to seek Christ in the heart. The Christ who dwells in our hearts, for Augustine, is not life-giving flesh nor human soul but the eternal Wisdom of God.

To turn inward is, for a Platonist, necessarily to turn away from bodily things. Consequently, Augustine's inward turn is necessarily a turn *away from* the flesh of Christ as well as a turn *toward* his divinity. Augustine emphasizes this point early in the *Confessions*, in a passage designed to prepare us for the inward turn in book 7. Once again his question is where to find God, and once again his answer is "within": "See where he is, where one knows Truth. Deep in the heart he is, but the heart has strayed from him. 'Return, you transgressors, to the heart!'"[28] Before transposing this call of inwardness into a Christological key, Augustine plays on central themes of ancient philosophy, the search for happiness and the contrast between immortality and the perishable world of bodies—a contrast all the more moving because he is concluding a long meditation on the death of a childhood friend and the meaning of grief:

> Seek what you seek, but it is not where you seek it. You seek a happy life in the region of death. It is not there. For how can there be happy life where there is no life?[29]

Having thus set the inward turn in the context of the problems of ancient philosophy, Augustine turns to the Incarnation. It is as if eternal Life has invaded the region of death, shouting like a conqueror. But its stay down here was only temporary:

> Our Life itself came down here, took our death and killed it out of the abundance of his own life. And he thundered, shouting for us to return to him in that secret place from which he came forth to us first into the Virgin's womb, where he wed the human creature, mortal flesh, so that it may not be forever mortal.

The Incarnation is God taking human flesh as his bride in order to transfer it from the region of death to immortality. We are not far from the notion of Christ's life-giving flesh, yet this is as far as Augustine gets: flesh can receive life but not give it. For what really matters is not Christ's flesh but "that secret place" (*illud secretum*) from which he came forth into the external world via the womb of Mary.

> And from there [i.e., the womb] "as a bridegroom coming forth from his chamber, he exulted like a great man to run his course." For he did not delay but ran, shouting by words and deeds, death and life, descent and ascent, shouting for us to return to him.[30]

Return to his flesh? Of course not. Augustine has already told us where to return. It is in that same place that we find Christ our Life: "And he parted from the eyes, that we may *return to the heart* and find him. For he departed—and see, he is here!"[31] Christ can be found, as eternal Life and Wisdom can always be found, within the heart that knows Truth.

Christ was in a hurry to run his race in the flesh so that he could pass through this region of mortality and "return to where he never departed," that is, to eternity, where we can find him in our hearts. The same metaphor of Christ running through his earthly race and leaving it behind is expounded more fully in Augustine's treatise *On Christian Doctrine*, written at about the same time as the *Confessions*:

> Hence it can be understood that nothing should detain us on the road, when the Lord himself, insofar as he deigned to *be* our road, did not want us to be detained but to pass on, so that we should not cling in weakness to temporal things (even though they are taken up and borne by him for our salvation) but rather that we should eagerly run through them to reach or deserve to reach his very self, who freed our nature from temporal things and placed it at the right hand of the Father.[32]

Christ's flesh is the temporal road or course (*via*) through which we run, but the goal we hope to reach is eternal life, not anything temporal—hence not flesh, not even Christ's flesh. In passing beyond Christ's flesh to something more permanent we are only running the course that Christ himself ran before us. Hence the Christ we find in our hearts is the goal, whereas the Christ we see in the flesh and in history is only the road—and only temporary. To cling to Christ's flesh, it seems, is not to cling to Life, but only to delay and turn aside from the race we are to run. We are seeking eternal life, and it is not there outside but "here" within—not in Christ's flesh but in our hearts. This is not the last word Augustine has to say about the significance of Christ's flesh, but it is the word that fits most naturally with his project of inward turn.[33]

Wisdom by Another Name

The inward turn in Augustine is a Christological theme, but it is no less philosophical for that. On the contrary, it is in the inward turn that we can see most clearly how Augustine's Platonist philosophical convictions shape his understanding of Christ. Christology in fact is precisely the ground on which Augustine sees the deepest unity as well as the clearest distinction between Christian faith and the philosophical pursuit of wisdom. For although the pagan philosophers did not know or accept the Incarnation of God in Christ, they did pursue eternal Wisdom, which is in fact Christ. Ancient philosophy and Christian faith thus converge upon Christ, whom Paul, in a passage that is of central importance for Augustine's early Christology, calls "the Virtue of God and the Wisdom of God."[34] It is thus the very nature of philosophy, which (as Augustine never tires of reminding us) is by definition the love of wisdom,[35] to seek that ultimate and eternal Wisdom that Christians call by the name "Christ." Of course Christians and philosophers are one on this point only to the extent that the flesh of Christ and his human identity are not in view. Hence when Augustine compares the content of "the books of the Platonists" with the content of the gospel, he emphasizes that Platonist philosophers knew and taught (though "not of course in these words") that "In the beginning was the Word, and the Word was with God and the Word was God" (John 1:1), but what they did not know or believe was that "the Word became flesh" (John 1:14) and all that followed from this Incarnation of the Word.[36] In other words, the Platonists knew about the divine nature of Christ but not his human nature: they saw the Christ who is found in the heart but not the man who lived and died and rose again in the land of the Jews.

The way Augustine tells it, his search for God was never separate from his philosophical search for eternal Wisdom and Truth. His heart was first turned toward God, he says, when he read an exhortation to philosophy written by Cicero:

> This book changed my prayers, and made my devotion and desires different. Suddenly I despised all vain hope and longed with unbelievable warmth of heart for immortal Wisdom, and began to "arise to return" to You.[37]

As with the later conversion scenes, our investigation here is primarily concerned not with the nature of the historical event to which Augustine is referring but with his present understanding, as the author of the *Confessions,* of the relation of philosophy to Christ. Like "the books of the Platonists," Cicero's exhortation to philosophy taught Augustine to seek God—and succeeded in this, he thinks, because it taught him to seek that true and eternal Wisdom that Christians know by the name of Christ.

For philosophy and Christianity love the same thing, but under two different names. Hence what delighted Augustine in Cicero's book, he tells us, is not the doctrines and formulations of any particular philosophical school; rather "I was stirred by that discourse to love and seek and pursue and possess or strongly embrace *Wisdom itself, whatever that might be.*" And in the great fire of longing ignited by Cicero's words, "only one thing held me back: that *the name of Christ was not there,*" a name that "my heart of tender years had piously drunk in even with mother's milk, and deeply retained still."[38] So, seeking the thing to match this name held in his heart, he went from Cicero to the Bible, but he soon gave up on the latter because its language and style were too humble to satisfy his pride.[39]

The next thing he tells us is how he was snared by the Manichaeans, proud madmen whose only advantage was that they raved in the right words, "in whose mouth were the snares of the devil and a birdlime mixed of the syllables of Your name and the name of the Lord Jesus Christ and of the Paraclete, our Comforter the Holy Spirit."[40] Augustine plainly wants us to notice the contrast with Cicero: whereas the heretics had the right name but not the thing itself (*res ipsa*), the philosopher pointed him toward the real thing but did not know its Christian name.

The attraction of the Manichaeans, as Augustine paints it in the *Confessions,* is precisely that they offered him a way to unite Christianity and philosophy. For they spoke not only the names of Christ and the Holy Spirit, but also the names Truth and Wisdom:

> These names did not leave their mouths, but this was mere sound and the noise of the tongue, and otherwise their heart was empty of truth. And they said, "Truth, Truth!" and said much to me about it, and it was never in them, but they spoke falsely not only about

You, who truly are Truth, but also about these elements of the world, your creatures. . . . O Truth, Truth, how inwardly did the very marrow of my mind sigh for You, when they sounded You so much and so often in mere words, and many huge books! And these were the platters on which they put before me, hungering for You, *the sun and the moon*— beautiful works of Yours, but Your works, not You.[41]

The curious reference to the sun and moon at the end of this passage has to do with the peculiar Manichaean variation on the ancient belief in the divinity of the heavens. We hear of it from a Manichaean teacher debated by Augustine years later, who is quoted in the transcript of the debate as saying, "the apostle says Christ is the virtue of God and the wisdom of God, and we believe in fact that *his virtue dwells in the sun, his wisdom in the moon*."[42] As a Manichaean, therefore, Augustine would have been taught that the name "Christ" referred to the sun and the moon—an identification he now derides as ridiculous and sacrilegious. Yet this Manichaean Christology did leave something permanent with him, namely the apostle's words themselves, "Christ the Virtue of God and the Wisdom of God," which from the very beginning of his career as a Christian writer he takes to be the cornerstone of Christian philosophy.[43] Given what he tells us here in the *Confessions*, we can infer, I think, that it is the oldest element in his theology, the thread of longing that marks his path from Manichaeanism to Christian Platonism and on to the very end of his life.

Ideas in the Mind of God

The distinction between name and thing, *nomen* and *res*, is crucial to Augustine's synthesis of Christianity and Platonism, which is based on the premise that the two are concerned about the same thing under different names. Hence his most explicit treatment of Platonic Forms, the essay "On Ideas," begins by drawing attention to precisely this distinction.[44] Answering questions from African friends (perhaps from his hometown in the "Bible belt") who might be suspicious or puzzled by the fancy philosophical theories he had picked up in the big city at Milan,[45] Augustine wants to convince them that Christians can and should believe in the existence of Platonic Forms, even though no such thing is mentioned in the Scriptures. Hence his first move is to suggest that wise men from other nations than Greece could have seen the same *things* as Plato but called them by different *names*. He evidently has in mind the prophets and apostles of the Bible, especially Moses and the patriarchs, whom Ambrose (following the Alexandrian tradition of Origen and Philo) painted in terms strongly resembling Stoic and Platonist portrayals of "the wise man." Augustine also mentions Plato's travels in search of wisdom, thus hinting that he might first have learned about the Ideas from those foreign wise men. This suggestion is based on another conviction of Ambrose, that Plato learned his doctrine from the writings of Moses when he was visiting Egypt.[46]

Having done what he could to deal with the problem of historical pedigree, Augustine is ready to turn from name to thing—but first he does a very clever bit of naming. Noting that several names for Platonic Forms were in use—not only "Ideas" (*idea*) but also "Forms" (*formae* and *species*)—he adds that "Reasons" (*rationes*) is a good name for them too, even though the word (*ratio* in the singular) translates the Greek *logos* rather than any of Plato's technical terms for the Ideas. This turns out to be a key move in his argument to persuade Christians to accept Plato's Forms, for among the many meanings of *ratio* is "plan," in an architectural sense (like a modern blueprint)—that is, the model by which a builder or artist makes something in the visible world.[47] Hence he argues that any Christian, believing in the doctrine of creation, will surely believe that God had a such a plan in mind as he created—else he created without reason and therefore irrationally (*irrationabiliter*).[48] And the Forms are simply those eternal plans or models in God's mind, by which he creates the world.

The argument is so apt that the West accepted it without demur for over a millennium.[49] The Eastern Orthodox tradition, by contrast, anathematized Plato's doctrine of Ideas—but that was on the assumption that it had to take the form found in the *Timaeus*, where the Ideas are located outside the Creator.[50] Augustine firmly agrees in rejecting this (genuinely Platonic) form of the doctrine, calling it sacrilegious, for it would mean that God was guided or ruled by something outside himself in creating. That by which God creates must be internal to God, which means not something lower and lesser than God but something integral to the divine being itself. All this Augustine has clearly in view when he takes the Neoplatonist position[51] that Plato's Forms are located nowhere else but the divine Mind. As any Neoplatonist could tell you, the ideas in the Mind of God are not other than God himself. They are not "in" God like pebbles in a box or even ideas in a human mind (at least not if one has a modern empiricist view of how concepts get in our minds, rather than an ancient Neoplatonist view of intelligible Form). Nor are they "parts" of God, for of course God is not made up of parts like a material thing. Rather, their being or substance is no different from the being or substance of God.[52]

This means, of course, that to see Platonic Ideas is to see God. That is indeed the point of Augustine's Platonist project. His aim is to show—and to see for himself—that the human mind, in gaining insight into things that are immutably true, catches a glimpse of the eternal Truth that contains them and is their very substance. This commitment to the intelligibility of God grounds Augustine's inward turn, whose aim is to catch a glimpse of how the mind catches a glimpse of God. In his early philosophical dialogues Augustine is a practitioner of such glimpses, watching himself and his interlocutors as they achieve momentary and partial insight into divine Truth. Like Plotinus's fallen souls, Augustine and his friends in the dialogues see only in part, even though the intelligible truth they see is integral to an indivisible whole. But just as the Plotinian soul turning inward sees nothing less than the divine Mind, so Augustine insists that the wise see nothing less than the Ideas that are the very substance of the one God. Without such vision there is no wisdom, Augustine says in the opening paragraph of "On Ideas," and his conclusion at the end of the essay is that such vision is what makes the soul truly happy. Beatific vision, in short, is simply the fullness of intellectual vision.[53]

The claim that in seeing Platonic Ideas our mind sees God emerges quite clearly in the essay "On Ideas." But it is not the direct object of the argument (which is the thesis that Ideas exist and are located in the Mind of God). The indirect argument for this claim is grounded on Augustine's definition of Ideas, which assigns to them three basic properties: they are immutable, they are the formative models by which mutable things are formed, and they are intelligible, being visible to the eye of the rational soul when it is pure. If ideas are immutable and formative, then their substance is no different from the very substance of God, and if they are intelligible, then we can see them—and thus see the very substance of God—with the eye of the intellect.

These three properties have been essential to the definition of Ideas ever since Plato, but Augustine is the last orthodox Christian of any stature who keeps all three of them together, as properties of the same thing. He is apparently the first Christian in the West to argue explicitly that Platonic Forms should be located in the mind and very substance of God, and he is the last in West or East to believe that the substance of God is intelligible. His commitment to intelligibility as the great clue to the relation between God and the soul makes his brand of Platonism unique in the orthodox Christian traditions.

The Intelligibility of God

I have noted an apparent disagreement between the Western and Eastern Christian traditions about Platonic Ideas, but I think we will see the difference between them more clearly if we see this disagreement as mainly verbal and regard Augustine's idiosyncratic commitment to divine intelligibility as the key strain of theological difference between East and West. The East will not speak of Platonic Ideas but is not averse to locating eternal formative principles in God, which amounts to much the same thing.[54] What the East consistently avoids is attributing intelligibility to God or to anything in him. And on that point the West agrees—all except Augustine.

Where Augustine differs from the rest of orthodox Nicene Christianity is in attaching the Platonist predicate "intelligible" to the divine side of the Creator/creature distinction. Like all orthodox theologians, he regards God as the Creator, not created (hence God is uncreated and eternal), in whom belongs the immutable formative principles that give form to the mutable created world. But Augustine alone adds that the eternal formative principles in God are of a nature intelligible to the human mind. This is the respect in which he stands with Plato and Plotinus against the rest of the Nicene Christian traditions. Aquinas, for instance, will follow Augustine's language but not his thought on this point. He calls God "intelligible" but adds that what is intelligible in itself or *per se* is not necessarily intelligible to us. God is indeed infinitely and supereminently intelligible, which means he is intelligible to himself but not to us, being beyond the natural power of our intellect to grasp.[55] Thus in Aquinas the being of God is not intelligible in the original Platonist sense of the word (i.e., not by nature intelligible to our intellects) and therefore by the same token neither are the Ideas in God.[56] What Plato had joined (Idea and intelligibility) Christianity put asunder—again, all except Augustine.

Augustine's idiosyncracy is not that he is a Christian Platonist but that he retains the Platonist notion of intelligibility, with its assumption that there is a deep kinship between soul and divinity manifested in intellectual vision. Augustine formulates this kinship using equivalent language borrowed from Plotinus, saying that the soul is closer or nearer in nature to God than anything else is.[57] This closeness is clearly based on the soul's capacity for intellectual vision: because the rational soul can see God, it is higher up on the hierarchy of being than things that cannot.[58] And higher means closer to God.

The result of this line of reasoning is a three-tiered hierarchy of being: God, soul, and bodies, with soul in the middle between the intelligible world (God) and the sensible world (bodies).[59] For the soul is higher than bodies because of its intellectual capacity, but lower than God because it is mutable and created. The double movement of Augustine's inward turn takes place on the conceptual landscape of this three-tiered ontology: turning inward means that the soul turns its attention away from the lowest level of being, the external world of bodies, and toward itself at the middle level. But then to gain real happiness, the soul must look above itself to the highest level of being, gazing at the immutable Truth that is above the mutable soul, as the Creator is above what he created.

This three-tiered hierarchy of being, combined with the portrait of the Mind of God in Augustine's essay "On Ideas,"[60] yields a rather striking comparison with Plotinus. Plotinus's universe has four levels: One, Mind, Soul and Bodies. Chop off the highest of these, and you get something very much like Augustine's three levels: God, soul, and bodies (with God being identified as the divine Mind). The crucial and essential departure from Plotinus is that Augustine regards the soul as a creature, not an emanation from what is above it, so that the soul is not divine. But the really striking thing, for our purposes, is what Augustine omits: Plotinus's concept of the One either disappears or else melts into the divine Mind.[61] For it is very clear that in locating the Ideas in the Mind of God and insisting on their intelligibility, Augustine is identifying the Christian God with the Plotinian level of Mind rather than the One. The reason for this identification seems clear: to identify God solely with the One would make him incomprehensible rather than intelligible, lifting him above that kinship between soul and divine things that is at the heart of Augustine's Platonist project. And that would spoil everything that Augustine is working for with his inward turn. Finding God within requires, for Augustine, that special closeness between the soul and God that is marked by the Platonist concept of intelligibility.

It is important to see that a Christian Platonist who is not committed to an inward turn is free to reject the premise that God is intelligible and thus to construct a picture of the hierarchy of being that draws the line between Creator and creature differently. This was in fact done by Pseudo-Dionysius, the fifth- or sixth-century Eastern Orthodox theologian known to the West as Denys. Using Plotinus's four-tiered hierarchy as the point of comparison between Augustine and Denys, we can see what is distinctive about Augustine's Platonism. What Augustine in effect proposes is to draw the line between Creator and creature at the boundary between the divine Mind and the Soul. Denys, on the other hand, clearly draws the line at the boundary between One and Mind, as he firmly identifies the Triune God of Christianity with the incomprehensible One of Neoplatonism, above the realm of intelligible being:

> The One, the Unknown, that which is above being, the Good itself, precisely this, I say, is the Trinitarian Unity—equally Deity and equally Good, which cannot be spoken or understood.[62]

The intelligible world of Plotinus's divine Mind thus becomes in Denys a created realm, below the level of what is strictly divine (though occasionally a Christian, speaking loosely, can call it "divine" in the old pagan sense of "immortal"). It is a celestial realm of immortal intelligences, but it is not God. In other words, when looking at the second level of Plotinus's hierarchy of being, Augustine thinks he sees the Creator and Denys thinks he sees creatures. In fact Plato's intelligible world, which in Augustine becomes the Mind of God, becomes in Denys the realm of the angels.

The developments in the Platonist tradition that led to this contrast are fascinating and worth a brief digression. Between Plotinus and Denys stands the metaphysics of fifth-century pagan Neoplatonism, best represented (among extant texts) by the writings of Proclus. In this metaphysics, Plotinus's conception of the divine Mind is elaborated in a striking way. The Middle Platonist pattern of proliferating divine Minds makes a comeback, reinforced by Plotinus's notion that each Platonic Form or Idea is a subject as well as object of knowledge, so that the realm of Mind is populated not merely by intelligible ideas but by intellects or intelligences. In Proclus these are organized in a vast hierarchy.[63] In Denys, this becomes the celestial hierarchy of angelic intelligences, immortal and unembodied minds—but emphatically creatures, not the Creator. Thus by the time they reach Denys, Plato's intelligible Forms have mutated into angels.[64] When Denys (or other Eastern Church Fathers, for that matter) speak of "the intelligible world," they are referring to the incorporeal world of angels or created intelligences, not the world inside the Mind of God.

The Incomprehensibility of God

Augustine and Denys represent the two fundamental conceptual alternatives available to an orthodox Christian Platonist, and it is a matter of historical importance that Denys's alternative eventually won the day in the West as well as the East. Unanimously supported by the Eastern Orthodox Fathers,[65] the doctrine that the essence of God is incomprehensible came to be accepted as Christian teaching in the Latin Middle Ages as well, by Platonists and Aristotelians and everyone else. But it is the Platonist version of the doctrine, as we find it in Denys, that shows most clearly what is idiosyncratic about Augustine's Platonism. Augustine's project is to turn from sensible things to intelligible things, and thereby to see God. But for Denys there is another whole level to go after the intelligible world:

> For just as intelligible things are not grasped or contemplated by the senses . . . so the infinity above being transcends all that is, and the unity which is above mind transcends all minds.[66]

To arrive at God we must therefore leave behind not only the sensible but also the intelligible, in order to achieve "a union . . . with what is beyond being and knowing."[67] Hence, although our minds or intellects can know something about God as First Cause through the things that he has made, we cannot know the divine nature directly; the true and proper and most divine knowledge of God is rather "a union above mind, knowing through unknowing."[68]

All this fits straightforwardly into Plotinus's conception of the One, as Augustine's notion of Ideas in the Mind of God fits straightforwardly into Plotinus's conception of Mind. It is precisely Augustine's commitment to the intelligibility of God that makes for this difference. For as we have noted in passing, Augustine can make use of the Neoplatonist conceptuality of the One in articulating the unity of the Trinity just as Denys does, while for his part Denys can accommodate the notion of formative rational principles in God that Augustine argues for in "On Ideas." What Denys cannot accommodate, and Augustine cannot give up, is the notion that the very substance of God is intelligible, accessible to the vision of the mind's eye. It is as if the two of them had climbed out of Plato's cave into the light, and Denys followed Plotinus in the belief that the Sun shining above was too bright to look at, while Augustine agreed rather with Plato that the soul is of such a nature, with the right discipline and purification, to gaze straight at the Sun and understand it.[69]

The contrast should not be blurred by the vicissitudes of terminology. Just as Aquinas affirms the intelligibility of God while emptying the term "intelligible" of its original Platonist meaning (i.e., understandable to the human mind), so Augustine can apply a word like "incomprehensible" to God but mean by it quite a bit less than Denys and the rest of the orthodox tradition mean when they affirm the incomprehensibility of God. For Denys God is incomprehensible precisely in that he is not intelligible.[70] Of course he is unintelligible only in the sense of being *above* intelligibility, not below it. (He is like the sun, too bright to be seen, not like darkness, which is too unreal and void of light to be visible.)[71] Augustine, by contrast, applies the Latin term *incomprehensibile* to God in a way that is meant to uphold, not negate, his intelligibility:

> God is for the mind to understand, as body is for the eye to see. But do you think you comprehend body with the eye? No way. Whatever you look at, you're not looking at the whole. When you see a man's face you don't see his back at the same time, and when you see his back you don't see his face. So in seeing, you don't comprehend.[72]

This line of reasoning depends on a rather literal interpretation of the verb "comprehend" (*comprehendere*) as "to grasp all together." For Augustine God is incomprehensible to the mind only in the sense that bodies are incomprehensible to the eye: we cannot grasp all sides of them at once. But of course this no more puts God above intelligibility than it puts bodies above visibility. This weak Augustinian sense of the *word* "incomprehensible" becomes standard in the Western tradition,[73] along with the affirmation of a *concept* of divine incomprehensibility that is much stronger, coming from Denys and the other Eastern Fathers.

One last point of terminology. The words "incomprehensible" and "ineffable" are often said in one breath, but they do not mean the same thing: the one puts God beyond the reach of our mind, the other beyond the reach of our words. Hence it is quite consistent for someone like Augustine, who thinks our mind can see far beyond what words can express, to affirm that God is ineffable while denying that he is incomprehensible. Words, for Augustine, are sensible things, and therefore cannot give adequate expression to intelligible things; they can signify them but not give knowledge of them. For in general, signs do not teach things but rather the reverse: knowledge of the thing signified must come first, so that we can then come to know the significance of the sign.[74] Hence in Augustinian hermeneutics the Scriptures do not mediate knowledge of God's nature, but rather are properly understood only by those who have already perceived the incorporeal nature of God and can thus avoid carnal interpretations of its language.[75]

Consequences of Nicaea

Since the West agrees substantially with the East in regarding God as incomprehensible rather than intelligible, a serious problem arises for Western readers who want to interpret Augustine in conformity with the rest of the orthodox tradition on this issue—a problem which must be discussed in the next chapter. Suffice it to say for now that Western Christianity has a long, complex and immensely fruitful history of misreading Augustine, and that this particular problem contributes to one of the deepest misreadings of all, that of the Thomistic nature/grace tradition.

Our focus in this chapter is on Christological issues, and in this respect the doctrine of divine incomprehensibility poses no problem, but rather takes its place within a prior and overarching solution—the fundamental orthodox Christian solution to the problem of how the divine is mediated to mortals. One might wonder, of course, how anyone could ever know anything at all about an incomprehensible God. In Platonist terms, the question is one of mediation: how is knowledge of an incomprehensible Creator to be mediated to the creature? The orthodox answer to this question lies in the doctrines of the Trinity and Christology developed in the ancient ecumenical councils beginning with Nicaea in 325. It was in the course of these developments that a clear commitment to the doctrine of divine incomprehensibility arose, alongside an irreversible commitment to an exhaustive distinction between Creator and creature.

The Creator/creature distinction, so essential to Christian theology and so different from the pagan Neoplatonist scheme of emanation, took its definitive shape for Christianity in the course of the complicated developments between the Council of Nicaea in 325 and the Council of Constantinople in 381 (the decade of Augustine's conversion). In rejecting the heresy called Arianism, Nicene theologians affirmed that the divine being of Christ (which of course is different from his humanity) is no different at all from the divine being of God the Father. Since he is "of one substance with the Father,"[76] he is no less God than the Father is. Hence he does not belong at an intermediate level between the Creator and the creation. Being coequal with the Father and Holy Spirit, he is not a lower divinity mediating between the First Principle and the visible world.

The Nicene doctrine of the Trinity thereby rules out one very natural form of Christian Platonism. In Nicene theology it is no longer possible to assign Christ, as the eternal Word and Wisdom of God, to the level of intelligible Mind, while locating God the Father at the top level of the ontological hierarchy as the incomprehensible One. The Nicene Trinity is coequal, not hierarchical. To make Christ the intelligible image of the incomprehensible Father is (especially in a Platonist milieu) to subordinate him to the Father in a way that is incompatible with the Nicene affirmation that they are of one being or substance.[77] In the wake of Nicaea, an orthodox Christian Neoplatonist must locate the whole Trinity, Father, Son, and Holy Spirit together at the same level of the ontological hierarchy. Hence if one of them is incomprehensible they all are, and if one of them is intelligible they all are.[78] Thus Nicaea makes it impossible to affirm both the intelligibility of the divine Word and the incomprehensibility of the divine nature. Faced with the choice, every Nicene theologian except Augustine retained the incomprehensibility of God and gave up the intelligibility of Christ, the eternal Word.

One more consequence of Nicaea caused problems for Christian Platonists. In eliminating Platonist hierarchy and subordination, Nicaea also eliminated Platonist mediation. Nicene theology has no place for a *tertium quid* or intermediary kind of being that can mediate between Creator and creature. Hence in the orthodox Christian traditions, the Creator/creature distinction is logically exhaustive: everything in existence is either Creator or creature, and there is nothing in existence that is not one or the other. There is, however, a distinctively Christian mediation between Creator and creature, because even though there is no kind of being between Creator and creature, there is one thing in existence that is both Creator and creature at once, the man Jesus Christ, who is God in the flesh—a human being who is also the eternal Word and Wisdom of God. Nicaea, in effect, leaves Christianity nowhere to turn but him. Of course that is one reason why orthodox theologians tend to regard it as the greatest achievement of the Christian theological tradition.

In Eastern Christianity, under the pressure of Nicene thought, the Platonist concept of intellectual vision underwent a transformation as astonishing as the mutation of Platonic Ideas into angels in Denys. For the East, beatific vision is not anything a Plato or Plotinus would recognize, for the light that beatifies both body and soul originates ultimately from the life-giving flesh of Christ. The Transfiguration, the episode in the Gospel when divine light shone from Christ's human body and was perceptible to bodily eyes,[79] becomes the model for beatific vision.[80] It is as if the light of the knowledge of the glory of God were found not in that Platonist "other world" where the intelligible Sun shines, but rather, as Paul says, in the face of Jesus Christ.[81] This becomes a standard pattern of Christian theology and piety in both East and West: a God who is by nature incomprehensible is mediated to us by one man's flesh. In the West, Word and Sacrament, Gospel and Eucharist and Church, are understood as containing or conveying, revealing or proclaiming this life-giving flesh of Christ, as if all divine goodness flowed with the blood and water from his pierced side.[82]

Augustine's inward turn provides the most important alternative within the Nicene traditions to this fleshly pattern of piety. His inward turn is not a turn away from Christ, but it is a turn away from Christ's flesh. He thinks such a turn is possible because he believes in the intelligibility of God and thus can conceive of a form of access to God that leaves Christ's flesh behind, turning inward to find Christ as God in the heart. Because of Augustine's immense prestige and influence in Western Christianity, an inward turn remains a permanent possibility for orthodox piety in the West. But because Augustine is so reticent about the Plotinian philosophy that admonished him to find God within himself, the heirs of Augustinian inwardness often conceive of an inner relation between God and the soul that is nothing like Platonist intelligibility. From medieval mysticism to contemporary theologies of religious experience, the West has conceived of the God within the self as beyond the comprehension of mere intellect. But Augustine could not have conceived of this inner self in the first place without believing in the special kind of closeness between God and the soul described by the Platonist metaphor of intellectual vision.

PART II

AUGUSTINE: INVENTING THE INNER SELF

5

Inward Turn and Intellectual Vision

This chapter presents the Augustinian version of two Platonist concepts, inward turn and intellectual vision, which form the context of other developments in Augustinian inwardness, such as inner space. Augustine's inward turn, as illustrated in Confessions 7, is conceived as a turning of the soul's attention toward itself, in order to found a project of philosophical inquiry in which the soul examines its own cognitive powers, ascending from sense perception to intellect and finally looking above its own mind to the intelligible Truth. The point of this project is missed if one tries to read Augustine in light of the Thomistic nature/grace distinction, which cannot allow that seeing God is a natural function of the human mind. I propose that the experience of vision for Augustine is best understood not as mysticism but as a form of what we would call insight. It is the sort of experience one can train for by getting a good education.

A Turning of Attention

Augustine's inward turn is first and foremost a way of directing the mind's attention, and on that basis it is also a form of conversion and a project of philosophical inquiry. The language of conversion (Latin *conversio*, Greek *epistrophē*) is based on verbs that mean "to turn one's attention."[1] What conversion is about, for Augustine as well as for Plotinus and Plato, is turning one's attention to look in a different direction from before, in order to find what is divine and ultimate.[2] To turn *inward*, as Plotinus and Augustine do, means looking for the divine in the self (and of course specifically in the soul) and therefore requires a view of the soul and its relation to the divine that would make sense of directing one's attention that way. Hence a commitment to turning inward generates a conception of inner space, a dimension of being within the soul where one can turn to look for God.

For Plotinus, as we have seen, the inner space of the soul is none other than the intelligible world, which is the divine Mind. For Augustine, on the contrary, the inner space of the self is not divine—in Christian theological terms, it is created rather than uncreated, creature rather than Creator—and precisely so it is the soul's *own* inner space in a way that Plotinus's inner space was not: it is the first version of what we in the West now call "the inner self." The rest of my study is devoted to tracing how this new conception of the self emerged within the context of the overarching project of inward turn: how Augustine, wanting to heed Plotinus's admonition to turn "into the inside," found that he had to conceive that inner realm rather differently from Plotinus.

Augustine came to the concept of inner self by exploring thoughts that were new to him, and this involved quite a bit of fumbling around and poking into blind alleys. But what stood fast for him in all the fumbling and poking was the conviction that some sort of turn to the soul was necessary, because God could not be found in the world of bodies. Amid all his confusion and changes of mind about the nature of the soul and how to turn to it, he never doubted the negative side of the inward turn: that he must turn away from bodies. Hence we can begin to see the shape of Augustine's inward turn by starting with what it turns away from. The inner space of the soul emerges as an alternative to the literal space of the bodily world.

To begin with, we can return to *Confessions*, book 7,[3] and look more closely at the problem to which the inward turn was a solution. The problem is where to find God, but more specifically, it is how to conceive of God in non-bodily terms. Where can one turn, where direct one's attention, to find a thing that occupies no space in the bodily world? The answer is Plotinian in inspiration: one must awaken to a different kind of vision, one that has been going on all along in the soul without being noticed.[4] Augustine's inward turn is a project of awakening oneself to that vision; it is an epistemology, a pedagogy, and an ethics for the mind that desires to see God.

The problem, he tells us at the outset of book 7, is that he could not conceive of anything but bodily existence, which he in effect defines as existence that takes up space in the sensible world (the kind of existence that Descartes would later call *res extensa*). As a result of this inability, he says, "I was forced to think of something corporeal, either permeating the space of the world or spreading infinitely beyond it."[5] He could not conceive of anything that was "neither extended over some spatial distance nor capable of being diffused and thinned out or condensed and packed tighter."[6] Hence even the omnipresence of God he pictured as a kind of distention, a spreading out part-by-part through the spaces of this world like water in a sponge—as if one part of God was in one area, another in another area, and so on.[7] For unless he conceived of God spread out in space, he could not conceive of God at all, since "*apart from such space I could see only nothing*, absolutely nothing, not even an empty space."[8]

The author of the *Confessions* proposes a diagnosis of this failure to see what is to be seen. As with Plato and Plotinus, it is moral uncleanness, the culpable love of bodily things, that hinders vision, like an impurity or disease in the eye. His mind or heart is carnal, fixed on things of the senses, even though he would rather see something better. Hence his soul's vision is clouded by *phantasms,* imaginary mental pictures derived from the senses, which he knows are carnal and misleading but which he can no more get rid of than he can permanently sweep a cloud of gnats from his sight with a wave of his hand.[9] This problem of freeing the mind from phantasms, which is part and parcel of the ethical problem of freeing the heart from love of bodily things, is a recurrent theme of Augustine's early works.[10]

The author of the *Confessions* is convinced that the way to lead the soul beyond its fascination with the senses is to turn its attention inward to get a reflective grasp of its own incorporeal nature. If the soul could only see *itself*, it would begin to see what non-bodily things are like. Hence in the *Confessions* Augustine traces his difficulty with conceiving God back to a lack of self-knowledge. If the soul was only pure enough to see itself and understand what it was already doing, then it would not seem so inevitable that every form of existence must be bodily and spatial. "For my heart ranged over the same kind of images as the forms to which my eyes were accustomed"—that is to say, over images of corporeal things—"and I did not see that the very attention [*intentionem*] which formed these same images was not such a thing as they were."[11] Turning inward means, to begin with, attending to the soul's own attention, which is not a bodily thing and thus is closer to God than the bodily things the soul is used to seeing. As with modern versions of the "turn to the subject," of which Augustine's project is the ancestor, it is not what the soul sees but the soul's seeing that is the great clue for philosophers to follow.[12]

Hence Augustine's inward turn, as he sketches it in book 7 of the *Confessions*, turns from bodies to look at the soul's cognitive powers, beginning with how it handles sense-perception.

> And so [I passed] step by step, from bodies to the soul that perceives by means of the body, and then to that interior power [*vis*] to which the bodily sense announces exterior things (this much the beasts are capable of) and then further to the reasoning power [*ratiocinantem potentiam*] to which what is taken from the bodily senses is referred for judgment.[13]

Thus begins a progression that Augustine describes in a later book of the *Confessions* by saying: "Through my soul itself I will ascend to him."[14] In both books he describes an inward turn that begins at the lowest of all the cognitive powers, the senses, in order to look at how the mind receives and judges their input. Then he passes quickly to something higher and more inward, the soul's interior sense (or what Aristotle called the "shared" sense), which correlates and unifies the diverse reports of the five external senses.[15] But this too is a function that our souls share with the irrational souls of beasts, so Augustine proceeds further up and further in, to the soul's rational power, which sits in judgment over the data of the senses, determining their truth or falsehood.

The progression is both inward and upward: not only from body to soul, but also proceeding within the soul itself from the lowest faculties, which can perceive only things of the body, to what is highest and best in us, our rationality, by which we can perceive intelligible and immutable things. The final stage of the inquiry thus focuses on the highest of our cognitive functions: reason's capacity for intellectual vision. In this inquiry, reason investigates itself. So Augustine continues:

> This also [i.e., the reasoning power], finding that it was mutable in me, raised itself to its own intelligence, and "drew thought away from habit," removing itself from the contradictory crowd of phantasms, to discover by what light it was sprinkled when without any doubtfulness it cried out that the immutable was to be preferred to the mutable: whence it knew the Immutable itself (which unless it somehow knew, it couldn't possibly prefer it with certainty to the mutable). And it arrived at *that which is* [see Exodus 3:14] in the stroke of a tembling glance. Then indeed I saw intellectually your "invisible things, by means of the things that are made" [Rom. 1:20].[16]

The judgment that immutable (hence incorruptible) being is to be preferred to mutable (hence corruptible) being is the one thing Augustine mentions that he was certain about in the quandary stated at the beginning of book 7. So here he reflects on the source of that certainty, and he can only conclude that it came from immutable Being itself, which is the light in which all certain knowledge is seen. This can be none other than what he has just called Truth:

> For, seeking whence I approved the beauty of bodies, whether heavenly or earthly, and what was present to me in judging correctly concerning mutable things and saying, "This should be so, that should not"—so, seeking whence I judged, when I judged so, I found the immutable and true eternity of Truth above my mutable mind.[17]

Here immutable Truth, there unchanging Being—and elsewhere eternal Beauty, unbroken Unity, incorruptible Good—all are names for the same God, who is the immutable light by which the mutable mind makes all its judgments, when it judges correctly about what is or what is true, what is beautiful or good or one. To see this light is to see the open secret of the mind, the Form that makes all judgment possible. This eternal and divine light has been present all along in the mind, unbeknownst to it, bestowing the very capacity for judgment by which it is a mind, as the light of this world bestows upon the eye the capacity for sight that makes it an eye.

A Philosophical Project

As with *Confessions* 7 generally, this description of a step-by-step ascent through the powers of the soul is important to us not because of what it says about the events leading up to Augustine's converson in 386 but because of how it spells out an inward turn that the author of the *Confessions* wants to tell us about in 400.[18] From that standpoint, its Plotinian sources are less important than its Augustinian ones. It reads like a summary of an earlier work of Augustine, the second book of the treatise *On Free Choice*, which also proceeds from the senses to the inner sense and up to the intellect and its ability to judge sensible things by the light of Truth, eventually ending with a glimpse of the intelligible Truth itself, which is above the human mind because it is immutable and the human mind is not.[19] This elaborate project of inward turn, ascending through an examination of the powers of the soul, is echoed elsewhere in Augustine's early work,[20] including three times in the *Confessions*,[21] and also shapes key elements in his later thinking, especially in the grand inquiry into the analogies of the Trinity in the soul in the second half of the treatise *On the Trinity*.[22] The glimpses of God that Augustine reports in *Confessions* 7 are summary statements of that ongoing philosophical project of inward turn—of arriving at an understanding of God through an examination of the cognitive powers of the soul ascending from senses to inner Truth.

Except for the much later inquiry in the treatise *On the Trinity* (an inquiry that is set in motion precisely because the vision of God as Truth and Good does not help us see God as Trinity)[23] the key moment in all these efforts to execute the project of inward turn comes when the mind or reason turns from looking inward to looking upward and discovers that immutable Truth is implicit in all its judgments. God is the light that makes intellectual vision possible, the Truth by which all truths get their truth, the Good by which we learn to prefer the better to the worse, the Beauty that is the source of all the loveliness that we love, the ultimate Unity that unites and thereby gives being to all that is.[24] Thus the inward turn, which begins with an examination of the wherewithal of human knowing, ends with the insight that it is Truth that makes all knowing possible, and this very insight is a glimpse of the nature of God.

To see the soul's seeing is thus necessarily to catch a glimpse of immutable Truth. For unlike the bodily sense organs, the rational soul is never a passive recipient of external stimuli. Because its very nature is to understand, it necessarily judges the truth of what it sees, and it can do that only in the light of the immutable Truth that is the standard of all that is true in the changeable, created world. Precisely by noticing this, the soul that has turned inward can subsequently look upward, at the immutable Truth in light of which it judges, and gazing straight at Truth can recognize that it is above itself, because Truth is immutable while the soul is mutable—Truth being wholly light like the sun, while the soul is a place that can be tainted by darkness.

At this point in fact something else happens: the eye of the soul, which is not yet pure, is dazzled by the brightness of eternal Truth and falls back to its accustomed semidarkness, bearing with it only a memory of that splendid moment of vision. So the double movement in then up is followed by a third movement, the fall back to the region of darkness, poverty, and unlikeness to God.[25]

But the momentary glimpse is enough to solve the problem of how to conceive of God. For now the soul knows from experience[26] that an incoporeal being that is not spread out in space is not necessarily "nothing, absolutely nothing." As Augustine's soul asks itself, "Is Truth nothing, just because it is not spread out through finite or infinite reaches of space?"[27] The being of Truth is of course the answer to all Augustine's questions, since Truth is God. As Augustine explains elsewhere,

> God is not distended or diffused through places whether finite or infinite (as if there could be more of him in one part than in another) but is present as a whole everywhere—*just like Truth*, which no one in their right mind would say is partly in this place and partly in that; *for after all Truth is God.*[28]

This conception of the integral omnipresence of the divine, its presence "as a whole everywhere" (*totus ubique*, in Augustine's oft-used technical vocabulary) was first formulated by Plotinus.[29] In Augustine it becomes the centerpiece of the Platonist alternative to his youthful materialism and a central conviction guiding him in his inquiries into the new dimension of the soul, the inner space that is not literally a space.[30]

Problems of Nature and Grace

At this point we need to make a digression on how Augustine's philosophical alternative contrasts with others—alternatives that he never heard of, because they came centuries after him. These alternatives are important to us, however, because they form the interpretive grid through which Augustine is read and misread. Augustine's inward turn must be contrasted with interpretations of Augustine that cannot admit the seriousness of his belief in the intelligibility of divine Truth.

The problem is that in the wake of Thomas Aquinas, Roman Catholic scholars must look askance at anyone claiming that it is natural for the soul to see God—and since they do not want to look askance at Augustine, they typically interpret him as if he never made any such claim. They interpret him, in other words, as if his theology conformed to the requirements of a specifically Thomistic doctrine of nature and grace. My procedure here is exactly the opposite: I interpret Augustine as if it never crossed his mind that human nature needs to be elevated by a supernatural gift of grace in order to see God.

Of course this does not mean that Augustine thought grace was unnecessary—he was after all the one gave the West its distinctive categories for thinking about grace by insisting, in his writings against the Pelagians, that we cannot overcome the effects of sin without the help of God's grace. But for Augustine grace was always divine healing and help against sin, not supernatural elevation required by the lowliness of our nature. Hence in his own treatise *On Nature and Grace*, the master-image is of God the great physician, healing the infirmities of our diseased nature and helping us on our way.[31] By grace God restores and purifies, redeems and justifies our nature so that it can perform its proper function, which is to enjoy the happiness of intellectual knowledge of God. And because of sin and its effect in us, we cannot hope to attain righteousness and the beatific vision without this grace. But Augustine describes grace as *healing* and *helping*, not supernaturally *elevating* nature. For it belongs to the very nature of the mind to raise its eye to gaze upon what is above it, the immutable Truth. Hence grace restores nature, healing it and helping it to attain the divine vision that is natural to it but was lost in the Fall.

The relation of nature and grace deserves our special attention because it has profoundly affected Roman Catholic interpretation of Augustine, which is far and away the most important tradition of Augustine interpretation in the past century. The contrast between Augustine and Thomas on nature and grace is subtle, as well as unfamiliar to those outside the Roman Catholic theological tradition. Moreover, it is not made any clearer by the complex formulations that arose from an agonizing controversy about nature and grace that preoccupied much of Roman Catholic theology in the middle decades of the twentieth century. But perhaps just here, in the last decades of a powerful neo-Thomism, is the clearest place for us to start.

In the 1950 encyclical *Humani Generis*, Pope Pius XII wrote against those who "vitiate the true *gratuity of the supernatural order*" by affirming that God *could not* make intellectual beings without ordering and calling them to the beatific vision."[32] To be "ordered to beatific vision" means to have as one's goal or fulfillment (*telos*) the vision of God. Augustine's belief in the intelligibility of God puts him on the wrong side of the pope's disapproval, for it implies that it is the very nature of intellectual beings to find their fulfillment in seeing God. For Augustine, God could no more make minds whose fulfillment lay elsewhere than he could make eyes whose fulfillment lay in the dark.

This poses great difficulties for Roman Catholic interpretation of Augustine. Many Roman Catholic theologians (including Pope John Paul II) follow Augustine in believing that the desire for God is a deep and ineradicable part of our very being.[33] Yet in defending "the gratuity of the supernatural order" Pius XII committed Roman Catholic theology to the view that God *could have* created a "pure nature," in the neo-Thomist sense, that is, a human nature whose orientation is solely toward this world and its temporal goods. However, precisely by making this commitment explicit, he also showed Roman Catholic theologians how to affirm the existence of this desire without compromising the gratuity of the supernatural order: the thing to do is affirm the *possibility* of a "pure nature" while denying its actuality (God *could have* created things this way but didn't).[34] Hence when speaking of Augustine and other Church Fathers, who of course had never heard of the Thomistic concept of the supernatural, a theologian who wants to be loyal both to the Roman Catholic teaching office and to the Fathers will speak in a way that sounds very strange to Protestant ears. The Fathers will be said to concern themselves with "concrete" or "actual" nature, by which is meant a human nature that is not "pure nature" but rather has the addition of the grace of a supernatural calling to beatific vision.[35]

As someone who respects but does not hold himself bound by the teaching office or *magisterium* of the Church of Rome, I will not adopt this carefully nuanced way of speaking. For in my judgment it obscures a key historical point: Augustine talks as if it is simply natural for the soul to see God. This does not mean he thinks it is easy or automatic, that it can happen without growth and discipline, hard work and virtue and righteousness, and above all the help of grace. Indeed for Augustine the road to happiness is long and arduous, and because of our sinfulness we cannot even get on the right road without divine assistance—but at the end of it we find a homeland that is natural to us. Moreover, it could not be otherwise. For Augustine there can be no intellect that is not by nature oriented toward enjoying the happiness of seeing intelligible Truth.

The point is stated clearly enough in Augustine's essay "On Ideas."[36] It is the nature of the mind's eye, when purified of sin and lust for sensible things, to see the Ideas in the divine Mind. For Platonic Ideas are the natural and proper objects of the intellect (it would be astonishing for a Platonist to say otherwise). In locating them in the divine Mind, Augustine places all that is really and truly intelligible on the Creator side of the Creator/creature distinction. All understanding of things other than God is less than full understanding (i.e., what the Platonist tradition calls opinion or faith rather than knowledge) and is made possible only because the divine light of Truth illuminates them—just as sensible things are visible only as illuminated by the sun, which is the light of the sensible world.

Roman Catholic scholarship on Augustine was affected long before *Humani Generis* by the fact that this Augustinian view of the mind's relation to Truth was prohibited by the Holy Office in 1861, in its decree against "ontologism." This is the Office's label for a nineteenth-century movement in Roman Catholic theology that attempted to combine an Augustinian view of the intelligibility of God with post-Kantian doctrines of intellectual intuition. The notion, roughly, was that we see all things in God. More precisely, the "ontologists" held that the human mind by nature understands things in the light of the divine Being, so that the divine Being is implicitly understood in every act of human understanding.[37]

The decree against ontologism was a decisive turn toward a more Thomistic view of the relation between God and the human mind. In Thomas's rather empiricistic version of Aristotelian epistemology (in contrast to Alexander of Aprodisias's more Platonizing interpretation of Aristotle) the universal forms that the human mind understands are intelligible species abstracted from sensible things[38] and hence are created things, not the uncreated Ideas in God. Thus we can understand the truth about created beings without catching a glimpse of the divine Being and Truth that is their ultimate ground.[39] For Augustine, on the contrary, all intelligible things (i.e., all things that are properly understood by the intellect) are contained in God, who is "the immutable Truth containing all that is immutably true."[40] Augustine's three-tiered ontology has no place for intelligible forms or species except at the top of the hierarchy of being—as uncreated Forms in the mind of God. Hence Augustine's cosmos has no room for the created forms that Aquinas calls "intelligible species."[41]

The official censure of ontologism has caused serious problems for Roman Catholic Augustine scholars, who have turned up abundant evidence that Augustine's account of intellectual knowledge is indeed ontologistic. Etienne Gilson, for example, defends Augustine from charges of ontologism in a long and subtle exegetical argument,[42] yet he is too insightful not to see how formidable are the obstacles to his exegesis, and in fact he points them out clearly enough to undermine his own interpretation.[43] He is acutely aware, for instance, that his attempt to divide Augustine's epistemology neatly into natural knowledge of created things and supernatural knowledge of God cannot be squared very easily with key texts in Augustine's treatise *On the Trinity*.[44] Johannes Hessen, a Franciscan and an influential expositor of Augustine's epistemology, has a similar problem. His interpretation comes very close to making Augustine an ontologist but swerves away from that conclusion at the last moment by appealing to a distinction between mere intellectual vision of Truth and a higher mystical-religious vision of God.[45] But this is a distinction that has no support in the texts. Augustine describes his deepest and most "mystical" experiences in terms of Reason's vision of God as Truth.[46] A more accurate account of Augustine's epistemology comes from a Protestant, Ronald Nash, who does not hesitate to conclude that Augustine really is an ontologist.[47] I myself am persuaded by Nash's interpretation, as well as his criticism of Gilson. However, it is not my aim here to prove that Augustine is an ontologist; the point rather is that unlike Roman Catholic scholars I have no commitment to *avoiding* interpretations that implicate him in ontologism.

Finally, it is important to note that the contrast between Augustine and Aquinas on nature and grace cannot be reduced to the contrast between Augustine's Platonism and Aquinas's Aristotelianism. For one thing, as we saw in chapter 2, the Neoplatonism to which Augustine is indebted got its account of Ideas in the divine Mind not from Plato but from Aristotle, by way of Alexander of Aphrodisias. Moreover, the Thomistic nature/grace distinction runs counter to Aristotle and indeed to all ancient philosophy in its implication that beatitude (i.e., ultimate human happiness or fulfillment) is not, strictly speaking, natural. One can only imagine Aristotle scratching his head over this implication and asking, "You mean to say, Thomas, that happiness—*eudaimonia*, the fulfillment of human nature—is not natural to it? But what could be more natural to a nature than its own fulfillment?"[48]

Thomas's way of distinguishing nature and grace is, I would suggest, a consequence not of his Aristotelianism but rather of his particular place in the history of the Christian traditions, at a point when the West was engaged with new intensity not only with ancient philosophy but also with Eastern Christian theology. Aquinas had many problems to solve in reconciling the theological legacies of East and West, and one of them arose from the contrast between Augustine and Denys we noticed in the previous chapter. On the one hand Thomas has the Augustinian legacy that conceives of beatific vision as the fullness of intellectual vision, but on the other he inherits Denys's emphatic doctrine of divine incomprehensibility. The problem is: how can our happiness consist in seeing God with our intellect if God is above intelligibility? In short, how can we have beatific vision of an incomprehensible God? The answer is that "seeing the essence of God belongs to the created intellect by grace and not by nature."[49] This is why a supernatural elevation is necessary for ultimate beatitude: even after the created mind is purified and its nature is restored to a sinless condition, it cannot see God. So grace functions not only to cleanse and restore the mind's eye but to give it a vision that is beyond its natural powers: grace not only heals and helps but supernaturally elevates.

This way of distinguishing nature and grace is a typical example of Thomas's procedure of reconciling diverse strands in the Christian traditions by making appropriate distinctions. But this particular distinction has had an especially long and influential life. For my purposes the important thing about it is that it reconciled Denys and Augustine by leaving Augustine's commitment to the intelligibility of God firmly behind,[50] and thereby making it difficult for later Roman Catholics to read Augustine with historical accuracy. Hence there are many aspects of Augustine's inward turn and its dependence on the concept of intellectual vision that, in my view, have yet to be clearly understood—for the richest tradition of Augustine scholarship in the twentieth century was not in a good position to see them.

The Experience of Insight

With Thomas's nature/grace distinction, the West leaves behind the ancient philosophical convictions (shared by Platonists, Aristotelians, and Stoics alike) about the sufficiency of Reason for ultimate happiness and takes a step toward modern, secularized conceptions of reason. In modernity "reason" comes to mean a function that is earthbound if not outright antireligious, something to be compared to grace and faith as lower is to higher (in both Thomism and Protestantism) or else contrasted with them as good sense is to superstition (in much of the Enlightenment). Taking such contrasts for granted makes it difficult to appreciate the whole ancient legacy of philosophy, as Augustine knew it, which assumed that reason was a divine function in human beings and that the goal of intellect was a divine knowledge. The true Augustinian spirit returns to the West in movements where a divine function is restored once more to Reason, as in post-Kantian idealism and the movements that Roman Catholicism repudiated under the names "ontologism" and *nouvelle theologie*. (The success of Rahner in particular was to revive the Augustinian elements in the Thomist synthesis without falling afoul of official Roman Catholic teaching in these repects.)

Slightly less true to the spirit of Augustine are theological movements whose focus is experience rather than reason, as in Protestant liberalism. The author of the *Confessions* is of course one of the great masters of those who want to take an experiential route to God. Among Roman Catholic scholars, this results in a tendency to interpret the key texts of the inward turn (especially those of Confessions 7) as a form of mystical experience. Both labels, "mystic" and "experiential," are misleading insofar as they tend to be set in contrast with "reason." For Augustine the workings of reason are profoundly experiential, as the vision of the intellect is the deepest and most divine experience we can ever have. If this is mysticism, it is the mysticism of one who thinks of God as a divine Mind rather than an incomprehensible One. Its aim is not a union that transcends all understanding but precisely the understanding of God: to see God with the mind's eye. Augustine's visionary experiences thus do not—by his own account at least—elevate his mind above its own rational functions but precisely fulfill its nature as mind, just as seeing is the fulfillment of the nature of the eye. Hence his is an ecstasy not of unknowing but of insight. For Augustine the vision of God is more like Archimedes discovering a deep truth of mathematics and shouting "Eureka! I've found it!" than like the transrational experiences reported by the medieval mystics.

Another way to put this is to say that Augustine is a rationalist, but in as odd and unmodern a sense as he is a mystic. To him Reason says, "I study to give you joy."[51] Hence the first grand execution of the project of inward turn in his career takes the form of a proof of the existence of God that concludes with a meditation on the theme that happiness is the enjoyment of Truth.[52] Augustine is not the sort of rationalist whose goal in life is to find proofs for God's existence, but rather one for whom the whole point of reasoning is to get us beyond proofs and words to see God for ourselves with the mind's eye. Hence his experience of God, unlike most forms of mysticism, is something nearly all thoughtful people have felt for ourselves. We all know what it is like to work hard at understanding a mathematical proof, pondering it, asking questions, trying various possible solutions, yet somehow we just don't get it—until suddenly, maybe after giving up and having turned our attention elsewhere, we are overtaken by a blessed moment of understanding. "Aha!" we say, in place of Archimedes' "Eureka!" and we speak of light bulbs turning on, while ancient Platonists speak of sudden illumination or kindling that bursts into flame.[53] It is a moment experienced as pure intellectual joy. Imagine what this must mean for a Platonist, especially one who believes that all unchanging truth is found in the very Mind of God. If only this flash of insight could become our permanent mode of being, we would be happy—ultimately happy, with no further happiness to seek. Such is precisely the beatific vision, which lifts us above all mortal pleasures and joins us to eternal Truth and Beauty. That is why a moment of insight is the climax of Augustine's inward turn, both subjectively and objectively: it is both the experience he aims to attain and the highest object of his investigation into the nature of the soul. Insight is the moment in time when the mind's eye glimpses immutable Truth; it is Time touching Eternity, a foretaste of eternal blessedness, an experience of God.

"Insight" is thus probably the best modern category to use in interpreting Augustine's epistemology, in hopes of avoiding the kind of misinterpretation that stems from imposing later categories and distinctions on an ancient thinker. A focus on insight can help prevent us from making inappropriate separations between Reason and Experience or drawing disciplinary boundaries between such forms of philosophical inquiry as epistemology, psychology, and ethics. For Augustine what human life is all about is achieving the blessedness of wisdom, and therefore what morality is all about is purifying the mind's eye, healing it of its defects and equipping it with the virtues it needs to see the Truth clearly. Hence the goal of human life is defined epistemologically (wisdom and understanding), the road is defined in ethical terms (virtue and purification), and the whole process must be understood psychologically (as a turning and journey of the soul). To separate these disciplines and discuss a topic like "Augustine's epistemology" apart from his ethics and psychology (not to mention his ontology and theology) is to make nonsense of it. If we see insight as the central experience of human life, then we will be much less tempted to take these separations seriously. Above all, we will understand that for Augustine Truth is the most inward object of desire, not a mere external or accidental fact that must be complied with, as if the only time we ever saw Truth was in proofs we did not understand or preaching we did not like.

However, while refusing to impose later distinction on Augustine we need to observe distinctions that Augustine takes more seriously than we do, especially that between soul and body, inner and outer. Unlike his interpreters, Augustine never forgets his belief that human beings are divided into two parts, body and soul, and that what is true of the one may not be true of the other. His focus is *not* on what theologians about a generation ago incessantly called "the whole man." His inward turn is emphatically and explicitly a turning of attention away from one part of the human being and toward another—a turn away from the body, in order to gain the tranquil joy of contemplation by the mind alone, unsullied by the lusts of our senses and the clamoring needs of our flesh.

Education for Vision

"There is nothing sweeter to the human mind than the light of truth" says Cicero,[54] in a saying so strikingly Augustinian that it is tempting to take it as a summary of Augustine's thought. It certainly does illuminate the dynamic unity of his philosophy, religion, ethics, psychology, and epistemology.[55] But what Cicero lacks, once again, is the name of Christ.[56] So the summary we need of the heart of Augustine's thought goes: *Happiness is seeing Truth, and Truth is Christ.* The one clause sums up what he learned from ancient classical thought, the other what he learned from the teaching of Church and Scripture. But the synthesis implied by putting these two clauses together is disrupted by Nicaea, which will not allow Christ to be the intelligible Truth that reveals the incomprehensible Father.[57] As a result, nearly every Nicene theologian but Augustine regards the whole Trinity, Father, Son and Holy Spirit, as incomprehensible rather than intelligible—shining with a glory that the mind finds dazzling and overwhelming rather than sweet. Thus for Aquinas reason is insufficient for beatific vision, and for Thomism, as for most of modernity, reason is something whose competence extends only to things of this world. This secularization of reason would surely have struck Augustine as terribly carnal, like a return to Stoic or even Epicurean views of the mind. In any case, it was a development he did not anticipate, and this makes him hard for modern readers to understand properly. But it also means that Augustine offers modern readers a distinctive excitement and beauty, as he holds together in a kind of original, almost unconscious unity, things that we are used to assuming must be far apart: reason and joy, inquiry and devotion, education and ecstasy, truth and happiness.

For Augustine these unities fall apart only because of sin and its penalty, ignorance.[58] Indeed part of the excitement of reading Augustine is that he offers explanations for separations we take for granted—including, as we shall see later, the separation of soul from soul in the privacy of the inner world. But the separation we must concern ourselves with now is the primary one overcome by the inward turn, the distance between us and beatific vision. If there is nothing sweeter to the mind than the intelligible light, then why do we find it so hard to learn Truth? The explanation lies with a key metaphor used to describe the cause of the third movement, the fall back down after the movement "in then up." Augustine speaks of his mind's eye being *dazzled*, unable to bear the brightness of the intelligible light. This talk of dazzlement is found frequently in his writings and evidently records a fundamental element of his religious experience.[59] Always the explanation he gives for it refers to some defect in mind's eye: it is unhealthy, made sick and weak by carnal desires, so that it cannot bear the brightness of the intelligible Sun above it but rather longs for the darkness of sensible things at the ontological level below it. Dazzlement, in other words, is a result not of our natural incapacity but of the sinful corruption of our nature.

Long before Thomism, Catholic theology was heading in quite a different direction from Augustine on this point. More than a century before Aquinas, Anselm of Canterbury attributed the dazzlement of the mind's eye to nature rather than sin. He certainly does not rule out sin as a factor that contributes to the phenomenon, but his emphasis clearly lies elsewhere. When he speaks of the "weakness" and "darkness" of the mind's eye, he seems to be thinking of its creaturely limitations, its "narrowness" and "littleness" compared to the God it seeks:

> Is its eye darkened by its own weakness or is it dazzled by your glory? Surely it is both darkened in itself and dazzled by you. Indeed it is both *obscured by its own littleness* and overwhelmed by your immensity. Truly it is both *constricted by its own narrowness* and overcome by your vastness.[60]

Thus from the dazzling phenomenon of the glory of God Anselm draws the conclusion, quite apart from our sin, that God is "more than any creature can understand."[61] For Anselm, as for Denys, the source of all light and visibility is itself too bright to be visible: so God, the intelligible Sun who gives light to the mind and therefore intelligibility to all being, dwells in a glory too dazzling to be intelligible.

For Augustine, things are quite different. He is convinced that "those endowed with vigorous, healthy and really strong eyes have nothing they would rather look at than the Sun itself."[62] It is as if Augustine were having an argument with Anselm (and Denys and Thomas) over whether it's ever safe to look straight at the sun, and Augustine is taking the position that the only ones who can't are those whose eyes are sick and weak. This means that once the mind is healed of its sin and cleansed of its evil desires, there is nothing further it needs in order to see God:

> So when you are such that none of the things of earth delight you at all, then believe me, at that same moment, at that very point in time, you will see what you long for.[63]

Purity of heart, interpreted Platonistically as a mind cleansed of desire for sensible things, is evidently all we need to see God.[64]

It is natural, Augustine thinks, to look straight at the intelligible Sun. But to say something is natural is not to say it is easy, as the analogy with natural processes of the body makes clear. It is natural for a human body to grow to healthy adulthood, but that does not mean that every child will live to adulthood or that a vigorous adulthood can be attained without proper nourishment and frequent exercise. What is more, if the body is weakened by disease or the ill effects of bad habit, laziness, and poor nutrition, then it will have to take its medicine, which may be unpleasant. Augustine will use all these metaphors to explain why the road to blessedness is arduous and long. The distance yet to be traveled is signaled especially by the metaphor of the dazzled eye, driven back into its wonted darkness by the radiance of a Sun that is too bright for its gaze. This dazzlement is a symptom of illness: "The eye loves darkness because it is not healthy."[65] Therefore, to be dazzled by the glory of God is not our natural condition but a weakness to be overcome by healing and further training—that is, by the kind of efforts that do not transcend our nature but restore and strengthen it.

To judge by the structure of the first book of the *Soliloquies*, where the treament of intellectual vision culminates in a discussion of how to strengthen weak eyes, it seems the metaphor of dazzlement played a large role in attracting Augustine to the Platonist metaphor of intellectual vision in the first place. While the talk of intellectual vision provides apt metaphors for Augustine's theory of knowledge and splendid descriptions of the soul's ultimate fulfilment, talk of weak, sick, and dazzled eyes provides even more apt metaphors for Augustine's morality and pedagogy: it suggests in all the right ways the obstacles preventing us from seeing God and how we are to overcome them. The obstacles are in ourselves: they are the ignorance, ill-health, and infirmity of our mind's eye, for which we are to blame because of our love of temporal things. It is as if our bad habit of staring at dim figures in the darkness has weakened our eyes and made them susceptible to all kinds of disease and corruption. Later Augustine combines this account of the obstacles to salvation with the conception that human nature in general has suffered a kind of corruption.[66] But in his early works the spotlight is on individual failure: each soul's vices account for its own particular distance from beatitude, each soul's carnal habits account for its own inability to bear the strong light of the intelligible Truth, and each soul's lack of training explains why it has not yet developed the ability to see God.

The opposite side of the coin from the metaphor of dazzlement is thus the program of strengthening weak eyes through education and moral purification. In *Soliloquies* Augustine aims to give a deep philosophical explanation of how and why this program is supposed to work. The key element in this explanation is taken straight from Plato's Allegory of the Cave: a good liberal education is the training that strengthens the mind's eye so that it can see the intelligible Sun. After describing how some eyes are healthy and strong enough to look straight at the Sun without flinching, the author describes what seems to be his own present condition:

> There are others, however, who are hit hard by the very radiance they intensely desire to see, and often they are glad to retreat into the darkness without having seen it. It is dangerous to want to show them what they are not yet capable of seeing, even though they are already such as may rightly be called "healthy." Therefore they need exercise first, a useful delay and nourishing of their love. To begin with they should be shown certain things that do not light up on their own but can be seen in the light, such as a garment or a wall or something of that sort. Next, something that shines more beautifully, not indeed on its own but in that light, such as gold, silver, and the like—but not so radiant that it hurts the eyes. Then perhaps, within limits, this earthly fire should be shown, then the stars, then the moon, then the glow of dawn and the brightness of the early morning sky. By these [steps] sooner or later—whether [proceeding] through the whole order or skipping some—getting habituated, each according to his own state of health, one will see the sun without flinching and with great pleasure. This is the sort of thing the best teachers do for those who are most eager [*studiosissimus*] for wisdom—not sharp-eyed but already seeing something. For the task of a good education [*bonae disciplinae*] is to attain this by a certain order—since without order it would be almost incredible luck.[67]

Thus for Augustine, as for Plato, the right studies in the right disciplines are just what the doctor ordered to cure the diseases of our minds' eye—or to strengthen those eyes that are in good health but have not yet reached their full potential. Since they fulfill their potential by gazing straight at the intelligible Sun, the First Principle of all things, it follows (for Augustine) that the point of a good liberal arts education is nothing less than to see God.

Such a view of education sounds absurd to modern ears, but it is part and parcel of the peculiar unity of Augustine's thought—the way he holds together reason and religion, epistemology and joy. It is also a view of education that would hardly have surprised the author of the Allegory of the Cave. Despite its influence on later views of mysticism and religious illumination, the Allegory is described by Plato himself not as an account of mystical experience but as an illustration of the nature of education.[68] The point—which is crucial to his whole program of training philosopher-kings in the *Republic*—is that a good education leads to a vision of the supreme Good. Precisely here, interestingly, Augustine ends up siding with Plato against Plotinus. Plato's theory of education makes no sense at all unless human minds can grasp the First Principle, which Plato calls here "the Form of the Good." Therefore he, like Augustine, thinks it natural for the mind's eye to gaze straight at the intelligible sun[69]—in contrast to Plotinus,[70] but also to most of the Nicene Christian tradition as represented by Denys, Anselm, and Aquinas.

While much of the epistemology sketched in the *Soliloquies* and the other Cassiciacum works is left behind in the writings of Augustine's maturity, intellectual vision remains central for him, defining the fundamental relation between God and the soul. Intellectual vision is the fundamental metaphor for intelligibility, the Platonist kinship between soul and eternal things that is the foundation for the Neoplatonist inward turn. Augustine inherits both concepts, intellectual vision and inward turn, from the Platonist tradition, and the themes of his own career as a Platonist mimic the order of development of these concepts in history: first intellectual vision, then inward turn—and then finally Augustine's concept of inner self. Hence the development of inwardness runs along two converging tracks: both Augustine's career and the Platonist tradition begin by being concerned with the concept of intelligibility (conceived as the vision of the mind's eye), and then in the course of investigating the nature of intelligibility develop a concept of inward turn. Then the final achievement of Platonist inwardness is Augustine's concept of the private inner space of the soul, which is fully developed by the end of his early period, in the *Confessions*. Each successive concept provides the context of inquiry in which the next develops: Plato's concept of intelligibility provides the conceptual framework of Plotinus's inward turn, and Augustine's adaptation of Plotinus's inward turn provides the context of problems that result in the new concept of soul as private inner space.

This chapter has introduced Augustine's concepts of inward turn and intellectual vision as the context for the development of his most original contribution to the history of inwardness: the private inner space. Once Augustine articulates his project of inward turn, it becomes the framework within which he conducts his investigation of the concept of intelligibility, which defines the relation of the soul to God. Before that time, we have what I call the "prehistory" of Augustine's inwardness—a set of themes, concepts, and problems that lead to the inward turn and the inner self but have not yet arrived there. The dominant context of investigation during this earliest phase of Augustine's career, when he is trying to understand intelligibility without an fully articulated project of inward turn, is a program of education in the liberal disciplines, modeled at least in part on that of Plato in the *Republic*, with the same goal as that expressed in the Allegory of the Cave: to gaze straight at the intelligible Sun without flinching. It is to this program that we next turn.

6

Explorations of Divine Reason

This chapter paints the developmental background of the inquiries in Augustine's early period that led him from inward turn to inner space. This "prehistory" of Augustine's inwardness begins at Cassiciacum, where Augustine takes the presence of Reason in the soul as the great clue to the relation between the soul and God. The developmental starting point of Augustine's inquiries is to be found not in Plotinus but in Cicero, whose philosophy includes, along with Stoic materialism, a Platonist turn from bodies to the soul, which would continue to affect the shape of Augustine's mature version of the inward turn. At the beginning of his career all Augustine's philosophical sources, and his Christology as well, were based on the premise that there was some divine power intrinsic in the soul. Hence the Cassiciacum dialogues conclude by sketching a program of education designed to remedy Augustine's own ignorance, and to reveal the divine nature of Reason.

Who Is Reason?

The inward turn comes before the private inner space. There is a project of inward turn in Plotinus (his exhortation for the soul to turn "into the inside") and even a conception of an inner world (i.e., the intelligible world) but no *private* inner space belonging only to a particular individual soul. Augustine was engaged in a fully articulated project of inward turn (a modification of Plotinus's inward turn) at least since the time of the second book of *On Free Choice*, about a decade before the writing of *Confessions*, in which he first elaborated the concept of a private inner space of the soul.

In book 2 of *On Free Choice,* Augustine examines the lower powers of the soul without invoking a picture of inner space, and when he comes to deal with the power of intellectual vision, the space he pictures is explicitly public. For the Truth the mind sees when turned inward is one and the same for all who see it; it cannot be anyone's private possession.[1] Nor does it need to be cut into pieces in order to be shared, like bodily things that must be divided among the many who are greedy for them. Augustine elaborates this contrast using an astonishing image: he pictures Wisdom as a beauty who has many lovers, all of whom can embrace her wholly without taking away from what her other lovers can have and enjoy of her.[2] Clearly at this point Augustine is still working with a Plotinian conception of inner space—an inner world that is the same for all souls. What we find within is common, not private property (*commune*, not *proprium* or *privatum*).[3]

Augustine develops the concept of a private inner space in the course of working through problems in this project of inward turn. For he wants to appropriate the Platonist tradition of divinity within but he does not fully understand it, and its relations with the Catholic tradition contain some pitfalls of which he is not yet aware. To see the roots of this development and its problems, however, we must go back before the second book of *On Free Choice* and examine what I call the "prehistory" of Augustinian inwardness, in the writings of Cassiciacum and the next year or so thereafter. In this chapter we need to familiarize ourselves with the context of this development—the soil, as it were, in which these roots were planted.

The most striking thing about the prehistory of Augustinian inwardness is that Augustine dramatized the inner space long before he conceptualized it. That is to say, before Augustine formulated a concept of an inner space of the soul, he wrote a drama staged in that space. It is an unprecedented kind of drama, and Augustine gives it the unprecedented name *Soliloquia* ("Soliloquies"), apologizing for the ugly sound of his neologism.[4] We should imagine the drama taking place mostly at night, as Augustine lies in bed at Cassiciacum thinking over the discussions of the previous day:[5]

> For a long time I had been turning over many and various things within myself, for many days searching for myself and my good, and what evil is to be avoided; and suddenly there spoke to me—either I myself, or someone else outside, or else inside, I don't know—for *this very thing is what I am working so hard to know.* So, R. said to me . . .[6]

From the *Retractations* we learn (what is easy enough to discover from the context) that "R," Augustine's dialogue partner, is Reason (*ratio*).[7] It is also easy to guess that the topic of the conversation to follow is none other than this opening question: who is it that speaks to Augustine in his solitary meditations? In other words, in the inner drama of the *Soliloquies* Augustine is discussing with Reason the question of what Reason really is. This is ultimately the same topic of discussion that is announced a little later on, when the philosophical inquiry is ready to begin—after Augustine, in obedience to Reason, has prayed for divine assistance:

A: There, I have prayed to God.

R: So what do you want to know?

A: Everything I prayed for.

R: Sum it up in brief.

A: I desire to know *God and the soul.*

R: Nothing else?

A: Nothing at all.[8]

If all Augustine wants to know is God and the soul, and the identity of Reason is the very thing Augustine was working so hard to know, then the conclusion has to be that Augustine thinks he will understand the nature of God and of the soul once he knows who or what Reason is. But of course the character named Reason does not just sit still and wait to be contemplated. In the *Soliloquies* Reason is not just the object of investigation but its guide—"Augustine" 's inner teacher. Hence the reasoning activity of the soul is simultaneously investigated and dramatized in the *Soliloquies*, and both the investigation and the dramatization are meant as clues about the relation between God and the soul.

Who Reason is remains throughout the *Soliloquies* an unanswered question—a topic of exploration and a problem to solve. In the Cassiciacum dialogues, as we shall see at the end of this chapter, Augustine has already explored a number of possible identities of Reason, and now in the inner dialogue of the *Soliloquies* (which was meant to be the crown of all his efforts at Cassiciacum but is left unfinished) his hope is to arrive at some definite solution to the problem, confident that once he understands Reason he will know himself and God.

"Augustine" 's partner in this inner dialogue is in fact a mysterious and rather formidable character. In contrast to that other character, called "A.," for "Augustine,"[9] this one does not bear the name of one born of woman, one who will eventually return to the dust whence he came. The name "Reason" suggests no temporal or historical origin, no fleshly or mortal end. And Reason's conduct in this conversation befits a being immortal and divine: whereas "Augustine" is the student, bewailing his ignorance and grasping at new insights, "Reason" speaks with unshakable certainty, like one who has always known. For anyone who comes to the *Soliloquies* after reading Plotinus, it is hard to imagine what this could be besides a dramatization of the life of the Plotinian soul, divided between a higher part that is immutable and unfallen and a lower part that has descended to this body of earth, blinded by ignorance and error, and contaminated by concerns about society, marriage, and death (concerns about which Reason interrogates "Augustine" in a kind of moral self-examination or examination of conscience that occupies a prominent place later in the first book of *Soliloquies*).[10] The dialogue between the anxious student named "Augustine" and the perfect intelligence named "Reason" seems intended to dramatize the temporal process by which the lower part of the soul gains hard-won insights into immutable Truth—the tortuous path of inquiry by which a lover of wisdom, not yet wise, comes to catch intermittent and partial glimpses of eternal Truth, through his contact with a part of himself whose ultimate identity is not temporal at all. The great moral and intellectual struggle of human life, according to Plotinus, is for the lower part of the soul to be called by the higher part away from its lusts and troubles in the material cosmos and back to the vision of higher and eternal things.[11] Augustine's *Soliloquies* reads very much like a dramatization of this struggle, with "Reason" taking the role of the higher part of the soul and "Augustine" the lower part.

But there is another possible identification of Reason to consider here. Several years later Augustine writes a treatise *On the Teacher*, which comes to a climax when Augustine discusses how we learn intelligible things. At this climactic point he speaks of an inner Teacher, whose counsel we listen to (*consulimus*) in our "inner man." That certainly sounds like his teacher in the *Soliloquies*. But in *On the Teacher* his name is Christ, the Virtue and Wisdom of God:

> But concerning the universals which we understand [*intellegimus*] we do not listen [*consulimus*] to anyone who speaks in outward sounds but rather to the Truth presiding inwardly over the mind itself—although perhaps by words we are admonished to listen. *We listen to him teach, who is said to dwell in the inner man, Christ the immutable Virtue and eternal Wisdom of God*, to whom indeed all rational souls listen, but who is available to

them only to the extent that they can hold [*capere*] him, according to their own good or evil will.[12]

It is important to bear in mind that for young Augustine, the explorer at Cassiciacum, both these identifications of Reason—Plotinus's higher part of the soul and Christ, the Virtue and Wisdom of God—are possible, and he might indeed be considering the possibility of combining them. If, as suggested earlier, his Trinitarian thinking still bore traces of subordinationism,[13] then it would not be so surprising for him to interpret Christ dwelling in the heart as the immutable and divine part of the soul, mediating to us knowledge of God the Father in his role as Wisdom and Truth. I must hasten to add: this is only a possibility, and it is not one that he eventually adopts. Yet by the same token, it is crucial for any sensitive interpretation of Augustine's earliest writings to be aware that this is a young man for whom many possibilities remain open—because, just like the character "Augustine" in the *Soliloquies,* he really is uncertain of where he is going and does not yet know which of the possibilities he is exploring will eventually be ruled out.

What he is certain of is that Reason is the crucial clue to what he is looking for. In a stroke of great boldness he puts a promise in the mouth of Reason: "Reason, who is speaking with you, promises to show God to your mind as the sun is shown to the eyes."[14] It is astonishing to think of Augustine writing this promise down. One wonders on what authority he thought he could put such words in Reason's mouth—the author Augustine promising the character "Augustine" that the fictional character named Reason can do all that he (Augustine!) says he can. There is great uncertainty in this young man, but there are also high hopes.

Ciceronian Point of Departure

As will become apparent at key points in our investigation of the prehistory of inner space, what Augustine does not know is a factor that any interpreter of his earliest writings must keep in mind—following the lead of Augustine himself, who portrays himself at Cassiciacum as one made deeply anxious by his own lack of learning. His ignorance at this time, it should be noted, embraces not only most of the Bible and the Christian tradition, but also Neoplatonism. At Cassiciacum he is only beginning to read and understand the books that would become the sources of his mature Christian Platonism. Hence it is misleading to place on a work like the *Soliloquies* the label "Augustine's early Platonism." This work is rather an exercise in which Augustine is still trying to learn Platonism as well as Catholic Christianity and is not yet getting either of them quite right. He is an explorer who has some blind alleys to poke his head into before he finds the right road.

To understand the aim of Augustine's inquiry into the identity of Reason at Cassiciacum, some positive idea of the starting point of his explorations is necessary. As interpreters of Augustine's earliest writings, we need a conception of his point of departure to replace the misleading label "Augustine's early Platonism." If the writings of Augustine's early period take a trajectory that arrives in the end at the mature Christian Platonism of *Confessions* and *On Christian Doctrine,* then how shall we mark its begining? What *terminus a quo* belongs at the other end of the trajectory from this *terminus ad quem*? "Ignorance" is not a sufficient answer, for in fact Augustine knew a great deal. Some of it he would rather forget, like the theology of the Manichaeans. But he also had a stock of philosophical knowledge on which he wanted to build, and this came mainly from Latin sources, especially Cicero.[15] Cicero's texts were, then as now, a centerpiece of Latin education—taught literally from grammar school, that is, in the school of the *grammaticus*.[16] Cicero also provided the central textbooks for the teaching of rhetoric, Augustine's old job.[17] It is obvious in the Cassiciacum dialogues themselves that there are no philosophical writings more familiar to young Augustine, more carefully studied and easily drawn on, than Cicero's.[18] It is in fact this Ciceronian point of departure, rather than Neoplatonism or Catholicism, that is most noticeable on the surface of the Cassiciacum dialogues.[19] The contrast with the *Confessions* is instructive, for it is just the opposite of what one is led to expect after hearing of "Augustine's early Platonism." In order to understand the *Confessions* the most important books to have on hand are the Bible and the *Enneads*, whereas in the Cassiciacum dialogues Cicero is far more frequently quoted, discussed, and relied on than any other author, sacred or profane.[20]

The young man writing at Cassiciacum is a professional rhetorician who has recently quit his job to devote himself full-time to philosophical inquiry, and he has learned most of his philosophy from Cicero, another professional rhetorician who took up philosophical writing after political events forced him into retirement. All this adds up to a very unprofessional philosophical training, as Marrou puts it:

> his philosophy teacher was not Plato or Aristotle but Cicero, that amateur. . . . Philosophically, Saint Augustine was an autodidact, with all that word evokes of persistent effort and also of irremediable imperfection.[21]

In the Cassiciacum writings we can trace the course of this philosophical autodidacticism, which reaches a peak of intensity in the *Soliloquies*, where Augustine has no teacher other than the Reason within him, in part because there is no teacher on earth who is ready and able to help him.[22] What he does have is some books that have changed his life and his mind. In the Cassiciacum works we can read Augustine's efforts to make a connection between the Ciceronian philosophy that had set him afire back when he was a student and the Plotinian philosophy that set him afire just that summer.[23]

In fact the move from Cicero to Neoplatonism is not as awkward as one might have thought, and Augustine is not the only one to have tried it. The most famous example of a project of Platonizing Cicero is Macrobius's Neoplatonist commentary on Cicero's *Scipio's Dream*. But Augustine had an example nearer at hand, in the sermons of the bishop of Milan. Some time before his conversion, he probably heard Ambrose's sermon "On Jacob and the Happy Life" (*De Jacob et Vita Beata*), which described the regenerative effects of baptism by borrowing from Cicero's Stoic portraits of "the wise man" and then by quoting large sections of Plotinus's treatise "On Happiness."[24] Augustine tries a similar but not so fully Plotinian movement from Stoic conviction to underlying Platonist ontology in the Cassiciacum dialogue *On the Happy Life*, where he argues that the (Stoic) imperviousness to the blows of fortune praised by Cicero is only conceivable if the wise man possesses something that is immutable (i.e., something like Platonic ideas).[25] This trajectory from Ciceronian Stoicism to Neoplatonism has its most important precedent, however, in Plotinus himself, whose many critical engagements with Stoic thought often end up with him appropriating Stoic concepts (purified, of course, of the Stoics' materialist ontology).[26]

Another reason why the transition from Cicero to Neoplatonism can be made rather smoothly is that there is a great deal of Platonism in Cicero himself. Cicero was eclectic in principle and in practice: an adherent of the moderate, "probabilist" wing of Academic skeptics (called the "New Academy"), he made it a principle to follow whatever impression or argument seemed most probable, which resulted in practice in his borrowing from a wide variety of sources, Academic, Peripatetic, and Stoic—a practice he justified also by claiming (along with the other wing, the "Old Academy") that all three of these schools taught basically the same thing in different words.[27] The *Hortensius*, for example, was modeled on Aristotle's early work the *Protrepticus*.[28] And one of the Academic sources from which he borrowed quite extensively was none other than Plato himself. We have in fact one book of Cicero, the first book of the *Tusculan Disputations*, that contains a fair amount of what could be called Cicero's Platonism.[29] This is the Platonism Augustine would have known before reading Plotinus and "the books of the Platonists" described in *Confessions* 7. As we shall see, there are reasons for thinking this Ciceronian Platonism had already attracted Augustine's interest before he read Plotinus. A glance at it will help us see what Platonist assumptions young Augustine already had in mind when he first read the great Neoplatonist—what kindling, as it were, was set afire by those "very few books of Plotinus." For when Plotinus's writings came into Augustine's hands in the summer of 386, they were received by a mind asking questions to which Plotinus seemed to have the answers.[30]

Cicero's Turn to the Soul

The first book of *Tusculan Disputations* argues for the immortality of the soul on the basis of an inquiry into the nature and composition of the soul. It contributed to both the language and the conceptuality of Augustine's inward turn, as Augustine himself signals by using Cicero's words to indicate a key step in the inward turn in *Confessions* 7. The reasoning power of the soul, Augustine says, rises up to examine its own intelligence as it "draws thought away from habit," by withdrawing from the contradictory crowd of phantasms (mental images drawn from the senses) in order to look at the mind alone, illuminated by the immutable Light.[31] He is echoing *Tusculan Disputations*, book 1, where Cicero says: "It takes great ability to call the the mind back from the senses and *draw thought away from habit*."[32]

Cicero says this at a turning point in his exposition. Up to this point, he had been arguing for the immortality of the soul on the grounds that all nations of the earth believed in it—a *consensus gentium* argument, based on the principle that "the agreement of all peoples [*consensio omnium gentium*] is to be accounted a law of nature."[33] The Stoics used this type of argument to prove the existence of the gods (on the premise that all the world believed in gods of some sort or other), and Cicero adapts it to make a proof of the immortality of the soul. At this point, however, Cicero turns from the agreement of all peoples to the reasoning of the wise—from the many to the few, as a Platonist would say—and builds a philosophical case for the divinity and eternity of the soul, in which Plato is called as chief witness.[34] Unlike the general run of the human race, who imagine the soul after death inhabiting the underworld as if it still had something like a body, the philosophers who follow Plato know how to call the mind away from the senses and its old habits of perception, in order to conceive of the soul as entirely separate from the body.[35] A few pages later Cicero translates a proof for the immortality of the soul from the *Phaedrus*,[36] then recounts the story of Socrates and the slave boy in the *Meno*, giving a brief exposition of Plato's Ideas or Forms that emphasizes their immutability and their connection with Platonic Recollection.[37] He wraps up his discussion of the Platonist view of the soul with a summary of the *Phaedo*, which he concludes by reiterating the importance of separating the soul from the body:

> What else are we doing when we call the soul away from pleasure, that is, from the body, and from the republic, from business of every kind—what, I say, are we doing but calling the soul to itself, compelling it to be with itself and leading it away from the body as far as possible?[38]

There is no inward turn here—no turning to enter an inward space of the soul—but this is certainly interesting preparation for someone to read Plotinus's inward turn. In addition to giving Augustine an acquaintance with Platonic Ideas and the doctrine of Recollection, this book would help him in the crucial business of taking the right things for granted: the real philosophers, Cicero is telling Augustine, all draw the soul away from the body and the senses. What is more, they all take the soul as a clue to the nature of God, for "there is in the human soul something divine."[39] The piety of these philosophers is thus obedience to the divine command, "Know Thyself," which both Cicero and Plotinus interpret to mean "know thy soul."[40] Our souls possess a "divine power" (*divina vis*) of which blood and bone are not capable. Hence Cicero is bold enough to say, like Plotinus, that the soul is a god.[41]

The notion that the soul turns to itself to find divinity is thus not something that Augustine must wait to hear about from Plotinus. Rather, he brings it to his reading of Plotinus and thus recognizes in the great Neoplatonist a deeper and more convincing version of these Platonist themes than he found in Cicero. Above all, Plotinus offers Augustine a much more powerful version of the turn to the soul, because Plotinus has a firm grasp of the key Platonist notion of intelligibility, which is strikingly absent from Cicero's writings. Cicero can give a definition of Platonic Ideas, but he says nothing about the power of the mind's eye to see them; he mentions Platonic Recollection, but he says nothing about the soul's capacity for intellectual vision, without which Platonic Recollection is merely mythology. Hence Cicero's argument for the immortality of the soul must in the end take quite a different route from the concept of kinship between soul and Form that is at the heart of the *Phaedo*.

In fact, Cicero's main proof of the immortality of the soul is still Stoic, even materialist—for without some sort of connection or kinship between soul and Form, there is in the end no alternative to conceiving of the soul as composed of material elements. This is something that takes a little getting used to, for modern readers: in the ancient world one could be a materialist and still believe in God and the immortality of the soul. Indeed, one could believe that the soul is divine, precisely because it is made of the same material as the gods.[42] In Stoic materialism, for example, the soul contains living, divine fire, just like the stars, which are celestial gods. When soul and body are separated at death, therefore, there is a separation of diverse kinds of elements: the body, made of the two lower elements, earth and water,[43] returns to the ground, but the soul, made of higher elements, fire and perhaps air, seeks its natural resting place on high.[44] For fire rises upward as naturally as stones fall downward: sparks and flames rise because they are gravitating toward their natural resting place, which is not on earth but in heaven, among the fiery stars. Hence according to Cicero, the soul after death quite literally *goes to heaven*, which is its true home.[45]

All of this continues to have an attraction for Augustine even in the days of his mature Platonism, but he takes it metaphorically and allegorically (the way a good Platonist takes much of the Bible). The soul is of course not literally made of fire, but the good soul does burn, as it were, with charity and as a result is borne upward toward God by a kind of spiritual gravitation, which Augustine sums up in his famous apothegm "My love is my weight."[46] In the realm of the will, to love God means to rise to God, as in the physical world the heat of a thing afire pulls it upward to the sky.

The Superiority of Soul in Cicero

It is worth seeing how Cicero, despite his materialist ontology, can affirm the soul's superiority to the body in a way that continues to appeal to Augustine even after he has imbibed Plotinus's Neoplatonism. Cicero in fact vacillates on the question of the composition of the soul, unsure whether it is made of Stoic fire or the Aristotelian fifth element (quintessence).[47] However, the same basic line of argument follows from both conceptions. In an earlier work, the *Consolatio*, Cicero had in fact based an argument for the immortality of the soul on the premise that the soul was made of the fifth element,[48] and it differed so little from the argument he undertakes in the first book of *Tusculan Disputations* that he incorporates the key passage of the former treatise into the latter. The basic argument is that

> There is nothing present in these natures [i.e., the lower elements, earth and water] that has the power [*vis*] of memory, mind, and thought, which retains the past and foresees the future and can embrace the present. These are wholly divine, and could not have come to the human being from anywhere but God. Therefore *that nature and power of the soul is unique*, and quite distinct from these familiar and well-known elements. So whatever there is that perceives and knows, lives and sees, is *celestial and divine*—and for that reason must be *eternal*. And indeed God himself, who is understood by us, cannot be understood except as a mind that is absolute and free, separated from all mortal admixture. . . .[49]

The nerve of this argument is a premise Cicero attributes to Aristotle in his account of the fifth element or quintessence.

> Aristotle . . . having accepted those four familiar kinds of elements, from which all things originated, was of the opinion that there was a fifth nature, from which came the mind. For thought and foresight, learning and teaching, the ability to discover [*invenire*] something and to *remember* so many other things, to love and hate, desire and fear, grieve and rejoice— these and the like he thought were not present in those four elements. . . .[50]

When the argument shifts from the Aristotelian premise of a divine fifth element to the Stoic premise of a divine fire, Cicero simply relies on the Stoic view that the two higher elements, fire and air, were the only ones with the power to act as efficient causes, while the lower, heavier elements, water and earth, were passive and causally inert.[51] Since the body is composed of the two lower elements (which make up blood and bone and the like) while the soul is composed of the two higher ones (for the soul is "a fiery breath," made of fire and air) all human activities must be caused by the soul rather than the body.[52]

As an example of this superiority of soul to body, Cicero offers an account of sense-perception:

> For even now [i.e., in the embodied state] it is not with the eyes that we discern what we
> see, nor is there any sensation in the body. . . . *It is the soul that sees and hears*, not
> those parts which are as it were windows of the soul. . . .[53]

Cicero supports this claim with psychological observations that are quite congenial to
Neoplatonism and its convictions about the causal superiority of soul to body. Most notable is an argument about the soul's power of "shared sense" (*sensus communis*),[54] by
which we compare the reports of various senses:

> For it is with the same mind that we comprehend dissimilar things, such as color, taste,
> heat, smell, and sound—which the soul could never recognize by means of those five mes-
> sengers [*nuntiis*, i.e., the five diverse sensory systems of the body] unless everything were
> referred to it and it alone was the *judge* of them all.[55]

The mature Augustine can adopt this line of reasoning with no appreciable modifications, using it to describe an early stage in the soul's reflection on itself in the inward turn.
As we turn to ourselves, the first and easiest thing for us to see is our own sensory activities, and Cicero's argument about the "shared sense" (which Augustine calls "the interior
sense") serves to show that even sense perception involves more than just the bodily organs. Augustine's first elaborate statement of the project of inward turn begins with a
rather lengthy treatment of the power of interior sense.[56] Later sketches of the inward turn
frequently include resumés of this earlier treatment, often formulated using Cicero's
vocabulary. For instance in the description of the inward turn in *Confessions*, Augustine
presents his examinination of the powers of his own soul as an ascent

> step by step from bodies to *the soul which senses things through the body*, and thence to its
> inner power, to which the bodily sense announces [*annuntiaret*] external things (and
> which the beasts also possess) and thence to that reasoning power to which what is taken
> from the bodily senses is referred for *judgment*.[57]

Both the language and the thought here are Ciceronian. The same power is again treated
briefly in *Confessions* 10 as the first step of the gradual ascent inward through the soul to
God.[58]

The fact that this Ciceronian reasoning survives intact into Augustine's mature work
is indicative of how little is required to Platonize it. Despite Cicero's materialist conception
of the soul, his argument about the "shared sense" already has the key conceptual feature
that a Neoplatonist account of the senses must insist on: it gives the soul absolute causal
superiority over the body. This is a point that modern readers may find hard to believe, but
it is important to recognize that from Augustine's point of view, all the important philosophical authorities (from Cicero to Plotinus), not to mention Reason itself, favored the
view that bodies can have no causal effect on souls. Thus, for example, in one of his early
accounts of sense-perception, his aim is precisely to show that even in sense-perception
bodies do not affect the soul.[59] This account is heavily indebted to Plotinus,[60] but the notion that it is the soul, not the body, that is active in sensation would have been familiar to
Augustine from Cicero.

Divinity in the Soul before Plotinus

What we see in the Cassiciacum works, I suggest, is Augustine, thoroughly persuaded by
Cicero's admonitions to turn from the body to the soul, working vigorously but cautiously

to assimilate newfound Plotinian doctrines about God and the soul. Plotinus's rigorously immaterialist account of the nature of the soul and its relation to the intelligible world offered a more cogent and thrilling account of the possibility of the soul's turning to itself than the one Augustine had originally learned from Cicero. What is new about Plotinus, for Augustine, is the Platonist concept of intelligibility and its promise of a powerful account of the inner relation between the soul and God. What is not new is the thought that, because there is something divine within, the soul should turn away from bodies toward itself.

In other words, for Augustine at Cassiciacum the divinity of the soul is an old familiar song, not a sudden, passing fad brought on by an overly enthusiastic reading of "the books of the Platonists." It has deep roots in a decade and a half of his thinking about the relation of God and the soul as a Ciceronian philosopher and as a Manichaean believer as well. It is the sort of thing one takes for granted in the cultured milieu of ancient thought, and at Cassiciacum Augustine treats it as a rather straightforward implication of the common definition of "human being" as "rational mortal animal." An *irrational* animal is of course a brute beast, while an *immortal* animal is classically a god (for *animal* is simply Latin for "that which has a soul," hence refers to anything that is alive, while "immortal" is nearly synonymous in classical usage with "divine"). The human being, understood as a compound of rational soul and mortal body, thus stands midway between these two levels of life, above the brutes but below the immortals (pagan gods or Biblical angels). Yet the soul is not supposed to rest content at this merely human level. Rather, the two characteristics, "rational" and "mortal," indicate two opposite directions of movement:

> I believe that by them the human being is admonished both where to return and what to flee. For as the progression of the soul toward mortal things is a Fall [*lapsus*], so the regress or return ought to be to Reason. By the one word, "rational," it is separated from the brutes, by the other, "mortal," it is separated from divine things. Unless it retains the one it will be a brute; unless it turns itself away from the other, it will not be divine.[61]

This is expressed in terms so commonplace that a Cicero, a Mani, and a Plotinus could all agree with it—hence I take it, in its very commonness, as a summary of the point of departure for Augustine's philosophical and theological development. How far it is from orthodox Christian teaching can be measured by noting that it stands in obvious conflict with the belief that we are brought to blessedness by the death of Christ or the resurrection of the body, both of which imply that mortality does not necessarily separate us from divine things.[62] The only feature of this definition of human nature and destiny that consorts better with Christian orthodoxy than with Cicero is the suggestion that the soul is not intrinsically divine but must become so (as in the Eastern Orthodox conception of deification).

That suggestion is in fact out of keeping with the rest of the Cassiciacum writings, where Augustine takes the more common philosophical position that even in its wayward and ignorant state, the soul contains something divine. For instance, in the preface to *Against the Academics* Augustine lets us know that his theme is the storm-tossed voyage by which "the divine mind [*animum*] inhering in mortals" makes its odyssey to "the port of wisdom."[63] The clear implication is that even a soul that is only seeking wisdom already has something divine in it. Thus a little later in the preface Augustine urges his patron Romanianus to awaken "that very thing which is divine in you."[64] In the debate that takes up the body of the book, Augustine defines the happy life as "living according to what is best in a human being." This is the part of the soul (*animi*) called "mind or reason" (*mens* or *ratio*), which ought to rule over everything else in the human being.[65] Later in the discussion his student Licentius (Romanianus's son) calls this "the part of the soul [*animi*] that is divine."[66]

This way of talking about reason or the best part of the soul seems quite in keeping with the role of the character named "Reason" in the *Soliloquies*. Yet I do not think we are in a position to see what Augustine is getting at until we hear Licentius say "undoubtedly there is even in human beings a divine power [*virtus*]."[67] Once again it seems to me we must hear echoes of the apostle's description of Christ as "the Power [*virtus*] of God and the Wisdom of God" (1 Cor. 1:24). Christ is both the Wisdom of God whom we seek and the Power or Virtue of God that makes it possible for us to seek him, as we saw in the treatise *On the Teacher*.[68] No other interpretation of these passages makes sense in connection with Augustine's biography: for although Augustine at Cassiciacum is not as orthodox a Catholic as one might expect, and he may always be much more of a Platonist than most orthodox Christians could wish, he is never simply a pagan. As he could not give himself wholly to a pursuit of wisdom in which "the name of Christ was not there,"[69] so he could not desire a divinity in himself that did not bear the name "Christ." Hence at Cassiciacum, the divinity of the soul is a Christological theme—just like the concept of finding God in the soul in Augustine's mature version of the inward turn. In fact the latter is the successor to the former in Augustine's development: it is what replaces the divinity of the soul once Augustine reaizes that no version of the intrinsic divinity of the soul, even a Christological one, is compatible with Catholic teaching.[70]

The exploration of the identity of Reason in *Soliloquies* is an attempt to work out a concept of divine presence in the soul that will help Augustine preserve the best of what he learned from Cicero while appropriating the exciting new things he is learning from the texts of Plotinus and the Christian Neoplatonists in Milan. At this point he does not quite realize that orthodox Catholic teaching has no place for the divinity of the soul, and in fact his prime worry about orthodoxy lies elsewhere. In addition to the aims of preserving the best of Cicero and constructing a Christian Neoplatonism, the Cassiciacum writings pursue the project of repudiating Manichaeanism and overcoming the old habits of thought associated with it.

The Manichaean heresy is the negative side of Augustine's point of departure, the thing he wants to leave behind. Interestingly, the habit of mind he most fervently wants to overcome is something Manichaeanism had in common with Cicero: materialism. "The greatest and almost sole cause of my inevitable errors" in his Manichaean days, Augustine tells us, was his inability to conceive of a non-bodily reality—so that "when I thought of my God, I did not know how to think of anything but corporeal bulk, and it did not seem to me that anything existed which was not like that."[71] His other errors were "inevitable," he thinks, because they followed by logical necessity from this chief error.

This is another thing that may take a little getting used to. Nowadays the Manichaeans are remembered mainly for their dualism, but Augustine thinks their errors flowed ultimately from their materialism.[72] According to Augustine's portrait of them, the Manichaeans thought everything that exists has a corporeal and spatial mode of being—that is, it takes up space in what we would nowadays call "the physical world."[73] Consequently, both Good and Evil were a kind of stuff or material substance, and the whole world was divided into the Good Stuff and the Evil Stuff.[74] From this materialist ontology follow two consequences, one about Evil and the other about Good, that were targets of Augustine's repeated criticism.

The first consequence is that in conceiving both Good and Evil as material substances, the Manichaeans put them on the same level ontologically: the Evil Stuff had been around as long as the Good Stuff and would continue to exist as long, and therefore Evil was just as real as the Good. This means that God (who is made of the Good Stuff) was no more real than Evil. Evil was as old as God, existing eternally in its own right independent of him, something he neither created nor had providential control over. For Catholics, who believe that God created all that exists and governs it with justice and wisdom, this was a wholly unacceptable conclusion. The objectionable feature, however, is not the dualism of Good and Evil *per se* (for of course Catholics too believe that it is important to distinguish between good and evil) but the raising of Evil to the ontological status of a substance existing independent of God—and this is the consequence specifically of Manichaean *materialism*, which makes evil a kind of stuff or material substance.

This consequence is done away with in Neoplatonist ontology, according to which the lower, sensible world is good, not evil, precisely because it is not independent of God but rather reflects and participates in his goodness, though in a lower and lesser way. Thus everything that has any positive existence is good, having its origin in the one and the same First Principle, while evil is only a corruption or defect in existing things that mars and destroys them.[75] Evil is emphatically less real than Good, indeed it is unreality itself. Evil is nothing but a defect or corruption in that which exists, a lack of being, goodness, beauty, or truth.

The second consequence of Manichaean materialism is that the Good Stuff, having its being in space, can be pierced and torn asunder.[76] Evidently, this was precisely what it was threatened with in the great cosmic battle that, according to Manichaean mythology, led to the formation of the present evil universe. Augustine's friend Nebridius discomfitted the Manichaeans by pointing out that the very possibility of God's being threatened by Evil implies that God is corruptible—a consequence that nobody, least of all the Manichaeans, really wanted to accept.[77] Hence this implication becomes one of Augustine's most powerful weapons in debate against them.[78] In order to secure the incorruptibility of God, Augustine is convinced, one needs something like the Platonist doctrine of the immateriality, immutability, and non-spatiality of intelligible things.

Augustine's dissatisfaction with the Manichaeans' view of the soul is of a piece with his dissatisfaction with their view of God. Like Cicero and the Stoics, the Manichaeans believed that God and the soul were made of the same stuff, the luminous heavenly material that we can literally see with our eyes.[79] The Manichaeans taught that the soul was divine and heavenly in origin, a portion of the Good Substance that was unfortunately trapped in this evil world of bodies. The story goes[80] that in the beginning the evil "race of darkness" was separate—literally, spatially separated—from the good realm of light. Things started going wrong when the evil race attacked the region of the good, threatening God himself and forcing him to respond with a sort of counterattack. So God sent a portion of his own substance—our souls—willy-nilly into this dark world. Here they were captured, as it were, behind enemy lines and imprisoned in the darkness of mortal bodies.

The whole story made no sense, as Nebridius pointed out, unless somehow the race of darkness threatened God with harm—and if God could be harmed then he was corruptible. Furthermore, if the story is true, then the very fact that the soul is suffering in this dark world means that the divine substance actually is suffering harm and is therefore corrupt-ible. Thus in the two earliest appearances of Nebridius's argument in Augustine's writ-ings, Augustine relies on the premise that the soul is divine, reasoning from the (universally admitted) fact that the soul is presently in an evil state to the (scandalously unacceptable) conclusion that God is corrupted, by way of the Manichaean premise that the soul is a frag-ment of divine substance.[81] Some scholars have seen in these passages Augustine rejecting the divinity of the soul,[82] but that is not the case. In both passages Augustine's harsh words are all reserved for the "impious" and "ridiculous" view that God is corruptible, while the premise of the divinity of the soul is accepted, at least for the sake of the argu-ment, without demur.

We must bear in mind that Augustine borrows this argument from Nebridius, his friend and fellow ex-Manichaean, not because he is a heresy hunter but because he is working to free himself from errors that were once his own—and the divinity of the soul is plainly not the error from which he is most anxious to be freed. His objection against the Manichaeans, rather, is that their materialism makes both God and the soul vulnerable to external threats. The whole point of affirming that there is a divine element in the soul is to make the soul immortal and unshakable, not to make God corruptible and subject to suffering.

The connection between God and the soul was thus a theme that lay in Augustine's heart ever since his Manichaean days, and the attraction of Platonism is that it gave a more satisfactory account of this connection than any he had encountered before. Instead of linking God to a fallen and vulnerable soul, it linked the soul to an incorruptible and im-mutable God. The central argument of the *Soliloquies,* as we shall see in the next chapter, is a kind of conceptual reversal of Nebridius's argument, using the same mediating premise of the divinity of the soul: whereas in Manichaeanism the corruptibility of the soul "rubs off," as it were, on God, in the "true philosophy" Augustine has found at Cassiciacum the immutability of God "rubs off" on the soul. This argument, aiming to reverse the great fail-ure of Manichaeanism, is "Reason"'s answer to "Augustine"'s plea near the beginning of the *Soliloquies,* where he asks to learn about God and the soul and nothing else. The note of anxiety and determination in this plea arises from Augustine's glance back at the pit of heresy he is escaping and from his high hopes for the truth toward which he is journeying. But common to both the Manichaean past and Neoplatonist future is the premise that the soul's nature and destiny is bound up with the nature and attributes of God.

A Program of Education

At Cassiciacum, Augustine conceives the divine mind or reason inhering in mortals as both the subject and object of investigation. Reason makes its homecoming by coming to understand what reason itself is. Hence Augustine's intellectual journey at Cassiciacum has a definite direction and path. The first dialogue, *On the Happy Life,* an exhortation to philosophy in the spirit of Cicero's *Hortensius,* argues that happiness consists in Wisdom, the mind's finding of Truth.[83] The next dialogue, *Against the Academics,* rejects the claim that merely seeking after truth is sufficient for happiness (book 1) and then refutes the Aca-demics' skeptic claim that truth can never be found (books 2 and 3). Having cleared away the skepticism that would make true knowledge (and hence true happiness) impossible, Augustine turns to deal with our actual situation of ignorance in the last of the Cassiciacum dialogues, *On Order*. Here the problem of human ignorance is placed in a cosmological setting, as the central instance of the problem of the place of evil in the providential order of God.

In the first book and a half of *On Order*, Augustine's student Licentius is portrayed as making significant but hesitant progress in understanding this problem, guided by divine inspiration but also falling back at times into the darkness of ignorance.[84] But at a crucial juncture in the middle of the second book, it is clear he can go no further.[85] The problem that stumps him is the same one that Augustine himself found most intractable, according to the *Confessions*: the origin of evil (*unde malum?*).[86] In fact not only Licentius, but the whole company of Augustine's friends, relatives, and students struggles in vain to understand the origin of evil in the providential order of God.

There are quite definite reasons for this moment of dramatic perplexity in the dialogue, on the part of its author as well as its participants.[87] The question Augustine is faced with here is one that both Manichaeans and Platonists answered by telling about the Fall or descent of the soul into bodies. Augustine (the author as well as the dialogue participant) does not know exactly how to go on from here, for he has not finished sorting out the differences between the two.[88] If a human being is the rational, mortal animal who should flee from the mortality shared with the brutes to seek the immortality of Wisdom by means of Reason, then it would be impossible for a good Creator to have have made us this way originally, wrapped in the ignorance and mortality of the body. So how then did embodiment and its attendant ills come about? Augustine rightly spies great difficulties and dangers in this topic, and he is not yet prepared to discuss it.[89]

Thus the predicament of the little group at Cassiciacum is Augustine's own predicament as well: none of them are really prepared to answer the question they are presently faced with. Into the troubled silence of the whole company Augustine speaks, therefore, announcing an end to the present discussion, which is getting "out of order," and proposing that the question be put off until their minds are better trained.[90] Accordingly, at this moment of dramatic crisis, when the situation of this company of inquirers serves as a perfect illustration of their intractable intellectual problem (ignorant of the source of their own ignorance and its place in the providential order established by divine Wisdom) Augustine helps them all out by proposing what appears at first to be a change of subject. Instead of talking about the providential order of things in the cosmos (the *ordo rerum*) he will tell them of a curriculum or order of studies (an *ordo disciplinae*) that will prepare them to understand the ontological order of things.[91] In other words, Augustine, who is not yet ready to solve this dangerous problem in theory, proposes a solution in practice, sketching a program of education in the seven liberal disciplines whose purpose is to lead us from our current state of ignorance to a knowledge of the Truth. The program culminates in the study of philosophy, which is mainly concerned with issues of Platonist ontology such as the nature of evil and the relation between God and the soul.

The discussion of the order of studies that takes up the rest of *On Order* thus shows, in effect, how the mind is to be trained to understand and articulate the (Plotinian) insights into the nature of evil that Licentius and others had had earlier in the treatise. It represents Augustine's programmatic first stab at assimilating his newfound Neoplatonism, combining it with his previous knowledge, and harnessing it to solve longstanding intellectual problems. Well aware of his own ignorance and lack of learning, he is formulating a plan to educate himself by writing textbooks in all the liberal disciplines.[92] His goal is to ascend step by step from knowledge of corporeal things to knowledge of incorporeal things.[93]

The notion that the way to reach a vision of ultimate realities is through a program of liberal education goes back of course to Plato, particularly to the Allegory of the Cave in the *Republic*. But there is a distinctively modern flavor to this enterprise as well: Augustine's project amounts to an attempt to provide philosophical foundations for the culture in which he was raised.[94] His curriculum of studies would introduce students to the fundamental achievements of the ancient classical tradition and then trace them back to the timeless truths of reason. For the study of the liberal disciplines is to lead us from the sensible world to the intelligible world. In *On Music*, the one textbook that Augustine actually completed, the first five books contain a discussion of poetic meter (i.e., audible numbers) and then the last book ascends from these to a Platonist-Pythagorean vision of the formative power of eternal numbers. Presumably something similar was in store in Augustine's treatment of the other disciplines: an ascent from teaching about sensible things to insight into the intelligible things that are their ultimate source. And as we shall see, the climactic discipline, philosophy, has the task of uncovering the nature of the Reason that is at the foundation of all the others.

Only a fraction of this vastly ambitious program ever saw the light: the big six-book study *On Music*, a lost book *On Grammar*, an unfinished book *On Dialectic* that is still extant. We can in addition get an idea of what Augustine might have said about geometry in *On the Quantity of the Soul*, which contains an extended geometry lesson (which it seems to me must be modeled on the *Meno* itself) complete with explicit conclusions drawn about the psychological basis of recollection. However, our interest here lies not in Augustine's attempts to execute the program but his sketch of it in *On Order*, for this provides the immediate context of his exploration of the identity of Reason in the *Soliloquies*, as well as the crucial background for understanding the very strange argument for the immortality of the soul that is its central concern.

The Self-examination of Reason

Augustine introduces his proposed curriculum of studies by way of an allegorical narrative in which a personified Reason founds the seven liberal disciplines.[95] In the beginning, Reason invents words as a means of expression, to bind soul to soul in society.[96] Then it proceeds to establish the three arts of language: grammar, dialectic, and rhetoric (the medieval *trivium*). First comes grammar, the basic art of literacy, which includes both the study of language *per se* and also the interpretation of literature.[97] Then comes dialectic, the art of argumentation that we now call logic, whose task is "to define, distinguish, and draw conclusions."[98] Finally there is rhetoric, about which Augustine, the recently retired teacher of rhetoric, has scarcely a good word to say.[99]

Before proceeding to the next group of disciplines (Augustine's version of the medieval *quadrivium*) Reason has a wild thought:

> At this point Reason wanted to be caught up [*rapere*] in blessed contemplation of divine things. But lest it fall [*caderet*] from on high, it sought gradual steps, and constructed for itself a road through its own possessions, an *order*.[100]

Perhaps the language of fall in this passage is meant to be a hint as to how Augustine was thinking of developing a doctrine of the Fall. If so, then to fall is to be overly ambitious, intellectually hasty, trying to know more than one is ready to understand.[101] In any case, Augustine clearly desires an order of studies that will preserve the soul from falling out of order and being mislead by its own premature speculations. He tells the participants in the dialogue that they cannot solve the problem of evil because they are themselves "out of order," trying to understand deep philosophical subjects without the proper education.[102]

Augustine evidently regarded his own seduction by Manichaeanism as due to a similar failing, a kind of rationalistic overconfidence abetted by his lack of learning. In his twenties, as a bright and inquisitive young man escaping from the hidebound traditionalism of the African church, he had trusted his own insightfulness rather than the authority of Catholic teachers who actually knew more than he did about the way of wisdom, and therefore he was easily taken in by Manichaean promises of rational explanations in place of the Catholic Church's insistence on putting faith before understanding.[103] He suggests on several occasions that he would not have been taken in by their crudely materialist views if he had had a good liberal education.[104] The disciplines, it seems, furnish effective weapons against heretics and their carnal, materialist errors.

So Reason wisely restrains its wild thought, defers the beatific vision, and proceeds instead to found the mathematical disciplines of music, geometry, and astrology. The first of these means specifically the study of poetic rhythm or meter—which in Latin (and until a couple of centuries ago, in English as well) was called "numbers."[105] The discipline of astrology requires a slightly more lengthy comment. When Augustine reviews his early program in the *Retractations*, some three decades later, he silently replaces astrology with arithmetic on the list of disciplines in the curriculum. In fact not long after Cassiciacum Augustine devised a rather famous criticism of astrological determinism.[106] Yet it is not surprising that astrology was on the original list at Cassiciacum, for it had recently been instrumental in freeing him from Manichaean mythology. Classical astrology encompassed, along with a great deal of what we now regard as superstition, a fair amount of sound astronomy, including calculations of planetary movements and eclipses that were precise enough to refute the cosmological myths of the books of Mani, which the Manichaeans insisted on taking very literally.[107]

All these disciplines, however, are merely steps on the way up to philosophy, which stands at the peak of the liberal arts. The discipline of philosophy takes up the results of the previous disciplines and investigates their ultimate source. Its agenda is set by the twofold question of God and the soul.[108] This of course is precisely the agenda Augustine himself takes up in his next work, the *Soliloquies*, which represents his private inner investigation of philosophical issues that his students and companions at Cassiciacum are not ready for. But here in *On Order* he makes this much clear to the whole company: philosophy is the discipline that will answer their vexing questions about evil and much more besides.[109] For "the order of studies of wisdom" is aimed at fitting us to understand the order of things in general,[110] and the ultimate aim of this understanding is nothing less than the vision of God, who is "the very fount whence flows everything that is true, being himself the Father of Truth."[111]

These philosophical goals are to be reached through Reason's finally achieving self-understanding. Reason is at the basis of all the liberal disciplines, but only in philosophy does it turn to investigate its very self. As it looks back upon the rationality of the lower disciplines and is especially impressed with the role that number and measure play there, it conceives of a daring new project:

It ventures to prove the soul immortal. It has diligently treated all subjects, and has clearly perceived itself capable of many things—and whatever it is capable of, it is capable of through numbers. It is moved by a kind of astonishment, and begins to suspect that perhaps it is itself the number by which everything is numbered—or if not, at least *there* is what it is trying so hard to reach.[112]

So at the culmination of the program of education in the liberal disciplines, Reason has an insight that leads to the central project of *Soliloquies*, the proof of the immortality of the soul. It has attained this insight by examining its own role in the other disciplines, being led back from the disciplines themselves to its own role as their founder—hence in effect from Augustine's curriculum of liberal education to the question at its heart, "Who is Reason?"

In pursuing these questions, Augustine sketches a precursor of his project of inward turn. After his account of the twofold question of philosophy Augustine describes the philosophizing soul:

> So the soul, holding onto this order and now given over to philosophy, begins by looking into itself [*primo se ipsam inspicit*]. And now that this learning [*eruditio*] has convinced it that *Reason is its own, or is itself*, and that either there is nothing better or more powerful in Reason than number, or else Reason *is* nothing other than number, then it speaks with itself thus: "I, by some secret and inner motion of mine, can distinguish and connect [i.e., by relations of logical consequence] the things that are learned [*ea quae discenda sunt*, i.e., the subject matter of the disciplines], and this power of mine is called Reason. . . ."[113]

The very idea of "soliloquy," of inner conversation between the soul and its Reason, begins here. What these two will converse about is precisely the question of who they are: are they identical with one another? Is one of them the same thing as the number by which all things are numbered?

This number of all numbers is, as any Platonist knows, One, from which all other numbers derive.[114] Hence the soul's awareness of its own power of distinguishing and drawing logical consequences (which Augustine had earlier made the special concern of the discipline of dialectic) leads it to consider the nature and power of oneness. Whatever needs to be distinguished is something that has no true unity, whereas that which is to be logically connected is something that thereby achieves its proper unity and being.[115] Evidently Augustine aims to ponder the Neoplatonist theme of Unity as the source of all beings via an examination of the logical unity and interconnection of the intelligible truths that are taught in the liberal disciplines, which is revealed by dialectic.[116] This passage is in fact a practice run for his later, deeply Neoplatonist accounts of Unity as the source of all being.[117]

The proof of the immortality of the soul that Augustine intended to be the crowning achievement of the *Soliloquies* is foreshadowed at the end of the soul's soliloquy in *On Order*.[118] The basic premise is that Reason, whatever it is, is immortal. Augustine's defense of this premise sheds light on the identity of Reason from a new angle:

> "One to two" or "two to four" is in the truest sense a reason [*ratio*], and this ratio or reason was no truer yesterday than today, tomorrow, or next year; and if this whole world fell in ruins, this ratio could not cease to be. For this thing is always such [*semper talis est*].[119]

The oddly phrased final sentence echoes Cicero's definition of Platonic ideas: "Plato thought that . . . that alone truly exists which *is always such as it is*, which he called *idea.*"[120] Reason or *ratio*, in the sense that Augustine uses it in this passage, thus clearly has the characteristics of Platonic Ideas—as he had learned about them already from Cicero, long before he read Plotinus. Cicero and Plotinus both point toward Platonic ideas as immutable things with which the soul, for all its apparent mutability and the threat of mortality, has some deep relationship—though Plotinus has far more interesting things to say about that relationship than Cicero. The conceptual problems surrounding that relationship are marked above all by the word "Reason," which designates both the soul's power of intellectual vision and the changeless, intelligible things it sees.

7

An Abandoned Proof

*The prehistory of Augustinian inwardness begins with the attempt to prove the immortal-
ity of the soul that Augustine presents as the crowning achievement of the Cassiciacum
works. Augustine's proof identifies Truth with the content of the liberal disciplines, on the
grounds that dialectic is the Truth by which all truths are true. The key claim is that discipline, like Reason, is inseparably present in the mind, so that the immutability of Truth
"rubs off," as it were, on the mind, making it immortal. The failure of this argument is
due to its insufficiently Platonist ontology, vitiated by lingering traces of materialism.*

An Astonishing Argument

The crowning task of the *Soliloquies* is to prove that the soul is immortal. Augustine's general strategy here is one that goes back to the *Phaedo*: he tries to establish a necessary conceptual link between the soul and that which is immutable and divine. He follows Plotinus
rather than Plato, however, in locating the immutable and divine *within* the soul. Hence
with this argument we see the earliest version of an Augustinian philosophical project that
bears the marks of an encounter with Plotinus's inward turn. It is not yet Augustine's inward turn, nor even an inward turn at all, but it takes the fundamental first step of locating
the immutable and divine within the soul. Hence in subsequent works he can conceive of
seeking God there.

Augustine's particular variation on the Platonist theme of the immortality of the soul
is an attempt to demonstrate that the immutability of Truth, present within the soul, has a
way of rubbing off on that in which it is present. The basic idea could have been suggested
by Plato himself, who wrote in the *Meno*, "If the truth of beings is always in our souls, then
the soul must be immortal."[1] But Augustine's precise way of going about this demonstration is startling to the point of being bizarre and is quite unlike anything else in either
Christianity or Platonism. We shall spend the rest of this chapter analyzing the structure of
this astonishing argument, which was too bold and foolish to remain very long at the center of Augustine's thinking. We can begin by looking at a striking identification made in the

basic premise of the argument—an identification characteristic of Augustine's whole procedure at Cassiciacum, and soon to be abandoned.

The argument is initially stated as follows:

> If whatever is in a subject abides forever, it is necessary that the subject itself also abide forever. And every discipline is in the mind [*animo*] as in a subject. It is necessary, therefore, that the mind abide forever, if the discipline abides forever. Now, *discipline is Truth*, and as the argument [*ratio*] at the beginning of this book demonstrated, Truth abides forever. Therefore the mind abides forever, nor can the mind be called mortal.[2]

This argument, which Augustine proceeds to elaborate and defend in the rest of the *Soliloquies*, is the culmination of all the inquiries at Cassiciacum, but it seems to have been passed over by most readers, who must have thought that Augustine cannot mean what he says. And reasonably enough: for it is hard to believe that anyone, much less a Church Father, could say that the liberal arts are God. But this is exactly the import of Augustine's key premise here. He flatly identifies *disciplina*, the word for studies in the liberal arts curriculum, with *veritas*, the Truth by which every truth (*verum*) is true—which, as the previous discussions at Cassiciacum make clear, can be nothing other than God.[3] This, together with the premise that the liberal arts reside permanently in the mind, yields the conclusion that the soul abides forever. The second premise may also seem surprising, since not everyone has been educated in the liberal arts, but Augustine defends it by alluding to the Platonist doctrine of Recollection: it may seem that the liberal arts are not always present in our minds, yet in fact knowledge of them does not come to us from without but rather is buried in our forgetfulness and "dug up" when we are reminded to do so by the right questions.[4] Thus it is the first premise—the identification of discipline with Truth—that really needs an elaborate explanation and defense.

We must bear in mind that Augustine is exploring here. Representing himself as speaking only to God and to Reason, Augustine is writing the *Soliloquies* in order to find out what Reason, Truth, and the Soul are. He has ambiguities to clear up, and one way he does this is by trying out various ways of identifying such entities as "Reason" or "Truth" and examining their consequences. Let us try to imagine why Augustine thought the identification "discipline is Truth" might work. To begin with we can use a distinction that Augustine himself would supply a year or two later: that between *signum* and *res*, sign and thing signified.[5] If we think of the liberal disciplines as a set of words (and hence of signs) that are heard by the ear or read in books, then the identification of God with the liberal disciplines is ridiculous—and quite abhorrent to a Platonist, for it would make God a sensible thing. But if we attend instead to the thing signified by the words, then we are brought into the realm of intelligible truths, and that is quite a different matter.

A concern with the truth signified by the words of the liberal disciplines is evidently what Augustine has in mind when he proceeds to argue that the disciplines are inherently true:

> Discipline gets its name from *discere*, to learn. Now, nobody who learns and retains something can be said not to know; and nobody knows what is false. Therefore all discipline is true.[6]

Again, the argument is, on the face of it, bizarre: the basic premise amounts to the claim that one can never learn anything false. Either Augustine is convinced that no one can ever acquire false beliefs[7] or else his premise ought to be read as a claim about the concept of "learning": any learning worthy of the name means finding truth, not falsehood.[8] The import of the premise would then be that in true learning we do not just come to believe that some sentence or other is true—as if learning was merely the acquisition of opinion not knowledge—but rather we catch sight of some intelligible truth.

If that is the meaning of the premise, then the really questionable part of the argument is the claim that the liberal arts actually consist of such learning. Why should we think that *disciplina* necessarily consists of *discere*, in this strong sense of learning to see the intelligible truth?

That this actually is the meaning of the premise is confirmed by the fact that Augustine laid the groundwork for his argument precisely by addressing the question: how can we say that everything in the liberal arts is true? The problem is that the liberal arts include not only mathematical disciplines such as geometry but also linguistic disciplines such as literature. As Plato warned, and Augustine the bishop later complains,[9] literature consists mostly of fiction. How then can this, the first discipline to be studied in Augustine's proposed curriculum, be true?

Augustine answers that the truth in literature lies not in the stories and fables of the poets but in the discipline that studies them.[10] In effect, literary criticism rather than poetry is the sober guard of truth here. But that means the discipline of literature must draw its truth from some other source than the poetic fancies it studies. That source, Augustine insists, is another discipline, "the discipline of argumentation" (*disciplina disputationis*) which is concerned with definition and distinction and hence with separating true from false. This is plainly a reference to the discipline of dialectic. However, the name "dialectic" is not actually used in the *Soliloquies*, but rather a series of related descriptions such as *disciplina disputandi*, *ars disputoriae*, and *ratio disputandi*.[11] This last phrase is especially interesting, as it plays into the open question of the identity of Reason in the *Soliloquies*. *Ratio disputandi* (literally, "the rationale or reason of disputing") is not only an apt name for the discipline of dialectic but also a fine description of the Reason (*ratio*) who is Augustine's inner dialogue partner in the *Soliloquies*. In addition, we should recall that Augustine would point out a few years later, in the essay "On Ideas," that "reason" (*ratio*) makes a good translation of Plato's word *idea*. Hence in calling dialectic by the name *ratio disputandi*, Augustine may be referring to something like the eternal Form that grounds or makes possible the temporal practice of argumentation—and it is surely not so odd to think that this might be Truth.

In any case, it is clear that one of the things Augustine is up to at this point in the *Soliloquies* is to explore the relation between Reason and the liberal discipline of dialectic. He is considering the quite plausible surmise that "the discipline of argumentation," or what we today would call logic, teaches us something important about the essential nature of Reason. If we distinguish once more between *signum* and *res* (i.e., between the words one hears while being instructed in logic and the intelligible truth one grasps when one really sees the point) then it is quite plausible to say that the *res*, the thing signified by instruction in dialectic, is nothing other than Truth.

According to *On Order*, Reason is "the activity [*motus*] of the mind which can distinguish and connect what is learned."[12] It is precisely such activity that sets a discipline in order and guards it from falsehood—and dialectic is the discipline that teaches this activity.[13] Hence Augustine has extraordinary things to say about the discipline of dialectic. It is the discipline of disciplines . . . it teaches how to teach and how to learn; in it Reason shows itself and manifests what it is, what it wants, what it can achieve. It knows how to know; it alone not only wants to make knowers but also can do it.[14]

This discipline of disciplines is the source of all other truths, distinguishing the true from the false in all other disciplines and connecting one truth with another within them.[15] It is because of this function of dialectic that Augustine identifies it with the Truth by which all the disciplines are true. This is an identification for which Augustine had prepared us in the Cassiciacum dialogues, when he claimed that perfected dialectic is the very knowledge of Truth.[16]

The Bizarre Identification

Augustine's argument is thus that dialectic, the discipline or *ratio* of argumentation, establishes what is true in all the disciplines, including itself; hence it is through its own self that dialectic is true—the point being that like the intelligible Sun, it shines by its own light, even as it lights up other truths and makes them capable of being learned. The identification of *disciplina* as a whole with Truth follows from this: discipline is Truth precisely because it includes within itself the discipline of argumentation by which all the disciplines (or discipline per se) is true. So we can say of *disciplina* as a whole what is said of the discipline of argumentation in particular: it shines by its own light.

Since the passage in which Augustine makes this argument is full of nuances and ambiguities that are difficult if not impossible to translate, I will quote it here in full, with commentary. The crucial ambiguity stems from the endemic problem that Latin lacks an indefinite article, so that it is often unclear whether the term *disciplina* in the singular means one of the seven liberal disciplines or "discipline" (i.e., learning) in general. There may indeed be a shift from one meaning to the other over the course of the argument, which is no insignificant matter, for the ultimate subject of the argument is not a plurality of disciplines but Discipline itself. Augustine's aim is to demonstrate that Discipline itself is not just a collection of truths but the one Truth by which the many truths are true—the equivalent of Plato's First Principle or Form of forms.

> R: . . . You said, and said truly, that no discipline occurred to you in which it was not the law of definition and distribution which made it [a] discipline. And if they are true precisely by that which makes them disciplines [*eo verae sunt quo sunt disciplinae*] then would anyone deny that Truth itself is that through which all the disciplines are true?[17]

This line of reasoning rests on several latent premises as well as the two premises it makes explicit. The first sentence gives us the explicit premise that it is dialectic (the law of defining and distributing) that makes a discipline a discipline (*ut disciplina sit, fecerit*). The second sentence begins by laying down the crucial premise that what makes a discipline a discipline is the very same thing that also makes it true. From a previous argument we know that it is Truth (*veritas*) that makes every true thing (*verum*) true.[18] Consequently, it is Truth that makes the disciplines true. The conclusion (implied but not stated) is that dialectic, which makes the disciplines discipline, must be none other than the Truth that makes them true.

"Augustine" finds this reasoning persuasive, but he hesitates. For isn't dialectic itself just one of the many disciplines, as much in need of Truth as the others?

> A: I am quite close to assenting, but this is what bothers me: we count the *ratio* of argumentation too among these same disciplines. That is why I rather consider that to be Truth by which this very *ratio* is true.

> R: An excellent and very alert answer. But I don't suppose you deny that it is true precisely by that which makes it [a] discipline?

> A: On the contrary, that's exactly what's bothering me. For I observed that it too is [a] discipline, and that's why it is called true.[19]

"Augustine" has seen all the essential points. He just needs to realize that dialectic's job of making the disciplines true is reflexive. Dialectic does for itself the same thing it does for the other disciplines: applying the rules of distinction and logical consequence to itself, it make *itself* true. That means that dialectic itself is the Truth by which dialectic is true.

> R: Well then, do you think there is any way this could be [a] discipline, if everything in it were not defined and distributed?

> A: I have nothing more to say.

> R: And if this job [*officium*] belongs to it, then it is through itself that it is [a] true discipline [*per seipsam disciplina vera est*]. Therefore, who will find it surprising if that by which all things are true is through itself and in itself the true Truth?[20]

In translating this I have adopted the most natural interpretation of Reason's conclusion, taking dialectic (i.e., *ratio disputandi*) to be the unexpressed subject of the clause *per seipsam disciplina vera est*. But this clause could also be read as providing its own subject, in which case it should be translated: "discipline is true through its own self." In that case the conclusion is that not merely dialectic, but discipline itself is Truth. This conclusion too could be supported by Reason's line of argument, which implies that Discipline in general is true by virtue of something internal to it, namely, the discipline of argumentation. Precisely because the discipline of dialectic makes all the disciplines true, Discipline in general makes itself true. Thus it seems that if dialectic is Truth, then Discipline also is Truth—and Augustine has succeeded in justifying the premise he needs for his proof of the immortality of the soul.

Though the identification "Dialectic is Truth" is on the face of it bizarre, it does seem clear that Augustine seriously intends to say that what we learn in the liberal arts is that very same Truth that is God. The really odd thing is the tight connection between the liberal arts and ultimate Truth—but this would not seem so odd to anyone working in the tradition of Plato's Allegory of the Cave, as I have suggested earlier.[21] If the project of learning to see God through a program of education appears absurdly pagan for a Christian writer, three considerations may lessen that appearance. First of all, Augustine is not the only Church Father to have suggested it.[22] Second, Augustine proves willing to be flexible about the kind of education involved: in his mature works Christian teaching replaces the liberal arts (Christian *doctrina,* as it were, steps into the place once occupied by liberal *disciplina*), but the notion that learning leads us to divine Truth remains.[23] Finally, the Truth that Augustine wants to learn is, as always, Christ, who is also probably the same as the inner teacher called Reason in the *Soliloquies*,[24] and whom Augustine calls "the discipline of God."[25]

Immutable Things in the Mind

Augustine's early attempt to prove the immortality of the soul in the *Soliloquies* becomes the model for a whole series of kindred proofs in the first part of his treatise *On the Immortality of the Soul* (sections 1–8), the immediate sequel of the Cassiciacum dialogues. It is in fact the rough draft or sketch of a planned third book of the *Soliloquies*, which Augustine never worked up into dialogue form. He had no intention of publishing it in the form we actually have it, but it fell somehow into the hands of people who circulated it against his will. The book is not much fun to read. As Augustine himself says, "Because of its abbreviated and convoluted reasoning it is so obscure that even my own attention flags as I read it, and I myself can scarcely understand it."[26] What we have in this treatise is the bare outlines of arguments: collections of premises and conclusions, objections and refutations.

It is clear, however, that the arguments sketched and defended here are modeled on the proof for the immortality of the soul in the second book of *Soliloquies*. The basic strategy is to locate something intelligible and therefore immutable in the soul (for example *disciplina*, *ars*, *ratio*, or *verum*), and then insist that whatever contains an imperishable thing must itself be imperishable. So, for instance, the opening sentence of the treatise presents the following set of premises:

1. Discipline exists somewhere.
2. Discipline can only exist in something that is alive [i.e., in a soul].
3. Discipline exists forever.
4. Something in which that which exists forever exists, cannot but exist forever.[27]

The conclusion at which these premises aim is plain: the soul in which discipline exists, exists forever. The most obvious objection to this line of argument, that the soul can be ignorant of the disciplines, is handled once again by a line of reasoning that goes back to Plato's theory of Recollection:

> But when we are reasoning with our own selves [as in the *Soliloquies*!] or else being questioned well by someone else about some of the liberal arts [e.g., in Socratic conversations such as Augustine presents in the other Cassiciacum dialogues] then what we discover [*invenimus*] we discover nowhere else than *in our own mind*. For to discover something is not to make or to generate it; otherwise the mind would generate eternal things through temporal discoveries (and it does discover eternal things: for what is as eternal as the principle [*ratio*] of a circle, which is grasped as never having a time in which it did not exist or will not exist?) So it is obvious that the human mind is immortal, and *all true reasons are in its secret places* [*omnes veras rationes in secretis ejus esse*], although because of ignorance or forgetfulness it may seem not to have them or to have lost them.[28]

Augustine's argument for the immortality of the soul clearly implies the divinity of the soul. For the crucial attribute of the intelligible things that Augustine locates in the soul is their immutability, and their presence in the soul makes the soul also immutable, at least in its higher or rational part. And for Augustine (as for all orthodox Christians of the time) immutability is the one attribute that is most clearly and certainly characteristic of deity, the characteristic that distinguishes God from everything else. According to Augustine's argumentation in *On the Immortality of the Soul*, therefore, this attribute belongs also to us, or rather to our Reason. Consider some of the premises Augustine collects in the second chapter of the treatise and the conclusion he is driving at:

> Reason either [1] *is* the mind or [2] is *in* the mind.
>> Reason is immutable.
>> [Therefore, if (1) is correct, then the mind is immutable.]
>> In no way can that which is inseparably in a subject remain unchanged, if the subject itself is changed.
>> [Therefore, if (2) is correct, then the mind is never changed, i.e., is immutable.][29]

Therefore, whether Reason *is* the mind or is only inseparably *in* it, the mind is immutable. That is to say, the rational part of the human soul is eternal, just like the things to which it is joined in intelligible knowledge. For the intelligible and immutable things that we understand are not gazed at from a distance, as in Plato's Allegory of the Cave, but are located nowhere else but *in* the rational soul:

> The things which are understood [*intelliguntur*] are understood to be located nowhere else than *in the very mind that understands them*, for at the same time they are also understood not to be contained in space [*non contineri loco*].[30]

This is the fundamental point of departure for the development of Augustinian inwardness. Augustine forges the conception of the self as an inner space in order to have a place where these immutable and divine things are found. This version of the divinity of the rational soul is thus the conceptual forerunner of Augustine's later talk of turning inward to find God.

The key notion here is Plotinian: what is found *in* the soul is nothing other than the intelligible world, the realm of Platonic ideas, eternal truths or *rationes* (as Augustine calls them) that we learn in geometry and the other disciplines. But specifying the sense in which Truth, Reason or Discipline is "in" the soul is a tricky conceptual problem that Augustine is not equipped to solve yet. That is, I suspect, the most important reason why the third book of the *Soliloquies* was never finished.

We can see why the main argument of the *Soliloquies* and its various elaborations in *On the Immortality of the Soul* were doomed if we look schematically at the basic structure of Augustine's reasoning. Let X be Discipline, Reason, Truth, God, or anything else immutable and intelligible. The basic template, as it were, of Augustine's various proofs for the immortality of the soul is approximately as follows:

1. X is immutable (or exists forever).
2. X is in the soul.

Therefore, the soul is immutable (or exists forever).

I have deliberately made this template a little too simple, in order to bring out the need for a crucial qualification that Augustine makes to the notion of "in" used in the second premise. Recall the objection, which Augustine has handled twice already, that the fact of ignorance seems to show discipline is not always in us. The point of that objection can be generalized: if Augustine's argument is to work, X cannot be in the soul only part of the time, for then the soul could lose it and become mortal. X must be a necessary and inherent part or feature of the soul. It is not enough to say simply that it is *in* the soul; it must be *inseparably* in the soul. Thus when Reason introduces the basic rule of inference that underlies the various proofs in the second and third books of the *Soliloquies*, it includes this crucial phrase: "Don't you agree that what is *inseparably in* a subject *cannot remain* if the subject itself does not remain?"[31]

This is where the argument goes fundamentally wrong. For if this rule of inference holds, and God or Truth is inseparably in the soul in this sense, then God cannot exist without the soul. This makes God's existence dependent on ours: Truth *cannot remain* unless the soul remains forever. It is important to appreciate that this conclusion was as repugnant to pagan Neoplatonists as it was to orthodox Christians. Neither tradition could stomach a line of reasoning that makes ontologically higher things dependent on lower things—in this case, the intelligible world dependent on the soul. The fact that Augustine's argument has this consequence is due not to his Neoplatonism but to his philosophical incompetence. He does not yet command the conceptual resources needed to make the argument work. By the time he does, he knows too much about the Catholic Church's rejection of the divinity of the soul to pursue it any further.

A Diagnosis

Consequently, Augustine abandons his proof for the immortality of the soul. But, very significantly, he does not abandon his project of finding the intelligible Truth *in* the soul—that is what the inward turn is all about. So the question remains: in what sense of the word "in" is it true that "Truth is found *in* the soul"? To see the shape of the problem this poses for Augustine, we can look at the concept he started with but had to abandon. In what sense is Discipline or Truth inseparably *in* the soul, according to the arguments in *Soliloquies* and *On the Immortality of the Soul*? And how, moreover, is this so different from the sense in which Plotinus could affirm that the intelligible world was *in* the soul?

Augustine approaches the problem by contrasting two ways we can say that something is *in* another thing. The first is the sense in which material objects are located in space, "such as this piece of wood in this place, or the sun in the East."[32] The other is the sense in which essential properties are inseparably in their subjects, "such as the form and appearance [*forma et species*] which we see in this piece of wood, or light in the sun, or heat in fire, or discipline in the mind."[33] This sense of "in" is one that "Augustine" claims is familiar to him from his school days.[34] It comes in fact from the one text of classical Greek philosophy that Augustine ever mastered firsthand (even if in translation), Aristotle's *Categories*.[35] Augustine is claiming that intelligible things are in the mind the same way a quality is in a substance as its subject. Thus God is "in" the soul in the sense of the word "in" defined by Aristotle's notion of a quality being "in" a subject: "By 'in a subject' I mean what is in something, not as a part, *being incapable of existing separate* from what it is in."[36] From a Platonist standpoint, this is a disastrous way to think about intelligible things, as it makes them ontologically dependent and secondary. The category of substance, for Aristotle, is ontologically primary, and the qualities that inhere in a substance (like color in a visible body, for instance) are ontologically dependent on the substance they are in.

Thus the philosophical concept Augustine uses to articulate the sense in which Truth is "in" the soul makes Truth ontologically dependent on the soul rather than the other way around. This is simply inept. For what Augustine obviously wants to do in his proof for the immortality of the soul is to show how the inherent imperishability of Truth "rubs off" on the soul in which it is present. His whole argument is therefore designed to show that the soul is dependent on Truth for its being, life, and immortality—not the other way around! Truth is supposed to endure even if the whole world were destroyed.[37] Yet the implication of Augustine's use of the phrase "inseparably in" is that without the soul as its subject Discipline or Truth cannot exist, for "that which is inseparably in a subject cannot remain if the subject itself does not remain."[38]

It is useful to compare this failure, this conceptual crudity in the prehistory of Augustine's inwardness, with the sophistication and subtlety of Plotinus's use of the little word "in." His use is largely metaphorical—and Augustine seems to have grasped the metaphor without quite grasping its limits. Much of the argumentation of Augustine's *On the Immortality of the Soul* makes more intuitive sense if we keep in mind the powerful Plotinian picture of a cosmos composed of concentric spheres.[39] At the center of everything is the One, from which radiates the intelligible world or Mind, around which the sphere of the Soul metaphorically revolves (either turning inward to contemplate intelligible things or looking outward to fall among bodies). The sensible world or material cosmos, the world of bodies, is furtherest out from the center. The word "in" applies literally only to this last sphere, for only the world of bodies is actually spatial in its mode of being, and only in space can one thing be literally *in* another. Hence Mind is not literally "in" the soul, nor is the soul literally "in" the body. Rather, the metaphor of "inward" and "outward" represents ontological similarity and dependence—the more inward things are, the greater their resemblance to the ultimate One at the center of the universe, while the farther out they are, the more they suffer division and manyness (as the divine Mind is more diverse and variegated than the One, and bodies are the least unified of all, being divisible in space, capable of literally falling apart). Thus in order to drive home the point about ontological dependence, Plotinus is perfectly willing to reverse the metaphor and say that lower things have their existence *in* higher things—for example, that body exists in soul and soul in the divine Mind.[40]

This reversal also has the implication that lower things are not really distant from higher things. Separation in space is only possible in space, after all. Therefore nothing is ever literally outside the intelligible world, and nothing is ever separated from it by spatial distance. Rather, the intelligible world is omnipresent: the whole divine Mind is present undivided everwhere in the material cosmos. Transcendence thus implies immanence: precisely because the intelligible is not limited by a spatial mode of being, it is present everywhere in space, in a way impossible for material objects, which are necessarily spread out part by part in space and contained in one place rather than another. Hence for Plotinus, the fact that the Divine is not a bodily thing is precisely what makes it more fully present in the material world than bodies themselves are. Even in the sensible world, immaterial being means *more* being, not less—fullness of presence, rather than the partial absence that is the necessary mode of being of bodies, which cannot be present one place without being absent in another.

The Plotinian doctrine of the omnipresence of the intelligible in the sensible is to play a major role in Augustine's thought, as we have already seen.[41] Soon Augustine will even toy with Plotinus' counterintuitive talk about the body being "in" the soul rather than the other way around.[42] But at this point it is clear that he has not quite seen the full import of

Plotinus's complex way of relating the sensible world to the intelligible, because his whole argument depends on Truth being *absent* from every place but the soul. If Truth exists also outside the soul, then the claim that it is inseparably *in* the soul, in the sense Augustine specifies, is undermined. Thus, in striking contrast to his latter views of the integral omnipresence of Truth, Augustine affirms that Truth does not exist anywhere in space (*non . . . in loco*) or in bodies (*non . . . in rebus mortalibus*).[43] Yet, Augustine insists, it has to exist *somewhere*, for "everything that is, must be somewhere."[44] This is precisely what a well-informed Neoplatonist would *not* say about the intelligible things. The intelligible exists everywhere in space, being omnipresent, precisely because it is not dependent on having any particular place or "somewhere" in which to exist.

Augustine soon realizes his mistake. Within a few years he asserts that "God is not somewhere" (*Deus non alicubi est*) and thence draws a conclusion that fits with Plotinus's reversal of the usual language of inside and out, saying, "All things are *in* Him."[45] From this point onward, when Augustine says that God does not exist in a place, he does not mean that God is absent from any place but that his mode of being is non-spatial and therefore he is omnipresent. This realization dooms the proof for the immortality of the soul that was the main line of argument in the *Soliloquies* and its sequel.

It is worth seeing exactly why. What does this realization change? If God is not somewhere, then the dictum "everything that is, must be *somewhere*" is false. Now where did that dictum come from? Certainly not from Plotinus. It is the sort of thing a materialist would say, and in fact it came to Augustine from the Stoics, via Cicero.[46] Variants of it recur in *On the Immortality of the Soul*,[47] where it is needed to establish the claim that intelligible things, not being located in space, have nowhere else to exist but in the mind.

The diagnosis, therefore, is that Augustine's argument fails primarily because it is insufficiently Neoplatonist. It is vitiated by his reliance on materialist concepts that he learned long before he encountered the books of the Platonists. More positively, we could count this abandoned proof of the immortality of the soul as a step on the road toward overcoming his old carnal habits of thought and formulating a fully Platonist ontology. In any case, what we cannot do, if we care to understand Augustine's explorations here, is make apologetics for him by supposing that this is merely an example of "Augustine's early Platonism," which will be overcome by his deepening Christian faith.[48] Rather, it is an example of old materialist habits of thought still infecting his newborn project of achieving a Christian Platonist view of God and the soul. It is doomed to be left behind because it is neither Christian nor Platonist enough.

8

Change of Mind

Augustine abandons the proof of the immortality of the soul he proposed at Cassiciacum, but he does not abandon the project of locating the divine in the soul—the result of which is Augustine's own original brand of inwardness. The crucial premise he must rethink is the claim that God is present inseparably in the soul. For if souls fell by their own will, then there is a kind of separation between God and the soul, in will rather than in space. In the first book of On Free Choice *Augustine tries to combine the premise of the soul's inherent immutability with the concept of a voluntary turning away from God. But within about a year he rejects the key premise of that attempt, thus opening the new path that would lead eventually to the inwardness of the* Confessions.*

Inseparably in the Soul

A striking feature of the prehistory of the inward turn, as we have been following it so far in Augustine's earliest writings, is that there is so little that distinguishes turning to the soul from turning to God. In the mature version of Augustine's inward turn, there are two distinct movements, first "in" then "up." In the second movement, the soul looks not at itself but *above* its mutable self to the immutable Truth. But this second movement is unnecessary if the highest part of the soul is immutable or if the immutable Truth is inseparably present *in* the soul. Hence at Cassiciacum, as in Plotinus, there is no sharp distinction between the soul turning into itself and the soul looking at God—for that, after all, is where God *is*. At Cassiciacum wisdom consists in "collecting oneself in oneself," and directing one's attention "to oneself and to God,"[1] and one can speak of the wise man being "with himself" and "with God"[2] as if these were equivalent or (more precisely) co-extensive terms—that is, as if whenever the mind is turned to itself it is necessarily turned to God, and vice versa. Later in his career Augustine becomes aware that this pattern of talk is not as Catholic as it should be, and in the *Retractations* he corrects it, indicating passages of the Cassiciacum works where he spoke of finding our highest good "in the mind" but should rather have said "in God."[3]

This development from the simple movement of the mind returning to itself to the double movement "in then up" is an important part of the story of the invention of the Augustinian inner self, as well as a crucial clue to its conceptual structure. In contrast to Plotinus, the mature Augustine comes to picture the inner space of the soul as something other than the intelligible world itself. This otherness (i.e., the soul's otherness from God) is marked by the contrast between mutability and immutability. In contrast to the changelessness of Truth, the soul is mutable, which means that it is vulnerable to changes for the worse—corruption and evil and perhaps even death. Yet the central purpose of the *Soliloquies* (as we have seen) was to prove that the soul could not suffer such changes. Hence Augustine's mature view on this subject represents a profound about-face from his early project. This about-face is worth tracing back to its initial stages, for that will in turn help us understand the role the concept of Will plays in the invention of the inner self.

In the first part of *On the Immortality of the Soul,* as we have seen, Augustine tries out various proofs of the immortality and immutability of the soul, based on the claim that Reason, Truth, or *disciplina* (each of which is immutable and intelligible) is inseparably present in the soul. However, in section 7 of the treatise, qualifications begin to appear. Augustine is willing to admit that there can be some kinds of change (*mutatio*) in the mind or soul so long as they are accidental rather than essential. The soul may be affected by passions, but these do not abolish its essence or change the soul into a non-soul, and therefore (since soul is in essence life) they do not subject it to death.[4] Thus the basic argument still stands:

> Therefore, as we said above, if the soul is a subject in which reason inseparably is, then *by that necessity by which it* [*reason*] *is shown to be in a subject*—and the soul cannot be soul without being alive, nor reason be in it without life, and reason is immortal—then the soul also is immortal.[5]

Henceforth everything turns on whether it can be shown that reason necessarily exists in the soul as its subject. Once that is established, the soul's own permanence as a living being is established, since "there is no way at all that Reason could remain immutable without its subject existing."[6] Therefore in the next section Augustine proceeds to turn "all [his] powers of reasoning" to the task of determining what Reason is.[7] He rehearses three possible identities of Reason: the *power* of intellectual vision (the *aspectus animi*), the *act* of intellectual vision (i.e., the actual contemplation), and the *thing seen* in intellectual vision (i.e., truth). The first two are obviously in the soul and thus support Augustine's line of argument, but "there is a great question about the third." The question is

> whether the truth [*verum*] which the mind beholds apart from the instrumentality of the body [i.e., without the senses] exists by itself and is not in the mind, or *whether it can exist without the mind.*[8]

If truth can exist by itself (*per seipsum*), without the mind (*sine animo*) rather than in it, then Augustine's whole early project is imperiled.

Here we come upon the same conceptual ineptness noted earlier: Augustine's commitment to the presence of truth in the human mind makes intelligible things dependent on the soul rather than the other way around. He proceeds to affirm that dependence by denying that truth can exist outside the mind. For in contrast to sensible things, which are perceived as existing outside us in space, intelligible things "are understood to be located nowhere else but in the very mind which understands them, for at the same time they are also understood not to be contained in space."[9]

Sensible things are outside (in space), intelligible things inside (in the mind): this tidy antithesis seems to have been guiding Augustine's thought up to this point. But once explicit, it immediately becomes apparent how questionable the antithesis is. So Augustine must proceed straightway to investigate exactly how the mind's vision joins it to the intelligible truth which it beholds.

> Either it is such that the mind is a subject and the truth is something in the subject; or else on the contrary the truth is the subject, and the mind is in the subject; or else they are both substances.[10]

The first of these possibilities is the one on which Augustine has been building up to now (the intelligible thing is in the soul inseparably as in a subject) while the second reflects the Plotinian reversal of the metaphor of inwardness according to which the soul is "in" the intelligible world rather than the other way around.[11] The whole trio of possibilities is based on Aristotle's *Categories*: intelligible truth is related to the soul either as essential quality to the substance in which it is present, or as a substance is related to an essential quality, or as one substance to another. Interestingly, Augustine does not seem to be aware of the possibility that for Plotinus is the literal truth about the relation between the mind and the truth it sees: they are identical. This too is an Aristotelian notion, but it comes from a part of Aristotle's work that Augustine did not know. There is reason to think he never did understand Plotinus's use of the Aristotelian theory that knowledge is a kind of identity between knower and known;[12] but even if he did, before very long his rejection of the divinity of the soul put that possibility off limits. For intelligible things are in the strictest sense divine, according to Augustine's teaching throughout his career. For him just as for Plotinus, the intelligible world is nothing other than the Mind of God. And while Plotinus can identify the human mind with the mind of God, the mature Augustine cannot.

At this point, however, Augustine sees more possibilities open than he later would. Of the three possible relations between soul and truth, the first two are acceptable in that they do not pose any threat to his proof for the immortality of the soul. Whether intelligible truths are in the soul or the soul is in them, the immutability of the one will rub off on the other. "So the whole remaining battle is about the third."[13] For if intelligible truth and the human mind are two different substances (which of course is what Augustine will soon come to understand as orthodox Catholic teaching) then the proof for the immortality of the soul that is the culmination of his early project cannot succeed. The way he defends his project at this point thus affords us a crucial view of what is to change after Cassiciacum: for it is precisely this defense that he must soon reject.

Voluntary Separation?

The problem Augustine is faced with concerns the relation between the mind and reason (*ratio*), where reason is understood in the third sense, as object of understanding or "true thing" (*verum*). As such it is evidently synonymous with "intelligible thing" and hence with Platonic "Idea." The "whole remaining battle," then, is about whether the human mind can ever be separated from Reason, taken in the sense of Platonic Idea or intelligible truth.

The first possibility Augustine considers in this "battle" is one he firmly and permanently rejects. It is a possibility suggested by the Manichaean myth of the Fall: perhaps the mind could be separated from reason by force (i.e., presumably by the assault of the "race of darkness").[14] But he can find nothing that is stronger than the mind that is joined to immutable reason: certainly no bodily thing has the strength to force them apart, nor could another soul have such power.[15] And Reason itself, in which there is no envy, would not push the mind away.[16]

But then Augustine considers another possibility: perhaps the mind separates itself from the truth voluntarily, by its own will (*voluntate*). This is the first time that the notion of a voluntary Fall comes up for discussion in Augustine's works, and it makes its appearance as an unwelcome possibility.[17] In order to save his proof, Augustine must show that such a thing is impossible. His defense boils down to a single claim about the concept of separation: there can be no separation between things that are not in space. Therefore, since both the mind and the truth have a non-spatial mode of being, they cannot possibly be separated from one another.[18]

This argument would be fine if the only conceivable kind of separation were by spatial distance, such as literally separates souls from the Realm of Light after the Manichaean Fall. But only a materialist is likely to believe that. Plotinus, by contrast, speaks frequently of a "separation that is not in space."[19] In fact Augustine later rejects his own argument here precisely because of its materialist assumptions, affirming on the contrary that there is indeed a kind of non-spatial separation between God and the soul: it is called sin. Though this conclusion can certainly be justified on biblical grounds,[20] it is clear that Augustine actually arrived at it by way of a deepening appropriation of Plotinian conceptuality. In Augustine's favorite passage from Plotinus, he learned that our flight to the intelligible Father is not a journey for the feet.[21] For the mature Augustine this non-spatial return to God the Father implies a prior non-spatial separation from God:

> In darkened emotions I was far from Your face. For it is not by feet nor by spatial distance that we journey from You or return to You. Neither did that younger son of Yours seek horses or chariots or ships. . . .[22]

These darkened emotions are the turning of our minds from light to darkness, from intelligible truth to outward things—the opposite movement from the inward turn.

The passage being discussed from *On the Immortality of the Soul* is the first time in Augustine's works that he reckons with the possibility that this downward and outward movement lying at the origin of all evil may be initiated by the soul itself—and he rejects the possibility.[23] But in the very next section he considers a possibility that comes ultimately to the same thing. This is perhaps inevitable, for he has left himself no acceptable alternative to explain how evil arose in the first place. If no outward force can separate the soul from the truth, then the origin of falsehood, evil, and ignorance can only be sought in the turning of the soul's own will:

> Precisely the turning away from reason through which foolishness touches the mind cannot take place without a defect in it. For if it is greater when turned to Reason and clinging to it—since it is clinging to that immutable thing, Truth [*veritas*], which is greatest and first of all—then in turning away from it, it has its own being in a lesser way, which is to be deficient. And all defect tends toward nothingness. . . .[24]

This is a fresh start, and it shifts the whole focus of discussion. Now the question is: given the defect of being that can indeed take place when the soul turns away from Truth, what prevents the ensuing tendency toward nothingness from going all the way to the extinction of the soul? This question assumes in effect that a voluntary separation between the soul and God is not only possible but has actually occurred—and now Augustine proceeds for the first time to examine the implications of this possibility. While he tries to argue here that the tendency toward nothingness can never proceed all the way to the destruction and death of the mind,[25] the important development, for our purposes, is the entrance of new ways of thinking that would later play a central role in his writing, such as the very notion of a "tendency toward non-being," which was developed at length in his brilliant philosophical essay *On True Religion*.[26]

From this point on, Augustine has in effect already given up the Cassiciacum project, or at least the proof of the immortality of the soul that was to be its crowning achievement. With this new metaphysics and psychology, in which the soul by the turning of its own will becomes less in being, closer to the divisibility and mortality of bodies, a whole new realm of dark but theologically fruitful possibilities opens up. The sense of paradox that runs throughout the *Confessions*—the soul fleeing from a God who is inescapably everywhere, who is indeed closer to the soul than it is to itself, because he is in us even when we are lost outside ourselves—stems from Augustine's sense that separation between God and the rational soul is well nigh impossible yet abominably real.[27] For how can the rational soul separate itself from Reason and yet remain rational? How can a mind be bereft of Truth and remain a mind? Yet that is somehow what has happened. The fact is, according to the mature Augustine, that the soul, the principle of life, is indeed subject to the power of death. For as the soul is the life of the body, so God is the life of the soul; separated from him the soul suffers—as the Scriptures testify—a kind of death.[28]

Immutable Good Will

These brilliant and familiar Augustinian themes lie in the future; our question in this chapter is how he got there from here. The main line of argument of *Soliloquies* and *On the Immortality of the Soul* is soon to be abandoned, but the project of locating God in the soul is not. There is a process of revision and rethinking that leads from Cassiciacum to *Confessions*; the inward turn is a major part of the process, and the concept of inner self is one of its chief products. For if it turns out that the soul really can separate itself voluntarily from God, then it would seem natural to suppose that it has a different kind of being from God, not of course corporeal, but not immutable either.

That is the conclusion Augustine eventually reaches, but it is not an inevitable one. Plotinus, for one, thought that a voluntary Fall of the soul was compatible with the the higher part of the soul remaining immutable and unfallen, and he argues for both these claims in the same treatise.[29] Hence on Neoplatonist grounds it is perfectly possible to affirm a voluntary Fall while retaining the divinity and immutability of the soul. And in fact the only possible way of making sense of Augustine's major treatise on the concept of Will is to suppose that at first he too wanted to do exactly that.

The first book of the treatise *On Free Choice* was written significantly earlier than the second and third, certainly within a year or two after the Cassiciacum dialogues. For purposes of understanding Augustine's development, this book should be treated as a separate production, for it represents a unique point of view that differs from the later books of the same treatise. In it we find Augustine's first attempt at overhauling the Cassiciacum program. Here he wants to develop the idea of a voluntary Fall, while retaining the Cassiciacum doctrine that part of the soul is divine and immutable. At least this is how we must interpret the book if we do not want to make it look wildly self-contradictory.

On any interpretation, to be sure, it is a wild book. One of the most brilliant and innovative pieces of philosophical writing in Western history, it is also a juggling act where Augustine scarcely knows how to keep all the balls in the air. In this one book Augustine not only introduces a profound new concept of Will,[30] he also fashions a new Platonistic understanding of the concept of Natural Law that he found in Cicero, proposing that there is an eternal law by which the changes and variations in the temporal laws of human communities are to be judged.[31] This eternal law also orders the changing world in general, apportioning to fallen souls the position in the hierarchy of the cosmos that their will, good or evil, has merited.[32] All this is by way of answering the question that had been incompletely discussed in *On Order*: what is the place of evil in the providential divine order that governs the changing world?[33]

The book concludes with a definition of sin that shows why evil need not be conceived (in the Manichaean manner) as an independent substance. Sin is what happens "when someone is turned away from divine things, things which truly remain, and is turned toward mutable and uncertain things."[34] The answer to the question "whence evil?" is therefore in essence quite simple: evil comes from the love of mutable things. Augustine hastens to point out that this does not mean (as a Manichaean might think) that mutable things are evil. They are good creations of God,[35] and when properly placed in the order he established they have a kind of beauty of their own, inferior to eternal beauty of course, but nonetheless real. The ethical point, however, is that they are not to be loved, for they are not the source of true happiness.

We can already see that some significant revisions will be required in this theory. For one thing, if sin means loving mutable things, then Jesus must have been commanding us to sin when he said, "Love thy neighbor."[36] Augustine will eventually redefine love so as to make love of neighbor permissible, by introducing his famous distinction between using things and enjoying them (*uti* and *frui*). Charity or well-ordered love can then include right use of temporal things as well as the desire to enjoy eternal things, so that one's neighbor can rightly be *used*, and (Augustine a little later concedes) even *enjoyed* "in God."[37]

But suppose we were to ask Augustine, at the time he was writing the first book of *On Free Choice*, what place love of neighbor had in his ethics? We should expect, I think, to get an answer based on the view of human love he had just recently sketched in the *Soliloquies*: "It is alright for me to love the reason in anyone."[38] Since loving anything mutable is sin, we must assume that the reason in us is not mutable—precisely the key premise of the argument in *Soliloquies* and *On the Immortality of the Soul*.

What the first book of *On Free Choice* adds to this argument is the claim that the *good will* in the soul is also immutable. For its central ethical argument is that all the virtues can be summed up in love for one's own Good Will.[39] It follows (unless Augustine is defining virtue as a sin) that the Good Will must be something immutable. Yet it is also unmistakably *ours*, "something we have *in* the mind," stemming from our ineradicable will to be happy.[40]

Thus we have, in an ethical register, the same conceptual framework that was operative at Cassiciacum:[41] there is something immutable in the soul, and as the soul's business at Cassiciacum was to understand that immutable thing, so its business in the first book of

On Free Choice is to love and enjoy it. This approach may have been suggested to Augustine by one of Cicero's remarks in the concluding book of *Tusculan Disputations*, which is a discussion of the nature of happiness, or *beata vita*:

> That supreme good which you seek is necessarily located in the best part of a human being. And what is better in a human being than a wise and good mind? This is the good we must enjoy [*fruendum est*] if we want to be happy. Now, a good mind [*bona mens*] is virtue. Therefore, virtue necessarily constitutes the happy life.[42]

Substitute "good will" for "good mind" and you have the central ethical claim of the first book of *On Free Choice*, book 1: "the happy man is the one who loves his own good will."[43] Evidently Augustine is still very impressed by the Ciceronian thought that the greatest good is present in the mind,[44] which he wants to develop here in a Christian-Platonist way. The term "good will" (*bona voluntas*) is central, first because it is the opposite of the evil will that turns to mutable things and thus causes the Fall and second because of its Biblical resonances. In works written within two or three years after Cassiciacum, Augustine takes "good will" to be the basis on which human beings merit happiness—for the song of the angels at the nativity of Christ tells us that there is "peace on earth for humans of good will."[45]

Soul as Creature

Once again, I would suggest, the guiding thread of Augustine's philosophical project is the Christology of 1 Corinthians 1:24, "Christ the Virtue of God and the Wisdom of God."[46] Just as at Cassiciacum the immutable Reason and Truth we seek to know is Christ the Wisdom of God, so in book 1 of *On Free Choice* the immutable Good Will we should wish to enjoy is Christ the Virtue of God. Thus even the conviction that the soul has voluntarily turned away from God does not prevent Augustine from locating something divine inseparably in our souls. For it seems clear in this book that even in the fallen soul Christ the Virtue of God is inseparably present, though perhaps forgotten and unloved.

Augustine's repudiation of the divinity of the soul must therefore take shape as a revision of his early Christology. This is apparent in the very early work *On the Morals of the Catholic Church*, which is the first treatise in which Augustine rejects the divinity of the soul. The importance of this treatise for understanding Augustine's development is often overlooked, however, because it is usually classed with the "anti-Manichaean" treatises rather than with the philosophical dialogues. This classification is quite accurate as regards genre but crucially misleading as regards chronology. Although the bulk of the anti-Manichaean treatises were written after Augustine's philosophical dialogues, this treatise was by Augustine's own reckoning (in the *Retractations*) written before any of the post-Cassiciacum dialogues were completed.[47] This gives the treatise (along with its sequel, *On the Morals of the Manichaeans*) a place of unique significance in Augustine's development, as a kind of theological interruption in the course of his original project of philosophical inquiry.

On the Morals of the Catholic Church is the earliest example in Augustine's work of a genre we could call "ecclesiastical treatise." This is the kind of writing that is most familiar to readers of Augustine the Church Father, composed to address an urgent concern of the Church rather than to pursue a roundabout course of philosophical inquiry. Instead of leisurely conversations between Christian laymen quoting Cicero and hinting at Plotinus, we hear in these writings the authoritative voice of apostle and prophet, with Augustine's own voice playing the role not of Socratic teacher but of exegete and polemicist. For of course the urgent concerns that called most of Augustine's ecclesiastical treatises into being were of a polemical nature: the purpose of this genre of writing is to refute heretics and schismatics, not lead students up step by step from corporeal things to intelligible things. The first time Augustine clearly rejects the divinity of the soul is thus when he begins writing as a responsible spokesman for the Church rather than as an independent inquirer seeking wisdom for its own sweet sake.[48]

Augustine's growing awareness of his responsibility to bring his search for wisdom into conformity with the authority of the Church made the difference between his early view of the divinity of the soul and the new brand of inwardness that he eventually bequeathed to the West.[49] Catholic orthodoxy cannot countenance belief in the divinity of the soul, as became increasingly clear after the triumph of Nicene theology, with its implication of a logically exhaustive Creator/creature distinction.[50] If everything that exists is either Creator or creature, then it is clear (for orthodox Christianity) that the soul is on the creature side of the ledger and therefore is not divine.

Ambrose insisted very frequently on the distinction between Creator and creature in his writings on the Trinity,[51] and I think we may infer that Augustine would have heard it in Ambrose's sermons,[52] so that it was known to him from the beginning of his career. But he may not have seen all its implications right away. Thus already in the first book of *On Free Choice* (probably the first thing he wrote after the Cassiciacum works) he clearly states the teaching of the Nicene Creed that Christ as divine Son of God is begotten, not created.[53] And the distinction turns up frequently in his early expositions of the Trinity, as we should expect.[54] It is only much later that he comes to appreciate its soteriological significance: that Christ has the role of Mediator between God and human beings not because of his divinity (for this is not something ontologically intermediate between God and the soul) but rather because of his humanity.[55] It is this that forces him to assign much more soteriological importance to the humanity of Christ than one would have expected from his early emphasis on Christ as the inner teacher. He must reckon with the orthodox Catholic teaching that Christ mediates between us and God not because he is inwardly present as divine Wisdom and Virtue, but because he is one of us, having a human soul and body.[56] Finally—what is most important for our present purposes—within about about a year of leaving Milan, Augustine realizes that Catholic doctrine does not allow him to conceive of the soul as divine and immutable, for everything that exists other than the Holy Trinity is created out of nothing and therefore is not eternal or immutable, but has an altogether different and lesser kind of being than God. It is this realization that we find spelled out for the first time in *On the Morals of the Catholic Church*, where it is closely connected with Augustine's decisive abandonment of the Cassiciacum project of locating divine things inseparably in the soul.

In this treatise, Augustine introduces the Creator/creature distinction while commenting on a passage of Scripture that might at first strike one as providing support for the proof of the immortality of the soul that he had been so intent on at Cassiciacum. The apostle Paul says,

> I am certain that neither death nor life, angels nor virtue, things present nor to come, height nor depth, *nor any other creature can separate us* from the charity of God which is in Christ Jesus our Lord.[57]

You might think this would reinforce Augustine's conviction that God is inseparably in the soul. Instead it provides an occasion for him to affirm that separation between God and the soul is possible, precisely because the soul is a creature and therefore a different kind of being than the Creator. Augustine fixes on Paul's phrase "nor any *other* creature" as an indication that the soul itself is a creature.[58] Then he issues a warning, which I take to be addressed primarily to himself: "we must be anxious lest the human mind, since it is counted among things invisible and intelligible, be thought to be of the same nature as him who created it."[59] Augustine states very exactly the source of his anxiety. The danger of confusing God and the rational soul stems from the fact that the soul too is not grasped by the senses, and therefore is in a certain sense an intelligible thing, like the intelligible Truth. But this similarity must not lead us to overlook the decisive difference, that the Creator is more excellent than the creature. The human mind must recognize that it is a creature, distinguished from the immmutable truth and wisdom of God by the possibility of error, folly, and ignorance that is intrinsic to its nature.[60] It can depart from God, not in space, but in its affections, its pride, its lust for things lower than God. Hence there is a kind of separation between God and the soul, and the soul must take care

> lest it be separated by love of some other creature, that is, of this sensible world, from the charity of God himself, by which it is sanctified that it may remain most happy. For *no other creature separates us* from the charity of God which is in our Lord Jesus Christ, since we ourselves are a creature.[61]

No *other* creature can separate us from the charity of God, for it is we ourselves (creatures that we are) who voluntarily turn away from loving God and thereby separate ourselves from him.

Here the project of proving God *inseparably* present in the soul is given up. In contrast to section 10 of *On the Immortality of the Soul,* Augustine here affirms that there is indeed a kind of separation between God and the soul but (as the *Confessions* puts it) a separation that is not in space but in dark and lustful affections.[62] The foundation for the startling rhetorical paradoxes of the *Confessions* is laid.

What lustful affections separate us from is "the charity of God, which is in our Lord Jesus Christ." This phrase, which in Paul means God's love for us, Augustine (as usual) takes to mean our love for God.[63] So the point is simple: in turning our love toward lower things, we separate ourselves from love of higher things. The proper object of charity is Christ, who, according to the familiar testimony of Paul (1 Cor. 1:24) and of Christ himself (John 14:6), is none other than Virtue and Wisdom and Truth, "Virtue which is inviolable and invincible, Wisdom which is never followed by foolishness, Truth which knows no turning, no being other than what it always is."[64]

I take it that Augustine is referring to the same thing here as in the first book of *On Free Choice,* where the proper object of love was named "Good Will." The difference is that he is now clear on the fact that in loving this we are not loving ourselves. This is the point of a very odd argument earlier in the same treatise, where Augustine spends a great deal of time demonstrating that when we pursue virtue we are following after something besides ourselves.[65] This argument must seem pointless until we recognize it as a correction of the ethical position taken in *On Free Choice,* book 1 (and by implication of the parallel line of epistemological argumentation in *Soliloquies* 2 and early in *On the Immortality of the Soul*). The virtue that we must seek is "something other" (*aliquid aliud*) than us, existing "apart from the soul" (*praeter animam*)—in contrast to our Good Will in the first book of *On Free Choice*. And it exists in and of itself (*per sese*), not merely in the mind (*in animo*)—in contrast to the proof of the immortality of the soul at Cassiciacum, which was threatened by the possibility that truth could exist without the mind (*sine animo*), and therefore had to contend *against* the idea that truth could exist in and of itself (*per seipsam*) rather than in the mind (*in animo*).[66]

Thus the argument here is not so much about the nature of virtue as about the nature of God, and its point is simply that God exists independently of us. Hence the conclusion is that to live rightly and happily we must follow after God rather than ourselves.[67] But until we get to this conclusion the discussion is couched entirely in terms of the nature of virtue, which makes the whole argument look very odd. Why would anyone doubt the common ancient view that virtue is a habit or quality in the soul, as Augustine does here?[68] The point is clear when we realize that "virtue" means Christ and that Augustine is denying that Christ belongs to the Aristotelian category of quality—the sort of thing whose existence is dependent on its presence in a substance as in a subject. This denial is necessary because, as we have seen, the main line of argumentation in the Cassiciacum writings had in effect asserted that the intelligible Truth (i.e., Christ) could only exist by being present in the rational soul the way a property is present in a subject.[69]

So Christ, the Virtue and Wisdom of God, is something other than the soul. (Amazing how much work it takes for Augustine to be able to say that!) Consequently the soul following God is doing something other than following itself—a conclusion that could not be drawn from the Cassiciacum dialogues, where (as we saw at the beginning of this chapter) there is no clear distinction between turning to the soul and turning to God. Yet notice that Augustine does not go on to say that Christ is *outside* the soul. The project of locating God within the soul is still on—and that is what will lead to the distinctively Augustinian conception of the inner space of the self. For although Augustine now recognizes Christ as something *other* than the soul, he still locates Christ *within* the soul rather than outside it, and this means the soul must have enough "room" within itself to hold what is higher and greater than itself. One can look inside the self to find what is not self. This is crucial for the doctrine of grace that Augustine develops later in his career: grace is inward, but not in our power—*in* us, but *other* than us. We can try to flee what is inmost in us, but we cannot succeed, for Christ is always present in the soul, even when the soul is separated from him: "The light of my eyes was not with me; for it was inside, but I was outside."[70]

That means something distinctive about the conceptual structure of Augustinian inwardness. We can be cut off from that which is most intimate to us, separated from the divine thing in our inmost soul. The fact that this most intimate and inevitable divine presence, the light of Truth that gives the rational soul the very possibility of being rational, can be both in us and separated from us means that the inner world is not what Plotinus thought it was. For Plotinus, there is a part of us that is never separated from the divine Mind. When we turn to it, we are *ipso facto* turning to God. For the mature Augustine, there is no such divine, immutable part of soul. Hence we can turn to the highest and best part of our self and still find nothing but our own solitary self.

9

Inner Privacy and
Fallen Embodiment

This chapter examines how the inner self became private, a development that stems from the key contrast between Plotinus and the mature Augustine. Because of the orthodox Christian doctrine of creation, the mature Augustine sees the soul as fundamentally other and lower than the immutable God. He thinks of embodiment as a good thing—a point he articulates by drawing on the less dualist strand in Platonism, which also helped him accept the doctrine of the resurrection of the body. For Plotinus and Augustine, the Fall is not the same thing as embodiment but rather means overinvolvement in the particularities of embodiment, which separate one soul from another, burdening us with individuality in Plotinus and inner privacy in Augustine. Since this privacy is an evil, it has no place in the soul's original condition in Adam or its final blessedness in heaven, though in the modern period it has often been regarded as essential to the very nature of the inner self, as for example in the philosophy of John Locke.

Soul as Mutable

At Cassiciacum Augustine had tried to find something immutable about the soul, while deferring consideration of its Fall. In his mature Christian Platonism he reverses this, emphasizing the Fall of the soul and firmly denying that the soul is immutable or divine. Within two years of Cassiciacum he explicitly rejects the divinity of the soul, then proceeds to work out a powerful Plotinian doctrine of its Fall.[1] His mature brand of inwardness takes shape within the constraints of this modified Neoplatonist framework. Plotinus's inward turn, with a Plotinian Fall but without the divinity of the soul, yields Augustine's notion of the private inner space. Or to put the equation more positively: a Plotinian inward turn plus a Plotinian doctrine of the Fall plus an orthodox Christian distinction between creature and Creator results in the concept of the individual soul as its own space, distinct from the divine intelligible world and separated from other souls.

The new concept of inner privacy results from Augustine's departure from Plotinus on inner divinity. For Plotinus, the true inner self is located in the intelligible world of Platonic Forms. Therefore in turning "into the inside," toward the highest and truest and best part of itself, the soul is turning to the world of the divine Mind, which is not private property but common to all souls who contemplate it. The mature Augustine cannot follow him here. Once Augustine fully understands the Nicene Creator/creature distinction, he can no longer consider the best part of the soul to be divine or immutable. The soul has its own kind of being, distinct from the immutable being of God above and from the spatial being of bodies below it, and hence it belongs at a middle level on the ontological hierarchy, beneath the intelligible world and above the sensible world.

In fact, it is the soul's distinctive kind of mutability that defines its place in the mature Augustine's three-tiered ontological hierarchy:

> There is a nature mutable in space and time, namely body. And there is a nature which is *not at all mutable in space*, but only in time is it also mutable, namely soul. And there is a nature which cannot be changed in space or in time, and this is God.[2]

The emphatic claim that the soul is "not at all mutable in space" means that the mature Augustine retains the last positive thesis argued for in the Cassiciacum dialogues, which is that the soul is immovable.[3] Originally, however, Augustine clearly intended the soul's immovability (and the non-spatial mode of being which that presupposes) to imply its immutability, its freedom from change of any kind. Movement means, by definition, passing from place to place in space,[4] and therefore something that exists above and beyond the possibility of movement exists without being circumscribed by a particular place in space. So immovability implies non-spatiality. Immovability furthermore implies immutability if (as Augustine claims soon after Cassiciacum) "there can be no change [*mutatio*] without movement."[5]

Augustine's mature three-tiered ontology, on the contrary, clearly premises that there is a kind of change that is not a movement in space—and hence a kind of mutability that does not imply movability. This is precisely the soul's own distinctive kind of mutability. Not subject to movement in space like bodies, the soul is nonetheless changeable—fickle, we could say—in time. This fundamental premise of Augustine's three-tiered ontology marks his definitive rejection of the Cassiciacum project. Accepting the premise of the soul's mutability means abandoning the peculiar method of proving the soul's immortality that he was working on in the *Soliloquies*, which relied on demonstrating that the immutability of intelligible things "rubs off" on the soul in which they are inseparably present, so that the soul too is immutable. Henceforth Augustine's ontology is built around the central possibility opened up by the soul's mutability: the separation between God and us that is due not to distance in space but to the turning of the soul's own will, which "lives in misery when inclined toward what is below, but in happiness when turned toward what is highest."[6] The soul's placement at a middle level between God and bodies is precisely its opportunity to turn above to divine Truth and eternal blessedness, as well its possibility of Falling, turning its fickle attention downward to bodies and thus to ignorance and misery, separation from God.

The distinctive mutability of the soul, changeable in time but not in space, is thus the key concept Augustine uses to integrate a Plotinian doctrine of the Fall with the Catholic doctrine of Creation (where everything mutable is creature rather than Creator). In fact, Augustine will most often mark the distinction between God and the soul by using the concept of mutability rather than the Creator/creature distinction. This is especially true in his discussions of the inward turn. The "in then up" structure of Augustine's mature inward turn is always accompanied by the remark that the human mind is mutable (capable of changing from wisdom to ignorance and back again) and therefore must look *above* itself to see the immutable Truth.[7] This follows, as we can see, from the fact that it is precisely the concept of mutability that determines what is higher and lower in the three-tiered ontological hierarchy. The more mutable something is, the lower it is in the hierarchy. Hence turning from the mutable soul to the immutable Truth means looking *upward*. Precisely because the whole soul is mutable, with no higher and eternal part of the soul as in Plotinus, the mature Augustine's search for God requires the double movement, first *in* then *up*.

The Varieties of Dualism

It is the nature of the "downward" turn that concerns us now, however, for that is what establishes the distinctively Augustinian conception of the privacy of the inner self. If the soul's relationship with lower things was what it should be, there would be no inner privacy. Privacy of the inner self is not natural to it but is a result of the Fall and the unnatural opacity that fallen embodiment interposes between one soul and another. The unnaturalness of inner privacy is a conclusion that follows from fundamental principles of Augustine's ontology, above all from the notion that the soul is non-spatial. Non-spatial things cannot be separated by distance in space but only by evil will, fallen desires, and culpable ignorance. Without sin there could be no separation of souls and therefore no inner privacy.

The way this works can be clarified by a closer look at Augustine's Plotinian doctrine of the Fall and how it intersects with a Plotinian account of embodiment.[8] Here the first thing we must note is a crucial and rather ironic contrast. Plotinus's ontology, as Augustine gratefully recognized, is more successfully antimaterialist than that of the Manichaeans. This means it possesses the conceptual wherewithal to make a sharper, cleaner distinction between the soul's mode of being and the body's and for that very reason is not so captive to harsh resentment of the body as are cruder dualisms like Manichaeanism.[9] Precisely because the Plotinian soul is so far superior to the body that it has a totally different (i.e., non-spatial) mode of being, a Plotinian Platonist need not feel so dreadfully trapped in the body as a Manichaean, for whom the fallen soul was quite literally *located* within the dark, filthy matter of the body. Thus a Neoplatonist is free to consider the possibility that some kind of link with the body is natural to the soul and that this link is attributable to the goodness of the visible world rather than to the Fall. This is why Neoplatonism, unlike Manichaeanism, can be made consistent with orthodox Christian teaching about the goodness of our embodied state.

Of course there are some very dualistic strands in the Platonist tradition, going all the way back to the *Phaedo*, where the ultimate destiny of the good soul clearly involves permanent separation from the body, which is an evil.[10] But there are also strands that clearly imply that some kind of embodiment is natural to the soul. The most important of these is found in the *Timaeus*, where Plato lays it down as a fundamental principle of his physics that the soul has the function of animating bodies and giving them movement, thereby perfecting the order and beauty of the visible cosmos. That this function is natural and not degrading to the soul is shown by the World-Soul itself, the highest, purest, and best soul of all, whose unending function is to move the whole cosmos in its regular celestial cycles.[11]

Thus, whatever Plato may have said in the *Phaedo* and the *Phaedrus*, in the *Timaeus* the fact that souls are embodied (or at least connected to bodies causally) is not a result of any kind of evil. Hence the *Timaeus* could be used as a resource by Christian theologians expounding the doctrine of Creation. Unlike Gnostic, Manichaean, and Origenist views of the Fall, the teaching of the *Timaeus* was compatible with the orthodox view that the Creator had always intended souls to animate bodies and that therefore those animated human bodies that we ordinarily call "ourselves" resulted from the good of Creation rather than the evil of the Fall.

Plotinus is aware of the tension between the cosmology of the *Timaeus* and the dualistic strands of Plato's thought, and in his treatise on the Fall (or rather, as he calls it, "the descent of the soul into bodies") he takes up the task of reconciling them.[12] Hence to the extent that he inherits the legacy of the *Timaeus*, Plotinus can be enlisted on the side of orthodox Christian Platonism against Gnosticism and Origenism[13] in affirming that the material world is good and the presence of soul in it is not an evil. In contrast to the crude dualism of Manichaeanism where the soul is a divine light involuntarily trapped in a dark, filthy body, a Neoplatonist can say that the soul's evil predicament in this world is due to its own fault, not to the evil outside it in the realm of bodies. Thus by the time he wrote the *Confessions*, Augustine was finding exactly the opposite sort of lesson in Plotinus than he had earlier found in Manichaean dualism: in place of a good soul fallen willy-nilly into an evil world, there is a sinful soul fallen willfully out of harmony with God's good creation.[14] Augustine's carefully nuanced adoption of a Plotinian version of the Fall is thus a crucial element in his correction of his former Manichaean dualism. This of course involved favoring some Plotinian themes over others—for example, Plotinus's anti-Gnostic defense of the goodness of the cosmos over his condemnation of matter.[15] But one of the advantages of having Plotinus as a philosophical resource is that this is easy to do: Plotinus's thoughts are so rich and many-sided (not to mention possibly inconsistent) that one-sided appropriations of them can still be powerful and convincing.

Resurrection Avoided Then Accepted

One must suspect, however, that the dualist side of Plotinus was what had originally attracted Augustine to "the books of the Platonists." Plotinus can insist as vehemently as any Manichaean that matter is both evil in itself and the source of all other evils,[16] and like the Manichaeans he pictures evil as external, sullying the soul's native purity only on the outside, like dirt covering pure gold.[17] This dualist optimism about the soul converges with the fundamental attraction of Manichaeanism to Augustine, as Peter Brown paints it: "For Augustine, the need to save an untarnished oasis of perfection within himself formed, perhaps, the deepest strain of his adherence to the Manichees."[18] It took a long intellectual journey and some fundamental changes of mind to get Augustine from this Manichaean optimism to the pessimism about human sinfulness for which he is famous, based on a doctrine of original sin according to which the very soul is born corrupted and impure.[19]

At Cassiciacum those changes of mind were still in the future. He still sought an "untarnished oasis" of immutable goodness in the soul, to which evil is attached as something external, like dirt or the body. The human being is rational in soul and mortal in body, but its destiny is to move from the latter to the former: to abandon the mortality of the body and realize the divinity of the soul.[20] So the soul surmises in the conclusion of its soliloquy in *On Order*:

Therefore, if reason is immortal, and I who distinguish or connect all these things *am* Reason, then *that by which I am called mortal is not my own.* Or else, if the soul is not the same thing as Reason, and yet uses Reason, and through Reason I am better, then one must *flee from worse to better, from mortal to immortal.*[21]

The prehistory of Augustinian inwardness, as can be seen here, is not merely a turn from the body but a flight from it, leaving it behind as something alien. The road to immortality in this text clearly does not pass through Christian hope in the resurrection of the body but rather relies on familiar philosophical reasoning about the immortality of the soul.

Such reasoning, which implicitly rejects resurrection of the body in favor of the survival of the "pure" soul, is a commonplace of ancient philosophy that Augustine would have learned from Cicero[22] long before he encountered "the books of the Platonists." But his attraction to it would help explain why he found these books so exciting when he came upon them. We should not be surprised to find at Cassiciacum doctrines that Mani, Cicero, and Plotinus had in common, and a view of the afterlife that had no place for the body is one of them. Hence Augustine speaks of how the best part of the soul, its power or *virtus*,[23] "having thrown off the burden of the whole body, will return to heaven"[24] and of what happens "after this life . . . that is, when you cease to be human,"[25] which can only mean, when you cease to be a compound of soul and body. To leave body and mortality behind and become pure soul is to be purely immortal and divine, and this is the hope with which the Cassiciacum works close, looking forward to how things will be "after this body."[26]

Doubtless Augustine did not mean to reject Catholic doctrine on this point but rather failed to understand that the resurrection of the body is in fact Catholic doctrine. Hence the first time he indicates his acceptance of the resurrection of the body is when discussing the authority of the Church and the importance of accepting "the things we are commanded to believe."[27] But in terms of Augustine's intellectual development, the important thing to realize is that his appropriation of "the books of the Platonists" helped him come to this acceptance. For in the same treatise where he first indicates acceptance of the resurrection, Augustine also gives a specifically Platonist reason for affirming that embodiment is a good thing:

who could justly resent that the soul is given to activate and manage the body, since there could be no better way to connect so great and divine an order of things?[28]

This argument has the ring of the *Timaeus* and its doctrine of the World-Soul.[29] Another year or two later, at the height of his assimilation of Neoplatonist conceptuality, he speaks of the ultimate blessedness of the soul as causing a "perfect vivification of the body"—that is, improving the relation of soul and body rather than severing it.[30] And by the time he writes the *City of God*, Augustine can skillfully play off the heritage of the *Timaeus* against the dualist strand in Platonism to yield an argument for the conceivability, even on Platonist terms, of an afterlife of unending embodiment that conforms to the Christian hope of the resurrection of the body.[31]

The Neoplatonist fallen soul theory thus helped rather than hindered Augustine in his move toward Catholic orthodoxy, and in two ways: it helped him affirm the goodness of creation, and it helped him accept the doctrine of the resurrection of the body. For Neoplatonism, unlike Manichaeanism, can make a crucial distinction required by Christian orthodoxy: embodiment is not the same thing as fallenness. It is thus precisely as Augustine comes to be a better Neoplatonist that he comes to accept the Church's belief that embodiment does not begin in sin nor end in heaven.

Falling into Division

For Neoplatonism, embodiment is not necessarily evil—though on the other hand a proper Plotinian embodiment does involve a much looser coupling between soul and body than any modern thinker, Christian or otherwise, is likely to conceive of. Some kind of link with the body may be natural to the soul, but deep involvement with bodily things is not. Souls should rule over bodies effortlessly, with their attention turned to contemplation of eternal things rather than mired in the particular details and worries of this lower world. If all was well we would rule over our bodies as easily as the World-Soul rules over the visible world—without anxiety or lust, curiosity or frustration. The Fall (or as Plotinus more often puts it, "the descent of the soul") makes the difference between us and the World-Soul on this score.[32]

It also makes us individuals, which is not a good thing. We can see why this is so if we compare Plotinus's view of the Fall to its predecessors. First, there is the founding myth of the *Phaedrus*, where the soul is depicted as falling from heaven to earth—a Fall in the literal sense of a spatial movement from a high place to a lower place.[33] Plato certainly did not take his own myth literally, but there were plenty of crude versions of the Fall, such as in Manichaeanism, which involved a literal descent of the soul from heaven to earth. More sophisticated were those doctrines of the Fall that interpreted "higher" and "lower" as metaphors for states of being—the purity of the disembodied soul in contrast to its entrance into the body through lust and sin. At this level of sophistication "the Fall" means not a tumble from the sky but rather embodiment. The spatial character of the Fall is demythologized but not its temporal character: one still talks as if there was a time at the beginning of the world when souls were disembodied—even if that time is incongruously called "eternity." This type of Fall theory is represented by Origen and the more sophisticated forms of Gnosticism. All of them have as an unavoidable (and often explicitly welcomed) consequence the conclusion that the material world either would not exist or would not contain souls, if it were not for the Fall.

For Plotinus, on the contrary, the Fall is not a change in space or time, although it has many consequences in the spatio-temporal world. Precisely because the "descent of the soul" has its point of departure in the eternal, intelligible world, the picture of "descent" or movement or change of any kind cannot be taken literally. As Plotinus notes, Plato often speaks mythologically, presenting eternal realities as if they occurred in a temporal sequence, "setting forth a successive manifestation of things that are [in fact] *always* happening or being."[34] Thus the literal truth is not that the soul was once eternal and disembodied and is now trapped in bodies, but rather that the soul has its ontological origin in eternity. That origin is not lost in its past but is still fundamental to its nature. To speak metaphorically again, the soul remains fastened to its divine Center by its best and highest part, which is still "there" in the intelligible world. The "fall into embodiment" is a myth representing the lower and mutable part of the soul's turning toward perishable things, taking an inordinate interest in governing particular human bodies, being captivated by bodily needs, lusts, and perceptions.[35] The Fall is nothing other than this "outward turn," which is itself a metaphor for the sensual activity of "individual" souls.

Hence for Plotinus much of what we think of as essential to our individuality is a result of the Fall. What we nowadays would call "individual" souls are for Plotinus *divided* souls. Since all being stems from Unity, all division and separation (i.e., all lack of unity) involves a diminution of being, imperfection, lack, or defect. The Fall therefore means that the soul, which like each of the divine hypostases is inherently one, proceeds "outward," away from intelligible unity and into the realm of division and separation, that is, into the spatial world of bodies. This occurs as the lower part of the soul turns from contemplation to action, directing its attention away from the beatifying and unifying presence of the intelligible world to the fragmentary and diverse possibilities of movement among bodies. This means not that the soul itself begins to be spatial and movable, but rather that by its interest in the sensations of particular bodies it becomes emotionally attached, as it were, to what particular bodies are doing and suffering. Instead of sovreignly giving life to bodies by its superior power, the soul is torn by its involvement with diverse bodies and their diverse, often conflicting needs. Thus the result of the Fall is a plurality of souls divided by deep attachments to their own separate bodies. It is not the Fall that makes souls plural to begin with,[36] but the Fall does give each soul its particular history, thus accounting for much of what (for us moderns) must count as its individuality. The fact that souls are separate, divided, in conflict with one another—even, it would seem, the fact that they are separate centers of consciousness, each looking upon the material world from its own distinct standpoint—is not natural to them but a defect due to their excessive attachment to particular bodies.

Against the background of Plotinus's concentric picture of the universe (the One at the center, the divine Mind revolving around it, Soul surrounding the divine Mind and looking into the inside, and finally the material cosmos at the periphery, furthest out from intelligible unity) we can picture the Fall as a turn outward, away from the primal unity at the center of being and toward the separation of one body from another that characterizes the periphery, where death, decay, and destruction are possible. The tragedy of the fallen soul is that its desires and hopes are dispersed through this perpetually disintegrating realm rather than focused on the eternal and necessary coherence of the intelligible world. All the soul must do to overcome this dispersal and disintegration is turn back "into the inside," where there is no separation and division of bodies. That is why there is no private inner space in Plotinus. Since the only thing that divides souls is their attachment to diverse bodies, the turn away from the body leaves behind everything that separates, including separate consciousness and diverse experiences, feelings and desires. The Plotinian inward turn thus necessarily overcomes all separation of souls: there is no logical possibility of turning inward and finding a separate, much less a private space. It is as if the Soul were a single sphere with many faces on the surface: all one has to do is turn into the inside and look to the center, and one sees that there really is only one inner space of souls.[37]

Original and Final Unity

The inward turn cannot mean this for Augustine, at least not after he recognizes that there is no third category besides creature and Creator. The inner space of the soul cannot be identified with the uncreated intelligible world but must have its own creaturely kind of being distinct from that of the divine Mind and its contents. Therefore what the soul sees when it turns into itself is first of all an interior that is its own: a created rather than divine inner self. It is not necessarily a private inner self, however. For sin is not necessary—and a soul without sin, having no evil will to separate it from God, could not possibly be separated from other souls either. If there were no Fall, we might have bodies but we would not have inner privacy. On the contrary, an unfallen inner space would necessarily belong to an inner community—an unclouded version of that fellowship which Augustine later calls "the invisible Church." This is a consequence, as we have seen, of Augustine's view that the only thing that can separate non-spatial things is evil will. The dividedness of our souls has the same root as our separation from God: lust, greed, ambition, and pride.[38] The dissension of that wills that divides the Earthly City, the diverse and competing desires, the conflict of souls each seeking its own private good, stands in contrast to the undivided unity of souls who live, free of sin and its punishment, in the original paradise or the ultimate blessedness.

Since the mature Augustine has no immutable part of the soul to anchor the fallen soul in eternity,[39] the unfallen state of the soul must be an occurrence in time—more precisely, at the beginning and the end of time, that is, when all souls were one in Adam (or, as Augustine occasionally says, when we all *were* that one man)[40] and when souls in the Heavenly City are united in the mutual consent of charity, seeing clearly into each other, no thoughts hidden by the opacity of fallen bodies.[41] Bodies indeed we shall have in the end, but they shall be heavenly and spiritual rather than fallen and mortal, so that "in the transparency and simplicity of heavenly bodies I do not think any motion of the mind shall be at all hidden."[42] The privacy of the inner self is thus a temporary phenomenon, not a necessary feature of the inner self but strictly a consequence of the Fall, a result of the ignorance and discord that divides soul from soul in our present state of sin and punishment. The opacity of our fallen bodies is a *result* of this fundamental division of souls rather than a *cause* of it; hence when souls are fully blessed, no longer divided by conflicting, evil wills, bodies also will no longer serve to divide one soul from another, and the inner world will not be private. Our inmost selves will be open to each other's gaze, as they were always meant to be.

Locke's Dark Room

The private inner self was born in sin. Augustine does not think this privacy is natural, much less a part of human dignity, and he can speak about it in tones of deep pathos. What a great evil it is that in this life we do not know what is in the hearts of our friends and neighbors![43] And how appalling that infants are born in such an immense darkness of ignorance, so contrary to the very nature of the rational soul! Surely this is a penalty of original sin, not the way God intended things to be.[44]

One of the most moving passages in the *Confessions* dwells on this theme, in connection with Augustine's own infancy. No sooner is Augustine done talking about mother's milk than he begins to describe the predicament of the child who does not yet have language to express himself.

> And behold, little by little I sensed where I was, and I wanted to show my wants to those who could fulfill them, and I couldn't, for those were within and these without, and they possessed no sense which would enable them to enter into my soul.[45]

Here is born a deep aspiration of Western thought: to be known is to have someone else sense your inner thoughts or read your mind, and to know other persons in the deepest sense is to enter into their souls—to violate privacy and penetrate the inner space of the self. Failing that, and lacking even the stopgap remedy of language, the infant lives in a profound inner isolation, locked up inside himself even when he is at his mother's breast.

One of the consequences of the Western secularization of reason is that the privacy of the inner self comes to be seen not as a tragedy attendant upon the Fall but as something essential and inevitable, as if it were the very nature of the human mind to be an inner room that no one else can enter. This concept of mind may have originated with John Locke late in the seventeenth century,[46] and in any case no one has ever painted it more vividly. Locke pictures the mind as a peculiar kind of dark room, which the Italians called *camera oscura*—the word from which we get our "camera." The room was in fact very much like a giant camera, windowless except for a small aperture in one wall that held a lens. Light passed through the lens and was focused on the opposite wall so that images of the outside world were projected on it, just as a modern camera lens projects images from outside onto the film in the back of the camera. In the *camera oscura*, however, there was no film, simply an image projected on the back wall as on a movie screen, so that someone inside the room could view it. And this, says Locke, is what the human mind is like, having no opening to the outside world but the senses:

> These alone, as far as I can discover, are the windows by which light is let into this *dark room*. For, methinks, the Understanding is not much unlike a closet wholly shut from light, with only some little openings left, to let in external visible resemblances or ideas of things without; would the pictures coming into such a dark room but stay there, and lie so orderly as to be found upon occasion, it would very much resemble the Understanding of man, in reference to all objects of sight and the ideas of them.[47]

Not only is each of us locked in our own separate little closet for as long as we live, but we don't even get to look out the window! We never actually see the world outside, but only its image projected on the inner wall of our private dark room. Hence all we are really certain of is what is inside our own minds. This thought has haunted a good deal of modern philosophy, especially in English-speaking countries.

It is important to see how this descendant of Augustine's private inner self differs from its ancestor. The inner space Augustine describes is not a little closet wholly shut from light, but broad halls and fields and vast courtyards.[48] We could in fact picture it as the inner courtyard of a great palace, for the crucial thing about it is that it has no roof: it is open to the light of the Sun above. In fact, it is the only place to go to see the Sun shining clearly. Outside, it is overcast at best, and one could wander long in the darkness. For unlike Locke, Augustine thinks it is easy enough to leave the inner space of the self. All you have to do is sin, as Augustine confesses:

> Behold, You were inside and I was outside, and there [i.e., among external things] I sought You, rushing about malformed among the well-formed things You have made. You were with me—but I was not with You. These things kept me far from You. . . .[49]

The result of all this rushing about, seeking the true Light and Beauty outside the self, is that "the Light of my eyes was not with me; for it was inside, but I was outside."[50]

By contrast, one would never think of finding God inside Locke's dark room, and that is by design. For a prime purpose of Locke's philosophy is to require conflicting religious claims to be adjudicated by reason alone,[51] ruling out any appeal to an inner light of divine illumination, such as was made by the religious radicals whom Locke and other members of the establishment called "enthusiasts." Locke did not deny that God could by special miracle bypass the little windows of the senses and inwardly illuminate the mind, as apparently happened with the biblical prophets long ago. But even a prophet has the responsibility to judge the ideas in his mind by sober reason, regardless of how they got there.[52] The result is a picture of the mind that is decidedly secular and modern. The notion of reason as a faculty of divine inner vision is obviously far from Locke's mind, and indeed a large part of his purpose is to make the very notion of divine inner vision seem irrational, even crazy. But in the process of putting the roof, as it were, on the inner space of the self, he also cuts it off from the outside world and other selves in a way that resonates profoundly with the pride and anxieties of modern individualism.

Locke's is of course not the only version of the inner self found in modernity. On the contrary, once the concept of a private inner space is available—and of course anything in Augustine's *Confessions* is widely available in Western thought—it can be put to a great many diverse, even contradictory uses. Moreover, old uses can be rediscovered. It is always possible to propose restoring to human reason the Platonist function of intellectual vision (or "intellectual intuition," as it was called by idealists after Kant). This would amount to a rediscovery of a more Augustinian view of the self, as was attempted by Roman Catholic "ontologists." Or if the starting point is already an Augustinian rather than a Lockean inner self (as in post-Kantian idealism or Protestant liberalism) then it is always possible to dig deep down, as it were, beneath the church of Augustinian inwardness and uncover the ruins of the ancient Plotinian temple buried under its foundation. This would amount to the "discovery" that the inner self is not merely the place to see God, but is in its highest or deepest part identical with God, as in Emerson or in today's "Protestant gnostics."[53] Hence all three versions of the inner self remain live options in modernity: the original, divine inner self of Plotinus and the modern, secular inner self of Locke, as well as the specifically Augustinian inner self occupying a conceptual middle ground: neither divine nor secularized, but the place to look to find a divinity that is other than the self.

10

The Origin of Inner Space

In this chapter we look at how Augustine constructed his distinctive concept of inner space. This construction takes place in his treatment of memory in Confessions, *book 10. Materials for the construction of this new concept come from three sources. First is the ancient rhetorical tradition with its arts of memory and invention, or "finding." Second is Cicero's* Tusculan Disputations, *book 1, which discusses the difficulty of finding the soul's place in the world and examines its powers of memory and invention as clues to its nature. Third is Augustine's own treatise* On the Quantity of the Soul, *containing a Neoplatonist elaboration of Platonist themes in Cicero's work. Precisely in emphasizing the non-spatiality of the soul, this treatise conceives of the soul as an alternative dimension, a "space" of its own. The same "space" becomes the inner world of memory in* Confessions *10, a place where God can be both hidden and present, sought and found within the human self.*

Memory as Inner World

In the previous two chapters we have seen that Augustine's mature brand of inwardness requires a conception of the human soul as a place in which to find God, that is neverthless not the same as God and therefore can be separated and cut off from him. Augustine needs to conceive the fallen soul as an inner space that is private—quite a different kind of place from the intelligible world, which is the inner self of the Plotinian soul. Hence in this chapter we must see how Augustine actually goes about conceiving or constructing this new kind of inner space. For of course it is not literally a space[1] and therefore it takes some special work to conceive of it. The crucial conceptual question about it is: in what sense of the word "in" are things present *in* it? Especially urgent for Augustine, of course, is the more specific question: in what sense can *God* be found in it?

We have seen that Augustine's initial answer to this question was conceptually inept and doomed to failure. No competent Platonist can believe that divine things are in the soul as an essential property is in a subject, for that reverses the proper order of ontological dependence.[2] The specifically Plotinian conception of inwardness is also off limits, however, for in making the rational soul identical with the divine things it contemplates (and thus in effect identifying the inner self with the mind of God) Plotinus violates the Creator/creature distinction required by Nicene orthodoxy. Consequently the mature Augustine locates God not only *within* the soul but also *above* it—and this means that the inner space of the soul must be roomy enough not only to enter but also to turn around in and look up. Moreover, according to the doctrine of the Fall Augustine develops after Cassiciacum, there can indeed be a separation between God and the soul, and this means that the soul's inner space can be in a profound and terrifying way its very own: private, isolated from other souls, and closed off even from the light of Truth. Some account must therefore be given of how it is possible to enter the inner self and *not* see God.

Here is that account, from the tenth book of the *Confessions*:

> A great power is that of memory, something awesome, my God, a deep and infinite multiplicity. And this is what the mind is, and this is what I myself am. What then am I, my God—of what nature am I? A variegated and multifaceted life, and utterly immeasurable. Behold in my memory the fields and caves and caverns innumerable, and innumerably full of innumerable kinds of things. . . . I scamper and flit through them all, and poke this way and that as far as I am [*quantum sum*] and there is no end of it—so great is the power of memory, so great the power of life in a human being living mortally![3]

Memory is literally a great power (*vis*) but pictorially a vast inner space, containing literally an infinite number of things. This power is what we *are*, at least in this mortal life—and this tells us something essential about what kind of life the fallen soul is and has. There is no end of its extent—not that it is spatially extended, but rather that it has the power to hold infinitely many things. It is an inner world, mirroring the innumerable variety of things in the external world.

The sense in which things are "in" the soul is therefore the sense in which they are *in* our remembrance. The inner space of the soul is primarily to be identified with the vast inner world called memory. This is a world specifically human, even mortal—animated by the mortal life of a fallen soul, not the divine life of immutable Truth. Yet this mortal space is also the first stop on the journey to God, and when God is eventually found, it is *here*—for this is where he was all along: "Late have I loved You, O Beauty so ancient and so new, late have I loved You! And behold, You were inside and I was outside. . . ."[4] Memory contains much that is merely human, temporal, and sensible; but as any Platonist would expect, it also has room for something greater—for eternal things, whose beauty is older and fresher and closer to the soul than anything external. It is in memory, then, that God is present in the fallen soul—not inseparably, but with the peculiar possibilities of separation that belong to memory: a truth forgotten yet not altogether unknown, and sought with sighs and regrets and inward searching. Memory is the perfect concept to articulate the inward presence of what we do not presently have: something intimately familiar but lost and longed for, making its presence felt precisely in its absence—like knowledge we have forgotten but hope to recall.

The lengthy discussion of memory in *Confessions* 10 focuses on the key question: in what way are various things "in" memory? When we remember sensible things, for example, it is not the things themselves but images of them that are present within us.[5] But with our memory of intelligible truths, such as are acquired by the liberal arts (*omnia quae de doctrinis liberalibus percepta*), including literature and dialectic (*peritia disputandi*), it is different: here it is the things themselves, not their images, that are present in memory.[6] The reasons (*rationes*) of numbers and measurements are likewise present themselves in memory, not merely represented there.[7] It is thus no surprise that Augustine finds God in memory as well:

> see how far I have traveled [*quantum spatiatus sum*] in my memory seeking you, Lord, and I have not found you outside it. For I have not found out anything about you which I did not remember from the point at which [*ex quo*] I learned of you. And from the point at which I learned of you, I have not forgotten you. For where I have found truth, there I have found my God, who is Truth itself, which I have not forgotten from the point at which I learned.[8]

In some ways this solution to Augustine's conceptual problem seems obvious: we find God in the soul the way we find the truths we have learned—even eternal Truth—in the memory. But it is not at all so obvious as it first appears. No writer known to me before Augustine talks of finding things in memory the way he does—as if memory were a three-dimensional space ample enough for us to enter and look for things within it. To conceive of memory as an inner space of the self is something new, one of the many innovations that are part of the specifically Augustinian legacy to the West. But of course Augustine did not create this concept out of nothing. Quite definite conceptual materials lay ready to hand for the construction of this new inner space, materials that were a familiar part of his education from long before his encounter with Neoplatonism. Indeed, they were not specifically philosophical concepts at all but belonged to the tools of his trade as a rhetorician.

Places in Memory

The conceptual connection between memory and space is very ancient. Ever since the Greek Sophists, orators had been using places as an aid to memory.[9] In preparing for a speech, they would memorize the order of subjects to be discussed, by imagining themselves walking through the rooms and alcoves of a familiar house in a definite order, and mentally "marking" each place with some image to serve as a reminder of the next topic of discussion.[10] As they delivered their speech, they would imagine themselves walking past those places again, and each image would remind them of what needed to be said next. Of course the images would change from speech to speech, as the subject matter changed. But the places and their order would remain fixed, being frequently rehearsed so as to keep them fresh in memory.

The rhetoricians compared these places to a wax writing-tablet and the images to the letters written on it. The images could be forgotten like letters erased from the tablet, but the places themselves remained in memory like a tablet ready to receive new writing. All three Latin sources on the ancient art of memory use this metaphor of writing on a wax tablet.[11] It is quite a different picture from Augustine's: instead of vast inner courts and fields, they pictured the places in memory as something you wrote things down on. Thus for the classical rhetoricians recollection was not like entering a three-dimensional space but like reading what is written on a two-dimensional surface. Of course the "places" they memorized were three-dimensional, but these were quite literally *places* in the physical world, not spaces within the mind. The ancient rhetoricians talked about these places in the same way we ordinarily talk about external objects, for that was what they were.

The fact that rhetorical "places" were not within the mind is strikingly illustrated by the rules the textbooks give for choosing apt places to memorize. The best kind of places for a rhetorician's purposes, according to one textbook, are well lit and not monotonously similar (i.e., not like the spaces between a row of columns). They should also be well spaced, about thirty feet apart, and the reason given for this is quite interesting: "for like vision, thought too is less successful when you move what needs to be seen too far away or up too close."[12] The Loeb edition of this text uses the phrase "inner eye" to translate the word "thought" (*cogitatio*) here. Evidently the translator, unlike the author, wants to picture our imagining or remembering as an inner act of looking at things in an inner space. And indeed, anyone who lives and thinks after Augustine is likely to find the suggestion of an inner vision in this text irresistible. Yet it is very significantly *not* irresistible for this anonymous ancient rhetorician, writing at about the same time as Cicero. If he had any inkling that memory was an inner space in which we saw things, he could have said so here, as his translator does. Instead, he draws a straightforward contrast between *aspectus* and *cogitatio*, that is, between literally seeing the places and thinking about them when they are no longer present. Neither of these is an act that he locates in a private inner space. This provides us with as nice a piece of evidence as we could wish for the contention that before Augustine, the people who had the most reason to think of memory as a kind of inner "place," the rhetoricians, did not in fact do so.[13] For them, recollection did not mean looking for something in the self's inner space but simply thinking about things that were no longer present.

So in the rhetorical tradition Augustine had materials for conceiving of memory as consisting of inner places, but the actual conception of the soul and its memory as an inner space was his own invention. One of the obstacles in the way of such a conception was that people in the pre-Augustinian era of Western culture did not find it at all obvious that the self, along with its acts of knowing and remembering, should be conceived as a kind of inner eye looking at an inner object in an inner space. The fact that this conception was by no means obvious to anyone before Augustine is indeed one of the most important lessons of this investigation.

But the novelty of the conception was not the only obstacle. The most widely accepted ancient theory of memory contrasts quite sharply with Augustine's picture. We have encountered it already in the metaphor of the wax tablet. Aristotle had suggested (evidently as an alternative to Plato's doctrine of Recollection) that we could conceive of the retentiveness of memory as something like the retentiveness of wax preserving the imprint of things impressed on it.[14] The empirically minded philosophers of the Hellenistic era adopted this metaphor, and it became a cornerstone of their epistemology. Augustine on the contrary needs a conception of memory that will support the claim that not only the imprint of sensible things but also the reality of intelligible things (the *res ipsae* of the intelligible world) are found within the mind. The metaphor of stamping impressions on wax, which had dominated both philosophy and rhetoric since Aristotle, must go.

The Art of Finding

One other element in the ancient rhetorical tradition also needs to be mentioned. The notion of "places" played a role not only in the rhetoricians' techniques of artificial memory, but also in the art of finding good arguments to use in a speech, which was called discovery or "invention" (*inventio*). The word translates the Greek *heurēsis*, which means literally "finding."[15] In Latin textbooks, "invention" was one of the five parts into which the art of rhetoric was divided, and memory was another.[16] "Places" in this sense (i.e., as part of the art of "invention" rather than of memory) also go back to the Sophists.[17] But the earliest documents we have extant on this point are Aristotelian. As an aid to finding good arguments, Aristotle listed some typical lines of reasoning, which he called "places," or *topoi*—from which we get our word "topic."[18] Because they could be applied to many different kinds of situations about which an orator might need to speak, these "places" came to be called *common* places, whence our "commonplace."[19]

The fullest explanation of how the notion of "places" came to be discussed under the heading of "invention" is Cicero's:

> Just as finding [*inventio*] things that are hidden is easy if the place is shown and noted, so also when we want to track down some line of argument, we ought to know the "places" [*locos*]—for so they were called by Aristotle, as being like the locations [*sedes*] from which lines of argument were drawn.[20]

A topic or *locus* in the art of "invention" is thus *a place to look* for what you want to find. Hence the rhetorical language of "invention" provides a natural vocabulary for Augustine's inward turn, whose basic premise is that the soul is the place we should look to find God. Augustine suggests something of the sort in his treatise *On the Trinity*, at the point where he has discovered that the place to look for analogies of the Trinity is in the soul, but he is just beginning his inquiry and there is much more to look for and find: "one usually finds the place [*locus*] where something is to be sought while it is not yet found—but one has already found *where* it is sought."[21] The first step in any inquiry is to find the place to look, and if what you want to find is God, the place to look is the soul.

"Places" are thus included not only in the art of memory, but in the art of finding or "invention," where they serve as the treasuries (*thesauri*) from which arguments are drawn.[22] The two arts, memory and invention, are distinct but not unrelated. For memory too is a treasury, a place to keep things that have been found (*thesaurus inventorum*).[23] Memory is indeed a treasury of all things (*thesaurus rerum omnium*), as it is "the keeper of words and subject matter which have been found and thought."[24] The metaphor of memory and "places" as treasuries or *thesauri* furnishes the most three-dimensional picture of memory in the classical tradition, although there is no hint that the self might somehow enter into such a treasury.[25]

Augustine indicates the relation between memory and invention at the very beginning of the *Soliloquies* when he points to memory as that which preserves what he hopes to find (*invenisse*) in the inquiry he is about to begin.[26] The verb "to find" (*invenire*) in fact plays a very prominent role in Augustine's early philosophical work, where his program of *finding* Truth and Wisdom is supported by the biblical maxim "Seek and ye shall find."[27] The verb "Seek" (*quaerere*) has strong overtones of "inquire"; hence the burning question of *On the Happy Life* and especially the first book of *Against the Academics* is whether the skeptic, whose whole life consists in inquiring after wisdom rather than possessing it—seeking truth rather than finding it—can be called happy. Thus Augustine's earliest philosophical inquiry, which is both epistemic (seeking truth) and ethical (seeking happiness), can be formulated in terms borrowed at once from the New Testament and the classical tradition of rhetorical instruction. Like orators who need to *find* arguments by looking in the right "places," Augustine is seeking to find the intelligible Truth and needs to know where to look. Hence the talk of "common places" that is central to the rhetoricians' art of "finding," together with the talk of "places" in the rhetoricians' art of memory, may have provided some linguistic if not conceptual materials for Augustine to use in formulating the concept of the soul as a "place" in which to find God. The two distinct arts of "find-ing" and of memory seem to have fused in Augustine's notion of *finding* the intelligible Truth within *memory*. The talk of "places" that these two arts have in common evidently served as a catalyst in this process of fusion, which expanded to include biblical notions of seeking and finding and philosophical notions of inquiry and discovery, prompting Augus-tine to think of memory as a place where the intelligible things that the lover of Wisdom seeks can be found.

That such a fusion actually underlies Augustine's new conception of the inner self seems more likely when we look at how Cicero himself put the notions of "invention" and memory to work philosophically, in his own version of the Platonist turn to the soul. For it turns out that in the *Tusculan Disputations* Cicero had a fair amount to say about the non-spatiality of the soul, which helped Augustine conceive the soul's own inner dimension as an alternative to external space.

The Location of the Soul

As we have already seen, Augustine's concept of the soul's non-spatial mode of being is closely related to the Plotinian concept of divine omnipresence, and Augustine's inward turn involves using the first as a clue to the second.[28] That the soul's (non-spatial and in-corporeal) mode of being is the clue to God's (non-spatial and incorporeal) mode of being is clear not only in *Confessions* 7 but also in Augustine's treatise on the Incarnation.[29] For the key question in this treatise is a variant of the question at the beginning of *Confessions* 7, about how to "locate" God. Augustine is faced with the problem that the Incarnation seems to mean that the eternal Son of God must abandon his reign in heaven and be con-fined to a body on earth.[30] Augustine's solution is premised on the Plotinian concept of omnipresence: being present as a whole everywhere, God is never tied down to a particu-lar spatial location and therefore never literally *moves* from place to place. Consequently, the Incarnation does not mean that God the Son literally descends from heaven to earth or is confined within the spatial limits of a human body. This solution, of course, requires us first and foremost to grasp the concept of integral omnipresence, according to which the divine nature is present everywhere as a whole, *totus ubique*, thus precluding any move-ment in space.[31]

This is no easy concept to grasp, especially for the carnally minded soul accustomed to thinking only about sensible things and their corporeal mode of presence in space. That is precisely why, Augustine argues (taking up the central theme of the inward turn in *Con-fessions* 7), the mind must learn to look at itself:

> The human mind [*mens*] is astonished at this [integral omnipresence], and since it cannot grasp [*capit*] it, perhaps does not believe it. But *let it for once be astonished at its own as-tonishing self*; let it take itself away from the senses a little bit, if it can, and from those things which it is used to perceiving by the body, and let it see what that very thing is which uses the body. But perhaps it cannot; for *"it takes great ability,"* as someone has said, *"to call the mind back from the senses and draw thought away from habit."*[32]

The talk of our astonishing self echoes the amazement Augustine expresses at the vastness of the inner space of memory in Confessions 10.[33] The "someone" mentioned here is Cicero, and the quote is the motto from the *Tusculan Disputations* that we previously found in *Confessions* 7.[34]

Like book 10 of the *Confessions*, book 1 of the *Tusculan Disputations* offers its readers a grand poetic overview of the visible world and asks us to consider its divine origin, arguing that although we cannot locate God in these things, they are still evidence of his existence.[35] Yet Cicero, like Augustine, thinks the soul finds the primary clue to the nature of God not by observing the world around it but by understanding itself. Unlike Augustine, however, Cicero has no inkling that the soul might be able to turn and look directly into its own self. Rather, the soul is like the eye, which can see everything but its own self.[36] Hence Cicero knows nothing of introspection, a looking within, but knows only of reflection— seeing the soul, as it were, reflected in things outside it.

In this respect, too, the soul is like God: it is known only indirectly, by examining its works and drawing inferences about the divine power that produced them.[37] Direct vision is impossible, because neither God nor the soul have a form to see, and there is literally no place to look for them:

> As you know God even though you do not know his location and appearance, so also your own soul ought to be known to you, even if you don't know its location and form.[38]

Here Cicero is taking account of the lively ancient debates about the soul's "seat" in the body: is it located in the head, the heart, the blood? Aristotle had answered that the soul is present as whole everywhere in the body[39]—an answer that made a major contribution to Plotinus's conception of intellible things being present everywhere as a whole in the sensible world. For it is natural for a Platonist to extend Aristotle's view to Plato's World-Soul, which would mean that the World-Soul is present as a whole everywhere in the material cosmos, its body.[40] It follows a fortiori that the divine Mind and the One are also present everywhere as a whole, since their being is even less qualified by relation to spatial things than the soul's.

That even the soul is in a way integrally omnipresent by virtue of its non-spatial mode of being is an implication that Augustine apparently understood and accepted. For immediately after quoting Cicero he insists on this implication, as part of his attempt to help his reader grasp the notion of the integral omnipresence of God. If, as Cicero says, it is hard to turn the mind away from the senses, then Augustine (ever the teacher concerned with leading his pupils step by step) proposes that we look first at the senses themselves. Rehearsing an argument that he had developed years earlier in *On the Quantity of the Soul*, he argues that the facts of sense perception show the soul is present outside the body. We see and hear things beyond the limits of our bodies, which shows (Augustine claims) that "we live outside our flesh."[41] This claim is designed to make it easier to see how the divinity of Christ is not confined within the bounds of his flesh.[42]

In the more detailed discussion in *On the Quantity of the Soul*, Augustine argues for this claim in terms that make his debt to Neoplatonism unmistakably clear. It is evident, says Augustine, that "there is no place in which the soul is contained."[43] For if the soul were confined to the body, Augustine argues, then it would be impossible to explain how the eye can see things far away. To perceive things at a distance or be aware of things that are absent is plainly impossible to mere bodies, unless they are blended, as it were, with the soul. Augustine's dialogue partner at this point expresses great confusion: doesn't this entail that our souls are not in our bodies? "If so, then am I not ignorant of where I am?"[44] Augustine does not answer the question but rather tries to reassure his friend by drawing a familiar (Ciceronian) moral: "This thought and consideration summons us to ourselves and plucks us away from the body as much as possible."[45] The unfamiliar (Plotinian) view that the soul is not literally *in* the body is then attributed to "certain very learned men."[46]

Obviously Cicero did not have in mind so sophisticated, not to say astonishing, a thesis about the "location" of the soul as Augustine develops under the aegis of Neoplatonism. But surprising things can happen when philosophers get really serious about calling the soul away from the senses of the body—something that Plotinus and Augustine were a great deal more serious about than Cicero. As we have seen, when the Neoplatonist conceptuality required to make sense of the inward turn is fully developed, one can no longer place the soul literally "in" the body or the Truth literally "in" the soul.[47] Where then, is the soul looking when it looks away from external things? It is of course exercising an altogether different kind of vision, which can be understood only by the mind because it is itself the vision of the mind alone. The "place" where it looks is thus not a location in space. Yet, in an irony that is not really so surprising in hindsight, once Augustine has thoroughly uprooted any traces of materialist attempts to locate the soul literally in space, he feels free to speak of the soul as a location unto itself, a non-spatial dimension—an inner space.

Powers of the Soul

Despite the fact that Cicero has no conception of an inner space for the soul to look into, his suggestions about how the soul is to gain knowledge of itself were something Augustine could use. If we want to understand the nature of the soul, Cicero suggests, we must look at its cognitive powers—just as Augustine does in the inward turn, ascending from sense-perception to the "interior sense" and finally to the mind.[48] Like Augustine, Cicero thinks of the powers of the soul hierarchically, ranking them higher if they are something we have in common with the gods, lower if they are shared with the beasts. Sense-perception, of couse, is not a good clue to the soul's divinity and immortality, because it is something the beasts also have. So he sets out to look for evidence of some divine power in us, which cannot be found in beasts and bodies.

Interestingly, Cicero does not make the usual move of pointing to the faculty of reason, but rather dwells on a pair of abilities that received systematic treatment by rhetoricians rather than philosophers: memory and invention.[49] We can see the divinity of the soul reflected in the works of these two powers, Cicero argues, just as we can see God in the works of nature.

> So it is with the mind [*mentem*] of the human being, although you do not see it, just as you do not see God—nonetheless, just as you recognize God from his works, so from the *memory and discovery* [*inventio*] of things and its quickness of movement and all the beauty of virtue you must recognize *the divine power of the mind*.[50]

Cicero describes these two powers in terms drawn from the rhetorical tradition,[51] but in his exposition he aims to give them weighty philosophical content. The memory he speaks of, for instance, is specifically the Platonic recollection of Ideas (else it would be something beasts also are capable of), and the discovery he mentions too is specifically human and is bound up with human culture. In fact it is to the power of invention that we owe human culture, Cicero says, beginning with the imposition of names upon things (the invention of language) and continuing with the gathering of human beings in cities (the invention of society), and then the assigning of letters to sounds (the invention of writing).[52] Cicero briefly reviews a whole parade of the arts of civilization, first the necessary and utilitarian ones like agriculture and house-building and then the arts that civilized people pursue in their leisure, including astronomy, poetry, rhetoric, and finally philosophy, "the mother of all the arts," which Plato calls the gift, Cicero the discovery (*inventum*) of the gods.[53]

Thus at the culmination of the arts we find the one true founder of human civilization; her name is Philosophy. Later in the *Tusculan Disputations* Cicero delivers himself of an apostrophe to Philosophy, in which he says that it was she who first brought human beings together in society and joined them by the bonds of speech and writing.[54] This later passage evidently impressed Augustine, for its imagery turns up in the Cassiciacum dialogues, where he speaks, like Cicero, of the "bosum" and "harbor" of philosophy.[55] More important, the picture of Philosophy founding or inventing language (thereby making human society possible) and subsequently inventing writing and then the arts seems to be the direct predecessor of Augustine's account of the origin of the liberal arts in *On Order*.[56] Simply change the name from Philosophy to Reason, and you have a resumé of Augustine's picturesque narrative of Reason inventing the liberal arts, beginning with language, society, and writing. In Augustine's narrative, too, philosophy appears at the culmination of the procession of arts and signals our discovery of what is at the bottom of them—for in Augustine's curriculum, as we have seen, what the soul studies in her philosophy lessons is precisely the nature of her own Reason.

Memory too is closely bound up with the liberal arts—though not so much with their origin as with our ability to learn them. For all such learning, Cicero explains, is recollection. And that tells us a great deal about the power of the soul:

> The soul has memory, which is infinite, of innumerable things. Plato in fact thinks it is a recollection of a previous life. For in the book titled *Meno*, Socrates asks a boy some questions in geometry about the measurements of a square. He answered just like a boy, and yet the questions were so easy that by answering step by step [*gradatim respondens*] he arrived at the same point as if he had learned geometry. From this Socrates drew the conclusion that learning is nothing other than recollection.[57]

This passage is clearly an important one for Augustine. His own descriptions of his early program of education frequently echo it, connecting learning with recollection and both with the method of question and answer, by which we are to rise "step by step" from sensible things to intelligible things.[58] Hence Socratic inquiry, such as Augustine attempts to represent in his philosophical dialogues, leads ultimately beyond Socratic perplexity to knowledge of ideas, made possible by Recollection. For "the soul could not get to know them once it was shut up in the body; it brings them known,"[59] which is to say, as Augustine in effect glosses this Ciceronian passage, "the soul brings all the arts with it" when it is born.[60]

Such recollection requires a different conception of memory than was current in the Hellenistic philosophy of Cicero's day. The metaphor of sense impressions stamped upon memory as upon on wax had provided an empiricist alternative to Platonic recollection ever since Aristotle, but here in the *Tusculan Disputations*, Cicero rejects it in order to go back to Plato. In conformity with his general line of argument, he must show that memory is a power greater than sense, one that the lower elements are incapable of. He does so in a passage that left numerous traces in Augustine's discussions of the non-spatiality of the soul:

> What this power is [*quae sit illa vis*] and whence it comes [*unde sit*] I think can be understood [*intelligendum*]. It is certainly not from the heart or blood or brain, nor out of atoms. . . . I ask you, does it really seem to you that so great a power [*vis*] as memory could be compounded or congealed from earth and its dark, cloudy sky? If you cannot see what it is [*quid sit*], then see what sort of thing it is [*quale sit*]. If not even that, then at least see how great a thing it is [*quanta sit*]. Come now, do we think there is some sort of capaciousness [*capacitas*] in the soul, as if it were a jug into which the things we remember are poured? Surely that's absurd. What sort of bottom [*fundus*] and what shape could the soul be understood to have, and how in the world did it get so much capaciousness? Or *do we suppose the soul to be imprinted like wax*, and memory to be the traces of things impressed on the mind? How could there be traces of words and of the things themselves, and what's more, how could there be such immeasurable size [*tam immensa magnitudo*] which could model so many of them?[61]

Much of this language is echoed in Augustine's treatment of memory in *On the Quantity of the Soul* and *Confessions* 10.[62] One can see why: Cicero is detaching memory from the senses by denying empiricist and materialist accounts of it, and in the process he denies that we can think of it as spatial—as if its capaciousness were like a jug with a bottom.

Yet precisely in denying that the soul has any size in the literal sense, he insists on its greatness in other respects. Memory is literally "infinite" because it contains "innumerable things."[63] The immense capacity of our memory provides an answer to Cicero's "how much" (*quanta sit*) question, which in turn helps answer his "what sort" (*quale sit*) question. This is important, because it narrows the range of possible answers to the all-important "what" (*quid sit*) question, the question about the very nature of the soul, to which Cicero admits he cannot give a sure answer—perhaps it is fire, perhaps breath, but in any case it is divine.[64]

The Size of the Soul

Cicero's treatment of memory is designed to help answer a whole series of questions about the soul and its powers: where does it come from (*unde sit*), what sort of thing is it (*qualis sit*), and what is its size (*quanta sit*)? These are precisely the questions Augustine sets out to answer in the oddly titled work *On the Quantity of the Soul* (*De Quantitate Animae*),[65] written shortly after the treatise *On the Morals of the Catholic Church* and containing his second repudiation of the faulty line of reasoning that was central to the Cassiciacum project. It is in this treatise that Augustine first gets his ontology of the soul right (or at least so he seems to think, judging by how frequently he has recourse to the ideas developed in it). Although the treatise does not itself contain a statement of the inward turn, many of Augustine's later versions of the inward turn draw on its discussions of sense, memory, and the non-spatiality of the soul.[66] Thus it is a matter of some importance for us that the inquiry it launches is formulated in terms of Cicero's questions.

The questions are put in the mouth of Evodius, Augustine's conversation partner, an old friend who is also a former Manichaean trying to overcome his materialist habits of mind. He asks: 1) whence is the soul (*unde sit anima*)? 2) what sort of thing is it (*qualis sit*)? 3) how big is it (*quanta sit*)? 4) why was it given to the body (*cur corpori fuerit data*)? 5) when it came to the body what sort of thing did it become (*cum ad corporem venerit qualis efficiatur*)? 6) and what sort will it be when it departs (*qualis cum abscesserit*)?

Augustine does not give much time to the last three questions,[67] but they too come from the first book of the *Tusculan Disputations,* forming part of Cicero's project of calling the soul back from the senses. The Ciceronian dictum about how hard it is to draw thought away from habit, which Augustine quotes in his treatise on the Incarnation, is part of Cicero's explanation of why so many people believe in disagreeable myths about punishment in the underworld. He offers a Platonist diagnosis: such myths are produced by the imagination of people who "cannot mentally comprehend that souls are alive per se, by their own selves."[68] Therefore Platonist philosophy calls the soul away from the senses in order to understand the immortal sort of thing that it itself really is:

> Many people . . . hand souls over to death as if they were sentenced for a capital crime. The eternity of the soul seems unbelievable to them, for no other reason than their inability to understand [*intelligere*], and comprehend in thought, what sort of thing [*qualis*] the soul is apart from the body. Indeed they scarcely understand what sort of thing the soul is even in the body, what its shape [*conformatio*], size [*magnitudo*], and place [*locus*] is. . . . Indeed I find it much more difficult to get a view of the nature of the soul, and the thought much more obscure, *what sort of thing the soul is in the body* as in a foreign dwelling, than *what sort of thing it is when it makes its exit* and comes into the free heavens as into its own home.[69]

Augustine's rephrasing of these issues (in Evodius's questions 4–6) suggests strongly that he agrees with Cicero that the soul lives independently of the body, survives apart from the the body after death, and moreover existed prior to being "given to the body." But at the time of writing *On the Quantity of the Soul* it appears he is not ready to discuss these issues. What he is sure of, however, is that the soul is non-spatial—that the answer to the question "how big is it?" (*quanta sit*) cannot refer to its literal size but to the greatness of its "power and virtue."[70] For him, as for Cicero, this is especially evident in the power of memory. Thus, after giving quick but weighty answers to the first two questions,[71] Augustine settles down to devote nearly the whole treatise to the question "how big," beginning with a discussion of memory.

Evodius, it turns out, has exactly the problem that Augustine describes himself having at the beginning of *Confessions* 7: since he cannot imagine anything that is not extended in space, he thinks anything that does not have spatial length and breadth must be altogether nothing.[72] Augustine's initial line of response is characteristic: he gets Evodius thinking about the hierarchical structure of being. He asks him to make a comparison of value between two beings, justice and a tree. If you take away spatial dimensions, the tree ceases to exist, but justice remains. Yet is not justice better than a tree, indeed "far more divine and far more excellent"?[73] The implication is that it is also more real, more truly existent. Yet it is neither long nor broad nor solid. "Therefore if justice is none of these things and yet is *not nothing*, why does it seem to you that the soul is nothing unless it has some sort of length?"[74]

Thus when we ask how big the soul is, we must not expect an answer in terms of spatial measurements—as if the soul was made of breath or air or wind, or was confined within the limits of the body. The soul is too great, too real, too powerful for that. This is shown by the phenomena of memory. Evodius can remember not only the city of Milan but also how much physical space now separates him from it (*quanto spatio terrarum nunc a nobis absit*). All this space, then, is seen by the mind (*animo vides*). Augustine couches the point in terms taken from the rhetoricians' art of memory: "the images of these places are contained in memory."[75] But how can there be so many images of such vast extent in so small a space—that is, so small a space as memory must be if the mind is merely a material thing inside the body? In order to press this point Augustine adopts the vocabulary and thought of the *Tusculan Disputations*, asking Evodius to consider more carefully

> how much [*quanta*] and how many things our memory contains, which are of course contained in the soul. What therefore is the bottom [*fundus*], the concavity [*sinus*], the immensity [*inmensitas*] of that which has room for these things?[76]

This is enough to convince Evodius that the soul cannot be made of a material substance such as air or wind; for air might fill the whole visibile world, but "the soul can imagine within itself *innumerable* worlds just as big—though in what space or extension it contains these images I cannot guess."[77]

The Lesson of Geometry

Through a Socratic pedagogy of refutation, probably modeled on the *Meno* itself, Augustine helps Evodius purify his mind from the carnal habit of conceiving of the soul as a corporeal quantity. But Evodius has not yet caught sight of the peculiar greatness of the soul:

> I am still disturbed by the question of how the soul can have room for innumerable images of such great extent, without any length, breadth or depth of its own.[78]

It is in order to answer this question that Augustine launches into his version of the *Meno*'s geometry lesson. Once again (as in *Confessions* 7) Augustine's approach involves the reflective attempt to get the soul to see what greatness is implied by the very power whose exercise distracts and stymies it. If we find it hard to conceive of something without length, width, and depth, let us conceive of *that which conceives* of length, width, and breadth—and see how much greater it is than what it conceives (just as memory is necessarily more limitless, more spacious, than the whole material world whose images it can contain).

The lesson begins with a question that signals Augustine's basic strategy: he asks Evodius to conceive of length without width, the way geometers do. Since no *body* has length without width, this is something incorporeal, understood by the mind alone.[79] As in *On Music*, where Augustine led his student to consider the eternal numbers that were the rational basis of the temporal numbers of poetic rhythm, so here Augustine leads his student to see the immaterial lines and figures that are the rational basis of the bulky and spatially extended bodies of the sensible world. But even in the incorporeal realm of geometry there is a hierarchy of value and power, which Augustine and Evodius spend most of the lesson exploring. Lines are better than two-dimensional figures, they decide, because they cannot be divided in as many ways.

This reasoning may seem bizarre to us today, but it is indispensable for us to appreciate it if we are to understand Neoplatonist ontology in general and Augustine's view of the soul in particular.[80] The indivisible is better, because it is more unified and therefore less vulnerable to disintegration. Consequently, the best and most powerful thing known to the geometers is the point, which is absolutely indivisible and therefore "does not admit of any sort of cutting apart."[81] Augustine thus lays bare one of the deepest convictions of Neoplatonist ontology: that which is extended in space is *less* than that which is non-spatial, because whatever is extended part by part can be cut up and divided from itself.[82] True being belongs to what is indivisibly one, of which a geometrical point is the easiest illustration to grasp. The geometrical point is therefore "the most powerful of all the things that have been demonstrated" in the geometry lesson, because it cannot be cut up into parts.[83] "The power of the point" can be seen in the fact that lines begin and end and are joined together in a point.[84] Augustine, like Plotinus, takes the center point of a circle as an image of ontological integrity and power.[85]

Augustine concludes the geometry lesson by returning to the question of the size of the soul, clinching his argument that the soul has no spatial dimensions at all. For it is obvious by now, he says, that the soul is better than a line—which is itself better than plane figures, since these stretch out or extend [*distendunt*] in more directions and therefore are more divisible than the line.[86] Being superior to the line, the least extended spatial thing, the soul must therefore be altogether unextended and indivisible, more like the center of a circle than its circumference. Yet like the pupil, the center point of the eye that has the power to take in the whole space of the sky, the soul has the cognitive power to take in the whole world, even though it has no quantity or magnitude that can be measured in bodily terms.[87] Here we come upon paradoxes (in the original sense of the word, surprising and counterintuitive opinions) that Augustine later exploits brilliantly in the *Confessions*. Just as God's non-spatiality implies that he is not absent from space but rather indivisibly present everywhere, so the soul's non-spatiality does not mean that it is shrunk to an infinitesimal point that has no place in the "external" world, but rather that, like the geometrical point in Platonist metaphysics, it contains virtually (i.e., by way of power) the whole of space and of the material cosmos. The soul is great not in spatial extent but in power, for it has the power to understand anything in geometrical space and remember anything in material space. Augustine thus tries to get himself and us to see (with our *minds'* eye, of course) a capaciousness of the soul that is not spatial but for which language suggesting vast and illimitable spaces provides the most apt metaphors.

What Is Found in Memory

Such is the dazzling language which Augustine uses to describe memory in the tenth book of the *Confessions*. Memory is a vast inner space, Augustine says, because its power and capaciousness are large enough to embrace the whole extent of the material world and beyond:

> Great is this power of memory, exceedingly great, my God, a secret place ample and limitless [*infinitum*]. Who can get to the bottom [*fundum*] of it? And this is a power [*vis*] of my soul, and belongs to my nature—and I myself cannot grasp [*capio*] all that I am! So *the mind is too narrow to possess itself.* And where is this thing, which hasn't enough room for itself [*quod sui non capit*]? Is it outside itself and not in itself? Then how is it that it doesn't have room for itself?[88]

The strange reversal at the end of this passage is Augustine exploiting, for rhetorical effect, one of the incoherences in the metaphor of inner space. If one can enter into oneself as into a hidden inner room, then the self must be both larger and smaller than itself, for the room that contains the self also *is* the self. Hence the self that enters the inner room appears too small to grasp or contain (*capere*) the room that is itself.

With these paradoxes Augustine is not merely indulging in rhetorical cleverness but is trying to suggest something about the strangeness of our self and its astonishing relation to what is not itself—the "outside" world and God. The self that cannot contain itself spends most of its time outside itself. The very fact that we need to enter ourselves means we are not usually in ourselves but rather are attached to external and perishable things, dwelling in what Augustine earlier called the region of impoverishment and unlikeness to God.[89] Our soul thus becomes carnal, accustomed to wandering around outside, a stranger to itself:

> And people go marveling at high mountains, the huge flood of the sea, the great breadth of flowing rivers, the circumference of Ocean and the revolution of the stars—and leave themselves behind! They do not marvel that when I spoke of all these things, I did not see them with my eyes; yet I would not be able to talk about them unless the mountains, rivers, floods and stars that I saw, and the Ocean that I believed, were all things that *I saw inwardly in my memory, in spaces as vast as those in which I outwardly saw them.*[90]

Inner vision, seeing within the inner space of the self, indicates what is closest to the soul but for the most part unknown to it. For the soul scarcely knows itself, much less the God within itself. This is part of what Augustine means when he confesses, "You were inside and I was outside."[91] The general principle behind this is explained by Augustine in a later work: the soul "is *in* those things which it thinks of with love."[92] Hence most of the time the soul, with its carnal loves, dwells not in itself but in the external world. This paradox of our being outside ourselves is of a piece with the paradox of our separation from the omnipresent God: "You were with me—but I was not with You."[93]

The opposite side of the coin from this paradox of separation and estrangement is the good news of inwardness. The soul is too small to contain itself, not just because it is large enough to be its own space but because when it enters within itself it finds it is large enough to contain God as well. The soul is too large to be contained by itself precisely because it is large enough to contain God, who is greater than the soul. Beneath the paradoxical language is the Plotinian point, which Augustine has now fully assimilated, that the soul is ontologically dependent on that which is "inside" it. If the soul is, in its non-spatial way, larger and more capacious than the spatial world itself, then by the same token God is larger and more capacious than the soul within which he is found. In both cases, that which is within is greater than that which is without, for the inner/outer contrast corresponds to the contrast of higher and lower in Augustine's three-tiered ontological hierarchy: what is more inner is also higher up on the scale of being and to that extent "greater." Hence to turn inward is not to move away from the real world but toward it: the spaces of memory in which we inwardly see things are a greater and higher reality than the external world of bodies, just as the intelligible world that is God's mind is the true and ultimate world, greater than our own inner space.

This is Augustine's attempt to explain how we can find in ourselves what is greater and better and other than ourselves. But why is this inner space, in which we find what is above us, identified as *memory*? Because we find God precisely as those who have once lost him, and our search for him is therefore like trying to recollect a truth that we have forgotten. And as Plato said in his answer to Meno's question, we cannot even seek a thing unless we already have in us the memory of what we hope to find. Augustine puts Plato's point thus: "We don't say we have found what was lost if we don't recognize it, and we can't recognize it if we don't remember it."[94] Using the language of memory and invention, he explains the point by interpreting a biblical parable of seeking and finding:

> For the woman lost her drachma and sought it with a lamp—and unless she had a memory
> of it, she would not have found it. For when it was found, how would she know whether
> this was it, if she had no memory of it?[95]

Even things we forget can be found only in memory, for "when we forget and seek to remember, where else do we seek but in memory itself?"[96]

Since we cannot seek what we have never known, to find God is necessarily to remember what we have forgotten. This is the ultimate fusion of memory and invention, in which we find what is higher and more inward than memory itself:

> I will go beyond memory too—and where will I find [*inveniam*] you, true Good and se-
> cure sweetness? Where will I find you? If I find you apart from my memory, then I am for-
> getful of you [*immemor tui*]. And how am I then to find you, if I do not remember you?[97]

God transcends memory, yet is not found outside it. For we seek him not as one unknown but as our very own life, our long-lost happiness. "For when I seek you, my God, I seek a happy life," says Augustine.[98] We all necessarily want to be happy, and therefore we all seek that happy life, which we could not seek unless it was somehow in our memory—and not just the *name* "happy life" but the thing itself, the *res ipsa*.[99] Hence "this is a thing which no one can say he has not experienced, because it is recognized as discovered [*reperta*] in memory, when the name 'happy life' is heard."[100]

The soul, turning into itself, finds both its divine source and its ultimate fulfillment, its Truth and its Blessedness. Thus within the inner space of the self is located both the origin and goal of human life. For the happy life that we all love is nothing else but to joy in Truth, from which we have our being.[101] Hence God is not only the primal Truth we have forgotten and desire to recall, but also the ancient Happiness whose taste we will recognize when it is ours again. The possibility of our remembering God is indicated by the actuality of our forgetting him, and the one helps explain the other. We lose God and find him as we forget and recover the memory of the home from which we have fled and to which we desire to return. The possibility of this fleeing and forgetting, returning and finding, is the very nature of the soul as portrayed in the *Confessions*. And as the fleeing means being outside itself among external things, the finding requires a return to itself. Hence the reason Augustine describes the soul as an inner space is of a piece with the reason he thinks it should turn inward and enter its own self: the point of Augustinian inwardness is to find once more the Truth and Happiness, the God that has always been within.

Conclusion

The Inner, the Outer, and the Other

It is hard to prove a negative, especially in history. To claim that someone was the first to do something is implicitly to make the negative claim that no one had ever done it before, and to demonstrate that would require a comprehensive survey of everything that was ever done up until then. Hence I do not think I have proved that Augustine was the first person ever to conceive of the self as a private inner space. I do hope, however, that I have come a long way toward showing that he *invented* the concept of private inner space, in the sense that he constructed the concept himself rather than finding it in anyone else's writings. This is not sufficient to prove that no one ever thought of it before, but does show that, even if someone else came up with it earlier,[1] Augustine gives the concept of inner self a new beginning. And I think it is safe to say that this Augustinian beginning stands at the head of the Western tradition of inwardness as it comes down to us. Whatever might be the case with an unknown predecessor, *our* inwardness originates from Augustine—and for a historian of Western thought, that is the important point. That is the point that I hope will illuminate our interpretations of Western philosophy, theology, and psychology, and indeed our interpretations of ourselves.

Though it falls short of proof, I hope I have offered strong evidence in favor of the claim that no one before Augustine conceived of the self as a private inner space, by demonstrating that this concept arose as the solution to a quite specific problem that no one before Augustine is likely to have had.[2] Augustine's problem is how to locate God within the soul, without affirming the divinity of the soul. He wants (like Plotinus) to find the divine within the self, while affirming (as an orthodox Christian) that the divine is wholly other than the self. He solves this problem by locating God not only within the soul but above it (as its Creator) thus modifying Plotinus' turn "into the inside" into a movement *in then up*—first entering within the soul and then looking above it. The concept of private inner space arises in consequence of this modification, for the place in which we find ourselves when we have entered within (and not yet looked up) is our very own space—an inner world of human memory and thought, not identical with the intelligible world of the divine Mind.

To see how and why Augustine invented the private inner space of the self is to understand something about the possibilities of self-understanding available to human beings in the West. We are people who are capable of thinking that we have found God by looking inside our little selves. We can talk of finding ultimate meaning within, as if such talk made perfect and obvious sense. And we are in the habit of finding problems with something called "the external world." For once you have conceived of an inner self, you think differently about the external and the other. If there is an inner world, then the world we all live in can be "merely external," and you can worry whether it is lifeless and meaningless like a Newtonian mechanism. You can even worry whether the external world exists. In the Western tradition one can write books about *Our Knowledge of the External World*, as if there were no question that we all start out in our own internal world and the real problem is to build an epistemic bridge to the external world.[3] Other cultures have entertained the skeptical thought that the visible world is illusory, but only in the West could such skepticism breed fears of solipsism. For only if you think of the visible world as "external" to your own inner space can you worry that if you fail to prove its existence you may turn out to be alone in a solitary world.[4] Only in the West could it be a major philosophic and cultural achievement to undo or deconstruct this problem—to unask, as it were, the question of solipsism.[5]

Thus a new concept can be used in contexts its author never imagined, and there beget new problems. We who inherit Augustine's legacy can ask questions about the inner and the outer that would not have occurred to him. We can think of our private inner space as something to escape from. We can worry that the world outside is barren and dead, a mere mechanism devoid of glory and intelligence. And we can think of our inner visions as a matter of faith rather than reason, and worry whether to believe what we see there. Or we can think of the inner world as a matter of experiences beyond or beneath reason, and seek there a divinity that does not shine with clear intelligibility but rather touches us in ways too deep for understanding, there at the hidden center of our being. We can, in other words, start with Augustine and reinvent something like Plotinus, as some medieval mystics and nineteenth-century idealists did and as contemporary American Gnostics are now doing.[6]

Above all, Augustinian inwardness bequeaths us a problem about otherness. If we look inside ourselves to find what we love most, how do we recognize it as *other* than our self? Or conversely, how can we find among "merely" external things an other who is really worth loving? Can we really know what is outside ourselves, much less love it? Can we really know and love the other *as other*? Lurking behind these questions, I think, is a concept that Augustine did not know but that shaped his view of the inner self all the same, because of its proximity to the Platonist concept of intelligibility: the Aristotelian and Neoplatonist notion that true knowledge is a kind of identity between knower and known. If Aristotle and Plotinus are right, then understanding must ultimately obliterate otherness. To know X is to be no other than X. Augustine would deny this, of course. His inwardness is precisely a project of finding an *other* in the self. But we can wonder whether he does justice to the otherness of what he loves when he deprives himself of the resource of saying his beloved is *outside* himself. "Outside" is a terribly handy word, if what you love about someone includes the fact that he is quite different from yourself. If our beloved is other than ourselves, should we not be glad to look for him outside our selves?[7]

I mentioned in the introduction that my study treats inwardness as a concept, not an experience. But it is a concept meant to turn our attention in a particular direction, and therefore it generates experiences—many important experiences in the history of Western culture. I am making a point of being critical of the concept, because the experiences worry me: I do not think that "inward" is the right direction to look to find what is other than the self. The very metaphor is incoherent: what eyeball can turn to look inside itself? Yet worse than incoherent, it is ugly: for what eye does not love to look outside itself? What lover desires to find her beloved by looking in her self? Though the thing cannot be done, the desire to do it is possible, maybe even common. And I think we would do better to desire what is outside ourselves.

An inward turn becomes attractive whenever the world outside seems the wrong place to find the good you're looking for—when the "external world" comes to look uninviting, dead, or meaningless. To some (not all) medieval mystics, alienated from the life of this world, it may have seemed inevitable that human flesh, being mortal and perishable, is a thing from which we must be freed; while to some (not all) modern philosophers it may seem inevitable that the physical world is lifeless and mechanistic, devoid of consciousness and thought—not the place to look to find ultimate meaning. In either case, dissatisfaction with the external world can provide a motive for looking inward, and the strange Augustinian metaphor of turning the eyes of the soul inward may appear to be exactly what we need. It is as if both medievals and moderns could stand with Augustine at the beginning of *Confessions* 7, looking out upon the external, spatial world in which we would ordinarily say we live, shaking their heads and saying to themselves, "No—whatever it is I want, it can't possibly be found here. But where else can I look?" At such a moment an inward turn appears inevitable. If the outer world cannot show me the good I seek, where else is there to look but the inner one?

Orthodox Christian belief in Jesus Christ undermines the motives of inwardness by making it seem much less inevitable that we must find the divine elsewhere than the external world. There is nothing more external than flesh, yet the Catholic Church since the year after Augustine's death has explicitly taught that in Christ's flesh we find the life-giving power of God.[8] Much has been built on this teaching: Eastern Orthodox use of icons, Roman Catholic devotion to the sacraments, and Protestant preaching of the Gospel—all understood as means by which God gives us life from Christ incarnate.[9] Founded thus on the flesh of Christ, Christian piety has long insisted on a kind of "outward turn." How Augustinian inwardness and other Platonist strands in the Christian tradition can be reconciled with this turn to Christ's flesh is the matter of some of the deepest and most interesting tensions of Christian thought.

These tensions are not least interesting in Augustine himself. Much of his career as teacher of the Church is concerned with articulating the importance and value of external things—even their necessity for our salvation. For although God is found within, we are outside,[10] and thus for Augustine the road back to the God who is inward and eternal requires the right use of external and temporal things. On this road, established by what he calls God's "temporal dispensation,"[11] we encounter or undergo many things that fit us for eternal life: the humility of Christ, the purification of the mind's eye, the building up of charity, justification by faith, and the authority of Christian teaching. How these lead us in the end to the blessedness of seeing God is a long story that Augustine could not tell without saying something positive about the relation between the inner self and external things.

The great limitation of this book is that I have not had space to discuss the positive relations between inner and outer in Augustine's thought. I have thus omitted what I love most about Augustine: how, in obedience to the external authority of the Church's teaching, he ended up making decisive concessions to the importance and even necessity of the external things of the faith. That story would make another book—longer, more complicated, and more surprising than this one. Here I have restricted myself to tracing his invention of the private inner space and its motives, and therefore have discussed only his desire to turn *away* from external things. But the story of Augustinian inwardness is not complete until the inner self is situated in relation to Word and Sacrament, Church and Incarnation. The surprises in the rest of the story stem from Augustine's consistent, resourceful, and increasingly subtle attempts to maintain the priority of inner to outer, precisely as the external things of the faith come to occupy center stage in his thought.

Lest misunderstanding arise from the truncated version of the story of Augustinian inwardness that I have told so far, let me in closing mention three of these surprises—fundamental themes for my further work—that are of great importance for understanding the shape of Augustine's intellectual development.

The first surprise is about the concept of signs. This concept is central to Augustine's account of the value of external things. Augustine originates medieval and modern semiotics by classifying both words and sacraments as a species of signs.[12] His is the first expressionist semiotics, in which signs are understood as outward expressions of what lies within. It is also a Platonist semiotics, in that the most important use of signs is to signify intelligible things. Of course, being by definition sensible and therefore external, signs cannot adequately represent the inner truth; for no Platonist would say that a sensible things can make intelligible things intelligible. Hence the surprise: for Augustine we do not learn things from signs, but the other way around—we come to understand the significance of a sign only after we know the thing it signifies.[13] Thus for example the proper interpreter of Scripture is one who already knows the spiritual things it signifies and therefore is not captive to a literal reading of its signs.[14]

The crucial theological implication of this surprise is that no sign—neither word nor sacrament—can be an efficacious means of grace. For no external thing can convey to us an inward gift.[15] The now standard Roman Catholic view that the sacraments not only signify but confer grace is a departure from Augustine, rooted in twelfth-century developments.[16] This medieval view of the sacraments, rather than Augustine's view, was in turn the ground for Luther's doctrine of the Gospel as an external word that bestows on us the righteousness it signifies.[17] Thus in regard to the crucial question of whether external signs can have salvific power, the crucial divide is not between Catholic and Protestant but between the medievals and Luther on the one side and Augustine and Calvin on the other. Calvin speaks for Augustine as well as for many Protestants when he warns us not to "cling too tightly to the outward sign."[18] But Luther speaks for many Roman Catholics when he insists that we can never cling too tightly to external means of grace such as the sacraments and the Gospel of Christ.[19]

The second surprise is about grace. Grace is an inward gift, inwardly given. It changes our will inwardly—not by coercion, but by attraction, like falling in love as depicted by Plato and Plotinus.[20] Augustine's doctrine of grace is thus not a break with philosophy but his epochal attempt to synthesize Platonism and Paul, *eros* and *agape*. The surprise is that for Augustine grace is originally connected with reason, not with faith. This can be shown by tracing key trajectories in the development of his thought. For example, Augustine's anti-Pelagian contention that grace consists in our being inwardly taught by God[21] can be traced back to his much earlier view of Christ as inner teacher,[22] which is a variation of the yet earlier theme of Reason as inner teacher in the *Soliloquies*.

An even more important trajectory concerns the steadily widening scope of grace. At first Augustine sees grace helping us only with our inward relation to intelligible things above us, but later in his career he sees grace as indispensable even in our use of external things, which are ontologically beneath the soul and therefore by nature under its power. Thus over the course of Augustine's career grace is necessary first for vision, then for love, and finally even for faith. The scope of grace widens from the most inward function of the mind (understanding of intelligible things) to that which is more external (faith in authoritative teaching).

To begin with *vision*: it was clear to Augustine from the very beginning of his career as a Christian writer that we cannot ultimately understand God unless our mind's eye, presently diseased and defiled by sin, is healed and cleansed by grace so that its inner vision is not distracted by attachment to external things. Otherwise what we experience when we look inwardly toward God is not beatific vision but dazzlement. But for some time Augustine thought that Christian *love* or charity has its ultimate source in our own will, since its function is not to understand eternal things but merely to seek them. All we have to do in order to love as we ought, Augustine initially thought, is to will to do so—and what could be more in the power of our will than the will itself?[23] But by the time he wrote *Confessions*, he thought differently. It is still true that all we need to do is will—yet he finds that we cannot will as we ought, unless we have the inner help of grace.[24] The mature Augustine, in other words, thinks that not only the success of our intellect but also the rightness of our will is dependent on grace. We sinners need God's help not only to see him, but even to want to see him.

Yet for a long time, even in the midst of controversies with the Pelagians, Augustine hesitated to affirm that *faith* too was wholly dependent on grace. Augustine's doctrine of justification spells out a process that begins with faith, engenders love, and culminates in understanding.[25] The process moves from outward to inward: from faith in the external teaching of Church and Scripture to love of inner things (using temporal things only in order to enjoy eternal things) to the final inner vision of God. Could not the beginning of this process, which concerns only external things, be determined fundamentally by our own will? Unlike eternal things, we have power over external things. So could it not be that the choice whether or not to believe is in our power? In the early stages of the Pelagian controversy Augustine had not yet taken a clear stand on such questions.[26] But near the end of his life he came explicitly to the conclusion that even the choice to believe is impossible for us sinners unless grace comes first.[27]

The final surprise is about faith and its relation to reason. For Aquinas, faith deals with things beyond the ken of reason, and for Luther faith is more inward than reason. Both these views are departures from Augustine—facilitated by Augustine's teaching that faith too is impossible without grace, but leading to misunderstanding if read back into Augustine's writings. First of all, Augustine frames the issue not in terms of faith and reason but rather in terms of faith and understanding, or authority and reason. In both these pairs, the first term is related to the second as external is to internal. *Authority* is a feature of external teaching, while *Reason* is the power of inner vision. *Faith* means believing what an external authority teaches, while *Understanding* is that seeing for oneself which reason desires.[28] The gist of Augustine's view of faith and reason is thus summed up in his use of the scriptural passage "Unless you believe, you shall not understand."[29] He takes this to indicate a temporal priority of faith to understanding—as if to say, faith is where we begin but understanding is where we end up. And of course it is the end, the goal or *telos*, which gives meaning to the beginning—for as Augustine insists very emphatically, the journey is pointless apart from its destination.[30]

In one of his latest writings, Augustine says, "It is begun in faith, but completed by sight,"[31] echoing one of his earliest works, in which he says, "Authority comes first in time, but Reason is first in reality."[32] If I am correct in interpreting Augustine's experience of intellectual vision as a form of what we would now call insight,[33] then the point of these sayings is not hard to see. The road to understanding often begins with our believing what our teachers tell us—as when we believe a mathematical formula on the authority of our math teacher, even though we cannot really see what it means. But of course if we are good students then we desire to understand the changeless truth it signifies—to see it for ourselves, with our own mind's eye. The mere external formula does not contain what we are looking for but is simply an external sign—a reminder of where to look, Augustine would say, admonishing us to direct our attention away from the world of the senses.[34] If, in studious love,[35] we seek to understand what the formula signifies, we may be rewarded with vision—that brief moment of insight when we say, "Aha! now I see it!" What we see is located within us, not in the external world. But what we long to see most of all is God, who is the changeless Truth containing all that is changelessly true.[36] Our goal is to leave behind the external authority of mere signs, words, and formulas, to enjoy an intellectual vision that is beatific—not transitory like earthly insight but enduring forever, the very substance of eternal life. Or at least so Augustinian inwardness would have us believe.

If I am right about these surprises, as well as those I have described at greater length in the text of this book, then Augustine is not what any of his successors—Protestant or Roman Catholic, authoritarian or liberal, me or my readers—want him to be. He not only made us who we are, but he is different from what we thought—which means perhaps we too are different from what we thought. To encounter him on his own terms is thus enthralling and liberating, dangerous and instructive, all at once. That is Augustine's fascination, beyond what any of us find in him to love or be dismayed about. I too am dismayed as well as enthralled by this great figure, my father in the faith who says many things I do not want him to say. Whether I have done justice to his many fascinations, both lovely and dismaying, I leave to my readers to judge.

Appendix 1

Chronology of Augustine's Writings

This list is provided for the convenience of non-specialists, who may on occasion want to place a particular work of Augustine's in the context of his career as a whole. The treatises are listed in the order Augustine gives them in the *Retractations*. The list is not complete but includes only works frequently cited in this book. Titles are given in Latin, as there is sometimes divergence in how they are translated. Also included are the abbreviations by which the works are cited in the notes.

Early Works (386–395)

WORKS SET AT CASSICIACUM (386–387):

Contra Academicos	*C.Acad.*
De Beata Vita	*De Beata Vita*
De Ordine	*De Ord.*
Soliloquies	*Sol.*

WORKS WRITTEN IN ITALY (387–388):

De Immortalitate Animae	*De Immort.Anim.*
De Dialectica	*De Dial.*
De Moribus Ecclesiae Catholicae	*De Mor. Eccl.*
De Moribus Manichaeorum	*De Mor. Man.*
De Quantitate Animae	*De Quant. Anim.*
De Libero Arbitrio, book 1	*De Lib. Arb.*

WORKS WRITTEN IN AFRICA BEFORE ORDINATION (388–391):

De Genesi contra Manichaeos	*De Gen. c. Man.*
De Musica	*De Musica*
De Magistro	*De Mag.*
De Vera Religione	*De Vera Rel.*

WORKS WRITTEN WHILE PRESBYTER (391–395):

De Libero Arbitrio, books 2 and 3	*De Lib. Arb.*
De Utilitate Credendi	*De Util. Cred.*
De Duabus Animabus contra Manichaeos	*De Duab.Anim.*
Contra Fortunatum Manichaeum	*C. Fort.*
De Fide et Symbolo	
De Diversis Quaestionibus octaginta tribus (388–395)	*De Div. QQs 83*

WORKS WRITTEN AFTER CONSECRATION AS BISHOP:

Contra Epistolam Manichaei, Quam Vocant Fundamentum	*C. Ep. Fund.*
De Doctrina Christiana (books 1–3:26)	*De Doct.*
Confessiones	*Conf.*
Contra Faustum Manichaeum	*C.Faustum*
De Natura Boni	*De Nat. Boni*
De Catechizandis Rudibus	*De Cat. Rud.*
De Fide Rerum Invisibilium	*De Fide Rer. Inv.*

Later Works Frequently Cited

MAJOR WORKS:

De Trinitate (399–419)	*De Trin.*
De Civitate Dei (413–427)	*Civ. Dei*
In Johannis Evangelium	*In Joh. Evang.*

ANTI-PELAGIAN TREATISES:

De Peccatorum Meritis et Remissione (412)	*De Pecc. Mer.*
De Spiritu et Littera (412)	*De Sp. et Litt.*
De Natura et Gratia (415)	*De Nat. et Grat.*
De Gratia Christi (418)	*De Grat. Christi*
De Gratia et Libero Arbitrio (427)	*De Grat. et Lib.Arb.*
De Praedestinatione Sanctorum (429)	*De Praedest.*

OTHER:

Enchiridion de Fide, Spe et Charitate (423)	*Ench.*
Retractations (427)	*Retract.*

Appendix 2

Two Key Texts of Augustine's Ontology

Augustine's Three-Tiered Ontology (from Epistle 18:2)

There is a nature mutable in space and time, namely body. And there is a nature which is not at all mutable in space, but only in time is it also mutable, namely soul. And there is a nature which cannot be changed in space or in time, and this is God. What I have suggested here is mutable in any way, is called creature; what is immutable is the Creator.

Now, since everything that we say exists, we would say exists insofar as it remains and insofar as it is one thing, and moreover unity is the form of all beauty, you can see in this arrangement of natures what is highest, what is lowest (and yet still exists) and what is in the middle, greater than the lowest and less than the highest.

The highest is Happiness itself; the lowest is that which can be neither happy nor miserable; but the middle nature lives in misery when inclined toward the lowest, in happiness when turned toward the highest. Whoever believes Christ does not love the lowest, is not proud in the middle, and thus is made capable of clinging to the highest—and that is all we are commanded, admonished, incited to do.

Augustine's Essay "On Ideas" (On Eighty-three Different Questions, section 46)

[46.1] Plato, it is maintained, was the first to speak of Ideas. Yet it is not the case that if this name did not exist before he instituted it, then the things themselves, which he called Ideas, did not exist, or that no one understood them. Rather, some called them perhaps by one name and others by another. For anyone can impose whatever name they wish on an unfamiliar thing which has no name in common use.

Now, it is not likely that there were no wise men before Plato, or that they did not understand whatever these things are that Plato, as was said, called Ideas—especially as such power is vested in them that no one can be a wise man without understanding them. Also, there were probably wise men in other nations besides Greece—something that Plato himself not only has sufficiently attested by traveling to perfect his wisdom, but also recorded in his books. So they (if there were any) should not be considered ignorant of the Ideas, even though perhaps they called them by another name. But so much for the name; let us look at the thing, which is what is most important to consider and become acquainted with, since words are assigned on the authority that everyone has to name the thing they have come to know however they want.

[46.2] Ideas, then, we can call in Latin "Forms" or "Species," if we want to render it word for word. But if we call them Reasons [*rationes*], we are of course departing from strict translation (for Reasons are called *logoi* in Greek, not "Ideas"), yet anyone who wanted to use this word would not be straying far from the thing itself.

For the Ideas are certain original Forms or Reasons of things—fixed and immutable, not themselves formed, and therefore eternal, being always the same way—which are contained in the divine intelligence. And while they never come into being or pass away, everything that *can* come into being or pass away is said to be formed in accordance with them, as well as everything that *does* come into being and pass away.

But the soul is denied the ability to see them, except the rational soul, with that part of itself by which it is superior, that is, the mind itself or reason—as if with a kind of inner, intelligible face or eye of its own. And as a matter of fact, not even any and every rational soul is held to be capable of this vision, but rather those which are holy and pure, that is, those which have kept that eye which sees them healthy, whole, undisturbed, and like to the things it aims to see.

Now what person who is religious, and imbued with true religion, even though not yet able to see them, would venture to deny—indeed would not rather affirm—that everything which exists (i.e., whatever is included in some nature appropriate to its own kind, in order to exist) is produced by God as its author, and that by the same author everything that is alive lives, and that the universal preservation of things—that very order by which things that change repeat their temporal courses in a certain controlled way—is held together and governed by the laws of the most high God?

This being established or granted, who would venture to say that God fashioned all things irrationally? And if that cannot rightly be said or believed, then it follows that all things are fashioned by Reason. And not the same Reason for a human being as for a horse—to think so is absurd. Hence individual things are created by Reasons appropriate to them.

And where are these Reasons supposed to be, but in the very mind of the Creator? For he was not looking at something located outside himself to set up what he set up in accordance with it—to believe that is sacriledge.

So if these Reasons of everything to be created (and everything already created) are contained in the divine mind, and nothing can be in the divine mind without being eternal and immutable, and these original Reasons of things are also what Plato called Ideas—then not only do Ideas exist, but they are true, for they are eternal, remaining the same way and immutable, and whatever exists is the way that it is by sharing [*participatione*] in them.

But the rational soul stands out above all the things God has fashioned, and it is closest to God when it is pure, cleaving to him in charity the more it perceives these Reasons (illuminated and saturated as it were by the intelligible light from him) not with bodily eyes, but with that chief part of itself by which it is superior, that is, with its intelligence—a vision which makes it utterly happy.

These Reasons, as was said, can be called Ideas, Forms, Species or Reasons; and it is allowed for many to call them whatever they want, but for very few to see what is true.

Notes

Preface

1. For this focus on traditions of inquiry I am indebted to Alisdair MacIntyre, though I do not share his particular approach to issues of relativism and the incommensurability of traditions.

2. The recognition that philosophers work from a heritage of problems goes back at least to Aristotle (for example, *Metaphysics* 3:1).

3. Notice that Genesis 3, which Paul (in Rom. 5:12–21) interprets as the story of the origin of sin and death, contains no mention of movement from a higher place to a lower. That the Christian tradition calls it "the story of the Fall" is due to the prevalence of Platonist exegesis in later interpretations. The original version of the Fall story is not in the Bible but in Plato's *Phaedrus* 246a–249c—see "The Other World" in chapter 1.

4. The exceptions prove the rule. In the Christian Bible only two extraordinary individuals, Elijah and Jesus, are described as going to heaven (apart from temporary visionary experiences). But these two are not dead. They are taken up bodily and alive, and they are expected to return. Of course Revelation 6:9–11 pictures souls in heaven, but only those of the martyrs, which must wait under the altar almost as if they were being held in storage until the consummation of the kingdom. The point about them is that they are not, in the traditional sense, "in heaven"—for *they are not happy* and they will not be until the heavenly City *descends* to earth so that God may dwell among human beings (21:2–4).

5. See Karl Barth's definition of theology at the outset of his *Church Dogmatics*, I/1: p. 4.

6. This approach I owe in large part, directly or indirectly, to Victor Preller's reading of Aquinas in *Divine Science and the Science of God* (see especially p. 25).

7. On this contrast, see Cullmann, "Immortality of the Soul or Resurrection of the Dead?"

8. Here and throughout this book I use the word "Catholic" in the ancient sense familiar to Augustine, which is roughly synonymous with "orthodox" (lower case). Hence "Catholic" here stands in contrast with "heretical" and "schismatic" but not (anachronistically) with "Protestant." Where I intend a contrast with Protestantism or Eastern Orthodoxy I will speak of "*Roman Catholicism*."

9. *De Trin.* 3:2. (All translations from ancient and medieval texts in this book are my own. For the manner of citation of Augustine texts, see page xvii. For the abbreviations of their titles, see appendix 1.)

10. O'Connell, *St. Augustine's Early Theory of Man*, chapter 4.

1. The Kinship of Soul and Platonic Form

1. See Alexander of Aphrodisias's preface to his treatise *On the Soul,* the opening of Plotinus's treatise "On the Soul" (*Ennead* 4:3.1; see also 5:1.1) and Cicero's interpretation of the god's command in his treatment of the nature and immortality of the soul, *Tusc.* 1:52. The same connection between self-knowledge and knowledge of the divine is found in the Nag Hammadi treatises (see Robinson, IX, 3,45.1–6, VII, 4,117.3–9, II, 7,138.16–18, II, 3,61.32–35, and XI, 3,56.15–20) and in Manichaean writings (see Brown, pp. 47–49).

2. *Discourses* 3:22.38–39.

3. Marcus Aurelius *Meditations* 7:59.

4. For example, Epictetus *Discourses* 1:4.18.

5. *Epistle* 41:1.

6. Ibid. 41:2 (guardian spirit) and 41:6 (divinity of soul).

7. For the Stoic contribution to inwardness see Aubin, pp. 62–63 and 175–176; Dodds, *Pagan and Christian,* pp. 80–81; Courcelle, *Recherches,* pp. 393–404; and Theiler, "Plotin und die antike Philosophie," pp. 155–156. These scholars agree in seeing the inwardness of the Roman Stoics as leading to Plotinus, where it is finally—and for the first time—incorporated into a systematic metaphysics of inwardness. Thus the language of inwardness evidently needs Platonist ontology if it is to be more than simply an intriguing metaphor. (Even when it appears in the Stoics it can be identified as part of a "Platonizing" trend in later Stoicism—see Pohlenz, pp. 320–323.)

8. It seems likely the "inward turn" originated in middle Platonism before Plotinus, although this depends on dating of the originals of various treatises from Nag Hammadi showing significant Platonist influence, where something like an inward turn seems clearly present (see for example Robinson, XI, 3,52.9–12, III, 2,66.24, and III, 5,128.2–5). In at least one case this is connected, as in Plotinus, with an identity theory of knowledge (II, 3,61.20–35)—a theory that was evidently known to the Valentinians (see I, 5,54.40–55.12).

9. Plotinus is acutely aware of the Stoic tradition and very concerned to spell out where he agrees and disagrees with it. See especially *Ennead* 1:4, which contains a critique of Stoicism as well as a great deal of the language of inwardness.

10. The *noetos topos,* in *Republic* 6:508c, 509d, and 7:517b.

11. *Phaedrus* 247b–e.

12. *Republic* 7:514a–515c; see also the "true heaven, the true light and the true earth" of *Phaedo* 108e–111c.

13. On the contrast between Plato and Plotinus on this point, see Theiler, "Plotin und die antike Philosophie," p. 155–156.

14. *Charmides* 160d. Socrates here urges young Charmides to "look into yourself" to discern what temperance is, since that is a virtue that everyone agrees Charmides has in his soul. The course of the conversation soon shows, however, that such firsthand looking is not a sure source of knowledge about the nature of one's own self or its virtues. Introspection is not the road to self-knowledge. By contrast, in the *Alcibiades* I (possibly spurious, but possibly one of Plato's early works), where temperance is defined as self-knowledge (133c), obedience to the divine command "know thyself" is possible because one can see oneself, in the mirror of a friend's soul: it is like seeing one's own eye reflected in the pupil of another's (132e–133b). Thus the odd metaphor of introspection or looking inward is rejected in favor of the more coherent metaphor of reflection.

15. *Republic* 9:591e.

16. *Theaetetus* 189e.

17. *Philebus* 38e–40c.

18. *Philebus* 39b.

19. *Sophist* 263e.

20. *Phaedo* 79d. The term for "akin" is *syn-genes,* which occurs frequently to designate the

soul's relation to the other world where there is no change and death: see *Phaedo* 84b. *Republic* 6:490b and 10:611e. The suggestion is not only that the soul is somehow like the Forms but that soul and Forms are in some way kin or family, having a common origin, so that in leaving the body behind at death and going to the changeless realm of the Forms, the pure soul is in effect returning home.

21. See *Timaeus* 90c.

22. See Snell, p. 8–9, and Kittel, 9:608–609.

23. *Phaedo* 64a–67e.

24. The Homeric picture of the fluttering psyche exiting the body with the last breath lies behind Cebes' question in *Phaedo* 70a. Socrates addresses Cebes' worry in 70d, which leads him into the discussion of the soul's kinship and likeness to the Forms, 77d–84b.

25. See Snell, chapter 1, on Homer, and Wolff, pp. 1–66, on the Hebrew Scriptures' use of the anthropological terms translated "soul," "flesh," "spirit," "heart," and so on.

26. The doctrine of Forms is related to the immortality of the soul as premise to conclusion. See especially *Phaedo* 76e: "if these things [i.e., Forms] do not exist, then the argument we've been conducting [i.e., about the soul] is pointless."

27. This is an attempt to render the untranslatable phrase *aei ōsautōs kata tauta echonti heautoi* (*Phaedo* 80b; see the similar phrasing in *Republic* 5:479a). Cicero also tries to render this phrase, with results that Augustine mimics; see "The Self-Examination of Reason" in chapter 6.

28. *Phaedrus* 248e.

29. See *Phaedrus* 250c (body as tomb), *Phaedo* 82e (embodiment as imprisonment), and of course *Republic* 7:514a–518b (life in the cave).

30. The Academy, the school founded by Plato, was dominated by skepticism during most of the Hellenistic period (Augustine's *Against the Academics* is an attempt to refute this form of skepticism). Cicero, who in addition to being an orator was an Academic skeptic and one of our most important sources for understanding the Hellenistic Academy (he was the only person educated there to leave us a significant body of extant philosophical writing), traces the Academy's skeptical theory and practice back to Socrates (*Academica* 1:44–45) and particularly to the reading of Socratic dialogues (*Academica* 1:46 and 2:74). For an overview of the history of the Academy told from this perspective see Sedley, "Motivation," (especially p. 10) and Long, *Hellenistic Philosophy,* chapter 3 (especially pp. 88–89). See also "Ciceronian Point of Departure" in chapter 6.

31. I take for granted here the common scholarly view that the *Meno* marks a transition from the earlier Socratic dialogues to the great middle dialogues such as *Phaedo* and *Republic,* as Plato starts to go beyond Socratic dialectic but has not yet formulated the doctrine of Ideas. For an introduction to this view of Plato's development, see Kraut, especially pp. 3–9. For details on dating the *Meno* in particular see Bluck's edition, pp. 108–120.

32. *Meno* 80d.

33. "Seeking and learning are wholly recollection." *Meno* 81d.

34. See the usage in *Meno* 85c and 86a, as well as *Phaedo* 73a. *Republic* 7:518c (in "The Allegory of the Cave") uses the same verb to describe the power of intellectual vision present in the soul.

35. Note how Socrates' comments on the slave boy's puzzlement in 84a–c parody Meno's description of his puzzlement in 80a–b.

36. *De Trin.* 12:24.

37. *Meno* 86a. The phrase "for all time" is *ton aei chronon,* which combines the words for time and eternity, literally, "for forever time."

38. Hence for the Platonist tradition "human" or "man" means soul and body together. The soul alone is not human, because it may be reincarnated in the body of a brute if evil and it has a divine destiny if righteous. Only the soul caged in a human body is both more than brute and less than god.

39. *Phaedrus* 246a–250c.

40. *Meno* 72c. See the similar formulations in *Euthyphro* 5d and 6d.

41. *Republic* 7:514a–519b.

42. *De Trin.* 12:24. "Artificer" is *Conditore,* a reference to God the Creator but also an allusion to Plato's Demiurge or cosmic Artificer in the *Timaeus,* which Augustine (like many Christians before and after) interprets as an approximation of the Christian doctrine of Creation.

43. See "Falling into Division" in chapter 9.

44. *De Lib. Arb.* 2:33—a phrase to which I will often return, as it indicates the heart of Augustine's Platonist ontology.

45. Compare *Phaedo* 65a–67a (the project of the soul investigating purely and by itself, apart from the body and its senses) with *Confessions* 7:1–2 (the project of conceiving of God in a purely incorporeal way, free from all contamination and distraction by the sense-based phantasms of the imagination). There is a recognizable continuity in the two projects, which will be of great importance to us later in this study.

2. *Identity from Aristotle to Plotinus*

1. *On the Soul* 3:8,431b20–432a2; see also 3:4,429b5 and 3:7,431a1.

2. See *Nichomachean Ethics* 10:7, especially 1177b26–31. The identification of mind and wisdom as the divine in us goes back to his *Protrepticus* (see Ross's fragment 10c, which Düring regards as the conclusion to the work)—whence it quite possibly reached Augustine via Cicero's *Hortensius.*

3. *Metaphysics* 12:9,1075b34; see also 12:7,1072b22. In this chapter I shall use the terms "mind" and "intellect" and "intelligence" as equivalents to *nous* (in both capitals and lower case), shifting from one term to another depending on context and on the historical connections I am trying to evoke. The related verb, *noein,* I shall translate as "understand" or "know" (in the specific sense of *intellectual* knowledge), avoiding the translation "think," which is frequently used in Aristotle translation but is in my view misleading because it suggests process and the possibility of error. "Contemplate" (rendering Aristotle's *theorein*) is used to indicate the act of knowing, as opposed to a piece of knowledge retained in memory but not under active consideration at present.

4. See Aristotle *On the Soul* 3:4,430a2–9, and more explicitly, Alexander of Aphrodisias *On the Soul* 86:14–23, which is basically an exposition of Aristotle on this point.

5. This is the point of Aristotle's remark that "in the individual, potential knowledge is temporally prior to actual knowledge, but in the universe as a whole it is not even temporally prior," *On the Soul* 3:5,430a21.

6. Ibid. 3:8,432a3–8.

7. *Metaphysics* 12:7,1072b14–25.

8. Ibid. 12:9.

9. This interpretation of Aristotle involves identifying the God of *Metaphysics* 12:7 with the "active mind" or "agent intellect" of *On the Soul* 3:5.

10. Cicero, on behalf of the Academy, makes the claim that not only Plato and Aristotle but even Zeno the Stoic taught substantially the same thing in different words; see "Ciceronian Point of Departure" in chapter 6.

11. The treatise is no longer extant. See Beutler.

12. The use of Aristotle in the later Neoplatonist schools is one of the central themes of A. C. Lloyd's work; see his contribution to the *Cambridge History* (followed up in the illuminating study by I. Hadot) as well as his *Anatomy.*

13. Düring and Owen trace Aristotle's course of development from the empiricism of his youth to something more like Platonism in his later thought. Ontologically, the development is from an early treatise like the *Categories* (where true being or *ousia* is identified with the concrete individual, e.g., Socrates) to the view of *Metaphysics* 7 (where the true being of a thing is its species-Form, e.g., "human"). The older view of Aristotle's development, represented most powerfully by Jaeger, argues that Aristotle moved in the opposite direction, starting out under the shadow of Platonism and ma-

turing into an Aristotelian empiricist. I prefer the former view, since the latter seems to me to underestimate young Aristotle's originality, critical ability, and logical acumen. After all, this was the young man who invented the discipline of logic.

14. Just to mention two points that will come up again later, there is the influence of Aristotle's critique of Platonic Ideas on Stoic materialism (see Hahm, pp. 7–8) and the influence of Aristotle's notion of a fifth element on the Stoic notion of divine fire (pp. 92–93).

15. See Owen, "The Place of the Timaeus."

16. For a modern interpretation of Aristotle along these lines see Lear, pp. 116–141.

17. See Moraux, *Alexandre,* p. xxiii, and Fotinis's edition of Alexander *On the Soul,* p. 155.

18. Alexander of Aphrodisias *On the Soul* 2:4–9. All the same, it is worth noting that this is Alexander's own treatise on the subject of the soul, not his commentary (now lost) on Aristotle's treatise of the same name.

19. See Moraux, *Alexandre,* p. xvi.

20. Porphyry *Life of Plotinus* 14. See Armstrong, "The Background," p. 406, and Merlan, "Greek Philosophy," p. 120.

21. Dillon hypothesizes for instance that this is the reason for the anti-Aristotelian polemics composed by the leading Athenian Platonist, Atticus, at about the time Alexander was beginning his career. In fact it is most likely that the target of this polemic was Alexander's teacher Aristocles, whose Platonizing interpretation of Aristotle would have threatened the distinctiveness of Platonist teaching (Dillon, p. 248–250). On the Peripatetics' ambiguous location on the spectrum between Stoicism and Platonism, see Merlan, "Greek Philosophy," p. 122.

22. "The separation [*chōrizein*] is the cause of all the unacceptable consequences concerning the Ideas," says Aristotle in *Metaphysics* 13:9,1086b7. For his full account of the origin and defects of Plato's theory of Ideas, see *Metaphysics* 1:9 and 13:4. Notice that Aristotle consistently calls the target of his criticism "ideas" (*ideai*). In this chapter I shall consistently use Plato's other term for them, "Form" (*eidos*), in order to stress the continuity between Aristotle's views and Plato's.

23. *ST* I, 79.7.

24. Alexander of Aphrodisias *On the Soul* 85.20–86.4.

25. For Alexander these two processes are basically identical, ibid. 85:15.

26. Ibid. 90:1–10. See Aquinas's rebuttal of this view, which he knew as Avicenna's, in *ST* I, 79.6.

27. *On the Soul* 90:11–19; see 81:1–13, which suggests that these two kinds of Forms may be the objects of the intellect in action and in contemplation respectively, which Alexander correlates with the (ultimately Platonic) distinction between opinion and knowledge.

28. Ibid. 89:11–21.

29. Ibid. 90:19–91:6.

30. Ibid. 88:24–89:11, alluding to the comparison of the Good to the sun in the Allegory of the Cave, *Republic* 6:507a–509b. Alexander is taking up a hint from Aristotle himself, who compares the agent intellect to light in his *On the Soul* 3:5,430a16.

31. The importance of the Aristotelian theology of divine Mind is a familiar theme in the scholarly literature on Middle Platonism: see Witt, pp. 125–126, Dörrie, pp. 202–205, Dillon, pp. 13 and 24, Armstrong, "The Background," pp. 402–404. The most illuminating representative figure here is the Middle Platonist Albinus or Alcinous (fl. 150 AD); see Dillon, pp. 282–283.

32. The great study of the concept of Mind or *Nous* in the Platonist tradition before Plotinus is Krämer's. Festugière's second volume is perhaps the most extensive study of the notion of God as World-Soul in this period; his fourth volume deals with the notion of an incomprehensible One prior to Plotinus.

33. For an excellent introduction to Plotinus's ontological hierarchy see Armstrong, *Architecture,* as well as the shorter and more accessible "Plotinus," especially pp. 236–258.

34. *Republic* 6:509b. See likewise the Allegory of the Cave, where the Good is pictured as *above* the other Forms, like the sun shining on the earth (7:516b).

35. *Parmenides* 137c–142a (the so-called "first hypothesis," a dialectical exercise concerning the notion of the absolute One, which concludes that such a thing cannot be spoken of, or known, or be—which Neoplatonists took to be a profound description of the First Principle through a kind of *via negativa*).

36. *Ennead* 5:3.5–6 and 5:9.5–8.

37. Whereas for Plato the soul is a self-mover (*Phaedrus* 245cd, *Timaeus* 36e–37b, *Laws* 10:895b–896c), for Aristotle the soul is an *unmoved* mover (*On the Soul* 1:3). Hence Aristotle's soul, unlike Plato's, is immovable—and thus that much closer to eternity and the immutable nature of the Forms. In this, as in several other points of psychology, Plotinus sides with Aristotle rather than Plato. His doctrine of the immutability of the higher part of the soul clearly owes more to Aristotle than to Plato: see how *Ennead* 1:1.1–3 develops the thesis of the immovability and impassability of the soul in Aristotle's *On the Soul* 1:4,408a29–408b32 (see also *Ennead* 3:6.1–5).

38. Plotinus explicitly mentions Aristotle's identity theory in *Ennead* 5:9.5, assimilating it to the Parmenidean identification of being and knowing and the Platonic theory of Recollection. Armstrong, in "The Background," seems to have been the first modern scholar to appreciate how important Aristotle's theory is in Plotinus.

39. The key text here is *Ennead* 4:8.4 and 8; but see also 1:1.10, 3:4.3, 3:8.5, 4:3.12, 5:3.4, 6:4.14. The concept of an unfallen higher part of the soul would have been conveyed to Augustine in *Ennead* 5:1.10, where it is identified as the divine part of the soul, "which Plato calls 'the man within' [in *Republic* 9:589a]."

40. *Enneads* 3:4.3, 6:5.7, 6:7.35, and 6:9.9.

41. In *Ennead* 1:2.4 Plotinus identifies the work of the four virtues with the task of conversion (i.e., turning) and purificaion. See how conversion, liberation, and purification—that is, turning, freeing, and purging—are equivalent in *Phaedo* 64e, 65a, and 66ab, respectively. In the same vein Augustine speaks of "those virtues which purify the soul by conversion" in *De Musica* 6:52.

42. *Ennead* 1:4.4; contrast *Eudemian Ethics* 7:12,1245b19.

43. *Enneads* 6:5.4, 6:5.12, and 6:9.6. For the full range of Plotinus's use of the term "infinite" to describe what is divine, see Sweeney, chapter 9.

44. Armstrong, "Plotinus' Doctrine of the Infinite," p. 56. This contrasts with Christian and Jewish theology, where the affirmation that God is infinite had long been commonplace, as "from Philo [of Alexandria] onwards, it was natural to believe that God was infinite and his infinity is stated without hesitations or reservations."

45. In fact *peras* is, by Plato's own account, the term for the boundary lines that define a geometrical figure, *Meno* 76a.

46. *Enneads* 5:1.7, 6:7.32.

47. For example *Enneads* 3:8.8, 4:3.17, 5:1.11, 6:5.5, 6:8.8, 6:9.8.

48. See *Ennead* 5:3.10: "It must be that . . . knowledge [*noesin*] is always in otherness as well as, necessarily, in identity. For the things that are principally known are both the same and other than the knower."

49. For example, ibid. 3:8.8–9, 5:1.4, 5:3.10, 5:6.2, and 6:7.41. The key point is stated succinctly in 6:9.2: "Since it [the divine Mind] is both knower and known, it must be dual and not simple, and is therefore not the One."

50. See ibid. 5:1.7; 5:3.11 and 15; 5:9.6.

51. Ibid. 6:4.3.

52. See ibid. 3:2.2.

53. The term "hypostasis," so suggestive of the Christian doctrine of the Trinity, is not found in Plotinus's writings but only in the title of *Ennead* 5:1.1 ("On the Three Principal Hypostases")—and Plotinus did not assign titles to his own treatises but left that to his students (Porphyry, *Life of Plotinus* 4). Hence I generally prefer to speak of three ontological "levels," mainly to indicate that different philosophical concepts come into play at each level of Plotinus's hierarchy.

54. This division of the soul among bodies is discussed by Plato in *Timaeus* 35a, a text that serves as a springboard for some of Plotinus's most important meditations on the nature of embodiment. See *Enneads* 1:1.8, 4:1, 4:2, 4:3.19, and 6:4.4.

55. *Ennead* 4:8.4.

56. See ibid. 4:2.1.

57. The doctrine that the higher part of the soul is by nature immutable and therefore unfallen is evidently unique to Plotinus. Proclus rejects it in *Elements* 211, and other Neoplatonists reverted to Plato's view that the soul is a self-mover (not an unmoved mover) and hence not immutable. See Macrobius's lengthy criticism of Aristotle's doctrine of the soul as unmoved mover in *Commentary on the Dream of Scipio* 2:13–17, which must have been cribbed from some Neoplatonist school text, perhaps by Porphyry (see Courcelle, *Late Latin Writers*, p. 43). Note Plotinus's explicit awareness of the fact that his doctrine of an immutable "higher part" of the soul is a novelty that "boldly goes against received opinion," *Ennead* 4:8.8.

58. *Ennead* 5:9.8. See the fuller discussion of intelligible part-whole relations in *Ennead* 4:9.5; for why this degree of unity among intelligible things nonetheless does not lead to confusion, see *Ennead* 5:9.6. Gurtler builds a very plausible systematic interpretation of Plotinus's philosophy around this analogy (*Nous* is to *noeta* as a science is to its theorems) and the "experience of unity" that results when this science is reflected in the knowledge of the soul.

59. "Each is all" and "all are together" are mottos that occur frequently to sum up Plotinus's discussion of the contents of the intelligible world. See *Enneads* 1:8.2, 3:3.7, 4.2.2, 5:3.15, and 5:8.4, as well as the references in note 60.

60. Ibid. 5:9.5–6 and 3:8.8. The fact that there are many minds or intelligences in the one Mind is the basis for Proclus's development of a hierarchy of divine intelligences and thence for the celestial hierarchy of angelic intelligences in Pseudo-Dionysius.

61. Plotinus develops the thesis of the unity of all souls in *Ennead* 4:9 and 4:3.1–8. This notion is not wholly alien to Augustine, as we shall see. Indeed, it is altogether a less out-of-the-way notion than one might expect. For the conceptual connection between the unity of Mind ("Averroism") and the oneness of all souls, see Merlan, *Monopsychism,* pp. 54–56, who shows that precisely parallel issues arise concerning the transcendental ego or *Bewusstsein überhaupt* in the Kantian tradition, which is on this score a conceptual descendant of Plotinus's view of the unity of all souls (pp. 114–124).

62. On the structural parallel between the realm of the divine Mind and the realm of Soul in respect of one and many, see *Enneads* 4:3.5, 5:9.6 (where the science/theorem analogy is applied to soul as well as Mind), and 6:4.4 (where the parallel is most systematically presented).

63. See Heiser, pp. 37–44, on the way that the embodied soul's characteristically discursive reasoning (*logismos*) breaks up into parts what in the realm of Mind is never divided.

64. See *Ennead* 6:5.7 on partial insight: "At first no doubt not all will be seen as one whole." See also 4:4.1.

65. 1 Corinthians 13:12.

66. See how Recollection is grounded in Identity in *Enneads* 5:9.5 and 6:9.11.

67. The phrase "into the inside" (*eis to eisō*) is so common in Plotinus it is almost a cliché. It often occurs together with the verb *epistrephein,* "to turn"—or as it would naturally be translated into Latin, "to convert" (*convertere*); see for example *Enneads* 1:6.8, 5:8.11, and 6:9.7. For Plotinus's very rich use of this verb, see Aubin, chapter 8.

68. What follows is a synthesis of several passages (listed roughly in order of importance for this purpose): *Enneads* 6:9.8–10, 5:1.11, 4:3.17, 6:5.5, 6:8.18, 3:8.8, 4:1 (Loeb 4:2), 1:7.1.

69. *Ennead* 6:5.7. (The "lucky tug" refers to Athena descending from heaven and coming up on Achilles from behind to yank him by the hair and pull him back from rash action, *Iliad* 1:194–200.) O'Connell (*St. Augustine's Early Theory,* p. 62–63) argues that this passage of Plotinus played an important role in the alchemy of Augustine's imagination up to the time of *Confessions.*

70. *De Ord.* 1:3 (note the metaphor of the center of the circle), *De Quant. Anim.* 69 (the soul is both many and one). Much later, the notion that there is an inner and invisible unity of souls plays an important role in Augustine's account of original sin in Adam and in his doctrine of the invisible unity of the Church.

71. See hereafter, p. 107. The Plotinian passage just discussed is the perfect illustration of why for Plotinus the inner self is *not* private.

3. *Augustine Reads Plotinus*

1. Ambrose was one of the most prominent exponents of orthodox trinitarianism in the West, devoting to the Nicene cause not only his formidable political skills but also his long treatises *On the Faith* and *On the Holy Spirit.* Augustine may not have read these treatises at the beginning of his career, but he would certainly have heard the same theology in Ambrose's sermons; see Williams, p. 151.

2. For what philosophical knowledge Augustine did have prior to reading Plotinus, see "Ciceronian Point of Departure" in chapter 6.

3. On the issue of Augustine's knowledge of Greek language and literature I follow Courcelle, *Late Latin Writers,* chapter 4. On his use of Latin writers the best guide is Hagendahl, reinforced by Marrou's magisterial study of Augustine's education, *Saint Augustin.*

4. See *Conf.* 4:28.

5. The *Timaeus* is the only work of Plato of which Augustine demonstrates more than a fragmentary knowledge. Augustine refers frequently to Plato's creation-story in *City of God,* noting its agreement with Genesis (*Civ. Dei* 8:11) and showing a special fondness for the speech of the supreme god in *Timaeus* 41a–b (see Hagendahl, pp. 131–138 for an extensive list of allusions and quotations). Hagendahl (p. 535) and Courcelle (*Late Latin Writers,* p. 169–170) concur in the judgment that Cicero's translation was the edition known to Augustine.

6. For Augustine's use of such sources in general see Solignac, "Doxographies et manuels dans la formation de saint Augustin."

7. For the importance of this Ciceronian book for Augustine's Platonism, see the second, third, and fourth sections of chapter 6 and the fourth, fifth, and sixth sections of chapter 10 hereafter. It seems to me rather likely that Augustine knew some of the geometry lesson in the *Meno* (as the inspiration for the geometry lesson in *De Quant. Anim.*) as well as the Allegory of the Cave (which seems to undergird the non-Plotinian aspects of Augustine's epistemology in *Sol.* 1:12 and 1:23, discussed in "Education for Vision" in chapter 5) through some—unknown and purely conjectural—doxography on theories of education; for education is a subject on which he is unusually well informed.

8. *Conf.* 7:13.

9. The debate was conducted on philological ground: not doctrines but phraseology was the basis for inferences that Augustine read this or that treatise. For reviews of this controversy and how to read its outcome see Solignac's introduction to the *Bibliothèque Augustinienne* edition of *Confessions;* O'Meara, "Augustine and Neo-Platonism"; and O'Connell, *Early Theory,* chapter 1.

10. Theiler, "Porphyrios und Augustin." See the criticisms by Courcelle, *Les Confessions de saint Augustin dans la tradition litteraire,* I,i,2.

11. I will take it as certain that Augustine read *Enneads* 1:6 ("On Beauty"), 1:8 ("What and Whence Evil?"), 5:1 ("On the Three Primary Hypostases"), and 3:2–3 ("On Providence")—there is little scholarly disagreement about these. In addition, I will take it as very likely that he read *Enneads* 6:4–5 (the treatise on Omnipresence), 4:7 ("On the Immortality of the Soul"), 5:8 ("On Intellectual Beauty"), 4:8 ("On the Descent of the Soul") and 4:3–5 (the treatise on problems regarding the soul). Less probable but still rather likely are *Enneads* 6:9 ("On the Good or the One") and 3:7 ("On Eternity and Time"). Last, for my own more unusual judgments: it seems to me probable that he also

read *Ennead* 1:2 ("On Virtues"), for reasons that will emerge in "The Intelligibility of God" in chapter 4 (note 57), as well as *Ennead* 1:3 ("On Dialectic") which I think must be in the background of his extraordinary views on the nature of dialectic in the *Soliloquies* (see "The Bizarre Identification" in chapter 7). The most important point to note, however, is that I will try to make my thesis independent of minor disagreements about which treatises belong on the list of those Augustine read, by showing that the Plotinian conceptuality I attribute to Augustine could have come to him from any number of treatises. Such concepts as the inward turn and the divinity of the soul are too pervasive in Plotinus's writings to be missed even by someone who has read very few of them.

12. *De Beata Vita* 4 (written only a few months after the event). Although most manuscripts have "a very few books of Plato," Henry has made a convincing and widely accepted argument (on the basis of the text-critical principle of *lectio difficilior*) that the reading found in a minority of MSS, *libri Plotini* in place of *libri Platonis*, is "absolutely certain," in *Plotin et l'Occident*, pp. 82–89.

13. Augustine tells of editing some manuscripts of Virgil while at Cassiciacum (*C. Acad.* 1:15 and 2:10) and of having his students there read the *Hortensius* (*C. Acad.* 1:4; see also 3:31); his extensive use of Cicero's *Academica* in his own treatise against the Academics suggests that he had that work on hand also.

14. For a judicious summary of these early developments in modern Augustine scholarship, see Nörregaard, pp. 1–14.

15. See especially Courcelle, *Recherches*, chapters 3 and 4, as well as pp. 251–255 of the conclusion.

16. See *De Beata Vita* 4 ("the sermons of our priest"), *De Util. Cred.* 20, and above all, *Conf.* 5:23–24.

17. This was first uncovered by Courcelle (*Recherches*, chapter 3) and extensively confirmed by later studies. See Nauroy, P. Hadot, "Platon et Plotin dans trois sermons de saint Ambroise," Solignac, "Nouveaux Parallèles," and Madec on the "Plotinian sermons" in his *Saint Ambroise*, pp. 61–71.

18. Among contemporary Augustine scholars, it is Robert J. O'Connell who does us the favor of emphasizing most consistently the fact that Augustine was constantly renewing and deepening his acquaintance with the books of the Neoplatonists, at least up to the time of the *Confessions* and probably beyond.

19. See "Ciceronian Point of Departure" in chapter 6.

20. So Courcelle, in his reconstruction of the summer of 386, *Recherches*, p. 157–167. This part of Courcelle's work strikes me as ingenious but questionable.

21. *Conf.* 7:13–14.

22. For a similar approach to this issue, see O'Connell, *Images*, chapter 2, especially pp. 115–118, 160–161, and 195–197.

23. Most notably, Augustine understands Platonist immaterialism far better in the *Confessions* than at Cassiciacum, where his main argument is in fact incompatible with the Plotinian doctrine of omnipresence—a doctrine that is central to his conception of the incorporeality of God in the *Confessions;* see "A Diagnosis" in chapter 7.

24. *Conf.* 7:16. The first clause is: "Et inde admonitus redire ad memetipsum, intravi in intima mea, duce Te."

25. *Ennead* 1:6.8 (the treatise entitled "On Beauty"). This passage (and its sequel immediately following) is interwoven with the parable of the Prodigal Son in *Conf.* 1:28 and alluded to again in *Conf.* 8:19, as well as quoted and praised in *Civ. Dei* 9:17, with explicit attribution to Plotinus (a rare thing in Augustine or any Christian writer). It may have become Augustine's favorite passage because he first heard it in a sermon of Ambrose, *De Isaac vel Animo* 78–79.

26. It should be emphasized that Narcissus's fate does not serve as a warning against self-love, but rather against loving one's image as reflected in material things like water or one's own body, which is a kind of image of the soul. The last thing Plotinus would disapprove of is the self-love of the

soul. A similar lesson is taught using the same mythic imagery in the context of a Gnostic story of the Fall in the first treatise of the Hermetic Corpus, *Poimandres* (*Hermetica* 1:14).

27. *Ennead* 1:6.8. Augustine picks up the reference to feet, chariots, and ships in his allusions to this text in *Conf.* 1:28 and 8:19. Closing one's eyes in order to attain true vision is another theme of *Poimandres* (*Hermetica* 1:30).

28. *Sol.* 1:7.

29. *Ennead* 4:7.10 (subsequent references to line numbers are from this chapter). For evidence that Augustine read this treatise, see Du Roy, p. 130 n.6, and Verbeke.

30. See also *Ennead* 3:4.3: "each of us is an intelligible world." On being identical with the Light within, see *Enneads* 1:6.9 and 6:9.9 (end).

31. This "golden soul" motif appears also in *Ennead* 1:6.5, the treatise that we are most sure Augustine read. A similar metaphor, describing the "spiritual man," was used by the Gnostics, according to Irenaeus, *Against Heresies* 1:6.2.

32. We must keep reminding ourselves of ancient conditions of reading: most of Augustine's "readers" were illiterate and would have heard these books read aloud. Hence they were quite literally an "audience," a set of hearers. See Brown's introduction to the Hackett edition of *Confessions*, p. xi, for an illuminating reconstruction of the conditions of readership in Augustine's era.

33. However, if O'Connell is right (in *Early Theory*, pp. 106–111) then there is one extraordinarily dense and allusive paragraph where Augustine hints at the kind of kind of idolatry he found in the books of the Platonists (*Conf.* 7:15)—though whom he expected to be able to decipher these hints is hard to imagine.

34. *Conf.* 7:16.

35. This use of one Platonist concept to correct another, so as to bring it in line with Catholic teaching is a method employed again in *Civ. Dei* 13:16 and 22:27.

36. See *Conf.* 7:23 where, after catching a glimpse of God "in the stroke of a trembling glance" Augustine finds himself too weak to gaze steadfastly at that dazzling light, and hence falls back to his usual self, "bearing with me only a beloved memory." But evidently it was such a memory that helped him solve the series of conceptual problems in 7:17–22. Compare the account of how a flash of insight is retained in memory and thence put into language in *De Cat. Rud.* 3.

37. Augustine affirms quite explicitly that pagan Platonists have seen God, *De Trin.* 4:20 (compare 12:23) and *Civ. Dei* 9:16.

38. *De Mag.* 46.

39. It is precisely for this reason that O'Connell, despite his strong emphasis on the Plotinian character of Augustine's thought, stands opposed to the thesis of Alfaric and others that Augustine's early writings are really Neoplatonist rather than Christian:

> Whether or not he was a Catholic must. . . be allowed to depend on his readiness to accept what the Church holds to be her belief, once it becomes plain to him what it is. And here there can be not the slightest question of his willingness to do that. Everything we have seen at Cassiciacum [i.e., his earliest writings] argues for it. (*Early Theory*, p. 260)

40. In the preface and first chapter of *Proslogion*, respectively. These formulas are often mistakenly attributed to Augustine. The latter does have a close precursor in Augustine's sermon 43:4, where he imagines himself saying "Believe, so that you may understand" to someone who would rather say "I understand, so that I may believe."

41. *De Trin.* 15:2.

42. *Enchiridion* 5.

43. In Augustine's early work, the moral cleansing of the mind's eye (needed to strengthen it to gaze at the bright light of Truth without flinching) is the essential function of Christian faith: see *Sol.*

1:12, *De Util. Cred.* 2, *De Fide et Symbolo* 25. The key scriptural text in this connection is Matthew 5:8 ("Blessed are the pure in heart for they shall see God"). But just as seeing God is defined by Platonist conceptions of intellectual vision, so purification of the heart is defined in Platonist fashion as a cleansing from the stain of sensible attachments (for the Platonist concept of purification of soul see for example *Phaedo* 64a–67d, *Enneads* 1:2.4 and 1:6.9, and Trouillard, especially chapters 10 and 11). Augustine's early emphasis on *purification* by faith is the precursor to his immensely influential interpretation of Paul on *justification* by faith (as one can clearly see in an early text such as *De Div. QQs 83*, section 68.3).

44. Augustine's whole ethics is based on the opposite of the common modern sentiment that the journey is more important than the destination, *De Doct.* 1:39.

45. For more details on how Augustine elaborates the relation between inward turn and external signs, see my conclusion.

46. *Ennead* 5:8. For the likelihood that Augustine read this treatise, see O'Connell, *Early Theory*, p. 167–168, and the whole of chapter 8.

47. See *Ennead* 6:9.11, describing the culmination of the ascent to contemplation of the One: "So then there was not two, but the seer himself was one with what he saw; it was not so much a seeing as a being-made-one." Metaphors of vision must be dropped as we ascend from the level of Mind to the level of the One, that is, from the realm of intelligible Forms to that which is above Being and Form. See likewise *Ennead* 6:7.34–35 (where Plotinus once again introduces a notion of inward vision only to say that this is more like unification than vision) and the helpful comments of Schwyzer, "'Bewusst' und 'Unbewusst' bei Plotin," p. 376.

48. In turning inward to be united with the One, the soul "arrives not at something else but at itself," as Plotinus says in *Ennead* 6:9.11.

49. See *De Mag.* 38.

50. See the similar description of separation from God at the end of *Ennead* 6:9.7. This striking metaphor is echoed in *Conf.* 10:38: "Late have I loved You, O Beauty so ancient and so new, late have I loved You. And behold, You were inside, and *I was outside*" (similarly *Conf.* 7:11 and 4:18). There is more than scintillating rhetoric here. According to Augustine we become united with what we love (*De Ord.* 2:48, *De Lib. Arb.* 1:33; see also *De Vera Rel.* 23—similarly *Ennead* 1:6.9). Consequently, in loving external things we ourselves become in an important sense "external," dwelling outside our own souls in the world of perishing bodies.

51. Similar Plotinian references to the (temporal) priority of faith to understanding and vision are found in *Enneads* 1:3.1 and 6:9.4. Augustine probably drew on these passages in his own formulation of the faith/understanding relation; see O'Connell, *Early Theory*, pp. 223–225.

52. Other treatments of this problem: *Enneads* 1:4.10, 4:8.8, and 5:1.12. The best scholarly discussion of Plotinus on this question remains that of Schwyzer, "'Bewusst' und 'Unbewusst' bei Plotin," especially p. 371.

53. See the similar remark in *Ennead* 4:7.10, quoted in "Some Plotinian Readings" earlier.

54. See likewise the function of faith in Augustine's early epistemology: by faith the soul "believes that what it should turn and look at is something that will make it happy or blessed, once seen" (*Sol.* 1:13) and

> so long as the soul is in this body, even if it fully sees, that is, understands God, yet because the senses of the body still perform their own function they can lead us into doubt if not deception—so faith can be said to be what resists them, and believes something else to be true. (*Sol.* 1:14)

55. *De Fide Rer. Inv.* The title is perhaps also meant as a biblical allusion (to Heb. 11:1) but this looks less likely in the Latin.

56. *Conf.* 10:34.

4. Problems of Christian Platonism

1. For the effect of this on Augustine's career, see "A Program of Education" in chapter 6.

2. See the third letter of Cyril to Nestorius, and the eleventh of the famous twelve anathemas appended thereto, conveniently found in Stevenson, pp. 284 and 288, or Hardy, pp. 352 and 354. This letter, with its anathemas, is traditionally included among the decrees of Ephesus 431, although there is some confusion about the content of the original Acts of the council and it seems likely that, like Cyril's second letter to Nestorius, this letter and its anathemas was read with approval but not formally adopted (see Grillmeier, pp. 414–415). For a fine introduction to the issues under discussion at the council, see Young, pp. 213–229.

3. It is useful to be aware that unlike the English words "flesh" and "carnal," which have their primary etymological associations with meat, the Greek word *sarx* (from which we get "sarcophagus") has its primary etymological associations with death and mortality. Hence "life-giving flesh" has the same paradoxical flavor as a phrase like "life-giving mortality."

4. *Ho esō anthrōpos*, Romans 7:22, 2 Corinthians 4:16, and Ephesians 3:16. The noun is the generic word for "human being," not the word for "man," but I have kept the traditional translation "inner man" in order to preserve continuity with previous discussions in the literature, and also because any other rendering (such as "inner self") is likely to be misleading or to beg important questions of this investigation.

5. *Ho entos anthrōpos, Republic* 9:589a.

6. See Wolff, pp. 40–58.

7. Ephesians 1:18. Most scholars think this "Pauline" letter was not actually authored by Paul himself but by someone in the Pauline circle. But it is enough like Paul's writing that I assume the author is, like Paul, a Hellenistic Jew and probably a native speaker of Greek.

8. For a fascinating and plausible speculation about where Paul got the phrase, see Jewett, pp. 391–401, who also gives a summary of the history of scholarly discussion on the subject. Jewett's suggestion is that Paul picked up the phrase from Gnostic opponents and put it to polemical use, in the process changing its meaning from the Gnostics' "spirit" or "spiritual man" (*pneumatikos*) to something more like the Hebrew "heart." Jewett's account, while more detailed and interesting, shares the key features of the account I am proposing here, namely, that the ultimate source of the phrase is Platonic but that Paul's use of it does not commit him to Platonism (much less to Gnosticism). With that in mind, I would add one more consideration in favor of Jewett's view: Plato's "man within" occurs in a passage that seems to have inspired Gnostic thinking about the three "races" of men ("spiritual," "psychic," and "earthly"). The importance of this Platonic passage for Gnosticism is confirmed by its appearance, in a garbled Coptic translation (without the phrase "man within"), in the Nag Hammadi library (IV,5). Hence the missing link between Plato's "man within" and Paul's "inner man" may be Paul's Gnostic opponents, who based some of their anthropology on this text of Plato—which subsequently became a standard text for some Gnostic groups and thus found its way into Coptic and thence into the Nag Hammadi collection.

9. A more striking version of the same phenomenon is the Epistle to the Hebrews, which makes extensive use of a Platonist contrast between the true temple in heaven, the place of eternal redemption, and its temporary shadow and imitation on earth (a contrast found in previous Jewish literature, e.g., Wisdom of Solomon 9:8 and Philo, *Who is Heir* 112) but then defies straightforward Platonist reading by speaking of the resurrected Christ—an embodied man, not a pure soul—as if he literally brought his own physical blood into the eternal sanctuary (9:12 and 9:24).

10. At least this seems to be the most plausible conclusion to draw from Eusebius *History of the Church* 6:19.6 (on Origen's philosophical education) combined with Porphyry *Life of Plotinus* 3 (on Plotinus's education). Both refer to an Alexandrian teacher named Ammonius, who was apparently an apostate Christian; see Dodds, "Numenius and Ammonius," p. 31; there are, however, some serious incongruities on the two accounts, and it is possible that two distinct Ammoniuses are in view; see pp. 35–36 and 43–44.

11. See "The Prologue to the Commentary on The Song of Songs" (in *Origen,* Greer, trans.), pp. 217–231. The identification of the inner man with the soul is explicit on p. 223.

12. See Rahner's study, "Le début," which cites and discusses the key texts. To these texts should be added, as Madec notes, Origen's "Dialogue with Heraclides" (see especially pp. 444–453).

13. Brown paints Africa as the corn belt and Bible belt of the Roman Empire, pp. 19–27; for the appeal of Manichaean sprituality in this environment, see pp. 42–45.

14. *Conf.* 5:23–24. On Ambrose's use of the language of interiority, drawn from Scripture, Origen, and Plotinus, see Madec, "L'homme intérieur." It is striking how much of this use is concentrated in works that originated at about the time Augustine was living in Milan and listening to Ambrose's sermons: the expositions on the Gospel of Luke, on Psalm 118, the *Hexameron,* and the sermon "On Isaac or the Soul." For the dating, see Courcelle, *Recherches,* pp. 123–124. According to Madec, Ambrose's concept of interiority is of a piece with his use of philosophical concepts in general: in a word, undigested. Ambrose is capable of transcribing words, phrases, sentences, and whole paragraphs from a philosophical source like Plotinus into his sermons (without attribution) and then polemicizing fiercely against "philosophy." One of Madec's conclusions about this puzzling phenomenon is that Ambrose is a fine pastor but no philosopher, as his rather mechanical and literal borrowings from philosophical sources contrast with Augustine's profound and personal integration of philosophical themes into Christian spirituality (see "L'homme intérieur," pp. 300–302, and the conclusion of his *Saint Ambroise et la philosophie,* pp. 346–347). From this I draw the further conclusion: Ambrose may well have been the one who initially provided Augustine with the language of inwardness (introducing Augustine to Plotinian inwardness in his sermons before Augustine read Plotinus for himself), but Ambrose could never have devised an original philosophical concept like the inner space of the self; that was Augustine's doing.

15. In *Ennead* 5:1.10, a treatise Augustine certainly read, Plotinus gives an exegesis of the phrase *ho eisō anthrōpos* ("the inward man"), which he explicitly attributes to Plato (though the phrasing is actually closer to Paul!). He alludes to Plato's phrase again in *Ennead* 1:1.10 (which it is much less likely that Augustine read).

16. See *De Beata Vita* 35 and *De Ord.* 2:7. Beginning with *Sol.* 1:12 talk of the mind's eye becomes programmatic and incessant.

17. For Augustine's considered view on the meaning of "inner man" language in Paul, see *De Div. QQs 83,* section 51, where he deals with exegetical issues (such as the connection between the "inner man"/"outer man" contrast and Paul's "new man"/"old man" contrast and Christ/Adam contrast) and places the concept of inner man in the context of his ontology and psychology—all without evoking an inward turn or inner space.

18. *Conf.* 10:8–9. This passage also alludes extensively to the five inner senses.

19. "Behold, body and soul in me are present to me, the one outwardly and the other inwardly," ibid. 10:9. The context is one in which Augustine is explaining not the inner powers of the soul but the objects of sensible perception and is preparing the transition from one to the other: "The inner man knows these things through external servants. I, the inner, know these things—I, I the soul, through the senses of my body."

20. See *De Trin.* 11:1, 12:1, 12:13, 13:4, 13:26, 14:4, 14:10. Most of these usages occur in the course of introducing or recapitulating some part of the overall inquiry.

21. See *De Mor. Eccl.* 36 and 80, where Augustine quotes the phrase from Paul (2 Cor. 4:16) but it does not lead him into any discussion of inwardness. This work is earlier than *De Magistro,* according to *Retractations.*

22. *De Mag.* 2. Similar phrasing recurs in section 38 ("Christ who is said to be in the inner man"), discussed in "Who Is Reason?" in chapter 6. Compare *De Ver. Rel.* 72, where *truth* "dwells in the inner man."

23. Eph. 3:16–17. The conflation is easy enough to achieve, as it could conceivably result just from an odd punctuation of the Latin, as follows: "ut det vobis secundum divitias gloriae suae virtute

corroborari per Spiritum ejus, *in interiore homine habitare Christus,* per fidem in cordibus vestris in caritate radicati et fundati." The standard punctuation is rather: ". . . per Spiritum ejus in interiore homine, *habitare Christus per fidem in cordibus vestris,* in caritate radicati et fundati . . ."

24. 1 Corinthians 3:16, as quoted in *De Mag.* 2.

25. See Romans 8:10, Galatians 4:19, and Colossians 1:27 (all second person plural). The first-person usage in Galatians 2:20 is unusual and therefore particularly striking.

26. See Romans 10:14–17.

27. For example *Conf.* 4:11 and 4:13.

28. *Conf.* 4:18. "Deep in the heart he is" renders *"intimus cordi est."* The quote is from Isaiah 46:8, mistranslating a Hebrew text that means something more like: "Call it to mind, you transgressors."

29. Ibid. "Happy life" (*beata vita*), it should be noted, is a technical term (taken from Cicero) translating the key term of Greek philosophical ethics, *eudaimonia.*

30. *Conf.* 4:19. The quote is from Psalm 19:5.

31. *Conf.* 4.19.

32. *De Doct.* 1:38. See Mayer, *Zeichen,* 2:249–261 for the *via/patria* scheme in Augustine's Christology and its relation to his ontology (especially the contrast between mutable and immutable being) and ethics (especially the contrast of *uti* and *frui,* things to be used and things to be enjoyed). The relation is basically quite simple: because Christ's humanity is mutable, not immutable (hence temporal, not eternal), it is way, not goal, to be used rather than to be enjoyed. Christ's flesh is not a thing for us to cling to.

33. The significance of external things—and how this coheres with Augustine's ongoing project of inward turn—is a subject for another study. See the conclusion.

34. 1 Corinthians 1:24. A more accurate rendering would be "Christ the Power of God and the Wisdom of God," translating Paul's *dynamis* with *potentia,* but Augustine always translates it with *virtus,* which can mean power but also ethical virtue. The philosophical attraction of this translation is obvious: it identifies Christ with two terms that are at the very center of ancient philosophy.

35. See for example *C. Acad.* 3:20, *De Ord.* 1:32, *Conf.* 3:8, *Civ. Dei* 8:1, *De Trin.* 14:2.

36. *Conf.* 7:13–14.

37. *Conf.* 3:7. The quote is from the parable of the Prodigal Son, a text that Augustine often associates with Plotinian themes of inwardness, and particularly with *Ennead* 1:6.8 (which he deliberately conflates with the language of this parable in *Conf.* 1:28). The prodigal son "comes to himself" and says "let me arise and go to my father," a double movement in which Augustine sees the in then up movement of the inward turn. See *Civ. Dei* 11:28 and *Retract.* 1:7.3 (in Migne, 1:8.3).

38. *Conf.* 3:8.

39. Ibid. 3:9.

40. Ibid. 3:10.

41. Ibid.

42. *C. Faustum* 20:9. Faustus is, of course, quoting 1 Corinthians 1:24.

43. 1 Corinthians 1:24 is referred to twice in the Cassiciacum dialogues (at a time when Augustine quotes the Bible very infrequently), and it stands at the head of Augustine's Christology in his early writings. See *C. Acad.* 2:1, *De Beata Vita* 34, *De Lib. Arb.* 1:5, *De Mor. Eccl.* 1:22, *De Quant. Anim.* 76, *De Musica* 6:52, *De Vera Rel.* 3, *De Mag.* 38, *De Div. QQs 83,* sections 11 and 26—and this does not count all the times Christ is simply referred to as "the Wisdom of God."

44. A complete translation of this brief treatise is found in appendix 2. It is actually section 46 of Augustine's answers to *Eighty-three Different Questions,* hence the usual citation is *De Div. QQs 83,* section 46. But for convenience most scholars refer to it under the title *De Ideis.* Hence I shall call it Augustine's essay "On Ideas."

45. For the genesis of *De Div. QQs 83,* see *Retract.* 1:26. For this period in Augustine's life, after

his conversion in Milan and return to Africa but before his forced appointment as a clergyman at Hippo, see Brown, chapter 13.

46. This historical fabrication is a patristic commonplace (see Justin Martyr *Ad Graec.* 20 [in *Ante-Nicene Fathers*], Clement of Alexandria *Strom.* 1:22, Origen *C. Cels.* [in *Ante-Nicene Fathers*], 4:39) of which Ambrose is particularly fond. See in Augustine *De Doct.* 2:43 (reporting Ambrose's views) and *Civ. Dei* 8:11 (backing away from some of the more implausible suggestions made in the previous text). On the lost work in which Ambrose makes this argument, see Madec, *Saint Ambroise,* pp. 249–279 and 323–337.

47. For this architectural usage see *De Ord.* 2:34.

48. See the very similar argument in support of the Platonist concept of "intelligible world," which Augustine makes near the end of his life:

> Plato indeed did not err in saying there was an intelligible world. . . . For "intelligible world" is a name for that eternal and immutable Reason by which God made the world. Whoever denies this, must say in consequence that God made what he made irrationally [*irrationabiliter*], or else that when he made it or before made it, he did not know what he was making, if there was with him no reason for making it [*ratio faciendi*]. But if there was—as indeed there was—then this seems to be what Plato called the intelligible world. (*Retract.* 1:3.2)

49. See for example Aquinas, *ST* I, 15.1. Notice that in handling the first objection Aquinas sides with Augustine against Pseudo-Dionysius (or Denys, as I call him hereafter), the most systematic Christian Platonist among the Eastern Fathers.

50. See the fourth and eighth of the "chapters of Italus," in the *Synodikon of Orthodoxy* (read every year in solemn liturgy on "the Sunday of Orthodoxy" in the Eastern Churches), in Gouillard's edition, p. 59 (ll. 198–200 and 220–224). See also Gouillard's commentary on pp. 194–195, which identifies the background assumptions.

51. Aquinas defends Augustine's essay "On Ideas" by pointing out that in locating Ideas in the mind of God rather than outside God, Augustine sides with Aristotle against Plato (*ST* I, 15.1, ad 1). This may be a surprise, but Thomas is quite correct: for Augustine got his doctrine of divine Mind from Neoplatonism, which got it from Aristotle via Alexander of Aphrodisias and others, as we have seen in chapter 2.

52. Augustine will even use the Nicene term *consubstantialis* in this connection, in *De Lib. Arb.* 2:32–33.

53. That all intellectual vision involves seeing God, even though not all intellectual vision is fully beatific, is a conclusion that follows from Plotinus's doctrine of the soul, sketched earlier (see especially the end of "Some Plotinian Readings" in chapter 3): for the fallen soul can have partial vision of what is indissolubly one (the dividedness belongs to the soul in its disunified state, not to the intelligible thing it sees). I use the word "glimpses" to designate this partial and fragmentary vision, which achieves only a partial and temporary happiness.

54. For instance Pseudo-Dionysius (or Denys) will speak of eternal models or exemplars (*paradeigmata*) "preexisting" in the unity of God as causes (*aitias*) or formative principles (*logoi*) in the one Logos (*On Divine Names* 824c and 872c). Maximus the Confessor, close student of Denys's texts and revered Eastern theologian, elaborates in some detail the concept of eternal formative *logoi* within the divine Logos, the second person of the Trinity (see Meyendorff, pp. 134–135). It would surely be plausible for Augustine to claim that these *logoi* are *rationes* by another name—which are in turn Platonic Ideas by another name. But unlike Augustine, Maximus insists that these are incomprehensible, in the sense of "beyond intelligibility," *akatanoeton* (*Ambigua,* PG 91:1080a).

55. *ST* I, 12.1 and 12.7. A similar usage occurs in Kant, where "noumenon" (which is Greek for the thing understood in intellectual knowledge) designates precisely what is beyond the scope of human understanding.

56. Whatever is true of the divine being will be true also of the Ideas, since "an Idea in God is nothing other than his essence." (*ST* I, 15.1 ad 3).

57. Augustine often insists that the soul is "nearer" to God than any other creature is (e.g. *De Quant. Anim.* 77, *De Mor. Eccl.* 1:18, *Civ. Dei* 11:26). This terminology apparently comes from Plotinus, who uses it as equivalent to Plato's talk of souls being "akin to" divine things in *Ennead* 1:2.2 (where he says the soul participates in Form more than bodies do because it is "nearer and more akin" to Forms than the body is). Augustine may have this passage in mind when he explains that the soul is nearer to the eternal reasons than bodies are, in *De Immort. Anim.* 24. Other Plotinian references to the kinship between soul and Form that would have been familiar to Augustine are found in *Enneads* 1:6.9 and 5:1.1.

58. See especially *De Div. QQs 83*, section 51.2.

59. See Ep. 18:2 (translated in appendix 2). This three-tiered ontology is never far from Augustine's mind when he is discussing the soul. For more detailed exposition, see Bourke, *Augustine's View of Reality* (pp. 3–7), as well as his anthology *The Essential Augustine,* pp. 43–66, where he provides a selection of passages from Augustine explaining the conceptual structure of this hierarchy of being and its three levels.

60. Translations of these two key Augustinian texts are provided in appendix 2.

61. Augustine is certainly aware of the Plotinian concept of the One, and in fact he uses conceptuality from that level elsewhere (most importantly in articulating the unity of the Trinity, e.g., in *De Trin.* 6:8 and *Civ. Dei* 11:10, where he uses a doctrine of divine simplicity that he explicitly attributes to the Platonists in *Civ. Dei* 8:6). But in the early period his focus is clearly on God as intelligible Mind. It is not clear why Augustine thought he could apply conceptuality from both levels to the Christian God without contradicting himself, but the possibility might have been suggested to him by a tendency in Porphyry to blur the distinction between the top two levels (detected by P. Hadot in *Porphyre et Victorinus,* 1:482–485).

62. *On the Divine Names* 1:5, 593b.

63. Proclus *Elements* 166–183. There is the complication that this proliferation extends even to the level of the One, where Proclus places a hierarchy of divine unities or "henads" (*Elements* 113–165). I take this to be an elaboration of concepts that from a Plotinian perspective belong properly at the level of Mind rather than One (for the latter ought to include no hierarchies, distinctions, or plurality). Hence I would trace Denys's angelic hierarchy back to Plotinus's Mind via a historical line of descent passing through the divine hierarchies of fifth-century Neoplatonism.

64. I do not mean to say that this was the first time. A similar mutation seems to have occurred in Gnosticism, whose heavenly realm, *pleroma,* is populated by beings called *aeons* or *archons* ("principalities"), which often look very much like a cross between Platonic Forms and Jewish angels. But Denys is separated from the gnostics by the same thing that separates him from Proclus: the orthodox Christian doctrine of Creation.

65. It should be emphasized that the doctrine of divine incomprehensibility is not an idiosyncracy of Denys's but has been the official teaching of the Eastern churches ever since the Cappadocian Fathers in the fourth century: see for example Basil *C. Eun.* 1:12 and Ep. 234, Gregory of Naziansen *Orat.* 28:3–4 (the 2nd Theological Oration) and Gregory of Nyssa *C. Eun.* 2:3 and *De Sanct. Trin.* (= Basil Ep. 189:6). This doctrine is not dependent on Neoplatonism, but it plainly has an "elective affinity" with Plotinus's doctrine of the incomprehensible One, an affinity that shows itself with particular clarity in the Neoplatonist Denys. (Note that the treatises just cited are not philosophical or mystical works but expositions of the doctrine of the Trinity.) The universal acceptance of this doctrine is evident in John of Damascus' seventh-century treatise *De Fide Orthodoxa* (see especially 1:4), a compendium of the teachings of the Greek Fathers that could also be called the world's first systematic theology text, which became highly influential in the Latin world beginning in the twelfth century (see de Ghellinck, pp. 374–404).

66. *On the Divine Names* 1:1, 588b.

67. *Mystical Theology* 1:1, 997b.

68. *On the Divine Names* 7:3, 872b.

69. For the respect in which Augustine's view of intellectual vision follows Plato rather than Plotinus on this point, see "Education for Vision" in chapter 5.

70. Denys is capable of saying that God is quite simply *un*intelligible (*a-noetos*), in *The Celestial Hierarchy* 2:3, 141a. If he is Mind at all, he is "unintelligible Mind," *nous anoetos* (*On the Divine Names* 1:1, 588b); he is neither an intelligible nor a sensible thing, neither *noeton* nor *aistheton* (*On the Divine Names* 7:3, 869c). Other vocabulary for incomprehensibility in Denys includes *aperileptos* and *akataleptos,* as well as *agnostos* (literally "unknown").

71. Even Denys's images of "divine darkness," such as those in the opening of the *Mystical Theology,* are meant to express the superabundance of light, not its absence.

72. Sermon 117:5. The passage begins: "Ad mentem Deus pertinet, intellegendus est. . . ."

73. For example in Aquinas, *ST* I, 12.7 "comprehend" means "know completely." However, one further complication of the terminological history should be noted. The medieval theologians could use the term *comprehensor* to describe the blessed, following the Vulgate translation of 1 Corinthians 9:24, "sic currite ut comprehendatis"—a usage Aquinas defends in *ST* I–II, 4.3. But this usage (which implies that God *is* comprehensible in some sense) is not one from which Aquinas draws any philosophical implications. When he calls God *incomprehensibile* it is normally the Augustinian sense of the word that he has in mind.

74. *De Mag.* 33–41.

75. *De Doct.* 3:9–13. See Augustine's hermeneutical debt to Ambrose as described in the *Confessions:* the reason why Ambrose did and Augustine did not understand the Scriptures is because the one could and the other could not "think of a spiritual substance" (*Conf.* 5:25) and thus read Scripture spiritually rather than literally (*Conf.* 5:24).

76. Also translated "of one essence" or "of one being" (Augustine uses the standard Latin translation *consubstantialem*), this is the famous *homo-ousios* clause of the Nicene creed, whose exact meaning has often been in dispute but which all the orthodox traditions agree excludes any inequality between Father and Son. For at the very least, the clause implies that the Son is not a different or lower *kind* of God from the Father.

77. This "subordinationism" was a much broader and more widely accepted form of doctrine than the Arian heresy. It was central to the Alexandrian theology of the third century (including both Clement and Origen) and was represented by such respectable churchmen as Eusebius of Caesarea, the famous Church historian. But along with Arianism, it was ruled out in the wake of Nicaea; see Young, pp. 17–18.

78. In the Cassiciacum dialogues, Augustine twice hints at the sort of *via negativa* that suits a theology of the incomprehensible One rather than the intelligible Mind: God is "best known by not knowing" (*De Ord.* 2:44), "of whom there is no knowledge in the soul, except to know how it does not know him" (*De Ord.* 2:47). Augustine never develops these hints any further, and indeed the latter flatly contradicts the project he pursues in the *Soliloquies,* his next work, which concludes with an attempt to prove that there *is* a divine knowledge in the soul. Their presence in Augustine's earliest writings is best explained, I think, in connection with the detection by Du Roy (the leading scholar of the doctrine of the Trinity in Augustine's early period) of traces of subordinationist thinking in these writings (Du Roy, pp. 154–168). Although even at Cassiciacum Augustine is already informed about Nicene doctrine and hence rejects in theory any hierarchy in the Trinity (insisting for instance that the third person of the Trinity proceeds "without any degeneration," *De Ord.* 2:16; see the same language in *De Beata Vita* 35), he does tend to associate the second person of the Trinity particularly with the intelligibility of God, in a way that suggests a kind of subordinationist substructure to his thinking. Thus he relates the Son to the Father, as Truth to "the Father of Truth" (*De Ord.* 2:51) and as Wisdom, which is "the measure of the soul" (*De Beata Vita* 33), to the "supreme Measure," which is unmeasured by any other measure (*De Beata Vita* 34). This suggests a Plotinian hier-

archy of the Father above Form giving Form to the Son who thereby mediates Form to the Soul. (See Du Roy, pp. 156–159, for likely Plotinian sources; in this scheme the Holy Spirit is identified with Reason in the Soul, Du Roy, pp. 130–143, a theme we shall see much more of later on.) My guess is that the scattered hints at negative theology in his earliest works were meant to be connected with the incomprehensibility of the Father but had to be dropped once Augustine had fully overcome the vestiges of subordinationism in his own thought.

79. Matthew 17:1–8, Mark 9:2–8, and Luke 9:28–36.

80. See Palamas, *Triads* 3:1.9–24 (Meyendorff, pp. 71–82).

81. 2 Corinthians 4:6.

82. See Aquinas *ST* III, 62.5.

5. Inward Turn and Intellectual Vision

1. Aubin, pp. 24–26 and 55–59.

2. See the metaphors of turning in Plato's *Republic* 518a 521c, 525c, and 532b. For "turning" in Plotinus, see "Turning into the Inside" in chapter 2.

3. See the earlier discussion in "In then Up" in chapter 3.

4. See *Enneads* 1:6.8, Augustine's favorite passage from Plotinus, quoted in "Some Plotinian Readings" in chapter 3.

5. *Conf.* 7:1.

6. Ibid. 7:2.

7. Ibid. 7:7.

8. Ibid. 7:1. The reference to "nothing" here is a leitmotif of Augustine's various formulations of this particular problem.

9. Ibid.

10. *Sol.* 2:34, *De Musica* 6:32 and 51–52, *De Vera Rel.* 18, and (using the term "false images") *De Ord.* 2:43. As the passage from *De Musica* makes particularly clear, the phrase "turning to phantasms," which for Thomas Aquinas signifies a natural and essential stage in human knowing (*ST* I, 84.7), can for Augustine only mean something pathological, tantamount to the Fall of the soul—its turning from higher to lower things.

11. *Conf.* 7:1.

12. On the continuity between Augustine and modern turns to the subject, see Taylor, especially chapter 7 (though I read the nuances of Augustine's Platonism rather differently).

13. *Conf.* 7:23. The phrase "I passed" is supplied in brackets, because the Latin sentence actually has no main verb.

14. *Conf.* 10:11.

15. *Conf.* 7:23 and 10:11. Augustine would have learned about this Aristotelian concept from Cicero; see "The Superiority of Soul in Cicero" in chapter 6.

16. *Conf.* 7:23. The phrase "drew thought away from habit" refers to the "carnal habit" mentioned earlier in 7:23 (to be discussed hereafter); it is also a quotation from Cicero, *Tusc.* 1:38 (discussed in "Cicero's Turn to the Soul" in chapter 6 and "The Location of the Soul" in chapter 10). The judgment that the immutable is to be preferred to the mutable is presented as an example of a truth so evident to the mind that no one (not even a Manichaean) could want to deny it (see the conclusion to *C. Faustum*, 33:9, where the conviction that God is incorruptible and immutable is presented as "naturally implanted in every human mind").

17. *Conf.* 7:23.

18. For this methodological perspective, which informs all my comments on the *Confessions,* see "Augustine on 'the Books of the Platonists'" in chapter 3.

19. *De Lib. Arb.* 2:8–39.

20. See especially the ascent from sense to memory to intellect, designed to prove the non-spatiality and therefore incorporeality of the soul and (*a fortiori*) of God, *C. Ep. Fund.* 40–41.

21. That is, *Conf.* 7:16, 7:23, and 10:8–38.

22. See especially the inward and upward movement announced in *De Trin.* 11:1 and 12:1.

23. We may glimpse God as Truth (see the end of *De Trin.* 8:2) and as Good (8:3) yet still have no hint of how to conceive God as the coequal Trinity taught by Nicaea. That is why Augustine seeks some analogy of the Trinity that will help us understand it (8:8), and it should be no surprise by now that the place he looks to find this analogy, this clue to the nature of God, is none other than the soul—just as in *Conf.* 7.

24. For the interlocking judgments of truth, unity, being, goodness and beauty, all dependent on the light of divine Truth, Unity, Being, Goodness and Beauty, see especially *De Vera Rel.* 52–60, but also *De Lib. Arb.* 2:22 (unity), 2:33–35 (truth), and 2:36 and 46 (good)—and note of course *Conf.* 7:17–21, the meditation on the goodness of all being that follows from Augustine's first glimpse of Truth.

25. So end both glimpses of God in *Conf.* 7 (i.e., 7:16 and 7:23).

26. See the summaries of what he learned from the books of the Platonists, in *Conf.* 7:26 and 8:1.

27. *Conf.* 7:16.

28. *Ep.* 118:23.

29. See especially his treatise on the topic (given the title "On Being being one and the same, everywhere at the same time, as a whole"), *Enneads* 6:4–5. For the influence of this treatise on Augustine see O'Connell, "Ennead VI, 4 and 5" and *Early Theory*, chapter 1.

30. See "The Lesson of Geometry" in chapter 10.

31. See especially *De Nat. et Grat.* 29.

32. Denzinger-Schönmetzer, section 2318.

33. See for example John Paul II, *The Splendor of Truth* 6–11, which unfolds a deeply Augustinian anthropology, and the new *Catechism of the Catholic Church*, part I, section 1, chapter 1, subsection 1, "The Desire for God."

34. Here, for example, is a classic formulation from Karl Rahner, in his essay "Nature and Grace" (p. 185):

> If someone affirms: I experience myself as a being which is absolutely ordained for the immediate possession of God, his statement need not be false. He will only be mistaken if he maintains that this unconditional longing is an essential element of "pure" nature or if he says that such pure nature, which does not exist, *could* not exist.

This unconditional longing has its source in the graced component of concrete human being that Rahner calls "the supernatural existential" in "Concerning the Relationship between Nature and Grace," pp. 311–317.

35. For this general strategy for reading the Church Fathers, see the discussion of "the ambiguity of nature," in von Balthasar, pp. 270–273, and the reference to *Humani Generis,* pp. 343–344.

36. See appendix 2.

37. For a thorough but highly unsympathetic study of this movement, as well as of the meaning of the official interventions against it, see Fonck; for a more sympathetic treatment of the movement in its historical context, see McCool, chapter 5. Not all the theses that the Holy Office rejects under the name "ontologism" apply to Augustine, but the first three are pertinent:

1. Immediate knowledge of God, at least in habit, is essential to the human mind or intellect, in such a way that without it nothing can be known; for it is the intellectual light itself.

2. The Being in which we understand all things and without which we understand nothing, is the divine Being.

3. Universals, considered in their objective reality [*a parte rei considerata*], are not really distinct from God (Denzinger-Schönmetzer, sections 2841–43).

Substitute "Truth" for "Being" in thesis 2, and you have the crowning insight of Augustine's inward turn. And of course you *can* substitute "Truth" for "Being," because for Augustine they are logically coextensive (or as the medieval logicians would say, "convertible," *ST* I, 16.3).

38. *ST* I, 85.1. Note the equivalence of "universal" with "intelligible species," which is a created component of things in the temporal world, quite different from the eternal Ideas in the Mind of God.

39. See *ST* I, 84.5, where Aquinas's interpretation of Augustine's essay "On Ideas" avoids Augustine's ontologist conclusions by imposing a non-Platonist epistemology at the decisive point.

40. *De Lib. Arb.* 2:33: "incommutabilem veritatem haec omnia quae incommutabiliter vera sunt continentem."

41. Contrast *ST* I, 12.11 ad 3, where Aquinas's argument against an Augustinian ontologist position is clinched by the observation:

Therefore just as to see anything sensibly it is not necessary that the substance of the sun be seen, so also to see anthing intelligibly it is not necessary that the essence of God be seen.

This comparison has no force against a position that locates all truly intelligible things in God—analogous to locating everything that is visible within the sun. And that is precisely Augustine's position: all intelligible truths are contained in the one intelligible Truth.

42. Gilson, *The Christian Philosophy of St. Augustine,* pp. 77–111.

43. Gilson's conscience as a historian seems to be nagging him when he writes:

I am prepared to admit that there is much to be said against my interpretation of Augustinian illumination. One might justly say that it oversimplifies both texts and doctrine in order to explain it more easily. However, I propose it only to the extent that the facts warrant its acceptance, and, in short, as a *psychological rather than an historical solution to the problem.* (Ibid., p. 88)

I am at a loss how to understand this last remark, except as a sort of verbal squirm of discomfort. Note also the extraordinary remark:

To be sure, Augustine made no mistake when he thought that he found a doctrine of divine illumination ready-made in Plotinus, *and yet he had no idea how far removed from it he was himself.* (Ibid., p. 109)

It seems we must regard Gilson's interpretation as a correction of Augustine's own understanding of the meaning of his thought.

44. Ibid., pp. 92–96.

45. Hessen, pp. 189–190.

46. Note the central role of the term "Truth" (*veritas*) in the classic "visions" of *Conf.* 7:16 and 7:23.

47. Nash, chapters 7 and 8 (the latter with detailed criticism of Gilson).

48. For divine contemplation as the fulfillment of what is best in human nature (i.e., not its mortal part, but rather reason or mind), see *Protrepticus,* fragments 6 and 10c (Ross), *Eudemian Ethics,* 7:15,1249b10–22, and *Nichomachean Ethics* 10:7,1177b16–1178a9. Thomas's way of accommodating such texts is to distinguish between two kinds of happiness, natural and supernatural, and to propose that the happiness Aristotle has in view is the merely natural sort, in contrast to the ultimate beatific vision, which is supernatural (*ST* I, 62.1). One can only wonder what Aristotle (or Alexander of Aphrodisias or Plotinus) would have made of such a distinction; in any case one can hardly call it "Aristotelian."

49. *ST* I, 12.4.

50. Of course the medieval tradition known as "Augustinian illuminationism" (represented by the older Franciscans and most influentially by Aquinas's great contemporary Bonaventure) remained closer to Augustine on this point than the Thomist tradition. Yet Gilson has a much easier time exonerating Bonaventure from the charge of ontologism than Augustine, because the key distinction he tries to impose on Augustine's texts is actually to be found in Bonaventure (*Philosophy of St. Bonaventure*, p. 362; see especially Bonaventure's *responsio* in *Disputed Questions concerning Christ's Knowledge*, question 4). The key distinction is that the eternal reasons in God are the *regulative causes* of our intellectual knowledge rather than its *immediate objects*. Consequently, intellectual vision (which does indeed involve some dim and indirect perception of the eternal reasons in God) is different in kind from beatific vision (where we actually gaze at the essence of God). Thus Bonaventure can affirm with Denys that in the final mystic ascent to God "all intellectual operations must be left behind" (*The Journey of the Mind to God* 7:7). Such mysticism, with its assumption of divine incomprehensibility, is foreign to Augustine; it means abandoning precisely the activity of the intellect in which, by Augustine's reckoning, the soul finds its ultimate happiness.

51. *Sol.* 1:9.

52. *De Lib. Arb.* 2:35–39.

53. See *De Cat. Rud.* 3 and *De Trin.* 8:3 (sudden illumination) and *C. Acad.* 2:5 and *Conf.* 3:8 (suddenly kindled fire—an image that Augustine seems to associate especially with his philosophical reading). Such metaphors have a history going back at least to Plato, Ep. 7 (344b).

54. *Acad.* 2:31.

55. See the Augustinian parallel, "For what does the soul more strongly desire than Truth?" *In. Joh. Evang.*, 26:5. This saying arises in the context of Augustine's theology of grace. He is explaining how divine grace moves the human will by attraction rather than compulsion: it reveals that which the soul most deeply desires, the Truth. The soul's innate desire for Truth is the reason why grace and free will are in harmony with one another rather than in competition. Thus Augustine's anti-Pelagian theology makes no sense apart from his Platonist epistemology.

56. *Conf.* 3:7. See "Wisdom by Another Name" in chapter 4.

57. See "Consequences of Nicaea" in chapter 4.

58. On ignorance and moral weakness as the penalties of sin, see *De Nat. et Grat.* 81. For Augustine there is something horrifying and *unnatural* about ignorance even in infants; see *De Pecc. Mer.* 1:67.

59. Just a sampling of the more important passages: *De Beata Vita* 35, *Sol.* 1:23, *De Mor, Eccl.* 3 and 11, *De Quant. Anim.* 25, *De Lib. Arb.* 2:42, *De Mag.* 21, *De Util. Cred.* 4, *Conf.* 7:16 and 7:23, *Civ. Dei* 11:2, *De Trin.* 1:4, 8:3, 12:23, and 15:10.

60. *Proslogion* 14.

61. Ibid.

62. *De Lib. Arb.* 2:36.

63. *Sol.* 1:24.

64. For use of this biblical motif (Matt. 5:8) see *De Div. QQs 83*, section 12 (which, Augustine informs us in *Retract.* 1:26, is a quotation from a treatise *On the Need for Purifying the Mind in order to See God*, by a Carthaginian Neoplatonist who died a Christian), and Ep. 147:26 (citing Ambrose: "God is not seen in any place but the pure heart").

65. *Sol.* 2:24.

66. See for example *On Nature and Grace* 22.

67. *Sol.* 1:23. See *Republic* 7:515e–516b, which describes the same process using very similar imagery.

68. *Republic* 7:514a. (Beware of translators who render *paideia* here as "enlightenment" rather than "education"!)

69. The final stage of Plato's ascent is when one is "able to see the sun, not its image in water

or some alien medium, but itself by itself in its own place, and contemplate what sort of thing it is," ibid. 7:516b.

70. Plotinus links his view of the incomprehensibility of the First Principle not to the account of the Good in the *Republic* but to the paradoxical dialectic on the One above Being in *Parmenides* 137c–142a (see e.g. *Ennead* 6:7.32).

6. *Explorations of Divine Reason*

1. *De Lib. Arb.* 2:27–28.

2. Ibid. 2:37.

3. For these Plotinian themes in *De Lib. Arb.* 2, see O'Connell, *Early Theory*, pp. 52–57.

4. *Sol.* 2:14.

5. See *De Ord.* 1:6 and *Ep.* 3:1 for Augustine's habit of solitary night-time meditation.

6. *Sol.* 1:1. These are the opening words of the dialogue.

7. *Retract.* 1:4.1. See "Reason who speaks with you" and "I, Reason," in *Sol.* 1:12.

8. *Sol.* 1:7.

9. I will put the name "Augustine" in quotes when referring to "A.," the character in the *Soliloquies*, to distinguish him from the author of the *Soliloquies* (the latter, not the former, is the source of the words spoken by "Reason").

10. *Sol.* 1:16–26.

11. *Enneads* 5:1.10, 6:9.8, 1.1:3.

12. *De Mag.* 38, alluding to Ephesians 3:16–17, "being strengthened in the inner man, that Christ may dwell in your hearts by faith" (see "Christ in the Heart" in chapter 4) and 1 Cor. 1:24, "Christ the Virtue of God and the Wisdom of God" (see "Wisdom by Another Name" in chapter 4).

13. See "Consequences of Nicaea" in chapter 4 (note 78).

14. *Sol.* 1:12.

15. Few scholars would dispute Courcelle's judgment that "[i]t was . . . Cicero who supplied St. Augustine with the most lucid information on ancient Greek philosophy. Furthermore, Augustine studied him very conscientiously" (*Late Latin Writers*, p. 167). For Augustine's direct acquaintance with classical Greek philosophy, which was never more than spotty, see "A Central Issue in Augustine Scholarship" in chapter 3.

16. See Marrou, *Saint Augustin*, pp. 17–19.

17. Interestingly enough, Quintilian has left no unambiguous trace in Augustine's writings (see Keseling), although it is hard to imagine Augustine teaching rhetoric all those years without some familiarity with Quintilian's *Institutio Oratoria* (see Hagendahl, p. 676).

18. Seneca, the only ancient Latin writer known primarily as a philosopher, left little impression on Augustine's writings, and Hagendahl concludes that except for a discussion of Seneca's treatise *On Superstition* in *Civ. Dei* 6:10–11, Augustine "took little, if any, interest" in him (Hagendahl, pp. 677–680).

19. For convenience of reference I shall restrict the term "Cassiciacum *dialogues*" to the three earliest works: *De Beata Vita, Contra Academicos,* and *De Ordine.* But the term "Cassiciacum *works*," as I shall use it, includes in addition the *Soliloquia,* which was also written at Cassiciacum but is not in the ordinary sense a dialogue. Because of this difference in genre and the difference in purpose that underlies it, there are a number of generalizations that hold for the three Cassiciacum dialogues but not for all four Cassiciacum works. In particular, "more Ciceronian than Platonist" is a description that fits the dialogues better than the *Soliloquies*—though as we shall see, the latter is in fact a good deal more Ciceronian and less Platonistic than has often been thought.

20. The first of the Cassiciacum dialogues, *De Beata Vita,* is probably modeled on Cicero's *Hortensius,* which Augustine quotes by name in *De Beata Vita* 10 and mentions also in 4 (describing the same stirring encounter that we hear of later in *Conf.* 3:4). The second Cassiciacum dialogue,

Contra Academicos, cites Cicero frequently as an authority on philosophy (see *C. Acad.,* e.g. 1:7, 2:26, 3:31, and 41), which is not surprising, since it is based on philosophical information provided in Cicero's *Academica.* The extent of Augustine's debts to Cicero can be measured by consulting Hagendahl and Testard, and is also evident in the excellent edition of *Against the Academics* by O'Meara, whose extensive notes are extremely alert to the Neoplatonist resonances of the text but emphasize quite rightly that the Ciceronian debts come first and foremost.

21. Marrou, *Saint Augustin,* p. 248 (ellipses in original).

22. *Sol.* 2:26. See *Conf.* 6:3–4 (Ambrose was too busy to answer his questions) and *De Util. Cred.* 20 ("If there were anyone [at that time] able to teach me, he would have found me most suitable and very ready to be taught").

23. Augustine himself suggests a deep connection between his reading of *Hortensius* as a student (*Conf.* 3:7–8) and the events of the summer of 386 in *Conf.* 8:17, describing both as being set afire or inflamed in *De Beata Vita* 4.

24. On the dating of the sermon see Palanque, pp. 154–156, 514–516. The Stoic themes are most noticeable in *De Jacob et Vita Beata* 1:23–24 and 1:35 (see Nauroy, p. 120). For the extensive borrowings from Plotinus's "On Happiness" (*Ennead* 1:4), which are especially prominent in 1:28–36, see Solignac, "Nouveaux parallèles."

25. *De Beata Vita* 10–11 and 26–28.

26. On Plotinus's critical engagement with Stoicism see especially Theiler, "Plotin zwischen Plato und Stoa," and note Porphyry's observation that "hidden Stoic doctrines as well as Peripatetic ones are mixed in with his writings" (*Life of Plotinus* 14).

27. See *De Nat. Deo.* 1:11–12, *Acad.* 2:99–100, and especially *Tusc.* 5:32–33, where Cicero defends his probabilistic eclecticism by referring to historiography of philosophy that he learned from the "Old" (anti-skeptical) Academy, headed by Antiochus, who claimed that the Academics, Peripatetics, and even Stoics all taught basically the same thing; see *Acad.* 1:17–18, 1:43, and 2:15, *De Fin.* 4:3, 5:22, and 5:74, and *De Legibus* 1:38 and 54–55.

28. See the testimonia cited in Ross's edition of Aristotle, 12:26. Ruch's reconstruction of the *Hortensius* situates it in the tradition of Aristotle's *Protrepticus,* pp. 18–27.

29. For the respect in which Cicero can be called a Platonist, see Gersh, 1:67–71.

30. Testard (1:157–176) gives us a picture of how a young man with a head full of the *Hortensius* might have responded to the Christian Neoplatonism of Ambrose's Milan (as portrayed by Courcelle). In the next section I take a similar tack with the first book of *Tusculan Disputations,* a book that had a less dramatic impact on Augustine's mind but that has the advantage of being extant. It will be clear from what follows that I agree with Hagendahl's judgment (p. 516) that "Testard underrates the influence of the *Tusculans*" on Augustine.

31. *Conf.* 7:23: "et abduxit cogitationem a consuetudine."

32. *Tusc.* 1:38: "Magni est autem ingenii sevocare mentem a sensibus et cogitationem ab consuetudine abducere." Augustine quotes this sentence in full in Ep. 137:5—discussed in "The Location of the Soul" in chapter 10.

33. *Tusc.* 1:30 (see also 1:35: "omnium consensus naturae vox est"). This part of Cicero's argument occupies *Tusc.* 1:26–37. Augustine's argument from the historical success of the Church, through which "all peoples have been persuaded to believe" is cast in the mold of a Ciceronian-Stoic *consensus gentium* argument (*De Vera Rel.* 6).

34. Cicero's proof for the *immortality* of the soul is couched as a proof of its *divinity* (*Tusc.* 1:38, 50, and 66–67; see the quote from *Hortensius* in *De Trin.* 14:26: "we have souls that are eternal and divine"). The two terms are, in classical usage, well-nigh synonomous: the immortals are the gods, and hence to prove the soul is immortal is to prove it is a god. Augustine, unlike most later Christians trying to prove the immortality of the soul, cannot ignore this classical usage.

35. *Tusc.* 1:36–37.

36. *Tusc.* 1:53–54 (translating *Phaedrus* 245d–246a).

37. *Tusc.* 1:57–58. For Cicero on Platonic Ideas, see "The Self-Examination of Reason," hereafter; for Cicero on Platonic Recollection, see "Powers of the Soul" in chapter 10.

38. *Tusc.* 1:75. The discussion of the *Phaedo* occupies *Tusc.* 1:71–75.

39. *Tusc.* 1:56: "inesse in animis hominum divina quaedam." Note the verb *inesse,* echoing the verb *eneinai,* which Plato uses in his "enlargement" of the soul; see "Enlarging the Soul" in chapter 1.

40. *Tusc.* 1:52 and *Ennead* 4:3.1 (the beginning of Plotinus's treatise on the soul, which nearly all scholars agree Augustine read).

41. And like Plotinus, he quotes a poet to do it, *Tusc.* 1:65. See *Ennead* 4:7.10, discussed earlier in "Some Plotinian Readings" in chapter 3.

42. Hence "if God is breath or fire, then so is the soul of man" (*Tusc.* 1:65) and "whether the soul is breath or fire, I would swear it is divine" (1:60).

43. In ancient physics the four material elements (earth, water, air, and fire) are arranged in a hierarchy that is ordered quite literally from lower to higher: earth at the bottom, then water on top of the earth, then air above the water, and fire the highest of all (unless, with the early Aristotle, one believes in a fifth element, which is a sort of hyperfire and the true constituent of souls and stars).

44. *Tusc.* 1:40 and 42–3. "Air" is added to fire here because there is some vacillation in the Stoic tradition (and hence in Cicero) about whether the soul is simply fire or whether it is *pneuma* ("spirit" or "breath"), which consists of hot air (and hence of both elements, fire and air). For a guide to the complexities of Stoic theory on this subject, see Long and Sedley, 1:281–280. Cicero translates *pneuma* as *anima;* hence in *Tusc.* his term for soul is not *anima* but *animus*—in contrast to Augustine, for whom *anima* means "soul" and *animus* means specifically rational soul or mind.

45. *Tusc.* 1:51. The same materialist ontology underlies Cicero's description of "going to heaven" in *Scipio's Dream* (i.e., *De Re Publica* 6:9–29). These two Ciceronian works are the earliest extant texts known to me that present a literal "going to heaven" as the normal form of afterlife for the good soul. The gradual development of this theme in the Jewish pseudepigraphal literature seems to take place later.

46. *Conf.* 13:10 (see also *Civ. Dei* 11:28). Cicero himself provides the key equivalences for this Augustinian allegory: the fire of the soul is its desire, and the heavenly desire is love of seeing truth (*Tusc.* 1:44).

47. Cicero is one of our most important sources for this early doctrine of Aristotle and the cosmology it implies. See, in addition to the quotations hereafter (which, together with *Acad.* 1:26, are counted by Ross as fragment 27 of Aristotle's lost dialogue *On Philosophy*), *De Nat. Deorum* 1:33 (fragment 26) and 2:42 and 44 (fragment 21).

48. *Tusc.* 1:65.

49. Ibid. 1:66.

50. Ibid. 1:22. On the significance of the pairing of "discover" and "remember" see "Powers of the Soul in chapter 10.

51. See *Acad.* 1:24–26.

52. *Tusc.* 1:42.

53. Ibid. 1:46.

54. The concept goes back to Aristotle (*On Memory* 450a10, *On Sense* 7, *On the Soul* 3:2), but it had evidently become rather commonplace by Cicero's time.

55. *Tusc.* 1:46.

56. *De Lib. Arb.* 2:8–12.

57. *Conf.* 7:23.

58. Ibid. 10:11.

59. *De Musica* 6:7–10.

60. For details see O'Connell, *Early Theory,* p. 166.

61. *De Ord.* 2:31. This ought to be recognized as the predecessor to the statement of Augustine's three-level ontological hierarchy in Ep. 18:2, which also contrasts two opposite directions of

movement, one above and the other below the human soul. See "Voluntary Separation?" in chapter 8 and appendix 2.

62. On the incompatibility of Augustine's earliest writings with the Catholic doctrine of resurrection, see "Resurrection Avoided Then Accepted" in chapter 9.

63. *C. Acad.* 1:1.

64. Ibid. 1:3.

65. Ibid. 1:5.

66. Ibid. 1:11: "illam divinam partem animi." For the context of discussion in which this notion of the divinity of the soul is raised, see Cary, "What Licentius Learned."

67. *C. Acad.* 1:22.

68. *De Mag.* 38—quoted earlier in the section "Who Is Reason?"

69. *Conf.* 3:8. See "Wisdom by Another Name" in chapter 4.

70. See "Soul as Creature" in chapter 8.

71. *Conf.* 5:19. This of course is the same problem formulated at the outset of *Conf.* 7— discussed earlier in "A Turning of Attention" in chapter 5.

72. Augustine shows how the Manichaeans' errors about the nature of Good and Evil are logically derived from their materialism in *Conf.* 5:20 (see also 7:7 and 3:12).

73. The Manichaeans themselves did not think of themselves as materialists, as they reserved the term "matter" (*hyle*) for the evil principle, so that the Good Stuff was in some sense non-material (see *C. Faustum* 20:3, where Faustus the Manichaean is speaking, and 20:14, where Augustine contrasts the Manichaean view of matter unfavorably with the Platonist-Aristotelian view). Nevertheless, as Augustine demonstrated quite convincingly in his debates with them, the Manichaeans were in fact committed to a materialist ontology, as they conceived of all that exists in spatial (and therefore bodily) terms.

74. See especially *C. Ep. Fund.* 16 and 19–26, where Augustine directs his antimaterialist critique of Manichaeanism against a text by Mani himself.

75. This Platonist account of evil, worked out (in conscious opposition to Christian Gnostics) by Plotinus, was preached by Ambrose (e.g. *De Isaac* 61, which is based on *Ennead* 1:8, as Courcelle points out, *Recherches,* p. 107) and no doubt was taught by various members of the Christian Neoplatonist circle in Milan (see pp. 153–156, 168–174). It becomes the ontological key to many of Augustine's anti-Manichaean polemics, for example, *De Mor. Man.* 1–11, *De Vera Rel.* 21, *De Nat. Boni* 1–6, *Conf.* 7:17–19. Notice that in all these passages, the evil of the rational soul stems not from its nature but from its will: evil results from a voluntary turning to lower (i.e., sensible) goods.

76. According to Augustine (*De Mor. Man.* 26) the Manichaeans cannot consistently deny that everything in the region of light is made of the Good Stuff, that is, consists of the divine nature itself. That means that when the race of darkness attacks the region of light it is threatening harm to the very substance of God (*C. Ep. Fund.* 26).

77. *Conf.* 7:3.

78. See especially *C. Fort.* 7–9, which is the record of a public debate where Augustine pressed this point ruthlessly against a hapless Manichaean opponent.

79. Hence as a Manichaean Augustine was taught that "You, my Lord God, the Truth, were a huge bright body, and I a fragment of that body" (*Conf.* 4:31). As Augustine points out (in *De Mor. Man.* 26 and *C. Ep. Fund.* 26), given the Manichaeans' dualism, the only alternative to being made out of the luminous Good Substance (the same as God) is to be made out of the gross Evil Substance (the same as "the race of darkness").

80. Augustine's fullest account of Manichaean cosmogony is found in *C. Ep. Fund.* 19–26. For a contemporary presentation (not obscured by Augustine's polemics) of ancient Manichaeanism on the nature and origin of the cosmos, see Bonner, pp. 162–170.

81. This version of Nebridius's argument occurs in the second half of *De Ord.* 2:46 and in *De Mor. Man.* 21–23. The latter passage is much clearer, and I read the former in light of it. For a careful reading of the former on its own terms, see O'Connell, *Early Theory,* pp. 124–130.

82. Most notably O'Meara, *Studies,* pp. 143–144.

83. *De Beata Vita* 34–35. Note that both Wisdom and Truth are explicitly identified here as "the Son of God" (see Cor. 1:24 and John 14:6, respectively).

84. Intimations of divine inspiration: *De Ord.* 1:10, 1:16–17, 1:19, 1:23, 1:28. Falling back into the darkness of ignorance: 1:29–30, 2:21. For the Cassiciacum dialogues as the story of Licentius's education see Cary, "What Licentius Learned."

85. *De Ord.* 2:23.

86. *Conf.* 7:7. Note that the Manichaeans had a very definite and astoundingly literal answer to this question: evil originated from a specific physical location, a region of darkness separated in space from the land of light, *C. Ep. Fund.* 19.

87. This moment of perplexity must be understood as a deliberate contrivance of the author, for the purpose of making a quite definite point. I take for granted O'Meara's contention (in the introduction to his edition of *C. Acad.,* pp. 23–32) that these dialogues, although no doubt based loosely on actual conversations at Cassiciacum, are fundamentally fictional and not historical compositions—just like every other philosophical dialogue written in antiquity. This is a matter of importance for anyone interpreting them: the course of these conversations and the views expressed by all the characters (not just Augustine) should be interpreted as the products of authorial intent, not the exigencies and accidents of actual conversation.

88. Augustine certainly does have the Neoplatonist doctrine of the Fall on his mind, as is especially evident in *De Ord.* 1:3 (see Solignac, "Réminiscences plotiniennes et porphyriennes dan le début du *De Ordine*"). On the nature of his hesitation, see "Voluntary Separation?" in chapter 8.

89. The difficulties and dangers never disappeared. Within two years of completing a magnificent ontological explanation of the fallenness of the soul in *De Vera Rel.* (c. 392) Augustine writes: "The soul—I have looked into the cause of it and I admit it is most obscure—errs and is foolish, as we see, until it achieves and grasps wisdom" (*De Util. Cred.* 14). The related question of exactly how the soul came to be in the body remains unanswered all his life, as he remarks a few years before his death in a review of his early works: "And as for what pertains to the origin of the soul and how it came to be in the body . . . I did not know then nor do I know to this day" (*Retract.* 1:1.3). Augustine has only warnings to offer those who would navigate the "treacherous waters of such a question" (*De Anima et Ejus Origine* 1:7), and given the rocks and shoals and potential shipwrecks that faced him in adjusting his doctrine of the soul to the demands of the controversy with the Pelagians, one can see why. See O'-Connell, *Origin of the Soul,* for a detailed chart of the shoals in those dangerous waters.

90. *De Ord.* 2:24.

91. *De Ord.* 2:24. It is useful to bear in mind that "order" in this dialogue is defined in dynamic and relational (and therefore hierarchical) terms: it is defined "downward" as God's conducting (*agere*) of the temporal world (*De Ord.* 1:28, 2:2, 2:11) and "upward" as "what leads to God" (1:27).

92. This is not the last time Augustine would learn his lessons by writing his own books about them. He defends his project of writing on the Trinity, for instance, with the admission: "I confess myself to have learned, by writing, many things I did not know" (*De Trin.* 3:1).

93. *Retract.* 1:5.3 (Migne, 1:6).

94. The picture of philosophers anxious to secure the foundations of Western culture is central to one of the most well-known postmodernist narratives seeking to characterize what is specifically modern in modern philosophy, Rorty's *Philosophy and the Mirror of Nature.*

95. This narrative was probably inspired by a similar account of the origin of human culture in Cicero, *Tusc.* 1:62–4 (see also the protrait of Philosophy as mother of language and literature, founder of law, and teacher of morality and *disciplina, Tusc.* 5:5)—discussed in "Powers of the Soul" in chapter 10.

96. *De Ord.* 2:35.

97. Ibid. 2:35–7. The equivalent Latin term for the discipline the Greeks call *grammatica* is, Augustine points out, *litteratura,* literally, the study of letters.

98. Ibid. 2:38.

99. Ibid. 2:38.

100. Ibid. 2:39.

101. See the allegory of intellectual pride in *De Beata Vita* 3, as well as the account of the origin of evil in *De Vera Rel.* 67–68. Licentius's wild speculations about divination and determinism earlier in the treatise provide an example of what can happen when the uneducated mind too eagerly draws conclusions from its brief flashes of insight (*De Ord.* 1:14–15). Notice that to this extent, Augustine retains the Academic skeptics' ethical disapproval of rashly giving one's assent to opinions.

102. *De Ord.* 2:24.

103. See *De Util. Cred.* 2 and 21, *C. Ep. Fund.* 6, *C. Faustum* 16:8. For the anti-intellectual traditionalism of Africa in Augustine's youth, see Brown, pp. 42–43. In his own self-portrait the young Augustine emerges as a fine specimen of the proverbial snot-nosed kid, taking pleasure in refuting his Catholic elders in order to make them look bad and promote his own self-conceit (*Conf.* 3:10).

104. For example *De Ord.* 2:46, *De Quant. Anim.* 63, *De Mor. Eccl.* 1, *De Util. Cred.* 16–17. Book 5 of the *Confessions* is organized around the contrast between the Manichaean "bishop" Faustus and the Catholic bishop Ambrose, the one a shallow pate who merely pretends to know the liberal disciplines, the other a genuinely learned teacher of Catholic truth who helps rescue Augustine from his errors. See especially *Conf.* 5:3, 13, and 24.

105. For Augustine's conception of "music," see Marrou, *Saint Augustin,* pp. 197–210.

106. *De Div. QQs 83,* section 45. For later and better known versions of the same criticism (based on the argument that by an astrologer's reckoning, the fates of twins should be indistinguishable) see *De Doct.* 2:32–34, *Conf.* 7:8–10, and *Civ. Dei* 5:1–7.

107. *Conf.* 5:3–6. See Brown, p. 57, and Ferrari, pp. 44–49.

108. *De Ord.* 2:47.

109. Ibid. 2:46.

110. Ibid. 2:47. "Ordo studiorum sapientiae" here reflects, as often in the Cassiciacum writings, a Ciceronian definition of one of Augustine's key terms: philosophy is *studium sapientiae* (*Tusc.* 1:1—see *C. Acad.* 1:20, *Conf.* 6:18 and 8:17).

111. *De Ord.* 2:51.

112. Ibid. 2:43.

113. Ibid. 2:48. The verb *inspicere* at the beginning of the passage means literally "to look into," but can often mean simply "to examine," precisely as when we say in English "I'll look into the matter." Hence it is not clear whether Augustine is actually thinking of the soul looking within itself here: he *could* be, and certainly in a few years he *would* be.

114. See *De Lib. Arb.* 2:22–23.

115. *De Ord.* 2:48.

116. Compare how in Plotinus the Unity and Multiplicity in the intelligible world are related as a science is to its theorems; see "Unity and Division" in chapter 2.

117. *De Mor. Man.* 8–9, *De Vera Rel.* 58–60 and 65–66.

118. Augustine marks the end of the soul's speech to itself very clearly by echoing the words he used to introduce it: "This and many other such things the well-educated [*bene erudita*] soul says to itself [*secum loquimur*]," *De Ord.* 2:50. Everything between this point and the beginning of the soliloquy just quoted (from *De Ord.* 2:48) should be placed in quotation marks, as representing the soul's speech to itself.

119. *De Ord.* 2:50.

120. *Tusc.* 1:58: "nihil enim putat [sc. Plato] esse, quod oriatur et intereat, idque solum esse, quod *semper tale sit, quale est; ideam* appellat ille." Cicero in turn is echoing Plato's way of talking about the immutability of the Forms (e.g. *Phaedo* 80b and *Republic* 5:479a); see "The Other World" in chapter 1. Cicero defines Plato's term *idea* also in *Acad.* 1:30, stressing once again its immutability, the fact that it is always "such as it is" (*tale quale esset*).

7. An Abandoned Proof

1. *Meno* 86b. See Pépin, "Une nouvelle source," pp. 54–55 (in "*Ex Platonicorum Persona,*" pp. 214–215).

2. *Sol.* 2:24. Augustine's terminology is rather fluctuating. His aim is to prove the immortality of "the soul" (*anima*), but the central term of the discussion is usually "the mind" (*animus*). The two words are of course very close in meaning, and he switches freely from one to the other (as in *De Immort. Anim.* 7). If I could have done so without intolerable awkwardness (and misleading suggestions of the presence of words like *rationalis*) I would have translated *animus* as "rational soul" and reserved the English word "mind" for the Latin *mens*. As it is, I have adopted the usual translator's compromise, using "mind" for both *animus* and *mens*.

3. The *Soliloquies* does not explicity identify God with Truth, yet it makes no sense apart from that identification, and there can be no doubt that Augustine is already well aware of this. For instance, the "argument at the beginning of this book" to which this passage refers (*Sol.* 2:2) is a proof that Truth would continue to exist even if the whole world ceased to be—which can only mean that Truth is God. Note also that the Son of God is unveiled as Truth at the climax of *De Beata Vita* 34, which precedes *Soliloquies*.

4. *Sol.* 2:34–35. The allusion to Platonic Recollection is more unmistakable in the sequel, *De Immort. Anim.* 6 (see the section "Immutable Things in the Mind" hereafter), as well as in *De Quant. Anim.* 34, and it is explicit in Ep. 7:2. Augustine indicates his later change of mind about Platonic Recollection (consistent with the critique of the *Meno* discussed in "Problems of Intelligibility" in chapter 1) in *Retract.* 1:4.4 and 1:8.2. Note, in this early endorsement of Recollection, Augustine's emphasis on the formula that I emphasized earlier, in "Enlarging the Soul" in chapter 1, as a precursor in Plato's writing of later inwardness: knowledge is present *in* the soul. Augustine briefly explores the connection between Recollection and Inward Turn in *De Musica* 6:34–36, where someone who is "reminded by being questioned" (i.e., in a Socratic/Platonic dialogue) about the discipline of music is said "to move himself inwardly in his own mind [*intrinsecus apud mentem suam movere se*] toward something from which he recovers what he had lost" (6:35), which means he "moves himself inward to God to understand unchangeable truth" (*sese intus ad Deum movet, ut verum incommutabile intelligat*, 6:36).

5. *De Mag.* 2. Note that for Augustine all words are signs (3).

6. *Sol.* 2:20.

7. Such a view, in addition to being outrageously foolish, is hardly likely to be Augustine's, because the previous half of the same book (i.e., *Sol.* 2:1–18) is devoted largely to an analysis of the nature of falsehood and error.

8. Augustine's argument here could be an adaptation of Cicero, *Academica* 2:26: "No one finds what is false" (*Nemo invenit falsa*).

9. *Conf.* 1:20–27; see also 3:2–4. He minces no words here, either, pointing out that a poetic story (*fabula*) is a lie (*mendacium*), *Sol.* 1:19.

10. *Sol.* 2:19.

11. *Disciplina disputandi* or *disputationis* is Augustine's formulation of the central term of the discussion in *Sol.* 2:19–21. He also speaks of *ratio disputandi* (2:21 and 2:27) and *ars disputoriae* (2:19). His usage here follows Cicero, who can refer to dialectic as the *scientia* or *ratio disputandi* (*De Part. Orat.* 79). Cicero's usage probably stems from the Stoic conception of dialectic as *ars*, *ratio*, or *scientia disserendi* (*De Fin.* 2:26, 4:8, and 4:10, *Tusc.* 5:72, *De Oratore* 2:157, *Topica* 6, *De Legibus* 1:62; see Diogenes Laertius 7:42).

12. *De Ord.* 2:30.

13. Ibid. 2:38.

14. Ibid.

15. The role of distinguishing true from false, as well as drawing valid conclusions, is one

Cicero regularly assigns to dialectic, following the Stoics. See *De Oratore* 2:157, *De Part. Orat.* 78, *De Legibus* 1:62, *Tusc.* 5:72, and especially *Acad.* 2:91, which indicates that the Stoics gave dialectic the job of judging what is true and false in other disciplines—a point that would have been reinforced for Augustine by his own studies in dialectic, in which he was dependent mainly on Stoic sources (see Pépin, *Saint Augustin et la dialectique,* pp. 72–98 and 180–187).

    16. *C. Acad.* 3:29: "perfecta dialectica ipsa scientia veritatis est."

    17. *Sol.* 2:21.

    18. Ibid. 1:27 ("si quid verum est, veritate utique verum est"). This straightforwardly Platonist premise is reiterated in 2:29 ("veritas . . . qua verum est, quidquid verum est").

    19. Ibid. 2:21 (immediately following the previous quote).

    20. Ibid. (immediately following the previous quote).

    21. See "Education for Vision," in chapter 5.

    22. See for example Gregory of Nyssa on the spiritual value of being educated in

> the disciplines [*mathemata*] by which the understanding is excited to virtue, geometry and astronomy, and the apprehension of truth through numbers, and all the methods of demonstrating what is unknown and confirming what is known, and above all, the inspired philosophy of Scripture. (*On Infants' Early Deaths,* PG 46:181C = NPNF ed., p. 378)

Clement of Alexandria says similar things about the liberal disciplines (see Lilla, pp. 169–173) in the context of an overall program of Christian appropriation of classical culture that bears many resemblances to Augustine's program at Cassiciacum (see in particular Clement's pre-Nicene, subordinationist doctrine of the Logos, which holds the whole project together conceptually, Lilla, pp. 199–212).

    23. Moreover, traces of Augustine's early interest in the liberal disciplines as guides to unchanging Truth remain in his more mature works, for example *De Doct.* 2:48–61 and *De Trin.* 12:23.

    24. See "Who Is Reason?" in chapter 6.

    25. The Son of God is "ipsa disciplina et forma Dei" (Ep. 12). See likewise the association of *forma* and *disciplina* with the second person of the Trinity in Ep. 11:4.

    26. *Retract.* 1:5.1. It is here also that Augustine tells us the work is a sketch for an uncompleted continuation of the *Soliloquies* ("quasi commonitorium . . . propter Soliloquia terminanda, quae imperfecta remanserant").

    27. *De Immort. Anim.* 1.

    28. Ibid. 6.

    29. Ibid. 2.

    30. *De Immort. Anim.* 10.

    31. *Sol.* 2:22.

    32. Ibid.

    33. Ibid.

    34. Ibid.

    35. See *Conf.* 4:28–29. On Augustine's use of Aristotle's *Categories* at this point see Du Roy, p. 178. It is worth noting that this early logical treatise represents Aristotle at his most un-Platonistic; see "Alexander's Interpretation of Aristotle" in chapter 2.

    36. Aristotle, *Categories* 2,1a24–6.

    37. *Sol.* 2:2.

    38. *Sol.* 2:22.

    39. For detailed discussion see "Turning into the Inside" in chapter 2.

    40. See especially *Enneads* 5:5.9 (where the general principle is explained), 6:4.2, and 4:3.20–22 (where the principle is applied to body and soul—the soul is not *in* the body, but the other way around!). Note also *Ennead* 5:1.10, where Plato's "inner man" (*Republic* 9:589a), the

higher part of the soul, is located "outside" the material cosmos and thus "outside of space altogether" like the World-Soul enveloping the cosmos "from outside" (in *Timaeus* 36e) or like the Ideas themselves, which are located metaphorically beyond the outermost heavens (in *Phaedrus* 247c).

41. See "A Philosophical Project" in chapter 5.

42. *De Quant. Anim.* 61; see "The Location of the Soul" in chapter 10.

43. *Sol.* 1:29. This contention not only is un-Platonistic but smacks of lingering Manichaeanism, as it implies that divine things are properly *absent* from the lower world.

44. Ibid.: "Quidquid est, alicubi esse cogitur."

45. *De Div. QQs 83*, section 20.

46. *Acad.* 1:24 ("Nihil est enim quod non alicubi esse cogatur"). See Hagendahl, p. 55. The ultimate source of this principle may have been a remark that Plato makes about the material world in *Timaeus* 52b.

47. That is, *De Immort. Anim.* 1 and 5.

48. For a sample of this sort of apologetics, which is a recurrent motif of modern Augustine scholarship, see Mourant, pp. 3–18.

8. *Change of Mind*

1. *C. Acad.* 1:23" "sapiens . . . se ipsum in semetipsum colligit . . . in se atque in Deum semper tranquillus intenditur." The words are put in the mouth of Licentius, Augustine's student, but they echo Augustine's own words in the preface to another of the Cassiciacum dialogues, where he takes lack of self-knowledge to be the great cause of error and says the way to know oneself is by "collecting the mind in oneself and keeping it in oneself," "animum in se ipsum colligendi, atque in se ipso retinendi" (*De Ord.* 1:3).

2. *De Ord.* 2:19.

3. *Retract.* 1:1.4; see also 1:1.2.

4. *De Immort. Anim.* 7–8.

5. Ibid. 9.

6. Ibid. 9. Note again that this makes Reason's immutable existence dependent on the soul.

7. Ibid. 10.

8. Ibid. 10.

9. Ibid. 10.

10. Ibid. 11.

11. For this reversal, see "A Diagnosis" in chapter 7.

12. See Pépin, "Une curieuse déclaration idéaliste."

13. *De Immort. Anim.* 11.

14. See "Divinity in the Soul before Plotinus" in chapter 6.

15. *De Immort. Anim.* 11. This freedom from external compulsion was soon to become the core of Augustine's early conception of will, in *De Lib. Arb.* 1:19–21 and *De Duab. Anim.* 14.

16. *De Immort. Anim.* 11. Augustine here echoes Plato's famous dictum that there is no envy or jealousy in the Creator, *Timaeus* 29e.

17. See "A Program of Education" in chapter 6, on Augustine's deliberate avoidance of this topic.

18. *De Immort. Anim.* 11. Augustine's statement of this problem and his response to it is condensed, ambiguous, and perhaps hesitant, and here is the whole of it:

> However, it would not be utterly absurd if someone said that the mind was separated from reason voluntarily [*voluntate . . . animum separari a ratione*], if there could be any separation from one another of things that were not contained in space.

It is not even clear that this is meant to be a rejection of the possibility until a few lines later, at the end of the paragraph: "Therefore the mind cannot be extinguished unless separated from reason; but it cannot be separated, *as we have argued above;* therefore it cannot perish."

19. For example, things in the intelligible realm "are separated by otherness, not by space [*ou topōi*]," *Ennead* 6:4.4 (and similarly *Ennead* 6:9.8); Plato's call to separate soul from body refers of course to a "separation that is not in space [*to chōrizein ou topōi*]" (*Ennead* 5:1.10), and likewise our flight from the evils of this world is "not in space" (*Ennead* 1:8.7). All these passages are from treatises that seem to have made a great impression on Augustine—but evidently they have not yet had their full impact at the time he is writing "On the Immortality of the Soul."

20. See *Retract.* 1:5.2, which comments on this passage and quotes as refutation Isaiah 59:2, "Your sins make a separation between you and God."

21. *Ennead* 1:6.8. ("Our Fatherland is that whence we came, and the Father is there. What then is our journey, our flight? Not by feet. . . . Nor should you procure horse-chariot or ship.") On the importance of this favorite Plotinian passage for Augustine, see "Some Plotinian Readings" in chapter 3. Plotinus's talk here of a flight "not by feet" would have reinforced for Augustine the reference to a flight "not in space" in *Ennead* 1:8.7.

22. *Conf.* 1:28.

23. Augustine has mentioned this downward and outward movement before (*De Ord.* 1:3) and associated it with the soul's appetite for the many rather than the one ("eo egestatem patitur magis [sc. anima], quo magis appetit plura complecti"). The more desire, the more division and impoverishment of soul—but that does not mean that desire is the cause. In fact the cause seems rather to be ignorance, and specifically lack of self-knowledge: "cujus erroris maxima causa est, quod homo sibi ipse est incognitus."

24. *De Immort. Anim.* 12.

25. Incidentally, this shows that Augustine has not yet fully understood the Catholic doctrine of creation out of nothing. For as Athanasius points out, if the soul is created out of nothing, then no metaphysical principle but only the kindness of God can prevent an evil soul from returning to its original state of sheer nothingness (*On the Incarnation of the Word* 3–5).

26. *De Vera Rel.* 21–28. An earlier and simpler exposition of the essentials of this ontology is worked out in *De Mor. Man.* 1–9. On the new metaphysical approach that Augustine takes here, see Du Roy, pp. 183–196.

27. The soul's paradoxical flight from omnipresence (*Conf.* 5:2; see 2:3) is futile because, for one thing, God is "more inward than what is inmost in me" (*interior intimo meo,* 3:11), so that the result of the soul's joining itself with external things is "You were inside and I was outside" (10:38; see 7:11). Hence "Your omnipotence is not far from us, even when we are far from You" (2:3).

28. The theme of God as the life of the soul—a life it can lose—becomes prominent very soon after this point and is central in the *Confessions:* see *De Mor. Eccl.* 19 (commenting on Paul's declaration that nothing can separate us from the love of God in Christ in Rom. 8:39, Augustine says, "that by which we love God cannot die, except by not loving God"), *De Lib. Arb.* 2:41 ("As the soul is the whole life of the body, so God is the happy life of the soul"), *De Vera Rel.* 25 ("The body flourishes by the soul, and the soul by the immutable Truth, who is the only Son of God"), *De Duab. Anim.* 1, *Conf.* 3:10, 10:29, and 12:13, *De Trin.* 4:5 ("As the soul dies when God leaves it, so the body dies when the soul leaves it") and 14:6 ("the soul also has its death, when it lacks a happy life"), *Civ. Dei* 6:12, 13:2, and 13:15, *De Pecc. Mer.* 1:2 ("the death of the soul which takes place in sin"). Of course any number of biblical passages testify that the soul is not, as Plato thought, immortal: for example, "the soul that sinneth, it shall die" (Ezek. 18:4).

29. *Ennead* 4:8.4–8.

30. I agree with Pohlenz (p. 457–458), Dihle (chapter 6), and Kahn in thinking that something new and epochal came on the scene with Augustine's concept of Will: he seems to have been the first to formulate the notion of a faculty of choosing that could not be reduced to some combination of reasoning and desire.

31. Cicero's conception of natural law is of course Stoic in origin, but (as is often the case with Cicero's Stoic conceptions) it is already partly Platonized: he describes the natural law as eternal and identifies it with the mind of God, saying that this is the true law, in contrast to the laws of human communities, which vary from place to place and time to time (*De Leg.* 2:8–11). This is the central idea developed by Augustine in *De Lib. Arb.* 1:11–15.

32. *De Lib. Arb.* 1:16–24. The question with which this passage concludes, about why our souls suffer the penalties of this mortal life, is not fully answered until 3:24–28, where Augustine describes how the divine order includes the punishment of sin by placing sinful souls in corruptible bodies.

33. See "A Program of Education" in chapter 6.

34. *De Lib. Arb.* 1:35. The verbs here, *avertitur* and *convertitur,* echo the description of the two possible directions of movement of the soul in *De Immort. Anim.* 12, where Augustine makes the fresh start described earlier in "Voluntary Separation?" Augustine is clearly trying to follow up the insights of that fresh start here.

35. Augustine is already clear on this key ontological implication of the doctrine of Creation: if God created all things, then all things that exist are good (*De Lib. Arb.* 1:4–5). See *Conf.* 7:18, "Whatever is, is good."

36. This startling implication is one of the many very odd features of this book that have been passed over in the scholarship. It is perhaps the starkest demonstration of the fundamental incompatibility between the ancient contemplative ideal of Platonism and the biblical gospel, and Augustine has the merit of both putting it in front of us in terms that are hard to miss and subsequently proposing a way of reconciling the two traditions that has become so deep a part of the Christian tradition that the incompatibility is nearly always missed. The incompatibility, in general, is this: Platonism attempts to leave mortality behind, both one's own and others'; whereas in the Christian Scriptures godliness means doing as Jesus does, which clearly includes indiscriminate love for the nearest piece of human mortality in the area, called "your neighbor." (Unfortunately this incompatibility has been obscured for decades by Nygren's attempt to interpret it as a contrast between selfishness and unselfishness.)

37. *De Doct.* 1:20–37.

38. *Sol.* 1:7. For a sample of Augustine's efforts to live out this view of human love in practice, which are both sincere and ambivalent, see Ep. 2.

39. *De Lib. Arb.* 1:27.

40. Ibid. 1:25. "Good will" here is defined in Ciceronian fashion as "the will by which we desire to live rightly and honorably [*honesteque*] and to reach the highest wisdom." Augustine connects this with the will to be happy, another notion he learned from Cicero. The argument of Cicero's *Hortensius* opens with the thesis "certainly we all will [*volumus*] to be happy" (as Augustine tells us in *De Trin.* 13:7). Throughout his life Augustine takes this to be a fundamental, necessary truth of the ethical life and an ineradicable feature of the rational soul (see e.g. *De Beata Vita* 10, *C. Acad.* 1:5, *De Lib. Arb.* 2:28, *Conf.* 10:29, *Civ. Dei.* 10:1).

41. The fact that *De Lib. Arb.* 1 aims to work out in an ethical register the same basic line of thought that *Sol.* 2 works out in an epistemological register is indicated by a striking parallel: while the crowning argument in *Sol.* begins by establishing the premise that *disciplina* is always true (2:20), *De Lib. Arb.* begins by establishing that *disciplina* is always good (1:2).

42. *Tusc.* 5:67.

43. *De Lib. Arb.* 1:28.

44. Cicero presents this as a point of view common to both Academics and Peripatetics (*Acad.* 1:22) as well as Stoics (*De Fin.* 3:30).

45. See *De Mag.* 38 and *De Mor. Man.* 10 (quoting Luke 2:14, and following the Old Latin and Vulgate mistranslation of *eudokias,* "well-pleasing," as *bonae voluntatis,* "of good will").

46. For the importance of this New Testament phrase in Augustine's early thought see "Wisdom by Another Name" in chapter 4 and "Divinity in the Soul before Plotinus" in chapter 6.

47. Of the post-Cassiciacum philosophical dialogues, only the first book of *On Free Choice* and (according to my conjecture in the note 48) the main body of *On the Quantity of the Soul* could possibly be earlier—although both treatises are listed later in the *Retractations*.

48. There is a clear repudiation of the divinity of the soul in a philosophical dialogue written at about the same time, *On the Quantity of the Soul* (sections 3 and 77), but this is tacked on to the beginning and the end of the treatise without playing any role in the main course of the argument. In *On the Morals of the Catholic Church*, on the contrary, the identification of Christ the Virtue of God as something distinct from and independent of the soul is part of the warp and woof of the argument.

49. From this point of view, the event that made Augustine into a Church Father was not his conversion in 386, by which he won the free time to philosophize, but rather his quite involuntary ordination in 391, by which he lost his free time and became a servant of the Church and of his unlearned congregation. Brown is particularly illuminating on the contrast between these two events, both in his biography of Augustine (chapter 14) and in his informative introduction to the Hackett edition of the *Confessions* (especially pp. ix–xi).

50. See "Consequences of Nicaea" in chapter 4.

51. See for example *De Fide* 1.14–16 and *De Sp. Sanct.* 1.1 and 5. Note especially the conceptual connection that becomes central for Augustine: "Every creature is mutable" (*De Sp. Sanct.* 1:5.63).

52. Some of Ambrose's anti-Arian work was preached as sermons before being published as treatises, according to Williams, p. 151.

53. *De Lib. Arb.* 1:5.

54. For example *De Fide et Symbolo* 5; *De Vera Rel.* 13.

55. For this soteriological implication of Nicaea, see "Consequences of Nicaea" in chapter 4. For Augustine's understanding of this point in his later works, see *Civ. Dei.* 9:14–15 (commenting on 1 Tim. 2:5, he says that Christ "is the Mediator in that he is man"). The Greek Church Fathers saw the same point quite clearly; see for example Gregory of Nyssa, *C. Eunomius* 2:12).

56. See "Christ in the Heart" in chapter 4.

57. *De Mor. Eccl.* 18, quoting Romans 8:38–39.

58. *De Mor. Eccl.* 20.

59. Ibid. 20. I take this warning to be addressed to himself, because it could not be addressed to his opponents in this treatise, the Manichaeans, who did not think of the mind as "invisible and intelligible."

60. Ibid. 21.

61. Ibid.

62. *Conf.* 1:28.

63. In general, when Augustine says "love of God" he means our love for God rather than God's love for us, unless he says something explicitly to the contrary; see Burnaby, p. 99.

64. *De Mor. Eccl.* 22.

65. Ibid. 9–10.

66. *De Immort. Anim.* 10; see the earlier section "Inseparably in the Soul."

67. *De Mor. Eccl.* 10.

68. Ibid. 9. Cicero defines virtue as a *habitus* of the soul in *De Inv.* 2:59. That such a definition was by then a commonplace and not the property of any particular school of philosophy is shown by the fact that this is a textbook on *rhetoric*. But of course this definition, as well as the closely related notion that virtue is a *qualitas* of the soul, do go back to Aristotle; see especially the treatment of virtue as habit (*hexis*) and quality (*poiotes*) in *Categories* 8,8a25–34, a treatise familiar to Augustine.

69. See "A Diagnosis" in chapter 7.

70. *Conf.* 7:11.

9. Inner Privacy and Fallen Embodiment

1. See *De Musica* 6:37–42 (the whole of book 6 is very illuminating—and very Plotinian) as well as *De Gen. c. Man.* 2:20–34. On the Plotinian character of the doctrine of the Fall in these books see O'Connell, *Early Theory*, chapter 6. For present purposes note especially *De Musica* 6:53:

> By pride the soul lapses into certain actions that are in its own power, and neglecting the universal law, it has fallen into doing certain things that are private [*privata*], and this is called apostasizing or turning away [*apostatare*] from God.

2. Ep. 18:2 (for full text, see appendix 2). See my discussion of this three-tiered ontological hierarchy in "The Intelligibility of God" in chapter 5.

3. See especially *De Ord.* 2:19. This discussion takes up the first part of *On Order*, book 2, before the conversation gets stuck on the question of the origin of evil.

4. *De Ord.* 2:18.

5. *De Immort. Anim.* 4.

6. Ep. 18:2.

7. *De Lib. Arb.* 2:14 and 33–35, *Conf.* 7:23 and 10:11: see *De Vera Rel.* 56–57, *C. Faustum* 20:7.

8. What follows is deeply indebted to the work of Robert J. O'Connell, especially *St. Augustine's Early Theory of Man*. My account of the development of Augustine's thought is substantially in agreement with O'Connell's, though I stress even more strongly than he the point that Augustine is *less* Plotinian at Cassiciacum than he becomes later (see pp. 193–197).

9. By "dualism" here I mean primarily *soul/body* dualism. However, in ancient thought this tends to shade over into "dualism" in the sense discussed in the section "Divinity in the Soul before Plotinus" in chapter 6, a sharp distinction between good and evil, where evil is closely associated with the body.

10. The body is "an evil" (*Phaedo* 66b), and the great reward of a good life on earth is for the soul to live forever without it (114c). Above all, the fundamental ethical metaphor of purification, defined as separation of soul from body (80c), implies that the body is dirt that does not belong on the soul and needs to be cleaned off.

11. *Timaeus* 36e–38a.

12. *Ennead* 4:8.1.

13. It may well be that on this point a distinction should be made between Origen himself and the Origenism that was condemned by later Church councils (especially the second Council of Constantinople in 553). Origen, like Plotinus, affirms that there was no time when the world of bodies was without souls (*De Princ.* 2:2.2; compare *Ennead* 4:3.9). However, Origen is not so clear that the embodiment of souls is a proper and inherent feature of the *goodness* of the cosmos (apart from the purpose it may serve as penalty or training for wayward souls). Plotinus, on the contrary, quite forcefully affirms that embodiment is a result of the outpouring of goodness from the intelligible world to the sensible (*Ennead* 4:3.13). Whether Plotinus's two-sided claim that the soul's descent is both necessary (a result of divine beneficence) and culpable (a result of willful arrogance) is ultimately consistent is another question (see *Ennead* 4:8.5).

14. The goodness of the creation, and the soul as the ultimate source of evil, are two of the most prominent lessons learned as a result of reading "the books of the Platonists," according to *Conf.* 7:17–22.

15. Note for instance how Plotinus puts in a good word for Matter in the same treatise where he insists on the soul's culpability in the Fall, *Ennead* 4:8.6.

16. See the condemnation of matter as the primal evil in *Enneads* 1:8.14 and 2:4.16.

17. See *Enneads* 4:7.10 and 1:6.7, which treat embodiment as dirty—discussed in "Some Plotinian Readings" in chapter 3.

18. Brown, p. 11 (on Manichaean optimism see p. 59). Augustine indicates that he did have

such a need in his Manichaean period by blaming himself for it in *Conf.* 5:18 (see the connection of this theme with divinity of the soul in *Conf.* 4:26).

19. *De Pecc. Mer.* 1:9–20. For the development from Manichaen optimism about the soul and pessimism about the material world, to Augustine's mature pessimism about the corruption of the soul and optimism about the goodness of the created world (where literally "whatever exists is good," *Conf.* 7:18)—in sum from psychological optimism and cosmological pessmism to the reverse— see Cary, "God in the Soul."

20. *De Ord.* 2:31, quoted and discussed earlier in "Divinity in the Soul before Plotinus" in chapter 6.

21. Ibid. 2:50.

22. See Cicero's picture of the soul literally going to heaven without the body, discussed in "Cicero's Turn to the Soul" in chapter 6.

23. For this concept, see "Divinity in the Soul before Plotinus" in chapter 6.

24. *C. Acad.* 2:2; and see 2:22, where the soul that has "grasped Truth" returns "to the region of its origin," that is, "will return to heaven." A soul that originated in heaven did not originate with a body, and returns there having been freed from it.

25. Ibid. 3:20.

26. *Sol.* 2:36. In Augustine's later works, this phrase would be a reference to this *mortal* body, which will be replaced by a spiritual body in the resurrection (see *De Pecc. Mer.* 1:2). But in this context the phrase means the human body *as such,* as can be seen in *Sol.* 1:14, where the phrase "while we are in this body" refers to the period of time when we have "senses of the body" that "perform their proper work." Augustine is looking forward to how things will be after that which is proper and essential to the human body, the senses and their work, is left behind.

27. *De Quant. Anim.* 76.

28. *De Quant. Anim.* 81. Note that the notion of the soul "activating" (*agendo*) the body parallels Augustine's early view of the Incarnation of Christ, where the eternal Wisdom of God "activates the man himself" (*ipsum hominem agens*), *De Ord.* 2:27 or "assumes and activates a body of our kind" (2:16).

29. For Augustine's interest in this doctrine, which is ambivalent but enduring, see Teske. Key passages on this topic include *De Ord.* 2:30, *De Immort. Anim.* 24, *De Quant.* 69, and *Retract.* 1:11.4—and, as Teske argues, the famous discussion of time in *Conf.* 11:17–41.

30. *De Musica* 6:51.

31. *Civ. Dei* 13:16–17 and 22:26.

32. *Ennead* 4:8.2–4.

33. *Phaedrus* 248c.

34. *Ennead* 4:8.4 (end).

35. Ibid. 4:8.4–8.

36. Like the intelligible world itself, the soul is inherently many as well as one; see "Unity and Division" in chapter 2.

37. See *Ennead* 6:5.7, translated and discussed earlier in the section "Turning into the Inside" in chapter 2.

38. Note the connection between the Fall and concern with "private things" [*privata*] in *De Musica* 6:53, and see O'Connell's discussion of the Augustinian theme of the individual soul's "own life" (*propria vita*) in *Origin,* pp. 15–16 and 340–350.

39. Evidently as late as the *Confessions,* Augustine still wants to conceive of the Fall of the soul as having its *terminus a quo* in eternity—as O'Connell shows in his reading of Augustine's famous inquiry into the nature of time in *Conf.* 11 (see his *St. Augustine's Confessions,* chapter 15). The anchor in eternity, however, is not an immutable and divine part of the soul but rather what Augustine calls "the Heaven of Heavens," a sempiternal, intellectual creature, mutable but not temporal (very much like an unfallen universal Soul, though not exactly a *World*-Soul, because it does not animate or move

any part of the world, not even the material heavens). This creature is the original and final home of our individual souls (chapter 16, on *Conf.* 12:1–21).

40. In his mature works Augustine hesitates and changes his mind about the origin of the soul, as O'Connell shows in some detail in *Origin*. The theory he ends up with (like several that went before) remains more hinted at than fully developed, but the keynote seems to be that in the beginning all souls were in some sense *identical* with "the first man": *Civ. Dei* 13:14, *De Pecc. Mer.* 3:14, *C. Jul. Op. Imp.* 2:177, *De Nupt. et concup.* 2:15, *Enarr. in Pss.* 84:7 (see O'Connell, *Origin*, pp. 299–304).

41. *Civ. Dei* 22:29.6. See also *De Bono Conjug.* 2, Ep. 92:1–2 and 95:8. The thought probably goes back to *Ennead* 4:3.18, as O'Connell argues in *Early Theory*, pp. 163–165.

42. *De Gen. c. Man.* 2:32.

43. *Civ. Dei* 19:5–7.

44. See *De Pecc. Mer.* 1:66–67. Augustine always spoke of the ignorance in which infants are born with a kind of sympathetic horror: see *Sol.* 2:36, *De Trin.* 14:7, *Civ. Dei* 21:14 and 21:22.

45. *Conf.* 1:8.

46. For the Lockean self as a watershed in modernity, see Taylor, chapter 9.

47. Locke 2:11.17.

48. *Conf.* 10:12 (*lata praetoriae* and *campos*) and 10:14 (*aula ingenti*).

49. Ibid. 10:38.

50. Ibid. 7:11.

51. For this fundamental aim of Locke's project, see Wolterstorff, "The Migration of the Theistic Arguments," pp. 40–56, or (for a much fuller account) *John Locke and the Ethics of Belief*, especially pp. 118–133.

52. Locke 4:195–16.

53. This contemporary American phenomenon is portrayed polemically by Lee and sympathetically by Bloom; what interests me of course is a point that the two portraits have in common, the divinity and eternity of the inner self. This rediscovery of the Plotinian divinity underneath the Augustinian self is not uniquely modern: something similar may have motivated the mysticism of Meister Eckhart.

10. *The Origin of Inner Space*

1. As Augustine is of course well aware: what lies within is in "an inner place, not a place" (*interiore loco, non loco*), *Conf.* 10:16.

2. See "A Diagnosis" in chapter 7.

3. *Conf.* 10:26. *Quantum sum* is one of many verbal echoes of Augustine's earlier treatise *On the Quantity of the Soul*, discussed hereafter in the section "The Size of the Soul."

4. Ibid. 10:38.

5. Ibid. 10:13.

6. Ibid. 10:17.

7. Ibid. 10:19.

8. Ibid. 10:35. The phrase *ex quo* ("the point at which") is often translated "from the time when." But it is important to observe that the Latin does not actually mention time and thus leaves open the question of whether Augustine first learned of God in time or in eternity.

9. The earliest documentary evidence of an artificial memory system is found in a fragment called *Dialexeis*, which is pre-Aristotelian and probably of Sophist origin (see Yates, p. 29). Yates's work remains the indispensable reference for anyone who wishes to understand the ancient techniques of artificial memory, and in what follows I am much indebted to her.

10. The clearest description of this procedure is Quintilian's, in *Inst. Orat.* 11:2.17–22.

11. See Cicero *De Oratore* 3:354 and 360; the anonymous rhetorical treatise (once ascribed to Cicero) called *Ad Herennium* 3:30; and Quintilian *Inst. Orat.* 11:2.21 (quoting Cicero).

12. *Ad Herennium* 3:31–32. For similar rules see Cicero *De Oratore* 2:358.

13. Mary Carruthers, in her extraordinarily rich study of medieval practices of memory *The Book of Memory,* occasionally reads post-Augustinian metaphors into pre-Augustinian texts. This seems to me to be happening, for example, when she writes, "Likening memory to an inner room or recess is also very common in antiquity" (p. 40). The only text she cites in support of this claim is Quintilian 10:3.30, where "thought should make for itself a private place" even in the midst of crowds and journeys and other company ("Quare in turba, itinere, conviviis etiam faciat sibi cogitatio ipsa secretum"). This is not an account of memory but an interesting nonce metaphor describing how we can be mentally "off by ourselves" even when surrounded by other people. It does not indicate a permanent aspect of the self but a technique of making some temporary privacy in which to hear ourselves think.

14. *De Mem.* 1,450a30–32. (Note also the reference to a memory system based on "places" in 2,452a14). The metaphor of retention in wax evidently originated with Plato, whose use of it in *Theaetetus* 191c–e and 194c–e suggests a different account of memory from the doctrine of Recollection, which he appears to deny a little later (197e).

15. Aristotle *Rhet.* 3:1, Diogenes Laertius 7:43. See the earlier discussion of the meaning of "invention" in my preface.

16. The five parts are: Invention, Arrangement (*dispositio*), Style (*elocutio*), Memory, and Delivery (*pronuntiatio*). See Cicero *De Inv.* 1:9, *De Oratore* 1:142, *Orator* 54, and the anonymous treatise *Ad Herennium* 1:3; Quintilian gives a history and defense of this fivefold division in *Inst. Orat.* 3:3.3–9.

17. Quintilian *Inst. Orat.* 3:1.12, traces the use of *communes locos* back to Pythagoras and Gorgias. See Marrou, *History,* p. 54.

18. See for example *Rhetoric* 1:2,1358a12 and 2:22,1396b28–1397a6 and *Topics* 8:1,155b8.

19. "We call those arguments which can be transfered to many cases, common places," Cicero *De Inv.* 2:48. For the history connecting these ancient *loci communes* with modern "commonplaces" see Ong, *Presence of the Word,* pp. 79–87. This book together with Ong's *Orality and Literacy,* makes fascinating reading for anyone interested in the psychological presuppositions of the literary culture in which Augustine's mind moved, including presuppositions about such things as memory and invention. Also immensely valuable in this regard is Carruthers's *The Book of Memory,* which corrects Ong at many significant points.

20. Cicero *Topica* 7. See also *De Part. Orat.* 1:3.

21. *De Trin.* 8:14.

22. Cicero *De Part. Orat.* 109, *De Fin.* 4:10.

23. *Ad Herennium* 3:28. The similarity with our words "thesaurus" and "inventory" is of course not accidental.

24. Cicero *De Oratore* 1:18.

25. Even in Augustine the *thesauri* of memory seem to be like a treasure chests in which things and images are stored and then taken out on demand, rather than an inner room one might walk around in (*Conf.* 10:12–14). See Carruthers, p. 35.

26. *Sol.* 1:1. Note also Augustine's use of the word *excogitata* to describe the thing found, which reflects Cicero's definition of *inventio* as "ecogitatio rerum verarum aut veri similium quae causam probabilem reddant" (*De Inv.* 1:9).

27. *C. Acad.* 2:9. The whole argument of this treatise is carried on using the two key terms "seek" and "find," as O'Connell points out, *Early Theory* p. 237.

28. See the discussion of the inward turn in *Confessions* 7 in "A Turning of Attention" in chapter 5.

29. This is what I shall call Ep. 137, which is Augustine's only book-length treatment of the Incarnation.

30. Ep. 137:2 (rehearsing questions originally put in Volusianus's letter to Augustine, Ep. 135:2).

31. *Ep.* 137:4 and 7. Plotinus is of course not mentioned by name, but the doctrine is unmistakeably his, as Augustine knows perfectly well.

32. *Ep.* 137:5.

33. See especially *Conf.* 10:15, quoted in the section "What Is Found in Memory" hereafter.

34. *Tusc.* 1:38; see *Conf.* 7:23—discussed in "Cicero's Turn to the Soul" in chapter 6.

35. The magnificent overview of the whole material creation in *Conf.* 10:9–10 serves the same argumentative purpose as the poetic evocation of the material cosmos in *Tusc.* 1:68–69 and is quite possibly modeled on it.

36. *Tusc.* 1:67. Augustine agrees with Cicero about the physical eye (*De Quant. Anim.* 44) but disagrees about the eye of the soul.

37. On Cicero's understanding of the relation between God and the soul, which is based on their being made of the same material, see "Cicero's Turn to the Soul" and "The Superiority of Soul in Cicero" in chapter 6.

38. *Tusc.* 1:70.

39. *De Anima* 1:5,411b19–27. Augustine accepted this view, as we can see from *C. Ep. Fund.* 20.

40. See *Ennead* 6:4.4 and 6:5.12. The omnipresence of the World-Soul is also suggested by Plato's talk about soul being distributed indivisibly among the divided bodies of the material world in *Timaeus* 35a, which serves as the textual jumping-off point of Plotinus's theory of omnipresence in *Enneads* 6:4–5. But once again it is worthwhile noting how much Plotinus (and through him Augustine) is indebted to Aristotelian psychology, and precisely in those places where Aristotle disagrees with Plato.

41. *Ep.* 137:5.

42. This is the *extra Calvinisticum* (so named by Lutherans who disagreed with it): the claim that Christ's divinity exists *extra carnem*, outside his own flesh (see Muller, p. 111). Augustine thinks we will understand why this must be true once we understand that something similar is true of our own souls: *extra carnem nostram vivimus.* Thus both divine Incarnation and ordinary human embodiment are examples of the way that higher things are present to lower things in the manner of Plotinian omnipresence—present in power and activity but not confined to a particular location in space. See O'Connell *Early Theory,* p. 274.

43. *De Quant. Anim.* 60.

44. Ibid. 61.

45. Ibid.

46. The "learned men" to whom Augustine refers include no doubt Plotinus and probably Porphyry, as well as perhaps some Christian Neoplatonists of Milan. See Henry, *Plotin et l'Occident,* pp. 73–75, and Pépin, "Une nouvelle source," pp. 56–70 (in *"Ex Platonicorum Persona",* pp. 216–230).

47. See "A Diagnosis" in chpater 7. Note especially the theory of embodiment in *Ennead* 4:3.22, where the body is located in the soul rather than the other way around.

48. See "The Superiority of Soul in Cicero" in chapter 6.

49. *Tusc.* 1:56–65.

50. *Tusc.* 1:70. A note on the two other features of the soul mentioned in this passage: "the beauty of virtue" is a theme Augustine met again, much more fully developed, in his favorite treatise of Plotinus, *Ennead* 1:6.4–6. "Quickness of movement" is in part an allusion to Plato's proof of the immortality of the soul from its power of self-movement in *Phaedrus* 245a–246a, which Cicero translated and incorporated into *Tusc.* 1:53–54. It also goes back to Cicero's explanation of how the soul manages to break free of this lower world to get to heaven: "nothing is faster than the soul" (*Tusc.* 1:43). This remark seems to have impressed Augustine enough for him to make the odd claim that God moves even faster than the soul (Ep. 118:23).

51. Cicero's descriptions of memory and invention in *Tusculan Disputations* echo his definition of them in his rhetorical treatise *On Invention* 1:9. In both, memory is "of things and words"

(*rerum et verborum* in *Tusc.* 1:65) and invention is treated as a *cogitatio* (*Tusc.* 1:61) or *excogitatio* (*De Inv.* 1:9). See Augustine's use of *cogitare* and its cognates in *Conf.* 10:18, describing how we re-collect things that have previously been found (*inventa*).

52. *Tusc.* 1:62.
53. Ibid. 1:64.
54. Ibid. 5:5.
55. *C. Acad.* 1:3 and *De Beata Vita* 1.
56. See "The Self-Examination of Reason" in chapter 6.
57. *Tusc.* 1:57.
58. Augustine's early endorsement of the theory of Recollection ("what is called learning is nothing other than recollecting and remembering," *De Quant. Anim.* 34) is formulated in words taken not from Plotinus or Plato but from this passage of Cicero (see Hagendahl, p. 143). Likewise, his later critique of the *Meno*'s doctrine of Recollection (*De Trin.* 12:24) owes so much to this passage that Courcelle can even suggest that Augustine's knowledge of Socrates' famous geometry lesson with the slave boy is derived entirely from this Ciceronian passage (*Late Latin Writers,* p. 171)—though I think that suggestion goes too far. For the pervasive thematic connection that Augustine sees between Socratic questioning, remembrance, the liberal disciplines, and gradual steps of ascent—all found together in this one Ciceronian passage—see for example *De Ord.* 2:39, *Retract.* 1:6 (some editions, 1:5.2), *De Immort. Anim.* 6 ("being well questioned [*bene interrogati*] by someone else about the liberal arts," which echoes the *bene interroganti respondentem* a little further on in the Ciceronian passage) and *De Mag.* 21 ("by gradations accommodated to our infirm steps"), and *De Musica* 6:1.
59. *Tusc.* 1:58. The last clause is pithy: *cognita attulit.*
60. *De Quant. Anim.* 34.
61. *Tusc.* 1:60–61.
62. *Fundus, capacitas,* and *immensa* recur in *De Quant. Anim.* 9 and *Conf.* 10:15–16 and 26. The questions Cicero raises in this passage, we shall soon find, are the questions with which *De Quant. Anim.* begins.
63. *Tusc.* 1:57. This language too is echoed repeatedly in *De Quant. Anim.* 9 and *Conf.* 10:12, 15, and 26.
64. *Tusc.* 1:60.
65. The title does not sound so odd, of course, if one has been reading a great deal of Cicero, who asks about the *magnitudo* of the soul in *Tusc.* 1:50 (quoted hereafter) and wonders how much memory or mind (*quanta memoria* or *quanta mens*) some people have in *Tusc.* 1:59—or a great deal of Plotinus, who often speaks of "a greatness that is not great in bulk" (*Enneads* 5:8.2, 6:4.5; see also the end of 4:3.9).
66. For example *C. Ep. Fund.* 20f, Ep. 137:5–6, and *Conf.* 7:1–16 and 10:8–38.
67. They are not so much answered as dismissed at the very end of the treatise, *De Quant. Anim.* 81.
68. *Tusc.* 1:37.
69. Ibid. 1:50–51.
70. *De Quant. Anim.* 4. Here Augustine uses *potentia* and *virtus* as equivalents (something he can also do in ethical contexts such as *De Musica* 6:55). *Vis*, the Ciceronian term for a "power" or faculty of the soul, which Augustine uses frequently in *Confessions* 10, is of course etymologically related to *virtus*.
71. Whence is the soul? From God (*De Quant. Anim.* 2). What sort of thing is it? Similar to God (3).
72. Ibid. 4.
73. Ibid. 5.
74. Ibid. 5. "Not nothing" becomes a leitmotif of Augustine's inquiries into non-spatial modes of being, as seen in "A Turning of Attention" and "A Philosophical Project" in chapter 5.

75. Ibid. 8: "Imagines ergo illorum locorum memoria continentur."

76. Ibid. 9.

77. Ibid. 9.

78. Ibid. 9.

79. *De Quant. Anim.* 10.

80. The metaphysics of geometry that underlies Augustine's inquiry here goes back ultimately to Plato's lecture on the Good, as reported in Aristotle's work *On the Good,* fragment of which are preserved in Alexander of Aphrodisias and other commentators (see especially Ross, fragment 2). The key intuition is that simpler and less divisible things are the first principles from which more extended things originate: the line is generated from the point, the plane from the line, and the solid from the plane. That is why the point is most powerful, containing "virtually" (i.e., by way of power) the whole world. See of course the geometrical construction of the sensible world in *Timaeus,* beginning at 53c.

81. *De Quant. Anim.* 19.

82. On the importance of this theme in Neoplatonism, see "Unity and Division" in chapter 2.

83. *De Quant. Anim.* 18.

84. Ibid. 19.

85. Ibid. 19 and 23. The imagery of circle and center is found frequently in Plotinus, as noted in "Turning into the Inside" in chapter 2, but Augustine here seems especially indebted to a discussion of the "shared sense" in *Ennead* 4:7.6, where it is specifically the human soul that is like the center of a circle: the soul is the unifying central point to which diverse senses lead, like radii leading from circumference to center. This use of the image of the point goes back to Aristotle's treatment of the shared sense (*De Anima* 3:2,427a10) via Alexander of Aphrodisias, who is the first to make the soul the *center* point to which all sensations are brought to be unified (see Henry, "Une comparaison," especially pp. 434 and 437). This seems to be the historical cornerstone of later talk about the sensible world as "the external world."

86. *De Quant. Anim.* 23. See the description of the life of the fallen soul as divided and "distended" in time, *Conf.* 11:38–39.

87. *De Quant. Anim.* 24.

88. *Conf.* 10:15.

89. "I became to myself a region of impoverishment (*regio egestatis*]" (*Conf.* 2:18), and "I found I was far from You in the region of dissimilarity [*regio dissimilitudinis*]" (*Conf.* 7:16), and likewise, "I have become to myself a land of difficulty [*terra difficultatis*]" (*Conf.* 10:25). In every case, the reference is not to the external world as such (which is good, because created by God) but to the soul in its carnal attachments, trying to find happiness by loving external things which, being perishable, must inevitably be lost.

90. Ibid. 10:15.

91. Ibid. 10:38.

92. *De Trin.* 10:11.

93. *Conf.* 10:38. The paradoxes of our being with and without God are a continuing theme of Augustine's work, from *De Ord.* 2:3–5 to *De Trin.* 14:16.

94. *Conf.* 10:27.

95. Ibid. See Luke 15:8.

96. *Conf.* 10:28.

97. Ibid. 10:26.

98. Ibid. 10:29. This builds on a thought he worked out many years earlier: "As the soul is the whole life of the body, so God is the happy life of the soul" (*De Lib. Arb.* 2:41).

99. *Conf.* 10:29.

100. Ibid. 10:31. "Experienced" is a term defined by a contrast that Augustine had earlier established (in 10:14) between what is experienced (*experta*) and what is believed (*credita*). The point is

that our memory of happy life is not taken on faith: it is not something we believe in because some-one told us but something we have tasted for ourselves. Augustine later changes his mind on this point. It remains true that everyone wants to be happy, and no one can love and seek what is utterly unknown, and therefoe "we all do know happy life" (*De Trin.* 13:8)—but only by believing the Scrip-tures and not by remembering it (*De Trin.* 14:21). Behind this change of mind lies a very complex evolution in Augustine's thought from a Plotinian Fall of the soul to his mature doctrine of original sin, which retained a number of Plotinian features (see O'Connell, *Origin,* pp. 265–281 and 337–350).

101. *Conf.* 10:33.

Conclusion

1. The most likely candidate for inventor of the private inner self before Augustine might be one of the Gnostics. The Gnostics indeed often show a decided affinity for the language of inward-ness (see in the Nag Hammadi corpus *Gos. Mary* 8:19–20, *Dial. Sav.* 125:2 and 128:3–5, *Gos. Truth* 32:20–40, *Gos. Thom.* 32:20–33:6, 37:27–26, 38:9–10 and 48:16–17, *Exeg. Soul* 131:14–28, *Gos. Eg.* 66:24–25, *Teach. Silv.* 94:28–29, 106:15, and 117:26–29, *Ep. Pet. Phil.* 137:22–23, *Allogenes* 52:10–13—this last sounding much like Plotinus). So far as I can tell (being no reader of Coptic), some Gnostics have something like a concept of inward turn, but none have any concept of private inner space.

2. The closest parallel to Augustine's problem I have found is in Gregory of Nyssa, the Greek Church Father whose interest in philosophical psychology is most like Augustine's. Gregory too is attracted to the Platonist language of inwardness but insists that the soul is not identical to God but only like him, created in his image. However, I do not find that Gregory's talk of what is within the soul goes beyond highly suggestive metaphor. To judge for yourself, see for example *De Virg.,* chap-ter 12 (searching for the lost coin "within oneself"), *De Opif. Hom.* 10:3–4 ("the city of the mind which is within us" as an inner container or receptacle filled by the operations of the senses) and *De Anima et Res.* 28c ("looking at the world within us," i.e., at the soul as microcosm). These passages can be found in the *Nicene and Post-Nicene Fathers* edition of Gregory's works, pp. 358, 395–396, and 433, respectively—but as always one must check the original Greek, which uses the language of inwardness less frequently than the Victorian translators do.

3. The book is by Bertrand Russell. For a classic introduction to this problem, see his *The Problems of Philosophy,* chapter 1.

4. For an impressive example of a philosopher taking the problem of solipsism with absolute seriousness, see the fifth of Husserl's *Cartesian Meditations.*

5. See G. E. M. Anscombe's testimony to the "medicinal" effect of Wittgenstein's argument against private language, in her *Metaphysics and Philosophy of Mind,* p. viii.

6. See the conclusion to chapter 9.

7. Levinas, *Totality and Infinity: An Essay on Exteriority,* has been a wellspring of thought on this issue. For an account of knowledge of other persons that avoids relying on inner/outer contrasts, see Cary, "Believing the Word."

8. See "Life-Giving Flesh" in chapter 4.

9. See "Consequences of Nicaea" in chapter 4. On Christ's deified flesh as the foundation of legitimate use of icons, see the first of John of Damascus's "Three Apologies against Those Who At-tack the Divine Images." On the passion of Christ incarnate as the source of the sacraments, see Aquinas, *ST* III, 62.5. On the Word of God as giving us Christ, see Luther's "Brief Instruction on What to Look for and Expect in the Gospels," *LW* 35:117–124.

10. The lamentation "You were inside and I was outside" (Conf. 10:38) comes immediately after Augustine's exploration of memory as the inner space in which we find God and leads into a discussion of the lifelong battle against temptation.

11. Augustine uses the term "temporal dispensation" (*dispensatio temporalis*) as equivalent to

the Greek theological term *oikonomia,* or economy of salvation (see *De Fide et Symbolo* 6 and 18 and the phrase *suscepti hominis dispensatio* in Ep. 11:4). It describes all of God's activity in history on behalf of our salvation and especially of course the Incarnation and historical life of Christ. On the place of the "temporal dispensation" in Augustine's Platonist ontology, see Mayer, *Zeichen,* 1:259–271.

12. The *locus classicus* for this classification is *De Doct.* 2:1–6, but see also *De Mag.* 1–4 (words as signs) and *Civ. Dei* 10:5 (sacraments as signs).

13. This is the key thesis of *De Mag.* 33–40. For the importance of this thesis in shaping Augustine's mature theology, see Mayer, "Philosophische Voraussetzungen" and "Taufe und Erwählung."

14. *De Doct.* 3:9–13; see *Conf.* 5:24–25.

15. The crucial conceptual point here is that causal efficacy always flows downward in Augustine's ontological hierarchy, from God to souls to bodies—and never in the reverse direction (hence never upward and inward). God can change souls, and the soul can move and animate bodies, but bodies can have no causal effect on souls. In fact, for Augustine, no body is an efficient cause of anything, for the only efficient causes in the universe are *wills* (*Civ. Dei* 5:9). That is to say, only things at the higher two levels of the ontological hierarchy can have causal efficacy—which rules out the possibility of any external sign being an efficacious means of grace.

16. See especially the twelfth-century *Summa Sententiarum* 4:1 (attributed to Hugh of St. Victor), which underlines the point that sacraments are signs that not only signify grace (as Augustine taught) but confer it.

17. For Luther the Gospel contains divine promises, as the Law contains divine commandments, and "the promises of God give what the commandments of God demand" (from the treatise on "The Freedom of a Christian," in *LW* 31:349). That Luther conceives the efficacy of the Gospel promise on the model of sacramental signs that confer what they signify is particularly clear in the 1519 treatise on "The Sacrament of Penance" (*LW* 31:3–23) where the Word of Absolution plays the role of sacramental sign. Later, the same Word of Absolution is called "the true voice of the Gospel" in Lutheran confessional documents (*Apology of the Augsburg Confession* 12:39, in Tappert, p. 187). For the development of this line of thought in Luther's early work see Bayer.

18. *Institutes* 4:14.16.

19. It will perhaps help my readers to know that I am a critic of Augustinian inwardness primarily because my thinking on Word and Sacrament derives from Luther's emphasis on the externality of the object of faith. See his Large Catechism, on Baptism:

> faith must have something to believe, something to which it may cling. . . . Thus faith clings to the water and believes it to be Baptism in which there is sheer salvation and life, not through the water . . . but through its incorporation with God's Word and ordinance and the joining of his name with it. . . . the entire Gospel is an external, oral proclamation. In short, whatever God effects in us he does through such external ordinances. (Tappert, p. 450)

20. The Platonist tradition (in contrast, for instance, to the Stoics) has always linked mind with love and has always portrayed love as something that comes over us unbidden, quite independent of our power of choice. Hence Plato attends to the phenomenon of falling madly in love in *Phaedrus* 244a–257b and *Symposium* 215a–219e, followed by Plotinus in his essay "On Beauty," *Ennead* 1:6.4 and 7 (see also *Enneads* 1:3.2 and 6:9.9). Augustine is thoroughly Platonist in believing that love of higher things is an inward gift flowing from the Beloved.

21. On being inwardly taught by God see *De Grat. Christi* 1:14, *De Praedest.* 13, and *In Joh. Evang.* 26:7. See also the theme of grace as the inward light of the mind in *De Pecc. Mer.* 1:37–38 and 2:5, *De Nat. et Grat.* 56.

22. *De Mag.* 38.

23. See *De Lib. Arb.* 1:26 and 3:7.

24. *Conf.* 8:20–21; see also *De Grat. et Lib. Arb.* 31.

25. This progression from faith to love to vision is the organizing framework of Augustine's argument in *De Sp. et Litt.* 51–59.

26. At this stage Augustine argues that faith is in our power (*De Sp. et Litt.* 54), but he also insists that it is a gift of God—leaving open the possibility that human choice is the decisive factor in determining whether this gift is actualy received (*De Sp. et Litt.* 60).

27. The issue of whether the beginning of faith (*initium fidei*) is due to grace or our choice is settled in *De Grat. et Lib. Arb.* 28–29 and *De Praedest.* 3 (see Augustine's account of his earlier views in 7).

28. For the Plotinian meaning of this contrast, see "Inner Vision and Faith" in chapter 3.

29. Isaiah 7:9, as translated by the Old Latin version from the Septuagint. This verse turns up frequently as a methodological principle in Augustine's works, for example *De Lib. Arb.* 1:4 and 2:6, *De Mag.* 37, *De Fide et Symbolo* 1.

30. *De Doct.* 1:4.

31. *Ench.* 5.

32. "Tempora auctoritas, re autem ratio prior est," *De Ord.* 2:26.

33. See "The Experience of Insight" in chapter 5.

34. For signs as reminders or admonitions, see *De Mag.* 36.

35. For studiousness as a form of love that desires to pass from sign to thing signified, see *De Trin.* 10:1–2.

36. *De Lib. Arb.* 2:33.

Bibliography

Primary Sources

Annotations here are to guide the non-specialist reader to the most useful translations and editions.

COLLECTIONS AND ANTHOLOGIES

Bourke, V., *The Essential Augustine* (Indianapolis: Hackett, 1974). Judicious anthology of short passages of Augustine on selected philosophical themes.

Catechism of the Catholic Church (Washington, D.C.: U.S. Catholic Conference, 1994).

Denzinger H., and A. Schönmetzer, *Enchiridion Symbolorum, Definitionum et Declarationum*, 36th ed. (Rome: Herder, 1976). Standard collection of Roman Catholic doctrinal formulations.

Fairweather, E., ed. and trans., *A Scholastic Miscellany: Anselm to Ockham*, Library of Christian Classics series (Philadelphia: Westminster, 1956).

Hardy, E., *Christology of the Later Fathers* (Philadelphia: Westminster, 1954).

Long, A. A., and D. N. Sedley, *The Hellenistic Philosophers* (Cambridge: Cambridge University Press, 1987). Vol. 1, *Translations of the Principal Sources, with Philosophical Commentary*. Vol. 2, *Greek and Latin Texts with Notes and Bibliography*. The most valuable collection of fragments and testimonia of the Stoics and Academics for non-specialists.

Migne, J.-P., *Patrologia Graeca* (Paris: 1857–1866) (abreviated *PG*). The huge, dated, but in many cases still standard nineteenth-century collection of all the available writings of the Greek Church Fathers in the original language (with Latin translation).

———, *Patrologia Latina* (Paris: 1844–1855) (abbreviated *PL*). The Latin counterpart of *Patrologia Graeca*.

Robinson, J. M., *The Nag Hammadi Library in English*, 3rd. ed. (San Francisco: HarperCollins, 1990).

Stevenson, J., *Creeds, Councils and Controversies* (London: SPCK, 1983).

Tappert, T., *The Book of Concord* (Philadelphia: Fortress Press, 1959). Translation of the Lutheran confessional documents, including Luther's *Large Catechism* and Melanchthon's *Apology of the Augsburg Confession*.

EDITIONS AND TRANSLATIONS

Alexander of Aphrodisias, *The De Anima of Alexander of Aphrodisias*, trans. A. Fotinis (Washington, D.C.: University Press of America, 1979).

Ambrose, *Opera Omnia* (Milan: Biblioteca Ambrosiana, 1979–). Critical edition of the Latin text with Italian translation, plus extensive notes on Ambrose's sources, including Plotinus and Cicero.

———, *Saint Ambrose: Selected Works and Letters*, trans. H. de Romestin, in *Nicene and Post-Nicene Fathers*, second series, vol. 10, reprint ed. (Grand Rapids: Eerdmans, 1979).

Anonymous, *Ad Herennium*, see under Cicero, *Rhetorica Ad Herennium*.

———, *Corpus Dionysiacum*, see under Denys.

———, *Hermetica*, see under Hermes Trismegistus.

———, *Summa Sententiarum*, see under Hugh of St. Victor.

———, *Synodikon*, see under Gouillard (secondary literature).

Anselm, *Proslogion*, in Fairweather, *A Scholastic Miscellany*.

———, *L'Oeuvre de Anselme de Cantobéry* (Latin text with French translation), ed. M. Corbin (Paris: Cerf, 1986–1990).

Aquinas, Thomas, *Summa Theologiae* (abreviated *ST*), 61 vols., Blackfriars ed. (London: Eyre and Spottiswoode, 1964).

———, *Summa Theologica*, trans. Fathers of the Dominican Province, 5 Vols. (Westminster, Md.: Christian Classics, 1981).

Aristotle, *Aristotle on Memory*, trans. and ed. R. Sorabji (Providence: Brown University Press 1972).

———, *Aristotle's Protrepticus: An Attempt at a Reconstruction*, ed. and trans. I. Düring (Göteborg: Elanders Boktryckeri Aktiebolag, 1961).

———, *The "Art" of Rhetoric*, trans. J. H. Freese, Loeb series (Cambridge: Harvard University Press, 1971).

———, *The Categories, On Interpretation*, trans. H. P. Cooke, Loeb series (Cambridge: Harvard University Press, 1973).

———, *De Anima*, ed. R. D. Hicks, reprint ed. (Amsterdam: Hakkert, 1965).

———, *The Ethics of Aristotle*, ed. J. Burnet (London: Methuen, 1900).

———, *The Metaphysics*, trans. H. Tredennick, Loeb series, 2 vols. (Cambridge: Harvard University Press, 1975).

———, *Der Protreptikos des Aristoteles*, ed. and trans. I. Düring (Frankfurt: Klostermann, 1969).

———, *On the Soul, Parva Naturalia, On Breath*, trans. W. S. Hett, Loeb series (Cambridge: Harvard University Press, 1975). Includes the little treatise *On Memory and Recollection*.

———, *The Works of Aristotle*, ed. W. D. Ross, 12 vols. (Oxford: Clarendon Press, 1910–1952).

Athanasius, *Select Works and Letters*, trans. A. Robertson, in *Nicene and Post-Nicene Fathers*, second series, vol. 4, reprint ed. (Grand Rapids: Erdmans, 1987).

Augustine, *Against the Academics*, trans. J. J. O'Meara, Ancient Christian Writers series (Westminster, Md.: Newman, 1950). The work of a leading Augustine scholar, this is a model of how scholarly translations ought to be done.

———, *Anti-Pelagian Writings*, trans. P. Holmes and R. Wallis, in *Nicene and Post-Nicene Fathers*, first series, vol. 5, reprint ed. (Grand Rapids: Eerdmans, 1980).

———, *Augustine: Earlier Writings*, trans. J. H. S. Burleigh, Library of Christian Classics series (Philadelphia: Westminster, 1953). Serves as a useful introduction, but Burleigh's translations are not close enough to be reliable for scholarly purposes. This book contains the most readily available English versions of *De Magistro, De Vera Religione,* and *Ad Simplicianum,* along with *Soliloquies, De Libero Arbitrio, De Utiliate Credendi, De Fide et Symbolo,* and *De Natura Boni.*

———, *Bibliothèque Augustinienne* (Paris: De Brouwer et Cie, 1949–; later numbers published by Études Augustiniennes). A prime resource for Augustine scholarship, this series contains critical Latin texts, French translations, and notes that are often major pieces of scholarship in their own right (see especially A. Solignac's introduction and notes to the *Confessions*).

——, *City of God*, trans. H. Bettenson (Harmondsworth: Penguin, 1972). A consistently reliable translation.

——, *Confessions*, trans. H. Chadwick (New York: Oxford University Press, 1991). Chadwick has a deeper understanding of Augustine's Neoplatonist background than any previous translator.

——, *Confessions*, ed. J. O'Donnell, 3 vols. (Oxford: Clarendon Press, 1992). Latin text with extensive commentary.

——, *Confessions*, trans. F. J. Sheed (Indianapolis: Hackett, 1993). The most eloquent translation this century, accompanied by Peter Brown's valuable introduction.

——, *Confessions and Letters*, trans. J. G. Pilkington and J. G. Cunningham, in *Nicene and Post-Nicene Fathers,* first series, vol. 1, reprint ed. (Grand Rapids: Eerdmans, 1983). Pilkington's translation of the *Confessions* is still reliable, and in its Victorian way does a fine job of rendering the poetry of the work. For a complete edition of the letters, see hereafter.

——, *Corpus Scriptorum Ecclesiasticorum Latinorum* (Vienna: F. Tempsky). This is the older, more complete series of twentieth-century critical editions of the Church Fathers.

——, *Corpus Christianorum, Series Latina* (Turnhout: Brepols). Containing the most up-to-date texts, this series is still far from complete in its editions of Augustine's works. However, it does include the *Confessiones, De Trinitate,* and *De Civitate Dei,* as well as the Cassiciacum works.

——, *De Dialectica*, trans. B. D. Jackson, with Latin text of J. Pinborg (Dordrecht: Reidel, 1975).

——, *Eighty-three Different Questions*, trans. D. Mosher, Fathers of the Church series (Washington, D.C.: Catholic University of American Press, 1982). A useful and close translation.

——, *The Happy Life, Answer to the Skeptics, Divine Providence and the Problem of Evil, Soliloquies*, trans. L. Schopp, D. J. Kavanagh, R. P. Russell, and T. F. Gilligan (respectively), Fathers of the Church series (New York: CIMA, 1948). Under perversely translated titles (what casual reader will recognize that "Divine Providence and the Problem of Evil" is a translation of *De Ordine?*) this volume contains the only complete and readily available English version of the Cassiciacum works. It is an uneven collection: the translation of *Soliloquies* is the best I know of, and *De Beata Vita* and *De Ordine* are reliably done, but the translation of *Contra Academicos* frequently turns precise and logically valid Latin arguments into English gobbledygook; it should be positively avoided in favor of O'Meara's edition.

——, *The Immortality of the Soul, The Magnitude of the Soul, On Music, The Advantage of Believing, On Faith in Things Unseen*, trans. L. Schopp, J. J. MacMahon, R. C. Taliaferro, and Luanne Meagher (respectively), and for the last work, R. J. Deferrari and M. McDonald; Fathers of the Church series (New York: CIMA, 1947). Taliaferro's is the only English translation of *De Musica* known to me.

——, *Letters*, trans. W. Parsons, Fathers of the Church series, 5 vols. (New York: Fathers of the Church, 1951–1956).

——, *On Christian Doctrine*, trans. D. W. Robertson, Library of Liberal Arts series (New York: Macmillan, 1958).

——, *On Genesis*, trans. R. J. Teske (Washington: Catholic University of America Press, 1991). Contains careful translations of Augustine's earliest exegetical efforts, *De Genesi contra Manichaeos* and *De Genesi ad Litteram liber imperfectus* (not to be confused with the mature work by the same title).

——, *On the Holy Trinity, Doctrinal Treatises, Moral Treatises*, trans. A. Haddan, W. Shedd, J. F. Shaw, F. D. F. Salmond, C. L. Cornish, and H. Browne, in *Nicene and Post-Nicene Fathers,* first series, vol. 3, reprint ed. (Grand Rapids: Eerdmans, 1988). Contains fine translations of *De Trinitate* and *Enchiridion*.

——, *Sancti Aurelii Augustini Hipponensis Episcopi Opera Omnia* (Paris: Beau, 1836). Prepared by the Benedictine Congregation of St. Maurus and hence known as the Benedictine or Maurist edition, this work is based on a tradition of Benedictine scholarship on the texts of Augustine that goes back to the seventeenth century and in turn provides the basis for Migne's edition in the *Patrologia Latina*. It is still the most compact and often the most accessible edition of the complete works.

———, *The Writings against the Manichaeans and against the Donatists*, trans. R. Strothert, A. Newman, J. R. King, and C. Hartranft, in *Nicene and Post-Nicene Fathers*, first series, vol. 4, reprint ed. (Grand Rapids: Eerdmans, 1983).

Aurelius, Marcus, *Meditiations*, trans. C. R. Haines, Loeb series (Cambridge: Harvard, 1930).

Basil of Caesarea, *Contre Eunome*, ed. and trans. B. Sesboue, 2 vols., *Sources Chrétiennes*, numbers 299 and 305 (Paris: Cerf, 1982). Greek text with French translation.

———, *Saint Basil: the Letters*, trans. R. J. Deferrari, Loeb series, 4 vols. (Cambridge: Harvard University Press, 1961).

Bonaventure, *Disputed Questions concerning Christ's Knowledge*, question 4, in Fairweather, *A Scholastic Miscellany*.

———, *The Journey of the Mind to God*, trans. P. Boehner and ed. S. Brown (Indianapolis: Hackett, 1993).

———, *Opera Omnia* (Florence: Ad Claras Aquas, 1882–1902).

Calvin, *Institutes*, trans. F. Battles and ed. J. McNeill (Philadelphia: Westminster, 1960).

Cicero, *Brutus, Orator*, trans. G. L. Hendrickson and H. M. Hubell (respectively), Loeb series (Cambridge: Harvard University Press, 1971).

———, *De Finibus Bonorum et Malorum*, trans. H. Rackham, Loeb series (Cambridge: Harvard University Press, 1971).

———, *De Inventione, De Optimo Genere Oratorum, Topica*, trans. H. M. Hubbell, Loeb series (Cambridge: Harvard University Press, 1974).

———, *De Natura Deorum, Academica*, trans. H. Rackham, Loeb series (Cambridge: Harvard University Press, 1972).

———, *De Oratore*, books 1 and 2, trans. E. W. Sutton and H. Rackham, Loeb series (Cambridge: Harvard University Press, 1967).

———, *De Oratore* [book 3], *De Fato, Paradoxa Stoicorum, De Partitione Oratoria*, trans. H. Rackham, Loeb series (Cambridge: Harvard University Press, 1968).

———, *De Re Publica, De Legibus*, trans. C. W. Keyes, Loeb series (Cambridge: Harvard University Press, 1970).

———, *L'Hortensius de Ciceron: histoire et reconstitution*, M. Ruch (Paris: Belles Lettres, 1958).

———, *Rhetorica Ad Herennium*, trans. H. Caplan, Loeb series (Cambridge: Harvard University Press, 1968). This ancient textbook of rhetoric was long attributed to Cicero but is almost certainly by someone else of about the same time.

———, *Tusculan Disputations*, trans. J. E. King, Loeb series (Cambridge: Harvard University Press, 1971).

———, *Tusculan Disputations I*, ed. and trans. A. E. Douglas, (Chicago: Bolchazy-Carducci, 1985).

———, *Tusculan Disputations II & V*, ed. and trans. A. E. Douglas, (Warminster, England: Aris and Phillips, 1990).

Clement of Alexandria, *Stromata* and other works, trans. A. C. Coxe, in *Ante-Nicene Fathers*, vol. 2, reprint ed. (Grand Rapids: Erdmans, 1989).

Diogenes Laertius, *Lives of Eminent Philosophers*, trans. R. D. Hicks, 2 vols., Loeb series (Cambridge: Harvard University Press, 1966).

Denys (= Pseudo-Dionysius), *Corpus Dionysiacum*, ed. B. R. Suchla, G. Heil, and A. M. Ritter, 2 vols. (Berlin: de Gruyter, 1990–1991).

———, *Pseudo-Dionysius: the Complete Works*, trans. C. Luibhead, Classics of Western Spirituality series (New York: Paulist Press, 1987).

Epictetus, *The Discourses, Manual, and Fragments*, trans. W. A. Oldfather, Loeb series (Cambridge: Harvard University Press, 1967).

Eusebius of Caesarea, *History of the Church*, trans. G. A. Williamson and ed. A. Louth (New York: Penguin, 1989).

Gregory of Naziansen, *Discours*, ed. and trans. J. Bernardi, *Sources Chrétiennes* series (Paris: Cerf, 1978-). Greek text with French translation.

——, *Select Orations* and *Select Letters*, trans. C. G.Brown and J. E. Swallow, in *Nicene and Post-Nicene Fathers*, second series, vol. 7, reprint ed. (Grand Rapids: Eerdmans, 1983).

——, "The Theological Orations," trans. C. G. Brown and J. E. Swallow, in Hardy, *Christology of the Later Fathers.*

Gregory of Nyssa, *Select Writings and Letters*, trans. W. Moore and H. A. Wilson, in *Nicene and Post-Nicene Fathers*, second series, vol. 5, reprint ed. (Grand Rapids: Eerdmans, 1979).

——, *Opera*, ed. W. Jaeger et al. (Leiden: Brill, 1960-1990).

Hermes Trismegistus (Pseudonymous), *Corpus Hermeticum*, ed. A. D. Nock and trans. A. J. Festugière, 2nd ed., 4 vols. (Paris: Belles Lettres, 1960). The only reliable critical edition of the Greek and Latin texts, with French translation.

——, *Hermetica*, trans. B. Copenhaver (Cambridge: Cambridge University Press, 1992).

Homer, *Iliad,* trans. R. Lattimore (Chicago: University of Chicago Press, 1951).

Hugh of St. Victor, *Summa Sententiarum*, in Migne, *Patrologia Latina,* 176:42-174.

Irenaens, *Against Heresies,* trans. A. C. Coxe, in *Ante-Nicene Fathers,* vol. 1, reprint ed. (Grand Rapids: Eerdmans, 1987).

John of Damascus, *Exposition of the Orthdox Faith* (known to the medievals as *De Fide Orthodoxa*), trans. S. D. F. Salmond, in *Nicene and Post-Nicene Fathers,* second series, vol. 9, reprint ed. (Grand Rapids: Eerdmans, 1979).

——, *On the Divine Images: Three Apologies against Those Who Attack the Divine Images*, trans. D. Anderson (Crestwood, N.Y.: St. Vladimir's Seminary Press, 1980).

——, *Die Schriften des Johannes von Damaskos*, ed. B. Kotter (Berlin: de Gruyter, 1969).

Justin Martyr, *First Apology, Exhortation to the Greeks,* and other works, trans. A. C. Coxe, in *Ante-Nicene Fathers,* vol. 1, reprint ed. (Grand Rapids: Eerdmans, 1987).

Locke, John, *An Essay concerning Human Understanding*, ed. P. Nidditch (Oxford: Clarendon Press, 1975).

Luther, "Large Catechism," in Tappert, *The Book of Concord.*

——, *Luther's Works* (abbreviated *LW*), ed. J. Pelikan and H. Lehman (Philadelphia: FortressPress, 1958-1986).

Macrobius, *Commentary on the Dream of Scipio*, trans. W. H. Stahl (New York: Columbia University Press, 1952).

Maximus the Confessor, *Opera Omnia*, in Migne, *Patrologia Graeca*, vols. 90-91.

Origen, "Dialogue with Heraclides," in *Alexandrian Christianity,* trans. and ed. J. E. L. Oulton and H. Chadwick (Philadelphia: Westminster Press, 1954) pp. 437-455.

——, *On First Principles* (*De Princ.*) and *Against Celsus* (*C. Celsum*), trans. F. Crombie, in *Ante-Nicene Fathers,* vol.4, reprint ed. (Grand Rapids: Eerdmans, 1982).

——, *Origen*, trans. R. Greer, Classics of Western Spirituality series (New York: Paulist, 1979). Includes "The Prologue to the Commentary on the Song of Songs" and *On First Principles,* book 4, as well as a fine introduction.

Palamas, Gregory, *The Triads*, selections, ed. J. Meyendorff and trans. N. Gendle (New York: Paulist Press, 1983).

Philo of Alexandria, *Philo*, trans. F. H. Colson and G. H. Whitaker, Loeb series, 10 vols. (Cambridge: Harvard University Press, 1958).

Plato, *Opera*, ed. J. Burnet (Oxford: Clarendon Press, 1900-1907).

———, *Plato*, trans. H. N. Fowler, W. R. M. Lamb, P. Shorey, and R. G. Bury, Loeb series 12 vols. (Cambridge: Harvard University Press, 1964–1975).

———, *Plato's Meno*, Greek text with introduction and commentary by R. S. Bluck (Cambridge: Cambridge University Press, 1961).

———, *Plato's Seventh and Eighth Letters*, ed. R. S. Bluck (Cambridge: Cambridge University Press, 1947).

Plotinus, *Ennéades*, trans. E. Bréhier, 7 vols (Paris: Belles Lettres, 1924–1938). Greek text with a French translation that is well worth consulting.

———, *Enneads*, trans. A. H. Armstrong, Loeb series, 7 vols. (Cambridge: Harvard University Press, 1966–1988). The standard scholarly resource for non-specialists.

———, *The Enneads*, ed. J. Dillon (New York: Penguin, 1991). A generous selection of *Enneads* from the famed translation by Stephen MacKenna, this is the only extensive (though not complete) collection of *Enneads* in paperback, and the place to go for readers who have no Greek but want to get immersed in Plotinus. MacKenna's translation is free but not misleading, and as elegant as English can make Plotinus. Includes Porphyry's *Life of Plotinus* and some first-rate scholarly introductions.

———, *The Essential Plotinus*, trans. E. O'Brien, (Indianapolis: Hackett, 1964). A small selection of *Enneads*, including some of those most important for Augustine (1:6, 5:1, and 4:3), in a translation I have found close and reliable.

———, *Plotini Opera*, ed. P. Henry and H.-R. Schwyzer, 3 vols. (Oxford: Clarendon Press, 1964–1982). The standard critical edition of the Greek text, smaller edition.

———, *Plotini Opera*, ed. P. Henry and H.-R. Schwyzer, 3 vols. (Paris: Desclée de Brouwer, 1951–1973). The standard critical edition of the Greek text, larger edition.

Porphyry, *Life of Plotinus* (found in all complete editions of Plotinus).

Proclus, *Elements of Theology*, ed. and trans. E. R. Dodds (Oxford: Clarendon Press, 1963). Greek and English.

Pseudo-Dionysius, see Denys.

Quintilian, *Institutio Oratoria*, trans. H.E. Butler, Loeb series, 4 vols. (Cambridge: Harvard University Press, 1969).

Seneca, *Moral Epistles*, trans. R. Gummere, Loeb series, 3 vols. (Cambridge: Harvard University Press, 1967).

Secondary Literature

Alfaric, P., *L'évolution intellectuelle de saint Augustin*, (Paris: Nourry, 1918).

Anscombe, G. E. M., *Metaphysics and Philosophy of Mind*, vol. 2 of her *Collected Philosophical Papers* (Minneapolis: University of Minnesota Press, 1981).

Armstrong, A. H., *The Architecture of the Intelligible Universe in the Philosophy of Plotinus* (Cambridge: Cambridge University Press, 1940).

———, "The Background of the Doctrine 'That the Intelligibles are not Outside the Intellect' " in Fondation Hardt, *Les sources de Plotin*, pp. 393–413.

———, *Plotinian and Christian Studies* (London: Variorum Reprints, 1979).

———, "Plotinus," in his *Cambridge History*, pp. 193–268.

———, "Plotinus' Doctrine of the Infinite and Christian Thought," *Downside Review* 73:231 (1954–1955), 47–58; reprinted in his *Plotinian and Christian Studies*.

———, ed., *The Cambridge History of Later Greek and Early Medieval Philosophy* (Cambridge: Cambridge University Press, 1980).

Aubin, P., *Le problème de la "conversion"* (Paris: Beauchesne, 1963)

Balthasar, H. U. von, *The Theology of Karl Barth* (San Francisco: Ignatius, 1992).

Barnes, J., M. Schofield, and R. Sorabji, eds., *Articles on Aristotle*, 3 vols. (London: Duckworth, 1975–1979).

Barth, K., *Church Dogmatics,* trans. G. Bromiley et al. (Edinburgh: T. and T. Clark).

Bayer, O., *Promissio: Geschichte der Reformatorischen Wende in Luthers Theologie* (Göttingen, Germany: Vandenhoeck and Ruprecht, 1971).

Beutler, R., "Porphyrios," in *Paulys Realencyclopädie der Classischen Altertumswissenschaft* ed. G. Wissowa et al. (Munich: Druckenmüller, 1980).

Bloom, H., *The American Religion: the Emergence of the Post-Christian Nation* (New York: Simon and Schuster, 1992).

Bonner, G., *St. Augustine of Hippo: Life and Controversies* (Philadelphia: Westminster, 1963).

Bourke, V., *Augustine's View of Reality* (Villanova, Pa.: Villanova University Press, 1964).

Brown, P., *Augustine of Hippo* (Berkeley: University of California Press, 1967).

Burnaby, J., *Amor Dei: A Study in the Religion of St. Augustine* (London: Hodder and Stoughton, 1938).

Carruthers, M., *The Book of Memory* (Cambridge: Cambridge University Press, 1990).

Cary, P., "Believing the Word: A Proposal about Knowing Other Persons," *Faith and Philosophy* 13/1 (1996).

———, "What Licentius Learned: A Narrative Reading of the Cassiciacum Dialogues," *Augustinian Studies,* 29/1 (Jan. 1998), 141–163.

———, "God in the Soul: Or, the Residue of Augustine's Manichean Optimism," *University of Dayton Review,* Summer 1994.

Courcelle, P., *Late Latin Writers and their Greek Sources,* trans. H. Wedeck (Cambridge: Harvard University Press, 1969).

Les Confessions de saint Augustin dans la tradition littéraire (Paris: Études Augustiniennes, 1963).

———, *Recherches sur les Confessions de saint Augustin* (Paris: de Boccard, 1950).

Cullmann, O., "Immortality of the Soul or Resurrection of the Dead?" in *Immortality and Resurrection,* ed. K. Stendahl (New York: MacMillan, 1965).

Dihle, A., *The Theory of the Will in Classical Antiquity* (Berkeley: University of California Press, 1982).

Dillon, J., *The Middle Platonists* (Ithaca: Cornell University Press, 1977).

Dodds, E. R., "Numenius and Ammonius," in Fondation Hardt, *Les sources de Plotin,* pp. 1–61.

———, *Pagan and Christian in an Age of Anxiety* (Cambridge: Cambridge University Press, 1965).

Dörrie, H., "Die Frage nach dem Transzendenten im Mittelplatonismus" in Fondation Hardt, *Les sources de Plotin,* pp. 194–223.

Du Roy, O., *L'intelligence de la foi en la Trinité selon saint Augustin* (Paris: Études Augustiniennes, 1966).

Düring, I., *Aristoteles: Darstellung und Interpretation seines Denkens* (Heidelberg: Carl Winter Universitätsverlag, 1966).

———, "Aristotle and Plato in the Mid–Fourth Century," *Eranos* 54 (1965), 109–120.

———, "Aristotle and the Heritage from Plato," *Eranos* 62 (1964), 84–99.

———, "Aristotle on Ultimate Principles from 'Nature and Reality'" in Düring and Owen, pp. 35–55.

———, "Did Aristotle Ever Accept Plato's Theory of Transcendent Ideas?" *Archiv für Geschichte der Philosophie* 48 (1966), 312–316.

———, and G.E.L. Owen, *Plato and Aristotle in the Mid–Fourth Century* (Göteborg: Elanders Boktryckeri Aktiebolag, 1960).

Duval, Y-M., ed., *Ambroise de Milan* (Paris: Études Augustiniennes, 1974).

Ferrari, L., *The Conversions of Saint Augustine* (Villanova, Pa.: Villanova University Press, 1984).

Festugière, A.-J., *La Révélation d'Hermes Trismégiste,* 4 vols., 2nd ed. (Paris: Gabalda, 1950–1954).

Fonck, A., "Ontologisme," in *Dictionaire de Théologie Catholique,* ed. A. Vacant, E. Mangenot, and E. Amann (Paris: Librairie Lefouzey et Ané, 1939), vol. 11/1, 1000–1061.

Fondation Hardt, ed., *Les sources de Plotin* (Geneva: Vandoeuvres, 1960).

Gersh, S., *Middle Platonism and Neoplatonism: the Latin Tradition,* 2 vols. (Notre Dame, Ind.: University of Notre Dame Press, 1986).

de Ghellinck, J., *Le mouvement théologique du XIIe siècle* (Paris: Descleé, 1948).

Gilson, E., *The Christian Philosophy of Saint Augustine* (New York: Random House, 1960).

———, *The Philosophy of St. Bonaventure*, trans. I. Trethowan and F. J. Sheed (Paterson, N.J.: St. Anthony's Guild Press, 1965).

Gouillard, J. "Le synodikon de l'Orthodoxie: édition et commentaire," in *Travaux et Mémoires*, vol. 2 (Paris: de Boccard, 1957).

Grillmeier, A., *Christ in Christian Tradition*, trans. J. S. Bowden, vol. 1 (New York: Sheed and Ward, 1965).

Gurtler, G., *Plotinus: the Experience of Unity* (New York: Peter Lang, 1988).

Hadot, I., "The Role of the Commentaries on Aristotle in the Teaching of Philosophy according to the Prefaces of the Neoplatonic Commentaries on the *Categories*," in *Aristotle and the Later Tradition*, ed. J. Annas (Oxford: Clarendon Press, 1991).

Hadot, P. "Platon et Plotin dans trois sermons de saint Ambroise" in *Revue des études latines* 34 (1956), 202–220.

———, *Porphyre et Victorinus* (Paris: Études Augustiniennes, 1968).

Hagendahl, H., *Augustine and the Latin Classics* (Göteborg: Elanders Boktryckeri Aktiebolag, 1967).

Hahm, D., *The Origins of Stoic Cosmology* (Columbus: Ohio State University, 1977).

Harnack, A. von, "Die Höhepunkte in Augustins 'Konfessiones' " in his *Reden und Aufsätze*, neue Folge (Giessen: Töpelmann, 1916) 3:67–99.

Heiser, J., *Logos and Language in the Thought of Plotinus* (Lewiston, N.Y.: Mellen, 1991).

Henry, P., *Plotin et l'Occident* (Louvain: Spicilegium Sacrum Lovaniense, 1934).

———, "Une comparaison chez Aristote, Alexandre et Plotin" in Fondation Hardt, *Les sources de Plotin*, pp. 427–444.

Hessen, J., *Augustins Metaphysik der Erkenntnis*, 2nd ed. (Leiden: Brill, 1960).

Husserl, E., *Cartesian Meditations*, trans. D. Cairns (The Hague: Nijhoff, 1960).

Jaeger, W., *Aristotle: Fundamentals of the History of His Development*, trans. R. Robinson, 2nd ed. (Oxford: Clarendon Press, 1948).

Jewett, R., *Paul's Anthropological Terms: A Study of Their Use in Conflict Settings* (Leiden: Brill, 1971).

John Paul II, *The Splendor of Truth*, Encyclical Letter, August 6, 1993 (Washington, D.C.: U.S. Catholic Conference, 1993).

Kahn, C., "Discovering the Will: From Aristotle to Augustine," in *The Question of "Eclecticism": Studies in Later Greek Philosophy*, ed. J. Dillon and A. Long, (Berkeley: University of California Press, 1988).

Keseling, P., "Augustin und Quintilian," in *Augustinus Magister* (Paris: Études Augustiniennes, 1954), 1:201–204.

Kittel, G., et al., eds., *Theological Dictionary of the New Testament*, trans. G. Bromiley (Grand Rapids: Eerdmans, 1964–74).

Krämer, H. J. *Der Ursprung der Geistesmetaphysik*, 2nd ed. (Amsterdam: Grüner, 1967).

Kraut, R., ed., *The Cambridge Companion to Plato* (Cambridge: Cambridge University Press, 1992).

Lear, J., *Aristotle: The Desire to Understand* (Cambridge: Cambridge University Press, 1988).

Lee, P., *Against the Protestant Gnostics* (New York: Oxford University Press, 1987).

Levinas, E., *Totality and Infinity: An Essay on Exteriority*, trans. A. Lingis (Pittsburgh: Duquesne University Press, 1969).

Lilla, S., *Clement of Alexandria: A Study in Christian Platonism and Gnosticism* (Oxford: Oxford University Press, 1971).

Lloyd, A. C., *The Anatomy of Neoplatonism* (Oxford: Clarendon Press, 1990).

———, "The Later Neoplatonists," in *Cambridge History*, ed. Armstrong, pp. 270–325.

Long, A. A., *Hellenistic Philosophy*, 2nd ed. (Berkeley: University of California Press, 1986).

MacIntyre, A., *Whose Justice? Which Rationality?* (Notre Dame, Ind.: University of Notre Dame Press, 1988).

Madec, G., "L'homme intérieur selon saint Ambroise" in Duval, pp. 283–308.

——, *Saint Ambroise et la philosophie* (Paris: Études Augustiniennes, 1974).

Marrou, H. I., *A History of Education in Antiquity*, trans. G. Lamb (London: Sheed and Ward, 1956).

——, *Saint Augustin et la fin de la culture antique* (Paris: de Boccard, 1938).

Mayer, C. P., "Philosophische Voraussetzungen und Implikationen in Augustins Lehre von den Sacramenta," *Augustiniana* 22 (1972), 53–79.

——, "Taufe und Erwählung: Zur Dialektik des sacramentum-Begriffes in der antidonatischen Schrift Augustins: *De Baptismo*," in *Scientia Augustiniana*, ed. C. P. Mayer and W. Eckermann, (Würzburg, Augustinus Verlag, 1975) pp. 22–42.

——, *Die Zeichen in der geistigen Entwicklung und in der Theologie des jungen Augustins* (Würzburg: Augustinus Verlag, 1969).

——, *Die Zeichen in der geistigen Entwicklung und in der Theologie Augustins, II. Teil: Die anti-Manichäische Epoche* (Würzburg: Augustinus Verlag, 1974).

McCool, G., *Catholic Theology in the Nineteenth Century* (New York: Seabury, 1977).

Merlan, P., "Greek Philosophy from Plato to Plotinus," in *Cambridge History*, ed. Armstrong, pp. 14–132.

——, *Monopsychism Mysticism Metaconsiousness: Problems of the Soul in the Neoaristotelian and Neoplatonic Tradition* (The Hague: Nijhoff, 1969).

Meyendorff, J., *Christ in Eastern Christian Thought* (Crestwood, N.Y.: St. Vladimir's Seminary Press, 1987).

Moraux, P., *Alexandre d'Aphrodise: exégète de la noètique d'Aristote* (Liège: Faculté de Philosophie et Lettres, 1942).

Mourant, J., *Augustine on Immortality* (Villanova, Pa: Villanova University Press, 1969).

Muller, R., *Dictionary of Latin and Greek Theological Terms* (Grand Rapids: Baker, 1985).

Nash, R., *The Light of the Mind: St. Augustine's Theory of Knowledge* (Lexington: University Press of Kentucky, 1969).

Nauroy, G., "La méthode de composition et la structure du *De Jacob et vita beata*," in Duval, 115–153.

Nörregaard, D. J., *Augustins Bekehrung* (Tübingen: J. C. B. Mohr, 1923)

Nygren, A., Eros and Agape, trans. P. Watson (Chicago: University of Chicago Press, 1982).

O'Connell, R. J., "*Ennead* VI, 4 and 5 in the Works of St. Augustine," *Revue des Études Augustiniennes* 9 (1963), 1–39.

——, *Images of Conversion in St. Augustine's Confessions* (New York: Fordham University Press, 1996).

——, *The Origin of the Soul in St. Augustine's Later Works* (New York: Fordham University Press, 1987).

——, *St. Augustine's Confessions* (Cambridge: Harvard University Press, 1969).

——, *St. Augustine's Early Theory of Man* (Cambridge: Harvard University Press, 1968).

——, *St. Augustine's Platonism* (Villanova, Pa.: Villanova University Press, 1984).

O'Meara, J. J., "Augustine and Neo-Platonism" *Recherches Augustininnes* 1 (1958), 91–111; reprinted in his *Studies in Augustine and Eriugena*, pp. 146–165.

——, Studies in Augustine and Eriugena (Washington, D.C.: Catholic University of America, 1991).

Ong, W. J., *Orality and Literacy*, reprint ed. (London and New York: Routledge, 1988).

——, *The Presence of the Word*, reprint ed. (Minneapolis: University of Minnesota Press, 1981).

Owen, G. E. L., "Logic and Metaphysics in Some Earlier Works of Aristotle," in Düring and Owen, pp. 163–190; reprinted in Barnes, Schofield, et al., vol. 3, pp. 13–32, and in Owen, *Logic, Science and Dialectic*, pp. 180–199.

——, *Logic, Science and Dialectic: Collected Papers in Greek Philosophy* (Ithaca: Cornell University Press, 1986).

———, "The Place of the *Timeaus* in Plato's Dialogues," in his *Logic, Science and Dialectic*, pp. 65–84.

———, "The Platonism of Aristotle," in Barnes, Schofield, et al., 1:14–34, and in Owen, *Logic, Science and Dialectic*, pp. 200–220.

Palanque, J-R., *Saint Ambroise et l'empire romain* (Paris: de Boccard, 1933).

Pépin, J., "Une curieuse déclaration idéaliste du 'De Genesi ad litteram' (XII,10,21) de saint Augustin, et ses origines plotiniennes ('Ennéade' 5,3,1–9 et 5,5,1–2)" *Revue d'Histoire et de Philosophie religieuses* 34 (1954), 373–400; reprinted in his *"Ex Platonicorum Persona,"* pp. 183–210.

———, "Une nouvelle source de saint Augustin," *Revue des études anciennes"* 66 (1964), 53–107; reprinted in his *"Ex Platonicorum Persona,"* pp. 213–267.

———, *"Ex Platonicorum Persona"* (Amsterdam: Hakkert, 1957).

———, *Saint Augustin et la dialectique* (Villanova, Pa.: Villanova University Press, 1976).

Pohlenz, M., *Die Stoa*, 2nd ed. (Göttingen, Germany: Vandenhoeck and Ruprecht, 1959).

Preller, V., *Divine Science and the Science of God* (Princeton: Princeton University Press, 1967).

Rahner, K., "Concerning the Relationship between Nature and Grace," in his *Theological Investigations*, vol. 1, trans. C. Ernst (Baltimore: Helicon, 1961).

———, "Le début d'une doctrine des cinq sens spirituels chez Origène" *Revue d'ascétique et de mystique* 13 (1932), 113–145; trans. (simplified and abridged) in Rahner, *Theological Investigations*, vol. 16 (New York: Crossroad, 1983).

———, "Nature and Grace," in his *Theological Investigations*, vol. 4, trans. K. Smith (Baltimore: Helicon, 1966), pp. 165–188.

Rorty, R., *Philosophy and the Mirror of Nature* (Princeton: Princeton University Press, 1979).

Russell, B., *Our Knowledge of the External World* (Chicago: Open Court, 1914).

———, *The Problems of Philosophy* (London: Oxford University Press, 1959), original ed. 1912.

Schwyzer, H., "'Bewusst' und 'Unbewusst' bei Plotin" in Fondation Hardt, *Les sources de Plotin*, pp. 341–378.

Sedley, D., "The Motivation of Greek Skepticism," in Burnyeat, pp. 9–29.

Snell, B., *The Discovery of the Mind in Greek Philosophy and Literature* (New York: Dover Publications, 1982).

Solignac, A., "Doxographies et manuels dans la formation de saint Augustin," *Recherches Augustininnes* 1 (1958), 113–148.

———, "Nouveaux parallèles entre saint Ambroise et Plotin. Le 'De Jacob et vita beata' et le 'Peri eudaimonias' Enn. I,4," *Archives de Philosophie* 19 (1956), 148–156.

———, "Réminiscences plotiniennes et porphyriennes dan le début du *De Ordine* de saint Augustin," *Archives de Philosophie* 20 (1957), 446–465.

Sweeney, L., *Divine Infinity in Greek and Medieval Thought* (New York: Peter Lang, 1992).

Taylor, C., *Sources of the Self: the Making of the Modern Identity* (Cambridge: Harvard University Press, 1989).

Teske, R., "The World-Soul and Time in St. Augustine," *Augustinian Studies* 14 (1983), 75–92.

Testard, M., *Saint Augustin et Cicero* (Paris: Études Augustiniennes, 1958).

Theiler, W., *Forschungen zum Neuplatonismus* (Berlin: de Gruyter, 1966).

———, "Plotin und die antike Philosophie," in his *Forschungen,* pp. 140–159.

———, "Plotin zwischen Plato und Stoa" in Fondation Hardt, *Les sources de Plotin*, pp. 65–86; reprinted in his *Forschungen,* pp. 124–139.

———, "Porphyrios und Augustin," in his *Forschungen,* pp. 160–251.

Thimme, W., *Augustins geistige Entwicklung in den ersten Jahren nach seiner "Bekehrung" 386–391*, 2nd ed. (Aalen: Scientia Verlag Aalen, 1973), 1st ed., Berlin: 1908.

Trouillard, J., *La Purification Plotinienne* (Paris: Presses Universitaires de France, 1955).

Verbeke, G., "Spiritualité et immortalité de l'âme chez Saint Augustin," in *Augustinus Magister* (Paris: Études Augustiniennes, 1954), 1:329–334.

Williams, D., *Ambrose of Milan and the End of the Nicene-Arian Conflicts* (Oxford: Clarendon Press, 1995).

Witt, R. E., *Albinus and the History of Middle Platonism* (Cambridge: Cambridge University Press, 1937).

Wolff, H. W., *Anthropology of the Old Testament*, trans. M. Kohl (Philadelphia: Fortress Press, 1974).

Wolterstorff, N., *John Locke and the Ethics of Belief* (Cambridge: Cambridge University Press, 1996).

——, "The Migration of the Theistic Arguments: From Natural Theology to Evidentialist Apologetics," in *Rationality, Religious Belief and Moral Commitment,* ed. R. Audi and W. Wainwright, (Ithaca: Cornell University Press, 1986).

Yates, F., *The Art of Memory* (London: Routledge and Kegan Paul, 1966).

Young, F., *From Nicaea to Chalcedon* (Philadelphia: Fortress Press, 1983).

Index